DOCUMENTING FIRST WAVE FEMINISMS
Volume II: Canada – National and Transnational Contexts

This book is the second of a two-volume anthology of primary source documents on feminism in the nineteenth and early twentieth centuries. Unique in its extensive treatment of the first wave feminist movement in Canada, it highlights distinct elements of the movement's origins and evolution.

The book is organized under thematic rubrics that address key issues, debates, and struggles within the first wave in Canada, as well as international influences and Canadian engagement in transnational networks and initiatives. Documents by Indigenous, Anglophone, Francophone, and immigrant female activists demonstrate the richness and complexity of Canadian feminism during this period. Together with the first volume, *Documenting First Wave Feminisms* reveals a more nuanced picture, attentive to nationalism and transnationalism, of the first wave than has previously been understood.

(Studies in Gender and History)

NANCY M. FORESTELL is an associate professor in the Department of History at St Francis Xavier University.

MAUREEN MOYNAGH is a professor in the Department of English at St Francis Xavier University.

STUDIES IN GENDER AND HISTORY

General Editors: Franca Iacovetta and Karen Dubinsky

Documenting First Wave Feminisms

Volume II:
Canada – National and Transnational Contexts

Edited by
Nancy M. Forestell with
Maureen Moynagh

UNIVERSITY OF TORONTO PRESS
Toronto Buffalo London

© University of Toronto Press 2014
Toronto Buffalo London
www.utppublishing.com

ISBN 978-0-8020-9135-2 (cloth)
ISBN 978-0-8020-9414-8 (paper)

(Studies in Gender and History)

Library and Archives Canada Cataloguing in Publication

Documenting first wave feminisms / edited by Maureen Moynagh with
Nancy Forestell.

(Studies in gender and history)
Includes bibliographical references and index.
Contents: v. 2. Canada – national and transnational contexts.
ISBN 978-0-8020-9135-2 (bound : v. 2)   ISBN 978-0-8020-9414-8 (pbk. : v. 2)

1. Feminism – History – 19th century – Sources.   2. Feminism – History – 20th century
– Sources.   3. Women's rights – History – 19th century – Sources.   4. Women's rights –
History – 20th century – Sources.   I. Moynagh, Maureen Anne, 1963–   II. Forestell, Nancy
M. (Nancy Margaret), 1960–   III. Series: Studies in gender and history

HQ1154.D63 2014   305.4209′034   C2011-906612-2

University of Toronto Press acknowledges the financial assistance to its publishing program
of the Canada Council for the Arts and the Ontario Arts Council.

 Canada Council   Conseil des Arts
for the Arts   du Canada

ONTARIO ARTS COUNCIL
CONSEIL DES ARTS DE L'ONTARIO
50 YEARS OF ONTARIO GOVERNMENT SUPPORT OF THE ARTS
50 ANS DE SOUTIEN DU GOUVERNEMENT DE L'ONTARIO AUX ARTS

University of Toronto Press acknowledges the financial support of the Government of Canada
through the Canada Book Fund for its publishing activities.

Contents

PART TWO: INTERNATIONALISM

PART THREE: SUFFRAGE

PART FOUR: CITIZENSHIP

PART FIVE: MORAL REFORM, SEXUALITY, AND BIRTH CONTROL

PART SEVEN: PACIFISM

Acknowledgments

We owe a debt of gratitude to several people and institutions for the support they gave to us and to this project. The Dean of Arts and the Academic Vice President and Provost at St. Francis Xavier University offered vital funding when it was most needed. The University Council for Research of St. Francis Xavier University provided research funding that enabled us to visit archives and hire research assistants. The librarians and staff at the Women's Library, London Metropolitan University, were welcoming and helpful. For Volume I, Janette Fecteau and Clare Mulcahy offered terrific research assistance, helping with permissions and literature searches, scanning and proofing documents, all the while sharing in our enthusiasm for the project. Additional research assistance was ably provided by Brandy McDougall, who searched the archives of the Pacific Collection at the University of Hawaii at Manoa for materials related to the Pan-Pacific Women's Association. For Volume II, thanks are due to Ryan Eyford, for his translation of Margaret Benedictsson from Icelandic; to Alison Norman for providing the Emily Grant document and biographical information about Grant; to Cecilia Morgan for assisting with Lally Bernard; to Peter Campbell for biographical information on Rose Henderson; to Jennifer Steel for her research on Québécois nationalism; and to Lynne Marks, Clare Fawcett, Rhonda Semple and Cecilia Morgan for reading portions of the manuscript. We are also grateful for technical assistance from Marie Gillis, secretary of the Department of English, Anne-Marie McPherson, secretary of the Department of History, and Betty MacNeil, secretary of the Women's Studies Program at St. Francis Xavier University. Finally, without the encouragement, enthusiasm, and unflagging support of our series editors Franca Iacovetta and Karen Dubinksy, this documents book would not have been published. Franca and Karen, thank you.

Permissions

General Introduction

NANCY FORESTELL AND MAUREEN MOYNAGH

Documenting First Wave Feminisms is a two-volume collection of essays, pamphlets, manifestoes, memoirs, petitions, reports, and resolutions documenting
the multiple forms of engagement and organizing within first wave feminism.
Our project is not primarily about recuperation, an undertaking that cannot be
embarked upon blithely given the deep implication of many first wave women
in structures of privilege and empire building. Rather, we seek to make more
readily available some of the documents of first wave feminism that make
especially evident its international linkages and its engagement with categories
of social location other than gender that were and continue to be so central to
women's organizing and feminist theorizing. Needless to say, the contours of
debates on questions of race, sexuality, nation, and so on were significantly
different at the turn of the last century than those that characterize the beginning of the twenty-first, but we anticipate that precisely those differences may
prove instructive.

The story of first wave feminism, as Christine Bolt has pointed out, is
"one of national distinctiveness within an international cause."[1] Our volumes
emphasize the international cause and an underrepresented national case,
respectively, and in making the "feminism" of our title plural we aim to signal
our conviction that there are multiple, overlapping stories of the first wave
to take account of. The emergence of "woman's rights" movements over the
course of the nineteenth century, concerned as they were with broadly similar
social and political goals – higher education, political enfranchisement, legal
reforms, moral reforms – made for the possibility of international collaboration. At the same time, the distinctiveness of feminist social movements within
different national and sub-national spheres means that any attempt to chart the
international can only be partial. Finally, accounts of national movements can
elide important ways in which key events were as international as they were
local or national, as is the case, for example, with the Seneca Falls Convention.

The primary focus of the first volume, *Transnational Collaborations and Crosscurrents*, is to document international feminist organizing, the overlapping and conflicting aims of feminists across the globe and the largely unacknowledged influence of minority women and women from the south on international feminist thought. Our aim in this volume has not been to abstract feminist organizing out of the material, political circumstances and embedded social relationships of specific localities, but rather to emphasize the ways that "local" feminist organizing was most often informed by what feminists were doing elsewhere, and the ways "local" issues frequently became international ones. Beyond specific instances of transnational collaboration like the financial assistance English and Irish women provided to US women abolitionists, or the support some British feminists loaned to Indian women who were in London to petition the colonial government, or the mentoring relationships forged between Uruguayan and other Latin American women, feminists also created formal international organizations to further their aims and pursued international legislation when that seemed the most fruitful course of action. Volume Two, *Canada – National and Transnational Contexts*, recognizes the participation of Canadian women in international feminist networks as well as the parallels and divergences between Canadian feminists and their counterparts around the world. The Canadian volume, moreover, will address and in some respects *redress* notable gaps in the historiography on first wave feminism in Canada. Certainly the situation of Canada as a white settler colony with a significant French-language minority had potentially far-reaching implications for international feminist political activism.

Our volumes also strive to document the first wave in ways that enable a critical apprehension of the dominant roles played by elite white women, and thus to reorient the scholarly focus by presenting evidence of a more diverse social movement than is conventionally associated with the first wave. The work of decentring first wave feminism entails attending not only to the usual dominance of Britain and the United States in the literature, but avoiding envisioning the peripheries as merely "writing back" – yet another way of placing the British Empire or the United States in the centre. Instead, we need to look at "south–south" relations, to use contemporary terminology, and to consider, for instance, alliances among Latin American feminists, organizations like the Pan-Pacific Women's Association, or Second-World alliances. Equally important are the ways that indigenous and other racialized women, within particular national contexts, contested dominant constructions of feminism that excluded them or positioned them as the objects of white feminist intervention. The transnational focus in particular enables us to take account of the dynamic interplay of individuals, organizations, and debates across a wide range of geographical centres. There are nonetheless significant gaps in our anthology, despite our aim to decentre the first wave. A documents book is inherently biased against oral sources, and in favour of those more privileged sectors of any culture that produced written texts. In our volume introductions and in our introductions to the thematic sections of each volume, we strive to make apparent the silences that persist and to historicize them.

While 1848 is often the starting point of accounts of the first wave, because the Seneca Falls Convention took place in that year, we have included texts that predate that moment as a means of recognizing texts and activism that resonated internationally in ways that were consequential for women activists in different national contexts. Our cut-off point, for the most part, is the Second World War. There was a significant expansion of internationalism after 1920, and a significant increase in the participation in feminist and nationalist movements of women in colonial settings that an earlier, more conventional cut-off date would elide. The Second World War not only interrupted transnational feminist organizing for a significant period of time; the world that emerged from the conflict was a much altered place, and feminist organizing significantly transformed as a consequence. Suffrage, for instance, receded as a leading principle of transnational feminist politics, even if it continued to matter in many national spheres. In the context of widespread decolonization around the globe, human rights arguably came to displace women's rights for a time in international spheres of organizing; transnational solidarity also arguably took new forms and acquired new objectives for many women in the global south. The Cold War that followed the United States also altered the terrain of international collaboration, making communication across "blocs" all but impossible.

We are, at the same time, conscious of the fact that thinking in terms of "waves" is not unproblematic, but we retain the term to distinguish the feminisms we are documenting from post-war feminism, which departs in significant ways from what went before. It is always problematic to establish a "beginning" and an "end point" for women's movements. While feminist historians once conceived of "waves" in these terms, more recent scholars have recognized the extent to which it makes more sense to trace patterns of continuity or transformation, and have argued that in fact the more established chronologies neglect the ongoing activism of some groups of women. Dorothy Sue Cobble, for instance, points out that women in the US labour movement were very active from the late 1930s through the 1960s, suggesting more continuity between the first wave and the second.[2] Another difficulty in a collection such as ours has to do with the tension between chronologies generated out of national women's movements and the international struggles in which many of these activists participated. While cut-off points are always somewhat arbitrary, the Second World War, in our estimation, constituted a significant enough interruption of the transnational collaborations we are attempting to track to warrant designating as different what came after the war.

Our use of the term "feminism" to encompass the thought and activism of many women around the world may well be perceived as problematic. Certainly many of the activists whose voices are documented here used different terminology. In the early nineteenth century "woman's rights" was the term most commonly in use; "feminism" was not used until the late nineteenth century, and even then was not embraced by all the activists involved in organizing for social change. We use "feminism" to indicate an awareness, on the part of women, that they are oppressed at least in part because of their sex, and to designate the analyses of oppression and the struggles for liberation conducted by and for women, whether or not the women in question used the term "feminism." In other words, we mean to designate as "feminist" concepts that manifest a critical, gendered consciousness. Where possible, we will indicate when alternative terminology was in use or where the term "feminist" was itself explicitly rejected or critiqued. For instance, socialist women were among those reluctant to use the term feminism because of its associations with the particular preoccupations of bourgeois women. Indian women were also reluctant to identify as feminists or suffragettes because of their sense that feminists were inclined to separatism, whereas Indian women saw themselves working together with men in the nationalist movement.

Our aim has been to produce collections of documents that reflect the more nuanced picture of the first wave that has been emerging in the recent work of feminist historians, literary critics, and political theorists. The influence of critical race and postcolonial studies, as well as efforts to consider links between feminism and globalization and an awareness of the need to be attentive to nationalism and transnationalism inform our anthology just as they inform the current secondary literature. Rather than constituting an anachronism, this approach promises to make more visible some of the features of the first wave that had been obscured in studies exclusively focused on gender as a category of analysis and dominated by attention to the work of European and Euro-American women, especially feminists in Britain and the United States. Although there have been editions that make more widely available material published in particular journals or documents pertinent to a given nation, or even collections focused on a particular theme, there has not yet been a first wave documents book that is transnational in scope. Estelle Friedman's important collection *The Essential Feminist Reader*, while transnational, is not focused on the first wave women's movement, but encompasses feminist documents ranging from the late Middle Ages to the present.[3] In the case of Canada, a number of documents books have been published, but with the exception of several impressive works that focus on Quebec, none has incorporated texts by both anglophone and francophone first wave feminists.[4] Nor has there been any attempt thus far to contextualize Canadian feminism within the overlapping frameworks of imperialism, internationalism, and transnationalism. Both of our volumes are intended to be used by researchers as well as in undergraduate and graduate classrooms as a complement to current historiographic, literary, and political studies.

Working on *Documenting First Wave Feminisms* has taught us a great deal about the ways earlier feminists understood their social worlds. While there is no denying that the first wave was dominated by privileged Euro-American women, these documents also suggest that feminist politics in this period were far more complex and interesting than this important acknowledgment betrays. The effort to organize transnationally, fraught and contradictory as it often was, exposed these women to other ways of conceiving feminism, other strategies for pursuing their goals, and other ways of understanding the world, even if many were not always open to the possibilities they encountered. We hope our readers will find these documents similarly engaging.

NOTES

1 Catherine Bolt, *The Women's Movements in the United States and Britain from the 1790s to the 1920s* (Hemel Hempstead: Harvester Wheatsheaf, 1993), 5.

2 Dorothy Sue Cobble, *The Other Women's Movement: Workplace Justice and Social Rights in Modern America* (Princeton, NJ: Princeton University Press, 2005).

3 Estelle Friedman, *The Essential Feminist Reader* (New York: New Library, 2007).

4 Micheline Dumont and Louise Toupin, *La pensée féministe au Québec: Anthologie, 1900–1985* (Montreal: Les Éditions du remue-ménage, 2003).

DOCUMENTING FIRST WAVE FEMINISMS
Volume II: Canada – National and Transnational Contexts

Volume Introduction:
Canada – National and Transnational
Contexts

NANCY FORESTELL

In preparation for the Paris International Exhibition in 1900 a handbook entitled *Women of Canada: Their Life and Work* was compiled by the main umbrel-
la group of female reform organizations in the country. This text documented
the many and wide-ranging accomplishments of women in Canada as well as
noted areas where they continued to face barriers or lacked particular rights.
In effect it served as an extended summary of many of the important achievements of the women's movement thus far and its future program of work. Of
additional consequence, the views of women and of feminism presented in this
handbook were projected at a "world" stage as it was intended for an international audience. The concluding summary of the contents of the text by Julia
Drummond is especially revealing of the multifaceted and at times conflicting
set of relations that shaped Canadian women's activism during this period:

> The volume closes with an invitation to the women of the old world, and a back-
> ward glance at the first women of the new. It was a good world in those days when
> the Indian women gathered in the harvest and sang their hymn of praise to the Sun,
> or gave their voice in the councils of war. It is a better world now; for the face of
> the Sun-god shines as it did of old; and the land is peopled by the children of two
> races who came hither from the old world and share under one flag the privileges
> of a great Empire.[1]

In this quotation, Drummond sought to capture the mix of cultural and political influences of old world and new, acknowledge the presence of both indigenous and settler populations, and even duly recognize the early prominent
stature of Aboriginal women within their communities. Yet at the same time,
the invitation extended to women of the old world was not open to all those of
European origin but rather to a select group of British immigrants. Moreover,

Aboriginal women were treated to only a "backward glance," with indigenous people more generally being surpassed by two races (and only two) of English- and French-speaking people in a now "better world." And certainly there were many francophones who would have contended that the privileges of the Canadian nation and British Empire were neither equally shared nor even desired.

This second volume of *Documenting First Wave Feminisms* focuses on Canada. The separate volume allows for an examination of feminist activism within a particular national context, while providing for recognition of transnational collaborations and cross-currents. This anthology is especially timely given that there has been renewed scholarly interest in first wave feminism in this country after several decades of relatively little historical research. Still, the Canadian historiography remains underdeveloped and it is intended that documents in this volume will address and in some instances redress ongoing gaps in the scholarship.

As of yet we still know all too little about the initial genesis of women's social and political activism in nineteenth-century Canada. Scholars here have often pointed to such factors as the origin of church-affiliated organizations, the quest for higher education, and the campaign to secure women's property rights as contributing to the creation of the "woman movement" in the second half of the century.[2] However, work covering the period before the 1870s is notably sparse, which raises questions about possible connections between women's involvement in the movement to abolish slavery, coordinated benevolence endeavours, and temperance activities early in the century to the emergence of feminism, connections which have been documented as crucial in other contexts.[3] As well, recent historiography has cautioned against a singular narrative for the beginnings of feminism and instead proposed the identification of a number of "origin stories"[4] which acknowledge national and international influences.

The Canadian scholarship remains underdeveloped in a number of other crucial ways. At a most basic level there is deficient information about an array of individuals, organizations, and forms of interaction or non-interaction.[5] The actual struggle for suffrage, for example, has elicited rather cursory study in recent decades. Incredibly, we have to go back over a half-century for our last comprehensive work on suffrage with Catherine Cleverdon's *The Woman Suffrage Movement in Canada*.[6] Of equal significance, we lack adequate analysis of how gender, race, ethnicity, class, religion, and colonial status intersected with one another in shaping ideas, actions, and interactions. And hence, as a case in point, little has yet been produced about what relationships developed, or did not develop, between white and racialized, working-class and middle-class, Catholic and Protestant, anglophone and francophone, or settler and Aboriginal women in the making and remaking of first wave feminism.

An issue which has resulted in extensive scholarly inquiry and discussion is the racial politics of feminists in the late nineteenth century and early twentieth century. More explicitly, scholars have considered the charge first made by Carol Lee Bacchi and later elaborated upon by Mariana Valverde, that first wave Canadian feminists were racist.[7] The debate which ensued, or what has been referred to as the entrenched polarities[8] which developed, resulted in some historians uniformly condemning the beliefs and actions of first wave feminism while others sought to defend them. A number of scholars have attempted subsequently to move beyond such polarization – to avoid both "the reductive conclusion that all first wave feminist writing promoted a monolithic racism" and arguments that early feminists not be judged so harshly for being "a product of their age."[9] Janice Fiamengo's analysis of the writings of various first wave feminists is one example of such an approach. Examining the race thinking of Nellie McClung and others, Fiamengo has discerned ambiguity, contradiction, and variation. Literary critics such as Fiamengo, Cecily Devereux who has also delved into the life and writings of McClung, and Jennifer Henderson who has explored racial thought among those she characterizes as "settler feminists," have been contributing much to our understanding of racialization and racism within the first wave, but we are still lacking richly detailed studies that are more attentive to the connections between discourse and action, and the broader political and social context, something that historians continue to do so well.[10] Questions also need to be raised about the racial politics not only of Anglo-Celtic women, but of francophone reformers as well.

Due attention to the national context is important for fully comprehending the origins and evolution of the Canadian women's movement. How reformers conceived of and acted upon various feminist issues was influenced by particular demographic, political, cultural, and linguistic features of Canadian society. The federal political structure created with Confederation, for example, had significant long-term ramifications as to where and how activists concentrated their efforts. The trajectory of economic development and of immigrant settlement patterns also had consequences for feminist thought and mobilization. Joan Sangster has maintained that taking the nation into account is essential for exploring the history of feminism as: "Nation states were and are the boundaries within which the law, policy and organizations of civil society shaped women's lives and attention to the way in which women were differently excluded, marginalized or punitively viewed by, and within the nation, are crucial ..."[11] Further, an in-depth understanding of the national context is a necessary foundation for making nuanced comparisons of similarities and divergences between the women's movement in Canada and elsewhere.

Taking national specificity into consideration also involves critically interrogating the very meaning, or more precisely meanings, of "nation" itself within the first wave.[12] The situation in Canada was especially complex, as the shift from colony to nation was protracted and uneven, and one in which indigenous people continued to be largely excluded from the rights and responsibilities of British subjects. There was also the added presence of a minority French-speaking population of European origin which had been colonized, as well as a non-British immigrant population which expanded dramatically at the turn of the century. In such a context it is thus hardly surprising that there was not a fixed or even singular conception of nation among women activists. Additional research is necessary that employs nation as a category of analysis, but without question multiple factors including race, colonial status, and language directly informed how women reformers variously formulated priorities for nation building, definitions of nationalism, and national identities.

At the same time, as an impressive body of recent historical scholarship has established, valuable insights can be garnered by looking beyond the immediate parameters of colony/nation to explore transnational influences and connections within the first wave.[13] And certainly questions related to colonialism and imperialism have been deemed intrinsic to such broader terms of reference. As Antoinette Burton has stated, "the category of feminism itself emerged from the historical context of modern colonialism and anti-colonial struggles."[14] Scholars in this country are just beginning to examine how long-lasting and significant British imperial ties shaped the women's movement; up to this juncture there has been relatively little dialogue between the feminist historiography of Canada and the historiography of the British Empire.[15] In a successful attempt to reinterpret the existing Canadian scholarship through an imperial lens, Adele Perry has eloquently postulated that, "in feminist hands, Empire gave political ballast to a striking range of equity claims, including arguments for the passage of dower laws to protect women's interest in prairie homesteads, campaigns to restrict public access to liquor, struggles for women's right to the vote, and local efforts to improve medical, social and legal services to children and youth."[16] And still other issues of ongoing concern for activists such as married women's citizenship, legal title for women to the designation of "persons," and Canadian engagement in military conflicts remained deeply enmeshed in British imperial politics.

Canadian historians will benefit from the extensive historiography that already exists which is attentive to exploring the contours of feminism in a British white settler society, most notably in Australia, New Zealand, and South Africa. Altogether such work has demonstrated the importance of investigating the historically contingent and contextually specific dynamics of feminism in a society with ongoing political, social, and cultural ties to empire; and further, the importance of understanding how contexts such as these shaped women's participation in feminist networks across borders.[17] Scholars of British settler societies elsewhere have drawn particular attention to the implications of the emergence of feminism alongside the displacement and oppression of indigenous peoples. Referring to feminists and their supporters in New Zealand and Australia, one scholar has noted that they "made their case for equity and justice for the female sex in societies immersed in negative constructions of indigenous peoples of both sexes."[18] A puzzling and seemingly distinct element of feminism in this white settler society was the way in which Euro-Canadian reformers for the most part avoided discussion of Aboriginal women. To the limited degree that Aboriginal women were the subject of feminist commentary, they were depicted in mainly pejorative and stereotypic terms. And otherwise, notably in terms of reformers expressing concerns about Aboriginal women (and Aboriginal men) being denied certain political and civil rights as well as experiencing extremely poor material conditions, one finds mostly silence. Such silence was not unique among female activists in white settler societies. Patricia Grimshaw has argued that Australian feminists, at least into the early decades of the twentieth century, completely ignored the plight of Aborigines.[19] Yet while most white feminists in Australia and in other settler societies continued to situate themselves in a position of superiority over indigenous women, over time many came to see themselves as colonizers, which resulted in indigenous women becoming the subject of study and the object of activism.[20] There is no indication of a similar shift in Canada; instead, Aboriginal people were primarily relegated to "religious missionary concerns while being marginalized from political processes and historical memory."[21] Further research is required to explain why exactly this was the case, but part of the answer might be found in the different settlement patterns and racial composition of Canada over the course of the late nineteenth century and early twentieth century. Sarah Carter has surmised that for white women on the Prairies, which could well be generalized for the country as a whole, "with the arrival of diverse white women, and as Aboriginal people became a minority isolated on reserves, white femininity no longer depended for its articulation on a sense of difference from Aboriginal women, rather a British-Canadian femininity was contrasted with negative assumptions about 'foreign' women."[22]

Imperial ties overlapped of course with international connections throughout the first wave. As one will observe in this documents anthology, Canadian feminists worked collaboratively on an individual and collective basis with activists elsewhere, often building upon existing personal and political ties, around issues of mutual interest or concern such as suffrage, prostitution, pacifism, women's legal rights, and socialism. There were a number of marked "axes of influence" that persisted over time with, most significantly, Canadians participating in and being shaped by a northern transatlantic network of Euro-American feminists from early on in the nineteenth century. Within this network British and American women continued to be a dominating presence to a degree that often accorded Canadian activists and their contributions a marginal status. However, on occasion reformers here proved more than capable of initiating transnational endeavours and innovations as well as assuming leadership roles in key organizations and campaigns. In terms of the trans-Pacific network that developed somewhat later around the turn of the century, Canadian women interacted primarily with their antipodean peers in Australia and New Zealand to begin with, but over time forged connections in South Asia and East Asia. It would appear that they were largely absent, however, from the attempts at hemispheric collaboration that occurred in the Americas during the interwar period.[23]

A related and important aspect of transnational engagement entailed participation in one or more of the international feminist organizations. A somewhat detailed discussion follows, as the historiography up to this point has lacked even the broadest of outlines about such organizational ties.[24] The first large multipurpose organization was the International Council of Women (ICW), formed in 1888, and in many respects Canadian involvement in the ICW was more extensive than any other women's international organization. Canada was not only the first country to create a national section – the National Council of Women of Canada (NCWC) – but its then president, Lady Aberdeen, went on to become the long-term president of the ICW (from 1893 to 1936, with only brief gaps from 1899 to 1904 and 1920 to 1922). In recognition of its prominent role in promoting and supporting the ICW, Canada was selected to host the quinquennial meeting in Toronto in 1909. After the war, a member of the NCWC served on the executive of the ICW throughout the 1920s, and others made regular and often significant contributions as national convenors on its various standing committees during the entire period. Involvement with this international body accorded council women in Canada a broader perspective on their own activities and goals. And certainly, they acquired valuable information about the strategies different countries were pursuing to address an array of social problems and forms of discrimination that variously affirmed their actions or challenged them. The ICW was by far the most conservative of the major international bodies, though, with its leaders avoiding issues that were potentially divisive among member countries, including, during the early years, female suffrage.[25]

Another prominent international organization with which Canadian feminists had involvement, at least initially, was the International Alliance of Women (IAW). This group originated as the International Woman Suffrage Alliance in 1904 as an offshoot of the ICW that would allow organizational support for those feminists who wished to openly advocate for enfranchisement. Canada was once again among the first countries to create a national section in 1906 with the Dominion Women's Enfranchisement Association (DWEA) and later the Canadian Suffrage Association (CSA) serving as the national auxiliary for the IAW. Well-known feminists such as Flora MacDonald Denison and August Stowe Gullen attended the organization's congresses before the First World War. However, even as the IAW broadened the range of issues it addressed and renamed itself the International Alliance of Women for Suffrage and Equal Rights in the early 1920s, Canadian contact with this group became rather sporadic. The attainment of the federal franchise in 1918 and the subsequent demise of the CSA was a significant factor, but so too was the dominating presence of Lady Aberdeen, who actively discouraged involvement in an organization that she perceived as being in competition with the ICW. As a consequence, links between Canadian activists and an international women's organization that was far more explicitly feminist and more willing to tackle controversial topics such as birth control and women's employment rights remained tenuous at best.[26]

An organization that garnered much more extensive Canadian participation was the Women's International League for Peace and Freedom (WILPF), which emerged out of the Women's Peace Conference held at the Hague in 1915.[27] With mainstream women's groups in Canada effectively boycotting the conference, a small contingent of feminists did attend, resulting in Canada being one of the thirteen founding national sections in WILPF. While the promotion of peace and intercultural dialogue remained the core purposes of WILPF, this group pursued a wide range of feminist issues and, as Leila Rupp has observed, "consistently took more radical positions" on topics such as imperialism.[28] And certainly of any of the women's organizations that operated during this period, WILPF attracted a far more diverse group of women in Canada. The largest and most active chapters, which were located in Toronto, Winnipeg, and Vancouver, had members who were principally middle class and university educated, but a number of working-class groups and the leading progressive farm women's organizations in the country, such as the United Farm Women of Alberta (UFWA) and the Women's Section of the Saskatchewan Grain Growers Association (Women's Section, SGGA) were officially affiliated. Most members identified as being socialist or social democratic. Canadian members of WILPF demonstrated a keen interest in world affairs and in ongoing ideological debates within their organization, although practical considerations limited their ability to forge extensive transnational networks of like-minded women or to assume a greater leadership role at the international level. Travel to WILPF conferences that were mostly held in Europe proved to be especially challenging. Far less affluent than their peers involved in ICW or IAW, many could ill afford an overseas trip. When the main congress of WILPF was held in Washington in 1924, it provided one of the few opportunities for a sizeable contingent of Canadian members to be present at such a gathering.

A final international organization worth mentioning is the Pan-Pacific Women's Association, formed in 1930 as part of the rapid expansion of feminist internationalism in the interwar period. The organization included countries from the Pacific rim such as New Zealand, the United States, Japan, China, Samoa, and Canada – along with India. The organization met every couple of years in various locations to promote cross-cultural understanding between East and West and to follow a social reform agenda aimed at establishing social and economic standards for urban and rural as well as islander women throughout the Asian Region. It represented a "less xenophobic internationalism [that] provided a new conceptual space for East/West internationalism."[29] Angela Woolacott has argued that Australian participation in the PPWA further decentred imperial feminism, allowing for a degree of cooperation, however tenuous, on women's issues across developed/developing divides.[30] While Canadian involvement was initially rather modest, by the mid-1930s there were a growing number of enthusiastic supporters, with a small group of female academics being among the most prominent. The dean of women at the University of British Columbia, Mary Bollert, who was a member of the PPWA from the outset, became its president in 1937, the same year Canada hosted the international meeting of this group in Vancouver.

In terms of formal connections with international women's groups, without question Anglo-Celtic middle-class and upper-middle-class women predominated. They, after all, had the financial means, time, and desire to engage in regular correspondence and to take long overseas trips. By the interwar period involvement in an international organization for at least some women also further solidified their identity as educated female professionals with the formation of groups such as the International Federation of University Women (IFUW) and the International Federation of Business and Professional Women (IFBPW). There is as yet little evidence of substantive organizational engagement by francophone middle-class women; and as one indicator, very few can be found among the Canadian representatives who attended conferences of the leading international women's groups from the late 1800s onwards. Micheline Dumont and Louise Toupin have argued that francophone feminists primarily concentrated on maintaining provincial women's groups and on struggles internal to Quebec, shifting their focus elsewhere only after obtaining the provincial vote in 1940.[31] Yolande Cohen has recently suggested that Quebec francophone groups such as the Fédération nationale Saint-Jean-Baptiste were influenced by British and American feminist networks and to some degree by the women's movement in France, but in-depth research is needed as to the precise links that were formed between individuals and groups.[32]

While working-class women and farm women were far more restricted in their ability to reach across national borders, they did so, albeit less frequently and on a more informal level than their middle-class peers. For labouring women, the North America–based Knights of Labour of the late nineteenth century and selected "international" unions (in reality composed of members from the United States and Canada) by the early twentieth century provided some degree of transnational dialogue and organizational support, especially on female employment issues and women's rights. So too would multi-country gatherings such as the International Congress of Working Women, which met annually for a number of years following the First World War, with representatives chiefly from Western industrialized countries, including Canada. And certainly left-wing feminists, many of whom were working class and immigrants, attempted to create "a new world for women" against the injuries of class inequality and female subordination, with many guided by directives and debates arising out of the Socialist International and later the Communist International. Organized farm women benefited from the efforts of prominent leaders such as Irene Parlby and Violet McNaughton, who created various links with feminist groups outside the country. Among a number of initiatives, McNaughton actually embarked on a campaign to create a Canadian section of the International Co-operative Women's Guild in the interwar period, although this was one that ultimately failed. As already noted, however, farm women were well represented among the membership of WILPF Canada.

Transnational engagement and cross-border influences were not just forged through organizational ties and solidified by attendance at far-flung conferences or congresses. Many activists, including those with modest educational credentials, read extensively and attended lectures and presentations about women's issues in the transatlantic and trans-Pacific worlds, along with those about a wide spectrum of topics related to "world affairs," such as slavery, international relations, disarmament, and communism. And of course, successive generations of immigrant women were by definition "transnationals," having made at least one and sometimes several global crossings from their homeland to arrive in British North America and later Canada. Scholars such as Donna Gabaccio, Franca Iacovetta, and Jennifer Guglielmo have been uncovering a rich history of proletarian feminism among women immigrants in various localities across the globe for whom connections between their homelands and communities abroad were many and ongoing.[33] The historical literature on female immigrant militants in Canada is far less developed, but work on Icelandic, Ukrainian, and Finnish women points to the development of activist networks, often premised on ethnic loyalties, which were concerned with local, national, and international issues.[34]

Organization of the Volume

As with the first volume, we have organized the source documents into thematic rubrics that address the central issues that encompassed the key debates and struggles within first wave feminism. We clearly cannot hope to address all the issues associated with the women's movement, any more than we can hope, given constraints of space, to be comprehensive in our selection of documents, but we are persuaded that the categories we have chosen are broadly representative. While documents related to imperialism and internationalism appear throughout this volume, we have devoted a separate section to each of these themes at the outset to establish in depth their significance to feminist thought and action in the Canadian context.

This volume begins with an examination of imperialism. Canadian feminism, as will be demonstrated, was profoundly influenced by ongoing connections to the British Empire and debates over imperial ideology. The political and social reform work devised and revised by women activists took place within a British white settler society where sharply drawn distinctions between settlers and indigenous peoples were the organizing grammar for governance and the operation of civil society. For the most part Euro-Canadian reformers drew upon pejorative imperial stereotypes in their limited depiction of indigenous peoples, leaving it up to select Aboriginal women to attempt to refute them. Anglo-Celtic feminists, who by and large continued to the dominate the women's movement, especially outside of Quebec, often viewed their endeavours as part of the larger "civilizing" project of British imperialism and as maintaining desired ties to the mother country. Support for the imperial project manifested itself in numerous ways, including public expressions of loyalty to the monarchy, and was further strengthened by travel to the metropole of London, where reformers interacted with British feminists and those from other settler countries. Much of the imperial feminist discourse produced by Canadian reformers, though, reinforced racial asymmetry and prejudice towards non-British immigrants. Another important facet of imperialism examined in this section is its close association with English Canadian nationalism, which not only viewed national responsibilities as synonymous with imperial obligations, but also depicted French Canadians and their nationalist aspirations in a negative light. In contrast, francophone feminists conceived of an enlightened citizenship shaped by French-speaking peoples and at some remove from English-speaking Canada and, by extension, Britain. Canadian feminist critiques of imperialism did occur, although less often than expressions of support.

The next section examines internationalism. Documents dealing with slavery and abolition have been incorporated here rather than constituting an entirely separate section, in part due to the limited scholarship that yet exists on this topic for British North America, but also to highlight the importance of the international struggle against human bondage in the origin of an organized women's movement in Canada. One can discern in these initial materials various forms of transatlantic influences as a collective political culture began to coalesce among women reformers in the colony, although one that was soon critiqued for its discriminatory practices. Over time an increasing number of female activists became involved in a variety of international feminist networks in which ideas and organizational initiatives constantly circulated. However, ties with the United States and Great Britain continued to define and to some degree delimit Canadian international involvement. Reformers gained much-needed encouragement and support from their cross-border collaborations, but many also willingly engaged in the dissemination of Western cultural imperialism, especially through their sponsorship of work in non-Western countries and among colonized peoples. Such pursuits, moreover, took place alongside efforts in Canada to minimize the influence, if not the actual presence, of certain international or "alien elements" in the form of non-British immigrants. Left-wing feminists pursued an alternative form of internationalism, with socialist and later communist women endeavouring to build working-class solidarity and secure female emancipation as part of what they conceived to be a global struggle. Women from select immigrant groups were notably well represented among these activists, while, more broadly, expressions of "gender consciousness" among the "foreign born" were influenced by political movements in their homelands and by challenges specific to their ethnic/racialized group in this country.

Suffrage was in many respects the defining issue of first wave feminism in Canada, especially as the struggle to secure it was so protracted, with women in Quebec gaining the provincial vote only after the outbreak of the Second World War. Canadian feminists retained close links with the well-coordinated international suffrage campaign, which they helped support and from which they drew inspiration. A number of documents related to the partial federal franchise during the First World War have been incorporated in this section, as the controversy surrounding this measure provides important insights into ongoing and significant fault lines within the Canadian women's movement and the ways in which it elicited differing responses within and from without the country. The arguments deployed by suffragists were numerous, but many employed a "progress" narrative that emphasized the attainment of equal citizenship and political representation for women as being essential in an "advanced" and "modern" country such as Canada. In the voluminous number of materials examined for this project, only fleeting reference was made in a couple of documents to the vote with relation to Aboriginal women, and even then they were only mentioned in order to exclude them from consideration.[35] Anglo-Celtic middle-class women based many of their qualifications for full political participation on selected and interconnected forms of privilege. Non-British immigrant and working-class women, however, made their own case for female suffrage and for their own benefit. And francophone activists often premised their arguments for suffrage on the accomplishments of French Canadian women and as a means of furthering a nationalist feminist project.

First wave feminists sought to achieve more than formal political rights, though; they also engaged in a much broader campaign to improve women's citizenship rights and to attain an equitable role in the nation state. The claims making of women reformers was premised in large measure on what they perceived to be the multiple contributions of women to nation building. The deep-seated legacy of colonialism served as an organizing frame for such claims making seemingly from the outset, however, leaving mostly unacknowledged the appeals of Aboriginal peoples for similar privileges and powers. Moreover, Euro-Canadian activists more often promoted rather than challenged discriminatory state policies and societal attitudes aimed at non-British immigrant populations. Nonetheless, female reformers from assorted racialized and immigrant groups proved quite capable of asserting their qualifications for full citizenship on their own terms. Various international citizenship campaigns, including married women's nationality rights, received sustained support from women reformers in Canada. And in their efforts to secure legal recognition for women as "persons" that had potential implications in the British Commonwealth and beyond, they actually assumed a leadership position.

The ensuing sections explore particular areas of citizenship-related activism and debate: moral reform (including sexuality and birth control), economic status and work, and pacifism. The unit on moral reform well illustrates that the contestation of citizenship went beyond legal and civil rights to include discussion of the morality of individuals, of communities, and of the nation. Frequently motivated by a combination of social reform and religious impulses, although the latter became more muted in the early twentieth century, numerous women activists assumed the mantle of community leaders who were engaged in a quest to raise the moral tone of Canadian society through the dissemination of "proper knowledge." A great deal of emphasis was placed on the attainment of a single moral standard, a common goal among most Euro-American feminists during this period, although there was not always uniform agreement on its precise meaning. Yet many of the organizational initiatives were directly informed by and helped to perpetuate a feminist discourse that more often upheld than subverted race and class hierarchies and was steeped in imperialist sentiment.

Women's precarious economic status, and more specifically the ongoing difficulties they faced as paid workers, was another important source of agitation. Social inequities once again shaped how concerns were formulated and responded to, but the opinions of working-class women arguably had greater influence on this feminist issue than any other. Working within but mostly outside the male-dominated organized labour movement, and at times in collaboration with middle-class allies, working-class feminists sought to combat oppressive working conditions and low wages. Protective labour legislation was deemed to be crucial to their agenda, but it garnered a rather tepid response from some middle-class reformers and even overt resistance from others. Once international labour standards were established at the turn of the century, they became a crucial benchmark against which to measure the situation of Canadian working women, although most female activists failed to note that these were standards that applied to the relatively economically privileged Western industrialized countries. That the economic interests of white working women were often viewed as being more important than those of "other" women and selected groups of men was also rarely questioned, either by working-class or middle-class feminists. Ongoing racial prejudice and the legacy of colonialism even meant that Aboriginal women's employment remained outside of discussions of "women's work." Agrarian reformers formulated the issue to fit their particular circumstances, reminding their urban peers that the financial well-being of women also depended on family enterprises such as the farm.

The promotion of peace was adopted as a key goal by many of the leading Canadian women's reform organizations from the nineteenth century onward. As with Euro-American feminist groups elsewhere, most supported the core principle that conflicts within and between nations should be resolved through negotiation, not armed conflict. But this principle was soon weakened with the outbreak of the Boer War and abandoned by many altogether with the First World War, when patriotic allegiance to nation and the British Empire was deemed to be more important than the goals of pacifism. Even so, a network of feminists with links to a pre-existing transnational women's peace movement endured and in time expanded with the formation of a Canadian section of WILPF. In the wake of the First World War, mainstream women's groups pursued a moderate approach to peace activism by espousing collective security, international cooperation, and disarmament, but the socialist and social democratic women who dominated WILPF assumed a far more explicit anti-militarist and anti-imperialist stance.

In the selection of specific documents for a given thematic section, preference has been given to less readily available materials on the principle that the more canonical texts can be found in most libraries. In some cases, however, short excerpts from canonical texts have been included because they are so central to the issue in question. Where possible we have avoided abridging archival documents or materials from out-of-print books, but we have been forced in one or two instances, again because of space considerations, to depart from this policy. We have been limited in our selection of documents that did not originate in English or French because of the challenges that getting such materials translated posed and due to limitations with the existing historiography. This documents project has revealed the need for further research on a range of topics and individuals, but most especially with regard to non-English- and non-French-speaking Aboriginal and immigrant feminisms. Nevertheless, we are confident that altogether the documents contained in this volume demonstrate the richness and complexity of the Canadian first wave feminist movement.

A Note on the Text

The original spelling conventions have been retained for all the documents collected in this volume. The texts translated from French follow the British convention. Errors in punctuation and obvious typographical errors have been silently corrected.

NOTES

1   D. Julia Drummond, "Introductory," in *Women of Canada: Their Life and Work, National Council of Women of Canada* (Ottawa: Queen's Printer, 1900; repr. 1975), 4.
2   See, for example, Alison Prentice et al., *Canadian Women: A History*, 2nd ed. (Toronto: Harcourt Brace, 1996).
3   Bonnie Anderson, *Joyous Greetings: The First International Women's Movement, 1830–1860* (Oxford, New York: Oxford UP, 2000); Clare Midgley, *Women against Slavery: The British Campaigns 1780–1870* (New York: Routledge, 1992); Patricia

D'Itri, *Cross Currents in the International Women's Movement, 1848–1948* (Bowling Green, OH: Bowling Green State University Popular Press, 1999).

4 Nancy Hewitt, "Origin Stories: Remapping First Wave Feminism," Sisterhood and Slavery: Transatlantic Antislavery and Women's Rights, Proceedings of the Third Annual Gilder Lehrman Center International Conference at Yale University, 25–28 October 2001, http://www.yale.edu/glc/conference/index.htm.

5 For a more extended discussion of deficiencies in the Canadian historical literature, see Nancy Forestell, "Mrs. Canada Goes Global: First Wave Feminism Revisted," *Atlantis* 30, no. 1 (Fall 2005), 7–20.

6 Catherine Cleverdon, *The Woman Suffrage Movement in Canada* (Toronto: U of Toronto P, 1950; repr. 1974).

7 Carol Lee Bacchi, *Liberation Deferred: The Ideas of English-Canadian Suffragists, 1877–1918* (Toronto: U of Toronto P, 1983); Mariana Valverde, "'When the Mother of the Race Is Free': Race, Reproduction, and Sexuality in First-Wave Feminism," in *Gender Conflicts: New Essays in Women's History*, ed. Franca Iacovetta and Mariana Valverde (Toronto: U of Toronto P, 1992), 3–26.

8 Veronica Strong-Boag, Mona Gleason, and Adele Perry, eds., *Rethinking Canada: The Promise of Women's History*, 4th ed. (Toronto: Oxford UP, 2002), 150.

9 Janice Fiamengo, "A Legacy of Ambivalence: Responses to Nellie McClung," in *Rethinking Canada*, Strong-Boag, Gleason, and Perry, 154.

10 Cecily Devereux, *Growing a Race: Nellie L. McClung and the Fiction of Eugenic Feminism* (Montreal: McGill-Queen's UP, 2005); Jennifer Henderson, *Settler Feminism and Race Making in Canada* (Toronto: U of Toronto P, 2003).

11 Joan Sangster, "Archiving Feminist Histories: Women, the 'Nation' and Metanarratives in Canadian Historical Writing," *Women's Studies International Forum* 29, no. 3 (2006), 260.

12 Ibid., 261–2; see also Micheline Dumont, "Can a National History Include a Feminist Reflection on History," *Journal of Canadian Studies,* 35, no. 2 (Summer 2000), 80–94.

13 See, for example, Katie Holmes and Marilyn Lake, eds., *Women's Rights and Human Rights: International Feminist Perspectives* (London: Palgrave, 2001); Mrialini Sinha, Donna Guy, and Angela Woolacott, eds., *Feminisms and Internationalism* (London: Blackwell, 1999); and Christine Bolt, *Sisterhood Questioned: Race, Class and Internationalism in the American and British Women's Movements, c. 1880s–1970s* (New York: Routledge, 2004).

14 Antoinette Burton, *Burdens of History: British Feminists, Indian Women, and Imperial Culture, 1865–1915* (Chapel Hill: U of North Carolina P, 1994), 6; see also Clare Midgely, "Gender and Imperialism: Mapping the Connections," in *Gender and Imperialism*, ed. C. Midgley (Manchester: Manchester UP, 2008), 1–18.

15 Adele Perry, "Women, Gender, and Empire," in *Canada and the British Empire*, ed. Phillip Buckner (Toronto: Oxford UP, 2008), 220.

16 Ibid., 234.

17 See, for example, Raewyn Dalziel, "Presenting the Enfranchisement of New Zealand Women Abroad," in *Suffrage and Beyond: International Feminist Perspectives*, ed. Caroline Daley and Melanie Nolan (New York: New York UP, 1994), 42–62; Patricia Grimshaw, "Settler Anxieties, Indigenous Peoples and Women's Suffrage in the Colonies of Australia, New Zealand, and Hawai'i 1888–1902," *Pacific Historical Review* 69, no. 4 (2000), 553–72; Marilyn Lake, "Frontier Feminism and the Marauding White Man: Australia, 1880s to 1940s," in *Nation, Empire, Colony: Historicizing Gender and Race*, ed. Ruth Roach Pierson and Nupur Chaudhur (Bloomington, IN: Indiana UP, 1998), 94–105; Louise Vincent, "A Cake of Soak: The Volksmoeder Ideology and Afrikaner Women's Campaign for the Vote, *International Journal of African Historical Studies* 32, no. 1 (1999), 1–17; and Louise Vincent, "The Power behind the Scenes: The Afrikaner Nationalist Women's Parities, 1915–1931," *South African Historical Journal* 40 (May 1999), 51–73.

18 Patricia Grimshaw, "Reading the Silences: Suffrage Activists and Race in Nineteenth Century Settler Societies," in *Women's Rights and Human Rights: International Historical Perspectives*, ed. Patricia Grimshaw, Katie Holmes, and Marilyn Lake (London: Palgrave, 2001), 33.

19 Ibid., 35.

20 See, for example, Marilyn Lake, "Childbearers as Rights Bearers: Feminist Discourse on the Rights of Aboriginal and Non-Aboriginal Mothers in Australia, 1920–1950," *Women's History Review* 8, no. 2 (1999), 347–63; and Fiona Paisley, "Australian Feminism and Indigenous Rights in the International Context, 1920s and 1930s," *Feminist Review* 58 (1998), 66–84.

21 Patricia Grimshaw used this phrase to describe the silence among Australian feminists about Aboriginal peoples in that country in the nineteenth century, but it is equally applicable to Canadian activists attitudes towards First Nations people well into the twentieth century. See Grimshaw, "Reading the Silences," 47.

22 Sarah Carter, "Britishness, 'Foreignness,' Women and Land in Western Canada," *Humanities Research* 13 (Nov. 2006), 45. Kurt Korneski also argues that local elites in Winnipeg tended to "ignore the situation of Aboriginals altogether." See Kurt Korneski, "Reform and Empire: The Case of Winnipeg, Manitoba, 1870s–1910s," *Urban History Review/Revue d'histoire urbaine* 37, no. 1 (Fall 2008), 55.

23 There is evidence that a small number of Canadian women attended congresses held by Latin American feminists in the 1920s, but as yet there is no indication of any form of substantive engagement.

24 A detailed account of Canadian feminist internationalism may be found in Nancy
    Forestell, "Transnational Citizenship in a Post-Suffrage Era?: Canadian First Wave
    Feminism, 1919–1939," paper presented at the annual meeting of the Canadian
    Historical Association, University of Saskatchewan, June 2007.

25 Leila Rupp, *Worlds of Women: The Making of an International Women's Move-
    ment* (Princeton, NJ: Princeton UP, 1997), 20.

26 Ibid., 24.

27 Canadian historians Veronica Strong-Boag and Thomas Socknat have closely
    examined the activities of WILPF during the interwar period, but their focus was
    more on matters internal to the country than on transnational connections and
    issues. See Veronica Strong-Boag, "Canada's Peace-Making Women: Canada,
    1919–1939," in *Women and Peace: Theoretical, Historical and Practical Perspec-
    tives*, ed. Ruth Pierson et al. (London: Croom Helm, 1987), 170–91; Thomas
    Socknat, "For Peace and Freedom: Canadian Feminists and the Interwar Peace
    Campaign," in *Up and Doing: Canadian Women and Peace*, ed. Janice Williamson
    and Deborah Gorham (Toronto: Women's Press, 1989), 66–88. WILPF first came
    about as a result of the Women's Peace Conference in the Hague, Netherlands. Out
    of that meeting an International Committee for Permanent Peace was established
    and later renamed WILPF.

28 Rupp, *Worlds of Women*, 33.

29 Fiona Paisley, "Cultivating Modernity: Culture and Internationalism in Australian
    Feminism's Pacific Age," *Journal of Women's History* 14, no. 3 (2002), 105–32;
    see also Fiona Paisley, *Cultural Internationalism and Race Politics in the Women's
    Pan-Pacific* (Honolulu: U of Hawai'i P, 2009).

30 Angela Woolacott, "Inventing Commonwealth and Pan-Pacific Feminisms: Aus-
    tralian Women's Internationalist Activism in the 1920s and 1930s," in *Feminisms
    and Internationalism*, ed. Mrialini Sinha, Donna Guy, and Angela Woollacott
    (London: Blackwell, 1999) 82.

31 Micheline Dumont and Louise Toupin, eds., *La pensée féministe au Québec:
    Anthologie, 1900–1985* (Montreal: Les Éditions du remue-ménage, 2003), 396.

32 Yolande Cohen, *Femmes philanthropes: Catholiques, protestantes et juives dans
    les organizations caritatives au Québec* (Montreal: U of Montreal P, 2010),
    64–5.

33 See Donna Gabaccia and Franca Iacovetta, "Women, Work and Protest in the
    Italian Diaspora: An International Research Agenda," *Labour/Le Travail* 42 (Fall
    1998), 161–81; Donna Gabaccia and Franca Iacovetta, eds., *Women, Gender and
    Transnational Lives: Italian Workers of the World* (Toronto: U of Toronto P, 2002);
    Jennifer Guglielmo, "Transnational Feminism's Radical Past: Lessons from Italian
    Immigrant Women Anarchists in Industrializing America," *Journal of Women's
    History* 22, no. 1 (Spring 2010), 10–33.

34 See, for example, Joan Sangter, "*Robitntsia*, Ukrainian Communists, and the
    'Porcupinism' Debate: Reassessing Ethnicity, Gender and Class in Early Cana-
    dian Communism, 1922–1930," *Labour/Travail* 56 (Fall 2005), 51–89; Varpu
    Lindstrom-Best, *Defiant Sisters: A Social History of Finnish Immigrant Women
    in Canada* (Toronto: MHSO, 1992); Frances Swyripa, *Wedded to the Cause:
    Ukrainian-Canadian Women and Ethnic Identity, 1891–1991* (Toronto: U of
    Toronto P, 1993); and Mary Kinnear, "The Icelandic Connection: *Freya* and the
    Manitoba Woman Suffrage Movement," *Canadian Woman's Studies* 7, no. 4 (Fall
    1986), 25–8.
35 Emily Cummings, "A Century of Progress: Discussion Continued," this volume,
    p. 123; and Edith Archibald, "Canada Notes," *Woman's Column* (Boston, MA), 8,
    no. 11 (1895), 2.

PART ONE
Imperial/National Feminisms

I am charged with the unpardonable sin of marrying a white man. I should like to know if you have a law in England that would deprive a woman of property left her by her Father's will, or if you please, inherited property? I ask have you a law that would deprive that woman of her property because she got married to a Frenchman?

The above quotation is drawn from a land claim submitted to British colonial authorities by Nahnebahwequa, also known as Catherine Sutton, in 1860. An Anishinabe woman who married an English immigrant, William Sutton, Nahnebahwequa protested against the dispossession of land that she considered to be integral to her indigenous birthright and called attention to the discriminatory nature of colonial policy towards Aboriginal women in her situation.[1] By "marrying out" Nahnebahwequa and other Aboriginal women were informed that their claims to and (co-)ownership of ancestral lands were abrogated; this policy would continue to be enforced for the next century and a quarter. Nahnebawequa also employed the explicit language of women's property rights, the focus of considerable reform efforts during the mid-nineteenth century, yet such grievances remained almost entirely outside the realm of feminist activism or even interest. The imperial foundations upon which the first wave feminist movement developed in British North America created sharp distinctions between the injustices of colonized and colonizer in ways that prevented most Euro-Canadian female reformers from perceiving this as a "women's issue." Moreover, the difficulties of Aboriginal women more generally received relatively little attention among women's rights advocates. Nevertheless, the very existence of this document and the precise argument used by Nahnebahwequa within it, provides important and tangible evidence that these imperial foundations were contested from early on and, of particular significance, by an Aboriginal woman.

Imperialism had a direct and enduring influence on first wave feminism in Canada. The women's movement originated and evolved in the specific circumstances of a white settler colony and later independent dominion with continued cultural, social, and political ties to the British Empire. Feminists' perceptions of themselves were constituted, as Marilyn Lake has argued in the similar of case of Australia, "within an imperialist framework, in terms of dichotomies drawn between the 'civilized' and 'primitive,' 'Europeans' and 'natives,' 'advanced' and 'backward.'"[2] Women reformers asserted their own entitlement to civil and other rights within a colony and, in time, a nation founded on "racial imperialism." In the particular case of Canada, there was the added dimension that not only had indigenous peoples been colonized, but so too had a population of non-British European origin – French Canadians. Anglo-Celtic feminists, who for the most part continued to dominate the women's movement, viewed their efforts as connected with the larger "civilizing" project of the British Empire, and were critical of what they perceived as the "narrow" and "backward" elements of French Canadian society. Furthermore, as Adele Perry has noted, the racial language of Empire "was always reshaped ... by the perceived threat non-British migrants posed to Canada."[3]

To the extent that Euro-Canadian feminists began to reflect on the situation of Aboriginal women, they tended to draw upon pejorative imperial stereotypes of indigenous peoples. Such was the case with Henriette Forget in her essay "The Indian Women of the Western Provinces" (1900). Forget depicted western tribes as uniformly savage and depraved, and as best exemplified by the widespread ill-treatment of Aboriginal women. This was a condition, she argued, that had been alleviated to a certain degree through the introduction of residential schools and the implementation of other assimilationist state policies. At the same time, she made clear that Aboriginal women remained less advanced than their Euro-Canadian peers. However, in the same publication, well-known Iroquois author and performer E. Pauline Johnson attempted to counter the generally negative characterization of Aboriginal women in most imperial feminist discourse. She did so by claiming that Iroquois women were equal to white women in many areas of accomplishment and, with regards to traditional political rights, in advance of them. Yet Johnson, who referred to herself as "One of Them," lauded the contributions and status of Iroquois women on the basis of their exceptionalism, being "superior in many ways to their unfortunate sisters throughout the rest of Canada."

The language of sisterhood was invoked often by first wave feminists as a rhetorical strategy for reaching across economic, cultural, and political divides, and to underscore the guiding principle that all women shared a universal set of common beliefs and values. Nonetheless, hierarchies of class, race, religion, and colonial status were far more often upheld than critiqued. The pamphlet published by the Presbyterian Foreign Women's Missionary Society, *Universal Sisterhood* (189?), offers an excellent example. Its author, Lucy Waterbury, appealed to Canadian women to assist their sisters in India, China, and "darkest Africa," although in doing so, she cast white Christian women in the superordinate role of rescuing heathen females in these "foreign lands." This "imperial saving role," as Antoinette Burton has characterized it,[4] was one that white women in Canada and throughout the Empire willingly adopted, and one that dovetailed well with feminist aspirations. Foreign women's missionary groups were key to the development of the women's movement in Canada, being among the earliest all-female organizations and acting as a springboard for involvement in other social-reform issues. These groups also provided the financial assistance for women missionaries, for whom these ventures represented, at least partially, the achievement of independence and a lifelong vocation.

Support for the British imperial project by Canadian feminists manifested itself in various others ways including public expressions of loyalty to the British crown. And indeed, on the occasion of the Diamond Jubilee of Queen Victoria in 1897, the National Council of Women of Canada (NCWC) not only pronounced its fidelity to the queen, but also linked the extended "beneficent" reign of this female monarch to the greater public role that women were then achieving. Moreover, as a tangible means of commemorating the jubilee, the NCWC assisted in the creation of the Victorian Order of Nurses, which provided visiting nurses to areas without access to medical services. Other women's organizations were also formed in Canada around the turn of the century whose principle purpose was patriotic support for empire. Such groups included the Victoria League, which first started in England, and the Imperial Order Daughters of the Empire (IODE) which became the largest women's organization in the country by the First World War. However, these patriotic women's groups were somewhat more conservative in their outlook than many other reform-minded organizations, and the argument can be made that more of their members identified as female imperialists than imperial feminists.

Lasting ties to Britain were maintained, and if anything strengthened, by the significant number of women reformers who travelled to the imperial metropole of London, some of whom became members of the Ladies' Empire Club, which the journalist Lally Bernard describes. In such a space, "colonial women" could participate in the "gendered community of nation and empire," as Cecilia Morgan has noted, in ways that enhanced both social and political networks.[5] A trip to London also afforded Canadian women the opportunity to take part in suffrage parades and rallies as well as to hear speeches by leading British feminists such as Christabel Pankhurst.[6] They engaged in various forms of "metropolitan activism," albeit to a lesser degree than those from elsewhere in the empire, especially when compared to feminists from Australia and New Zealand.[7]

While many of the leading women's reform groups advocated allegiance to the British crown and empire, this did not ensure that they accorded fair and equitable treatment to all loyal British subjects. Such was the case with a group of recent Jamaican immigrants in 1910 whom the Young Women's Christian Association (YWCA) in Toronto threatened to evict from its premises. In an appeal for assistance, one of the women called attention to her status as a British subject as she protested against being "badly used" by this organization. The YWCA only resolved the situation in time by constructing a segregated residence for Black women. Another instance arose in the years leading up to the First World War with the debate that took place over the immigration of South Asian women. The NCWC, among other leading women's groups, opposed government policy that barred the entry of Indian immigrants' spouses. As Ena Dua has insightfully pointed out, the NCWC did not advocate this position on the basis of fair treatment for South Asian women, but out of concern for the morality of South Asian men – out of fear that without female spouses present, Indian men would engage in sexual relations with white women.[8] Both of these episodes further illustrate the racial asymmetry often imbedded in imperial feminist politics and the widespread intolerance directed towards non-British immigrants more generally.

In the Canadian context, imperialism and English Canadian nationalism were closely intertwined. Within the women's movement Anglo-Celtic feminists presented their endeavours on behalf of women and nation as tied to the inevitable advance of British civilization while characterizing French Canadians and their nationalist aspirations in negative terms. Bessie Bullen-Perry's observations of Montreal while on an across-the-country trip in 1912 exemplified this. Bullen-Perry heralded the accomplishments of various anglophone women's groups, leaving aside entirely any mention of francophone feminist organizations. More significantly, she quoted the opinion of a well-regarded anglophone feminist that French Canadians were racially inferior, and deployed the anti-francophone cultural stereotype of the French Canadian mother with an overabundance of underfed children. A later 1918 piece in *Woman's Century* was especially explicit in its disavowal of French Canadian nationalism. The author went so far as to characterize the ethnic/linguistic identity of French Canadians as a form of divisive "racialism" that purportedly placed racial affinity ahead of loyalty to the nation.

Elsewhere, English Canadian nationalism took the form, as in the 1915 piece by Constance Boulton, of challenging efforts to disconnect national responsibilities from imperial obligations. Boulton argued that nationalism and imperialism were "synonymous," and praised the work of a women's group such as the IODE, which in her view promoted both ideals. Yet as an internal conflict that occurred within the NCWC at the end of the First World War demonstrated, even among Anglo-Celtic reformers there was not always uniform agreement about how allegiance to nation and empire should be affirmed, especially when complicated with international organizational ties. On this occasion the dispute arose over the national council's ongoing involvement with its international body so long as enemy countries such as Germany were in any way affiliated at present, or might be in the future. The executive of the IODE objected so strongly that they withdrew their group from its affiliation with the NCWC. While executive members of the order defended this decision as a patriotic gesture, a public affirmation of loyalty to country and empire, other women reformers disagreed. In an article entitled "National or Imperial?" Henrietta Muir Edwards accused the order of pursuing a narrow, national agenda at the expense of the remaining membership of the Canadian council, which, she asserted, advocated a collective imperial strategy.

Feminist critiques of imperialism in general and British imperialism more specifically did occur, albeit far less frequently than expressions of support. In a column published about her experiences as a British immigrant in Canada, Manitoba resident Gertrude Richardson lamented the suffering and dislocation of Aboriginal people as a result of colonization. Richardson was one of a small number of Canadian feminists who began to see how detrimental colonization had been for Aboriginal people and, equally important, to recognize themselves as directly implicated in the imperial project as colonizers. Other criticisms of empire took the form of objecting to the militaristic elements of British patriotism. In a 1927 editorial for the *Woman Worker*, for instance, Florence Custance rebuked those women's groups that promoted militarism in Canadian schools while ignoring other issues of direct concern to the working class. Left-wing feminists more broadly adopted an anti-imperial position especially from the end of the First World War onward.

There was also some Canadian involvement, at least initially, in the British Commonwealth League, formed in 1925, which brought together women reformers from across the empire for annual meetings in London. As the resolutions from its founding meeting indicate, the league attempted to situate women's issues within the broader framework of empire. They often did so with a view to comparing social and political conditions in the different dominions and colonies, taking a far greater critical stance than had been pursued up to that point. One of the most striking features of the British Commonwealth League was how it adopted what Angela Woolacott has referred to as a form of "Commonwealth feminism." She explains that "Commonwealth feminism (as opposed to imperial feminism) ... suggested that the enfranchised (white) women citizens of the dominions, not just British women, were responsible for their less fortunate imperial sisters."[9] The plight of indigenous women became the subject of extensive study and the object of activism within the league, yet for reasons that are not yet clear, Canadian engagement with this issue was virtually non-existent, and from the early 1930s no representative from this country attended BCL meetings.

For at least some Canadian feminists (further research may indicate a broader phenomenon), their stance on British imperialism was not simply one of support or opposition to imperialism, but rather of ambivalence and contradiction. No less a figure than Nellie McClung has been characterized as embodying a complex mix of conservatism and radicalism with regard to her positions on race and empire.[10] There were other activists such as Mary Bollert, who as a young university graduate in the 1910s was a staunch proponent of the IODE and served on its executive, but over the interwar period adopted a form of feminist internationalism that was critical of both militarism and imperialism. In a speech given to the Women's Teacher's Federation in February 1940, Senator Cairine Wilson, a friend and close feminist ally of Bollert's whose political views had followed a similar trajectory, disavowed the form of combined imperialist/nationalist sentiment in Canada that resulted in the discriminatory treatment of non-British immigrants, while advocating the form of non-violent nationalism/anti-colonialism being espoused at the time in countries such as India.

NOTES

1 For a more extended discussion of Nahnebahwequa's efforts to address this injustice, see Celia Haig Brown, "Seeking Honest Justice in a Land of Strangers: Nahnebahwequa's Struggle for Justice," *Journal of Canadian Studies* 36, no. 4 (Winter 2001/2002), 143–70.

2 Marilyn Lake, "Between Old Worlds and New: Feminist Citizenship, Nation and Race, the Destabilisation of Identity," in *Suffrage and Beyond: International Feminist Perspectives*, ed. Caroline Daley and Melanie Nolan (New York: New York UP, 1994), 234–51.

3 Adele Perry, "Women, Gender, and Empire," in *Canada and the British Empire*, ed. Phillip Buckner (Toronto: Oxford UP, 2008), 234.

4 Antoinette Burton, *Burdens of History* (Chapel Hill: U of North Carolina P, 1994), 101.

5 Cecilia Morgan, *"A Happy Holiday": English Canadians and Transatlantic Tourism, 1870–1930* (Toronto: U of Toronto P, 2008), 187.

6 Ibid., 188–9.

7 See, for example, Angela Woollacott, "Australian Women's Metropolitan Activism: From Suffrage to Imperial Vanguard to Commonwealth Feminism," in *Women's Suffrage in the British Empire: Citizenship, Nation and Race*, ed. Ian Fletcher, Laura Mayhall, and Philippa Levine (London: Routledge, 2000), 207–23; see also Fiona Paisley, *Loving Protection?: Australian Feminism and Aboriginal Women's Rights, 1919–1939* (Melbourne: Melbourne UP, 2000).

8 Enakshi Dua, "The Hindu Woman's Question: Canadian Nation-Building and the Social Construction of Gender for South Asian Women," in *Anti-Racist Feminism: Critical Race and Gender Studies*, ed. George Dei and Agnes Calliste (Halifax: Fernwood, 2000), 55–72.

9 Woollacott, "Australian Women's Metropolitan Activism," 121.

10 Janice Fiamengo, "A Legacy of Ambivalence: Responses to Nellie McClung," in *Rethinking Canada: The Promise of Women's History*, 4th ed., ed. Vernoica Strong-Boag, Mona Gleason, and Adele Perry (Toronto: Oxford UP, 2002), 149–163.

Nahnebahwequa – Catherine Sonego Sutton (1824–65) was born and raised on the Credit River Mission. Her Ojibwa parents converted to Christianity soon after her birth, and Catherine accompanied the English wife of her uncle on a year-long trip to Great Britain in 1837. Married in 1839 to an English immigrant, William Sutton, she moved with other Ojibwa families to establish farms and form their own band at Owen Sound in 1846. After spending time in northern Ontario and Michigan, Sutton returned to Owen Sound in 1857 to find her land offered for purchase by the colonial government. After years of protesting against the treatment she and other Aboriginals had received, she travelled to England in 1860 to meet with the colonial secretary and Queen Victoria.

Nahnebahwequa – Catherine Sutton

From "For a Reference" (c. 1860)

[...] I wish it to be understood that in 1857 at the time of the land sale I was prepared to purchase the land but unfortunately I was an Indian – and as such according to the laws of the Indian Department I could not enjoy the privilege of being a land holder.

And in 1858 I still had sufficient money left to pay the first installment. But in 1859 I could not do it. But if the department had paid my money claims I should have been prepared to meet their claims against me for the land.

Before the time arrived for the next distribution of money to the Indians I received a letter from the department informing me that as I was married to a white man I had no claims in common with the Indian and that my claims would not be allowed. In consequence of which I was now deprived of all hope of raising the whole amount required to pay the first installment of the land by the first of January in the year 1860.

The second week in January I received a letter from the department informing me that I had failed in my part to pay the first installment on the land. I could not have any more claims upon it and that if I did not send the money forthwith, the land would be sold to those individuals who had made application for it. I could not bear the idea of losing my home, a home that had cost us several years of toil and privation besides about 700 dollars in cash. And 200 acres of the land was my own and every honest man acquainted with the facts connected with it will consider it as such.

After considering the consequences of the two last letters from the department I concluded to come to England and if God would spare my life and health I would plead my own case there. I feel to shrink from the undertaking as my health is poor and feeble, and the winter cold and stormy, and I am but a poor Indian woman, and I shall be going to a land of strangers, but I hope I shall meet with this honest justice. And this hope keeps up my sinking spirits. I cannot bear to see my children deprived of their lawful home and inheritance.

In 1859 when I visited the Indian Department I had a number of papers with me which were of considerable importance to me, and which I was intending to take with me to England. But the Hon. Wm. Hogan, MPP, handed them to the Indian Department against my wishes and without my consent. He said they were the property of the department. Mr. Penneyfather said I could have a copy of them, but when I wanted to copy them, Mr. Turner would not allow me to do so, and it was five days before I got the privilege of copying.

The Indian Department have tried every dodge and quirk they could think of no matter how flimsy. At one time they have told me that I had no connection with the Owen Sound or Croker Indians but that I always belonged to the Credit tribe. At another time they have told me that I had no connection with any band or tribe of Indians because I had sold all right title and claims to Indian benefits. And then again that I had forfeited all my claims because I had been living in the United States. And lastly because I was married to a white man I could not any longer be considered as an Indian.

A Mr. Thorburn, who acts as visiting superintendent to the Credit tribe was present at the department office when they charged me with belonging exclusively to the Credit tribe. I asked Mr. Thorburn if their statement was true, and he informed the department that my name was not on their list, but that he had heard the Credit Indians speak of me and that they had told him I was connected with the Owen Sound Indians. This Gentleman further stated that the Indians had a right to give a portion of this land to any other Indian if they chose and he appeared to feel much hurt at the conduct of the department towards me at that time.

And as to the charge of my acting ... and selling my birthright they knew it was false. They no doubt referred to the time when I was transferred from the Credit to the Owen Sound band. For the Credit Indians paid me at this time two hundred dollars which was due myself and family as our shares for land payments. A part of the Credit Indians were unwilling to pay me so large an amount. Colonel Bruce, who saw the justness of my claims, assisted me in getting the money.

Colonel Bruce at this time understood well the nature of my transfer to the Owen Sound Indians, and he approved of the course I was pursuing.

And thirdly that I had forfeited all my Indian claims in Canada because I had been living in the United States. The Rev. Mr. Shaw having just commenced a new mission engaged my husband to assist him by erecting buildings and superintending farm labour.

Now I should like to know what crime I have committed by then living in the United States? Also I should like to know if there is any law in the British Dominions which will deprive a woman of her property and just claims for living under another government under such circumstances?

And lastly I am charged with the unpardonable sin of marrying a white man. I should like to know if you have a law in England that would deprive a woman of property left to her by her Father's will or if you please inherited property? I ask have you a law that would deprive that woman of her property because she got married to a Frenchman? Now if my husband was a lazy man and of poor morals there might be some excuse for the department's conduct towards me for wedding a white man but they know such is not the case. The honourable and responsible situations in which he has been should be a sufficient guarantee of his character. He was engaged by the Indian superintendent to teach the Saugeen Indians to farm. And next he was employed by Rev. S.S. Charron to superintend the working of a farm for the benefit of the Garden River Indians. And lastly he was employed by Rev. Mr. Shaw for similar purposes in the state of Michigan and where they would be glad to have him return.

I have a number of certificates to show my own standing in the Wesleyan Methodist church from several ministers of the gospel. And also from other gentlemen showing my moral standing in society.

I am aware that some years ago an act was passed and became law for the purposes of disinheriting Indian women who should get married to white men. I have been married 20 years and the law referred to was made several years afterwards. I therefore cannot be disinherited under that law.

Why did not Colonel Bruce and the Indian Department make me feel the affects of that law at the time of my transfer to Owen Sound instead of assisting me to get my share of land payments from the Credit Indians? Strange the department should never have thought of it until just now.

There have been 4 white men and 4 white women incorporated into the Credit tribe by marriage, some of them before me and some of them afterwards. Not only do the families of these white men and women continue to receive their shares of the benefits arising from the Indian funds, but even the white men and women thus married are considered as Indians and receive their shares accordingly. And the Allisewick Chief told me it was the same in his band. Why am I thus singled out as a mark for the special displeasure of the department? For almost 3 years I have been trying to get my just claims from them but all to no purpose. I ask no favours but I want justice.

[Source: Library and Archives Canada (LAC), RG 10, vol. 2877, file 177, 181, Catherine Sutton, "For a Reference," 7–10.]

The pamphlet below written by a woman prominent in the American mission field, Lucy Waterbury, was widely distributed to Presbyterian women in Canada. Lucy McGill Waterbury (1861–1949) served as a missionary with her husband in India in the 1880s. After her husband's death in 1886, Waterbury returned to the United States, where she accepted a position as home secretary for the Woman's Baptist Foreign Mission Society of the East. She held this position for the next eighteen years.

Lucy Waterbury
The Universal Sisterhood (189?)

I am writing to you concerning your sister who is in great need. I met her in India a few years ago. She was only a child in years, but very old in suffering. At the age of twelve she was married and before she was thirteen became a mother. Lying on the floor of a mud hut, which was her home, she met excruciating pain, aggravated by every form of torture that ignorant women could devise. After cruel treatment too sickening for words, a slow fire blistered her body for purification, and she lay for three days in a stupor with neither food nor drink, according to the Hindu custom. The baby was a girl and died; so many girl babies die in India that in some districts the proportion is eighty-one boys to nineteen girls. The number of girls is still further reduced later by frequent suicides; – poor little sisters! If you were there how you would stretch out your hands to save them as they turn their beautiful, despairing faces toward the deep well or stagnant pool.

But the saddest hour is not the hour of birth nor of death. More bitter is still the life of twenty-one millions of widows. Your sister is a widow, only thirteen, but a despised outcast, denied even the right of chastity, she wanders about an object of loathing. Ah, little sister, we could lighten your burden. We could give you the comfort of Christ if only we were *interested*.

Stand in the street of a heathen city and watch the swarms of children, naked, dirty, diseased. See the patient faces of those little girls, seven, possibly eight years old. In a week some will be married and a week later will lie in the hospital breathing out their little lives in an agony of pain – *murdered!* God help them and forgive those who will not help.

Is this the land, – where children are taught every form of vice from the cradle; where from idols, foul and obscene comes the only thought of God; where girls are sacrificed; where womanhood is dragged in the mire; where widow is the synonym for prostitute; is this the land where the "beautiful religion" of Hinduism flourishes? Where are the men who in priestly robes from public platforms in Christian lands proclaim the beauty of this beastly thing called religion? When these *priests* have released from vile heathen temples thousands of fair young girls whose lives are devoted to the horrible rites of heathenism, let them dare to speak before Christian women of this religion, whose very name if understood would cause a shudder.

Turn from your Hindu sister to that sister in China. She cannot come to you. Her feet are bound and her life is bound and fettered. From thousands of homes in that land rises a wail of pain. Shall we drown the sobs and moans with hymns. "Jesus, Lover of my Soul." "He Leadeth Me," are comforting and may shut out the sound, but God hears the cry from Chinese women above the hymns which we selfishly sing, and there is not praise but discord. Send help soon if you would not be too late, for "a million a month in China are dying without God."

No one has penetrated *darkest* Africa who has not entered an African woman's life. Born a slave, her life at the mercy of her husband, a believer in witchcraft, filthy, debased, naked, – meet your sister again. We cannot. We close our eyes and turn away from all these dreadful, pitiful faces, only to meet another face which we cannot shut out. His words ring in our ears, haunt our hearts: "Inasmuch as ye did it *not* unto one of the least of these, ye did it not unto Me."

Ah, but you say, "I gave my dollar." So you did but how many dollars did you spend straightway in some pretty trifle or pleasure trip?

Some of you refused even the dollar for your sister in foreign lands, because you believe in Home Missions, and of course you can't have Foreign Missions unless you keep up the work here; which system of financiering may seem very complete, but is so unsatisfactory to the one billion four hundred millions of men and women, beyond the touch of home-work. Or you peep into the slums of New York and Boston and forthwith say, "See, isn't there enough to be done at home?" Use that same logical brain to reason that if a lack of Christianity produces slums in America, the condition of whole nations, absolutely unreached, must be infinitely worse, especially as they have not within their own borders twelve millions of Christians to render personal service.

Perhaps you said, with no excuse at all, "I don't believe," or, "I am not interested in Missions." You said it not in a whisper, but to influence your daughter or your neighbor. How many things have you done today for love's sake, for duty's sake, in your kitchen, your sewing-room, your office, not because you feel any white heat of enthusiasm, but simply because it was your work, – hard work, discouraging, slow, but your work? Are you not bound by the command of Christ to do this work in which He certainly is interested?

You may say my statements are exaggerated. You can easily prove that they are all too true.

You may say, "No one has a right to dictate how I shall use my money." *Whose* money? Not, yours, if you are Christ's.

You may say, "I am too sensitive to listen to such horrors." And yet, – strange sensitiveness, – you will, by withholding help, force your sister to endure these horrors.

You may say, "I cannot help it; if they don't know they are not responsible." Try that plan with your own children. What of present suffering? What does God say? "When I say unto the wicked, thou shalt surely die, and thou givest him not warning, nor speaketh to warn him from his wicked way, to save his life, that same wicked man shall die in his iniquity, but his blood will I require at your hand."

You may say a hundred other things to excuse yourself from obeying a direct command of Christ, or you may say, and I trust that you will, my dear sister, for are we not His big family, and do we not believe in the Universal Fatherhood? – you may say, – "I have not done what I should have done for my unhappy sister. I have given little or grudgingly, or not at all. Forgive me, my Father, for the past, and the future shall be different. As a beginning; I take this box or envelope, and will put into it each day as I pray for my sister, or each Lord's Day as I go to His house, an offering, which shall make known His love to the uttermost parts of the earth."

[Source: Lucy Waterbury, *The Universal Sisterhood*, Women's Foreign Missionary Society, Presbyterian Church in Canada (Western Division) 189?.]

Ishbel Majoribanks Gordon, Marchioness of Aberdeen and Tremain (1857–1939) was born in London, England, and in 1877 married the Earl of Aberdeen. She lived in Canada from 1893 to 1898, the period during which her husband was governor general. An outspoken supporter of women's rights, Aberdeen spearheaded the formation of the National Council of Women of Canada in 1893 and the Victorian Order of Nurses in 1897. With the exception of several brief interruptions, Aberdeen served as the long-time president of the International Council of Women from 1893 to 1936.

Lady Ishbel Gordon, Countess of Aberdeen

Address from the National Council of Women of Canada to Her Majesty the Queen (1897)

Her Most Gracious Majesty the Queen:

May it please Your Majesty – We, of the National Council of Women of

Canada, a Society having for its aim the better application of the Golden Rule, and for its members all women within Your Majesty's Canadian realm who will follow and embrace that aim, would add our tribute to that world-wide expression of loyalty and devotion which it is the joy and privilege of your subjects to render Your Majesty, on the happy occasion of the completion of the 60th year of your beneficent reign. Your Majesty's reign has been marked by a maternal and social progress unparalleled in any age of the world. The ocean has become a high road for the commerce of nations, time and space yielded to steam and electricity, while the movement towards a permanent National unity for all parts of the British Empire is significant of a great consolidation and of the supreme part which the British race has yet to fulfil in the history of nations and the destinies of mankind. Yet, the movement toward National unity is but the sign and outcome of a larger impulse and awakening of that recognition of a unity underlying and transcending all difference, binding the nations of the earth and the children of men in a single humanity, which, during Your Majesty's reign has, with ever-growing intensity, stirred and animated the thoughts and deeds of men.

Through the constraining power of this idea, the fetters of the slaves have fallen, the sick and wounded have been tended, and men have seen in the realization of the human brotherhood the key to a universal harmony, and the highest good of the individual and the race. Coincident with this movement and inherent in it is the single and momentous advance in thought and opinion which has so heightened the ideas and enlarged the possibilities for women. And in that wider sphere of usefulness and activity now happily open to women no service is more honourable or more blessed in its results than that of the trained nurses – a calling which Your Majesty has done so much to elevate and promote – one which has been successfully organized and established in India at Your Majesty's request, and which in the British Isles and in Canada will ever be honoured by its association with your name.

As Your Majesty's subjects, sharing in the glory and prosperity of a great empire, we would tender the expressions of our unswerving loyalty and devotion. As women, we acknowledge our peculiar debt to Your Most Gracious Majesty, whose wisdom in judgment, charities of heart, and purity, simplicity and fortitude of personal life have set our womanhood on high, crowned and enthroned. That the Divine Blessing may rest upon your Most Gracious Majesty now and ever is the earnest prayer of:

Ishbel Aberdeen, President

On behalf of the National Council of Women of Canada, June 15, 1897.

[Source: Ishbel Aberdeen, "Address from the National Council of Women of

Canada to Her Majesty the Queen," *Yearbook of the National Council of Women of Canada*, no. 4 (1897), 30–1.]

Henriette Drolet Forget (1853–1928) was born in St-Hyacinthe, Quebec. In 1876 she married Amédée Forget, who served as a civil servant in various capacities in the Northwest, including Indian commissioner, before being named lieutenant-governor of the Northwest Territories in 1898 and lieutenant-governor of the new province of Saskatchewan in 1905. She was among a small but prominent group of francophone Catholic women who were involved in the NCWC at the turn of the century. She was on the national executive of the NCWC as representative for the Northwest Territories and president of the local council in Regina.

Henriette Forget
The Indian Women of the Western Provinces (1900)

In the Canadian West, that is in Manitoba, the North-West Territories and British Columbia, there are 46,289 Indians, of whom only 10,061 are pagans. The rest belong to one or other of the Christian churches, the Roman Catholic Church heading the list with 16,606 adherents. The Indians live on "Reserves," scattered at considerable distances apart over the area named, and are cared for by the Government in a very paternal fashion.

Twenty-five years have elapsed since Canada adopted this policy, and the results of a quarter of a century's contact with civilization are as evident from the condition of the Indian woman now, as compared with then, as from any of the other changes that have taken place. The Indians belong to various tribes, the principal ones being the Crees, Bloods, Sioux, Blackfeet, and Piegans. All the tribes have different customs, which are, however, identical in principle, the differences being only of detail. It is evident, therefore, that all that can be attempted in the space at my disposal is a rapid glance at a few general characteristics.

In order better to recognize the present status of Indian women, it will be well to recall their condition before the civilizing influences began to operate, – twenty-five years ago. Their lot was indeed hard. Polygamy was the general practice. The richer an Indian was (his wealth being horses), the more wives he sought, or rather bought, for the maidens were sold by their paternal relatives to become the wives of those who proffered the greatest number of horses in exchange. The prices ranged from two horses to twenty, according to the attractions of the bride. There might be love on the part of the young couple, and indeed a sort of courtship was common, but the purchase had to be made all the same; and the Indian regards the white people's custom of giving a dowry as a sign of weakness and folly. The attractions, too, of a young bride, in the eyes of the red man were not always such as would appeal to "the pale-faces." He often preferred quantity to quality.

> Wives were chosen as we choose old plates,
> Not for their beauty but their weight.

The marriage ceremony was as meager as the bride's dress – among some tribes nothing but a cedar-bark petticoat. The chief provision was a promise by the woman to be "chaste, obedient, industrious and – silent." After marriage the position of the woman was worse even than before. The lordly husband never worked, or rather his work was sport, hunting, trapping or fishing. The woman did all that had to be done, however laborious the task might be.

In the days of the buffalo, the more wives a man had the richer he became, because of the greater number of robes which could be dressed by his squaws. Divorce was as easy as marriage. A man, tired of his wife, could easily sell her to someone else. Whenever there was a death in the family, the women, for some reason unknown, were mutilated by being slashed with a knife, and the bent, decrepit and scarred forms to be seen at the present day are the living testimony to a horrible practice which exists no longer. The only compensation for the sad lot of the squaw was that she was queen over all her domestic affairs; that she claimed and received a sort of chivalrous respect, and that, among the Algonquins, of which the Crees are a branch, she had even the sole right of declaring war, or of permitting peace.

And now, after twenty-five years – what of the women? The visitor to the Canadian West sees bright-eyed, chubby, happy-looking damsels; though it must be admitted the matrons are still haggard and worn. The Industrial Schools, which have been established for the training of the young Indians, and the efforts of missionaries have had their effect. Horses, cattle, or other wealth are still sometimes given in exchange for a wife, but polygamy exists no longer, except among a few of the least civilized tribes. Most marriages are now sanctified by a religious ceremony, and just as the agricultural pursuits of the men are leading them to substitute houses for tepees (tents), so the cedar bark petticoat is being supplanted by the neat dress of modern make.

The Indian man has now an adequate inducement to work; but that has not relieved the squaw from any of her burdens. She has still to bear her share of the toil, and more than her share. The Indian, going to fish on the frozen lake, stands by while his squaw digs the hole in the thick and compact ice; and returns home on horseback, unencumbered by any impedimenta, followed by his wife on foot, heavily laden with the results of his skill. The Indian kills a steer, but it is the squaw who skins the carcass, carries it home, dresses the meat and cures the hide. The Industrial Schools are quietly giving the death blow to this sort of thing by teaching civilized methods of housekeeping. The Indians still enjoy boiled dog or roasted gopher, but the cooking is none the worse for the school training of his daughters; while sewing, knitting and even fancy work (to say nothing of the artistic productions of pen and pencil) are revolutionizing the home of the more civilized, where sewing machines, clocks, organs and other musical instruments are now to be found.

The belief in charms and love potions lingers among the squaws, as it does among Europeans, but promises to die more quickly among the red-skins than amid the "pale-faces." The women smoke quite as much as the men, and drink tea, – fifteen to twenty cups of "the only intellectual drink" in one day being quite common. The beverage is taken without milk or sugar and is imbibed for its toxic qualities.

No notice of Indian women would be complete without a reference to the papooses, that is the infants. These are cared for with the most motherly affection. The mode of carrying the youngsters is peculiar. The little one is strapped to a board, its feet carefully embedded in moss or soft grass, and there is an ample covering over all. Babe and board are then bandaged to the mother's back and the child is thus carried about, whatever the mother's task or however laborious the work. In this unique cradle the child, sleeping or waking, is in comfort, and is restless, only when not so cared for, ever crying for its cosy nest on the board, and immediately soothed on being hoisted on its mother's back.

[Source: Henriette Forget, "The Indian Women of the Western Provinces," in *Women in Canada: Their Life and Work*, comp. National Council of Women of Canada at the request of the Hon. Sydney Fisher, Minister of Agriculture, for distribution at the Paris International Exhibition (1900), 435–7 [reprint 1975].]

E. Pauline Johnson – Tekahionwake [Tekahioucoaka] (1861–1913) was born on the Six Nations Reserve, Canada West, the daughter of a Mohawk chief and an Englishwoman. In recognition of her Aboriginal heritage she later adopted the name Tekahionwake and developed a career as a writer and performer. Johnson published a number of collections of poetry including *The White*

Wampum (1895) and prose pieces in a variety of periodicals. She performed extensively throughout Canada and the United States as well as in London, England, where she recited her poetry to wide acclaim.

E. Pauline Johnson – Tekahionwake
The Iroquois Women of Canada (1900)

To the majority of English speaking people, an Indian is an Indian, an inadequate sort of person possessing a red brown skin, nomadic habits, and an inability for public affairs. That the various tribes and nations of the great Red population of America, differ as much one from another, as do the white races of Europe, is a thought that seldom occurs to those disinterested in the native of the western continent. Now, the average Englishman would take some offence if anyone were unable to discriminate between him and a Turk – though both "white;" and yet the ordinary individual seems surprised that a Sioux would turn up his nose if mistaken for a Sarcee, or an Iroquois be eternally offended if you confounded him with a Micmac.

Francis Parkman, that ablest and most delightful historian of the age, that accurate and truthful chronicler of North American Indian tribes, customs, legends and histories, concedes readily to the Iroquois all the glories of race, bravery and lineage that this most arrogant and haughty nation lay claim to even in the present day. In his phylogenetic and unbiased treatment of the various tribes of red men, Parkman declares the undeniable fact, which has been for many decades asserted by historians, explorers, voyagers and traders, that for physical strength, intelligence, mental acquirement, morality and bloodthirstiness, the Iroquois stand far in advance of any Indian tribe in America. The constitutional government of this race has since the time of its founder, Hiawatha (a period of about four centuries), had an uninterrupted existence, without hindrance from internal political strife; has stood the test of ages, and wars and invasions and subjection from mightier foreign powers. This people stand undemolished and undemoralized to-day, right in the heart of Canada, where the lands granted a century ago in recognition of their loyal services to the Imperial Government, are still known as the "Six Nations' Indian reserve of the Grand River."

That the women of this Iroquois race are superior in many ways to their less fortunate sisters throughout Canada, is hardly necessary to state. Women who have had in the yesterdays a noble and pureblooded ancestry, who look out on the tomorrows with minds open to educational acquirements; women whose grandmothers were the mothers of fighting men, whose daughters will be the mothers of men elbowing their way to the front ranks in the great professional and political arena in Canada; women whose thrift and care and morality will count for their nation, when that nation is just at its turn of tide toward civilization and advancement, are not the women to sit with idle hands and brains, caring not for the glories of yesterday, nor the conquests of to-morrow.

The Iroquois woman of to-day is one who recognizes the responsibilities of her position, and who makes serious and earnest efforts to possess and master whatever advantages may drift her way. She has already acquired the arts of cookery, of needlework, of house wifeliness, and one has but to attend the annual Industrial exhibition on the Indian reserve, an institution that is open to all Indians in Canada, who desire to compete for prizes, to convince themselves by very material arguments that the Iroquois woman is behind her white sister in nothing pertaining to the larder, the dairy or the linen press. She bakes the loveliest, lightest wheaten bread, of which, by the way, her men folk complain loudly, declaring that she forces them to eat this new-fangled food to the absolute exclusion of their time-honored corn bread, to which the national palate ever clings; her rolls of yellow butter are faultlessly sweet, and firm, her sealed fruits are a pleasure to see as well as taste, in, fact, in this latter industry she excels herself, outdoing frequently her white competitors at the neighboring city of Brantford, where the "southern fair" of Ontario is held annually. Her patch-work quilts, her baby garments, her underwear, her knitted mittens and stockings, her embroidery and fancy work are features of the exhibition that call for even much masculine attention, and yet while you gaze, and admire, and marvel at her accomplishments, she is probably standing beside you, her placid, brown face apparently quite unintelligent, her brown, deft hands devoid of gloves, her slight but sturdy figure clad in the regulation Iroquois fashion, a short broadcloth petticoat, bordered with its own vari-coloured self edge, over this a bright calico "short-dress" and plain round waist, her neatly braided black hair tied under a red bandanna handkerchief, her feet encased in coarse leather shoes, her only ornaments a necklace of green or yellow glass beads and a pair of gilt earrings.

Beside her is her daughter, who has long since discarded the broadcloth petticoat, the ill-shapen short dress, the picturesque head gear. Miss Iroquois has most likely arrayed herself in a very becoming stuff gown, made in modern style. She wears gloves and a straw hat, decorated with bright ribbon and a few pretty flowers. She is altogether like the daughter of one of Canada's prosperous farmers, save for her dark colourless skin, her extremely retiring manner and her pretty, tripping accent when she condescends to address you in English. Then, too, she has not been idly reared, for although the elder woman may have made the patchwork, and the butter rolls, the girl is probably "out at service," or teaches [in] one of the district schools. Then, too, if she is a member of one of the fifty-two noble families, who compose the Iroquois Government, she has this divine right in addition to woman's great right of motherhood – the divine right of transmitting the title, if she is in the direct line of lineage, for the Chief's title is inherited through the mother, not the father, which fact is a powerful contradiction, to the widespread error, that Indian men look down upon and belittle their women. Add to this the privilege, which titled Iroquois women possess, of speaking in the great council of their nation, and note the deference with which the old chiefs listen to these speeches, when some one woman, more daring than her sisters, sees the necessity of stepping into public affairs – then I think the reader will admit that not all civilized races honour their women as highly as do the stern old chiefs, warriors and braves of the Six Nations' Indians.

[Source: E. Pauline Johnson – Tekahionwake, "Indian Woman," in *Women in Canada: Their Life and Work*, comp. the National Council of Women of Canada at the request of the Hon. Sydney Fisher, Minister of Agriculture, for distribution at the Paris International Exhibition (1900), 440–2 [reprint, 1975].]

Mary Agnes Bernard FitzGibbon, aka Lally Bernard (1862–1933), returned to Canada in 1896 after fourteen years living abroad, much of it in England. Her return was precipitated by a failed marriage and she lived with her stepfather who was a lawyer and politician in Toronto. She later became a journalist and wrote at times under her mother's maiden name, Lally Bernard.

Lally Bernard
The Ladies' Empire Club of London (1904)

During the season of 1902, made memorable by the festivities which attended the coronation of Edward the Seventh, the Ladies' Empire Club sprang into existence under the auspices of the Victoria League, an organization of well-known women in the British Isles who joined forces with the idea of furthering the Imperial ideal in social as well as political circles.

Lady Jersey, the Hon. Mrs Alfred Lyttelton (wife of the present Secretary for the Colonies), and Lady Mary Lygon, who is attached to the household of the Princess of Wales, were among those mainly instrumental in originating and carrying out the idea. During the summer of 1903 the Club quarters were situated in Whitehall Court, and it became a distinguished rendezvous where visitors from all parts of the Empire met in an easy and informal manner the members of the various committees connected with the League, and the guests they invited to their weekly at-homes.

So eminently successful was the result of the efforts made by those interested, that it was decided to establish the club on a permanent footing, and thanks to the untiring energy of Mrs Herbert Chamberlain (formerly a Miss Williams, of Port Hope), to-day the beautiful club at 69 Grosvenor Street is the very centre of the social whirlpool of London life, and forms one of the most charming meeting grounds of all that is best in colonial and British society. Not ten minutes' walk from the town house of the High Commissioner for Canada, in Grosvenor Square, it is yet only a few yards from the fashionable shopping locality known to all Canadians, familiar with London, as Old Bond Street.

Formerly 69 Grosvenor Street was the residence of Lord Kensington, whose family name is Edwards, but to-day the Duke of Westminster is the distinguished landlord of the club committee. A typical town house of the best possible design, the rooms are spacious and well proportioned, and have retained a distinctly home-like air. It is to be regretted that among the photographs reproduced there is not one of the fine entrance hall, with its broad curving staircase and its cheerful welcome of crimson-tinted carpets, which shed a warm glow over the ivory panelling of the walls. The head porter has a snug little office to the right as you enter, and the telephone is not the least of the luxuries provided for the members. Opening off the hall on the ground floor is a well-proportioned dining-room, with soft green and ivory again for the scheme of decoration. Electroliers, softened by creamy silk shades, produce the mellow glow of candle light. Frequently one will find the round table in the dining-room set for a special dinner party, for several of the *habituées* of the club, and especially its colonial members, rent this room for their dinner parties, as by paying the sum of one guinea can secure it for the evening.

Opening off the dining-room is the lunch-room; here, again, is the same effect of ivory and green, which harmonizes well with the glitter of perfectly-kept glass and silver, and the snowy cloths which cover the numerous little tables, at which four or six people can be comfortably accommodated. Maids in the freshest of caps and aprons move quietly to and fro, and the buffet at the end of the room is set exactly as it would be in a private house, with cold joints and the inevitable "game pastie" of an English luncheon table.

Between the hours of one and two one will generally find the lunch-room filled with the *habituées* of the club; among them are Lady Aberdeen, who is often accompanied by her husband; the Duchess of Marlborough, the Duchess of Northumberland, Lady Edward Cecil, Mrs Laurence Drummond, Mrs Molson Macpherson, the Baroness Macdonald of Earnscliffe, Lady Brassey and the Hon. Mrs Howard. Mrs Everard Cotes (Sara Jeanette Duncan) and a lady who has lately arrived in London from Cape Town, are among the occupants of the club chambers at present. Strolling through the club drawing-room, of which a photograph is given, one will find groups of well-known people enjoying five o'clock tea in the pretty room with its comfortable furniture, covered with a rose-patterned glazed chintz, and its many dainty extras, which give it the air of a room in a private residence.

The room is so large that half a dozen small tea parties can take place at one time without danger of over-crowding. Here, again, there is a glow of deep rose, ivory and green. Opening off the drawing is the members' reading-room, furnished much on the same lines as the drawing-room, for when it is necessary for special entertainments these two rooms are thrown into one with excellent effect. However, on ordinary occasions you will find solitary members enjoying their tea in the quiet and seclusion which this room affords with its command of "Silence," which comes out so distinctly in the photograph. Tea is served in green earthenware sets, which contrast well with the dainty be-sprigged china, quite in keeping with the rose-patterned chintz of the furniture. On side-tables are to be found all the newspapers and periodicals of the hour and several colonial publications, *The Canadian Magazine* conspicuous among them. The writing-tables are fitted with the most up-to-date appointments, and one hears the ceaseless scratch of the fashionable "quill," for members evidently find it difficult to keep up with the eternal rush of correspondence which assails one in London. At the end of the corridor, on the same floor as the drawing-room and reading-room, is the smoking and card-room, where members may take their friends for a quiet cup of tea, while they smoke a veritable "cigarette of peace" or make up a game of bridge. After luncheon coffee is often brought up to this southern sunlit room with its mass of delicately-tinted windows. There is not a suggestion of the masculine smoking den, but pale green chintz takes the place of the rose-patterned glory of the drawing-room, and there is an air of cleanly, cheerful, home-like comfort. Coal fires blaze all day in the open grates, and hot-water coils keep the corridors and rooms at a temperature which Canadians in this land of fog and chill appreciate fully.

The bedrooms, of which no photographs are procurable, are furnished, like the rest of the club, with an idea of absolute comfort as well as beauty. Electric light, open fires, plenty of bathrooms with the latest and most luxurious appointments, and the best attendance to be had in London, are some of the advantages offered to members. Twenty-five servants are employed, and with the two secretaries, a manager and cashier, club chambers promise to be particularly comfortable.

Canada is represented in the list of members by about a hundred and thirty names, and the whole colonial list is over three hundred. The club committee which has to do with the entertainments decided to discontinue a series of lectures they proposed giving as they found that the club had so many members who used it regularly that the disturbance caused by special entertainments was to be avoided.

There have been now and then observations made regarding the objects of the club, which should be fully discussed in an article such as this; for it is undoubtedly established with the idea of bringing into close contact visitors from the colonies with the wives and daughters of men of prominence and distinction in Great Britain.

There have been those who asserted that making it so much a "matter of business" is to take away the most pronounced charm of social intercourse. But those who raise this objection fail to grasp that in so vast a world as London the season has always been managed upon more or less business-like lines. Unless colonial women who come to London have the advantage of either great wealth or the social prestige which surrounds the wife of a Minister of the Crown, they have little chance of finding themselves brought into close touch with those whom doubtless they consider it a pleasure and profit to meet. People, especially women, might spend months in this vast metropolis within a stone's throw of someone with whom they might find they had much in common, were it not for such a medium of communication like the Ladies' Empire Club, where there is a sub-committee whose work it is to make known to each other members of society from all parts of the Empire.

The work of the Ladies' Empire Club is to draw together all that is best in colonial and British society circles without reference to political official prestige; and anyone who has had experience of life in the great self-governing colonies will admit that this is a work worthy of encouragement. Now comes the practical side of the question; what renders one eligible for membership in the Ladies' Empire Club and what expense does it entail? The answer to this is very simple. By writing to the secretary a list of members may be procured, and if the person desirous of becoming a member can find the names of two of her friends or acquaintances on the list she can apply to them to propose and second her as a member, one of them writing a note of introduction to the secretary. On receipt of the notice of her election she will receive a note of the amount of the entrance fee, which is one guinea, and two guineas annual fee if in England, and only ten shillings and six-pence while resident in the colonies.

That its existence in its present and permanent form is mainly due to the untiring energy and administrative ability of a Canadian by birth is one, and certainly not the least, of the reasons why the Ladies' Empire Club should receive the cordial support and excite the interest of all Canadians who have the welfare of the Empire at heart.

[Source: Lally Bernard, "The Ladies Empire Club of London," *The Canadian Magazine* 23, no. 3 (July 1904), 195–9.]

Catherine Hay

Letter from a Jamaican Immigrant to Lady Aberdeen (1910)

The YWCA
79 Richmond Street
Toronto Canada

The Countess of Aberdeen:

May I please your ladyship to notice my brief and humble letter. Your appearance in Toronto a year ago was comfort to many strangers. I am a subject of Britain and native of Jamaica but according to the severe earthquake which we have had 3 years ago many of us have to leave as domestic for this country. Now we are badly used by the natives.

I am writing to ask your advice and that is could you kindly tell me the meaning of Young Woman's Christian Association? Does it mean protection of young women travelling abroad or is it for whites only? The Christian rules here is by far different to the Christian lives in Jamaica. My reason for writing. I have seen your solemn words published in the papers, of your speech in the Convocation Hall last summer, 1909: "Woman must be protected, it makes no matter what the colour." I am begging your ladyship, could you call upon a number of ladies of the Congress and guarantee forming an organization for us the Jamaicans so that we will be protected with a Christian institute. Especially when we are going to be out of a position. The Christian organization of Toronto actually want to dispose of us. The majority of us are well taught and brought up in religious work and we do stick to our principles. The only Christians that comfort us and strengthens us in good works is Mrs J.A. Brownghall and the Rev. Cannon Brownghall at St Stephen church. I can hardly realize to myself that this is British ground. I wrote to her Ladyship because I believe you are a true Christian. The Christian is always willing to help those that are trying to strive and who will not stumble the unbelievers. I expect and depend on you to do something for us, and a life of protection while we are here working for an honest living. Hoping you are quite well.

> Yours faithfully,
> Catherine Hay

[Source: LAC, MG 28,I245, vol. 33, Councils – Canada, Letter from Catherine Hay to Lady Aberdeen, 5 October 1910.]

Bessie Pullen-Burry (1858–1937) was a British writer who devoted her life to travel across the globe. She published a number of books on her travel experiences including *Jamaica as It Is* (1903) and *In a German Colony, Or, Four Weeks in New Britain* (1919). In recognition of her observations of the diverse cultures which she encountered in her travels she was made a fellow of the Royal Anthropological Institute and of the Royal Geographical Society. She lectured extensively about foreign countries and claimed particular expertise on the "Negro Race" in British colonies and the United States.

Bessie Pullen-Perry
From *From Halifax to Vancouver* (1912)

The interests of the first city of British America are not confined to the preservation of the *entente cordiale* between the French and the English, nor to the study of past mismanaged municipal finance, nor to the fact that the citizens of Montreal have so impure a water supply that it is necessary to buy drinking water. The English-speaking inhabitants of Montreal have led the way in many intellectual movements resulting in benefit to the community, of which by far the most important has been the formation of the *Men's Canadian Clubs*. It was found that business men, too fatigued after the day's work to attend public lectures, rarely found opportunities for hearing the topics of the day discussed by capable speakers, so an association was formed to arrange that during the luncheon hour men of note should on approved occasions address them on the needs, resources, history, and institutions of Canada. At the present day these clubs are invaluable factors in forming, educating, and determining public opinion on questions directly concerned with the welfare of the nation. Pledged to no course of action, they represent a body of thought – inspiring, educative, or otherwise.

This activity on the part of the men has been closely followed by the women of the Dominion in the cities; the members of the *Women's Canadian Clubs* propose, as in the case of the opposite sex, to encourage patriotism and to foster a spirit of inquiry into the historical and material treasures of their country. In the words of the constitution for that of Montreal, "The object is to give women opportunities of hearing orators and men of eminence speak on various subjects. It has therefore been resolved to invite speakers who will bring inspiration and instruction to address the members of the Club five times during the season (October till April). Before each address there will be a simple and informal luncheon." Such speakers as Viscount Middleton, Professor Adler, Mrs Humphry Ward, M. Bourassa, and Sir W. Laurier have addressed the club at various times, and its membership includes several hundred women.

One day during my stay at Montreal I was invited to a lecture at another Club known as The Montreal Women's Club. Organised in 1892, it claims to be the first Women's Club in Canada, and the object originally outlined, "to promote agreeable and useful relations among women of artistic, literary, scientific and philanthropic tastes," has certainly been achieved, for at the present day the ladies of Montreal, by their various affiliated associations, stand for all that appertains to culture in home life and activity in citizenship. The later phase of committee work has had actual results in the sphere of philanthropy. For four years its members laboured before they succeeded in the formation of a Medical Inspection of Schools Committee. Two years later they procured the appointment of a Pure Food Committee. The afternoon when I was present was devoted to Patriotism. The National Anthem and a vocal rendering of "Lest we forget," together with an interesting summary of Canadian history, when the speaker ("a daughter of the Empire") compared the infant colony to the ugly duckling, which only awakened maternal pride on reaching a respectable maturity, united to make an attractive programme.

Upon another occasion I was a guest at a council meeting of the Local Council of Women of Montreal, which was formed some fifteen years ago in the belief that the Association of Women's Societies, such as those already mentioned, into a general organisation would lead to mutual sympathy and united action in matters of general interest. The Women's Local Council of Montreal is at the present time affiliated with nearly forty such societies, its policy being to serve as a medium of communication and a means of prosecuting any work of common interest; but any society entering the Local Council in no way loses its independence in aim or method. An elementary knowledge of the public work connected with hygiene, education, the care of the sick and infirm, as undertaken by these representative Local Councils of women, to be found probably in every city in Canada, suffices to make one realise the importance of measures proposed, considered, and sent up by them to the National Council of Women (first established by Lady Aberdeen), which in its turn prepares a schedule of needed reforms or suggested improvements in Canadian legislation dealing with the physical and moral welfare of the community, which is sent finally, to the authorities of provincial legislative bodies, directly concerned, to read, mark, learn, and digest.

Reviewing the struggle going on in the British Isles to obtain justice for taxpaying, wage-earning women, one cannot sufficiently commend our Canadian sisters for having organised themselves so efficiently, thus, in their National Councils, representing a consensus of opinion which Canadian politicians are scarcely likely to oppose, or to ignore.

The Local Council of the Women of Montreal were discussing with much animation the success and plans for the continuance of their milk stations, which in view of the appalling infant mortality – 55 per cent dying under the ages of five years – were started in the summer months by Dr Ritchie-England, the capable president. Whilst infants were succumbing daily during the intense heat, out of those brought daily to the stations who had enjoyed its ministrations for a fortnight, none had died. I visited one of these excellent charities, where the nurse in charge, one of the Victorian order founded by Lady Aberdeen, said that they were then giving milk specially modified to over ninety babies, and during six months only three had died. I told her of the impression left upon me after a visit to the Foundling Department of the Grey Nuns, where everything apparently, which up-to-date methods and self-sacrificing efforts on the part of the sisters could do for the unfortunate little things was done.

"Well," said she, "my experience here has taught me to think that if it is so difficult a matter, to save some of these French legitimate babies, how almost impossible it must be for the nuns to rear the illegitimate infants, often wrapped up in newspapers and found in their doorway."

"But you give milk to other than French Canadian mothers?" I asked.

"Oh, yes; but the greater number are French. Comparing them with Jewish women and others, I consider that, at least in urban districts, the French Canadian are by far the weakest race."

A talk with Mrs Henderson, the newly appointed official to the Juvenile Court just established, was enlightening as to the growing evils of slum areas in Montreal.

"I would like to tell you," said she, "that two-thirds of factory labour in this province are done by women and children, and in connection with that fact, add this: that in no city, not even in New York, where I have worked in the slums, is there a greater proportion of girls between the ages of twelve and eighteen living immoral lives! Does that look as if they were sufficiently paid?"

"How are the men employed?" I queried.

"Many of them swell the ranks of the loafers and of the unemployed. It is scarcely their fault," she added; "the employers pay women and children, who can quite well manage the machinery, much less than they would pay men; in fact," she continued, "if monkeys could be trained to do it, we should then have all the women and children on the streets."

I told her the same economic difficulty obtains in older lands.

"The Labour members are fighting for an eight hours' day for factory workers, but it was thrown out by the owners. At present the women and children's working-week comprises fifty hours."

I alluded to the illness resulting from the bad water supply in Montreal.

"Well, that is the reason we have the largest percentage of typhoid on the American continent," she exclaimed; "and Dr Blackadder, who is a well-known, reliable, medical man, stated that in the province of Quebec occurs the largest proportion of deaths from consumption in any part of the civilised world."

Without entering into further details the unprogressive French regime at work in Montreal is apparent; from any humanitarian point of view it is absolutely appalling! A study of the internal affairs of this backward province is the strongest argument in favour of restricted families as well as for State intervention to prevent the marriage of tuberculous, unfit persons. Surely from every standpoint it is better to rear three or four healthy children than from eleven to twenty consumptive, rickety weaklings. No wonder that the convents are filled with so many congenital wrecks of humanity! Given ordinary hygiene, and enlightened conditions, the youthful generation should be healthy, sane, and self supporting [...]

[Source: Bessie Pullen-Perry, *From Halifax to Vancouver* (Toronto: Bell and Cockburn, 1912), 91–6.]

Gertrude Twilley Richardson (1875–1946) was born in Leicester, England. She became involved in pacifist politics in reaction to the Boer War and was a supporter of women's suffrage. She immigrated to Canada in 1911 and soon after married a farmer, George Richardson. Active in promoting female suffrage in her community of Swan River, Manitoba, Richardson soon developed close ties with feminists across the country. She was an outspoken critic of

Canada's involvement in the First World War. Her observations on her life in Canada were published in the *Midland Free Press*.

Gertrude Richardson
My Canadian Letter (1915)

I wonder whether I ought tell you some little happenings of our ordinary life, as I used to, before the Great War filled all our thoughts. I will just tell you about the "rural Survey" meetings. Some time ago, an expert (as he was called), came to Swan Valley to examine conditions. He must have made an exhaustive survey, for he is well acquainted with the economics, religion, educational, and political outlook. He has written a book which is very interesting and on Friday the meetings were held in Swan River, similar ones having been held earlier in the week in the smaller towns surrounding.

The Professor of the Agricultural College, also a clergyman working the Social Service Council, and the Methodist minister of the town were the speakers. Splendid addresses were given, lively discussions took place, and together the meetings were very interesting indeed, and very well attended. Very few were references to the war, and there were no flags or patriotic decorations. Nurses are being chosen now for the second contingent which is soon to leave for England and the third contingent is being recruited rapidly. I hope that strife will end before all of them are needed. My mother is here to-day, and she has just been looking at King Albert's book. She thinks it is very beautiful as must all who see it, and although I hope many will have the privilege of seeing it (as I shall see that they do), I do not think any will fail to be touched to the very heart.

Oh! How dreadful is war! I wonder how many can attempt to justify it. There has never been war in which the innocent ones have not suffered greatly. Our work, our nation, has had many great soldiers. How we reverence the memory of men like Havelock! But it is not true to assert that war makes them great. It merely reveals their greatness. Is our work never to rise beyond the hideous holocausts? We all know them to be utterly unchristian, though many of the truest Christians are bound to take their part in the horrors.

It is a subject of endless sadness to me to reflect on the story of Empire. How much we all have to repent of and to feel shame for is best explained by the simple touch words of the Indian poetess of whom I have already told you and who died a short time ago. I will explain (for the sake of those who do not remember) that this lady was the daughter of a Red Indian chief and a missionary's daughter. She loved the Indians as her own people always and bore an Indian and an English name (Pauline Johnson). Here are words – she was speaking of her conquered race, and trying to explain their pain and suffering.

> They but forget we Indians owned the land
> From ocean to ocean: that they stand
> Upon a soil, that centuries agone
> Was our sole Kingdom, and our right alone.
> They never think how they would feel to-day
> If some great nation came from far away
> Wresting their country from their hapless
> braves,
> Giving what they gave us, but wars and graves,
> Though starved, crushed, plundered lies our nation low
> Perhaps the "White-Man's God" has willed it so.

Do you not think we have need for repenting now? Do you think we have room to criticize too strongly the actions of other nations? Oh, let us think how far we all are from the true spirit of Christ, and recognize that in some measure we are responsible for everything that happens in the world. I am so thankful for the spirit that is animating the best of the world's womanhood. From Germany, Russia, Austria, Ireland, Belgium, come the voices of true-souled women of intellect and courage, cheering, strengthening, sympathizing with each other, and preparing to make a demand for peace. So there is hope, and gladness, love and kindness and forgiveness and charity in spite of all the hatred and slaughter. May God bless and comfort all who suffer everywhere, and may His will be done on earth as it is in Heaven.

God bless all my friends.

[Source: Gertrude Richardson, "My Canadian Letter," *Midland Free Press* (Midland, UK), 1915.]

Woman's Century Editorial
India and Canada (1915)

Speaking of the opportune arrival of the Indian troops in France Sir Francis Young said at a recent meeting of the Royal Colonial Institute: "Had we not been able to bring up these reinforcements from India, had our position there been so precarious that we could not afford to take them away and had we been under the necessity to send out more British troops to strengthen our position in India, then in all probability our troops in Flanders would not have been able to stay the German onrush, and our brave little army would have been swept off the Continent. That Indians were able to help the French, the Belgians and ourselves in stopping a blow which the Germans had prepared for years is a thing of which they may be proud, and for which we should always be grateful to them."

The Sikhs in India

There are about 2,000,000 Sikhs in India. They had their origin in the Punjab in the fifteenth century. Their first teacher, Nanak, was a reformer and taught the unity of God, the brotherhood of man and the equality of the sexes. He put aside caste, idol worship, and superstition, and prohibited the use of intoxicating liquors. The Sikh religion, in the words of Mr. Macauliffe's standard work, "inculcates loyalty, gratitude, philanthropy, justice, truth, honesty and all the moral and domestic virtues known to the holiest citizens of any country."

Since the annexation of the Punjab in 1849 the Sikhs have remained ever loyal to Great Britain. They have formed a distinguished part of the British army in India, and they saved the Empire at the time of the Mutiny.

The Sikhs are monogamous and do not countenance child marriage. They are active in promoting education among their own people and encourage the education of girls.

The Sikhs in Canada

The great majority of Indians who have come to Canada are Sikhs, and many of them have seen active service in the Indian army and wear medals awarded for special bravery.

They are employed in agriculture, railroad construction, land-clearing and in factories and lumber mills. By industry and enterprise they have succeeded in making a competency. They own their dwelling houses and other property in the Cities of Vancouver and Victoria, and round about these places, and have invested in British Columbia in real estate and business several millions of dollars.

The authorities have found them peaceful and law-abiding citizens. In regard to their suitability for citizenship, Dr Lawson, in *Daily Colonist*, Victoria, 1913, wrote: "It was my duty to make a thorough physical examination of each emigrant at Hong Kong. I refer in particular to the Sikhs, and I am not exaggerating when I say that they were 100 per cent cleaner in their habits and freer from disease than the European steerage passengers I had come in contact with. The Sikhs impressed me as a clean, manly, honest race. I have not yet seen one good reason why they should not be permitted to bring their families in as freely as European immigrants."

Almost all these Sikhs entered Canada between 1904 and 1908. When they came they had every reason to believe that they could bring in their wives and children, as do other immigrants, but in 1908 the Government put into force restrictive legislation which practically stopped immigration from India. This is shown by the fact that in the following years only 117 Indians have entered Canada and many of these after considerable litigation. Thus when, after some years, these British subjects and Canadian citizens wished to have their families with them in their adopted country, they found that the restrictive legislation had made this impossible.

In 1911 a deputation of three Sikhs and one Canadian approached the Canadian Government with a petition in which it was said: "The restriction that most presses and needs very immediate redress, is the regulation that makes it impossible for the wives and children of the Hindustanis residing in Canada to join them." In 1912 and 1913 similar petitions were presented. In 1913 three Sikhs were sent as representatives of the Indians in Canada to present their case to the Imperial and Indian Governments.

So far their efforts have been in vain. Only five wives have been admitted and these after much effort and litigation. These people, of noble religion and traditions, capable of excellent citizenship, are forced to live as a community of men with the attendant discouragements, temptations and lack of uplifting influences. Sikhs may fight in France for British ideals but in Canada they are denied that which is basic to the British nation – the family life.

The Time for Change

This situation has arisen in a young and rapidly growing country with large undeveloped resources, and the resulting conflict of economic, racial and class interests. It is one which is manifestly antagonistic to Canadian sentiments of humanity and justice and to Christian teaching. It is especially adverse to the moral ideals of Canadian women.

Is not this time for change? Now, when India has proved herself not only loyal but lavishly generous in this crisis of the Empire, when friends and relatives of Sikhs in Canada are fighting side by side with Canadians for a great common cause, would it not be peculiarly appropriate for Canada to freely accord this much petitioned-for right? Shall Sikhs fail to find in liberty-loving Canada the justice for which their countrymen are giving their lives in other lands?

What Is Needed

Without doubt the Canadian Government will pass the legislation necessary to give Indians now resident in Canada the right to bring in their wives and families if it be known to be the wish of the Canadian people. Upon such a question – one of justice, morality and Christianity, surely all Canadians can unite, irrespective of party, religion, class or other differences.

What is needed is that requests be sent to the Dominion Government from representative bodies throughout Canada asking for such legislation.

Will not Canadian women undertake to see that such requests are sent from all women's organizations and others which they can influence? Will they not study the question, disseminate information and organize so that the required expressions of opinion may be gained at the earliest date possible?

[Source: Editorial, "India and Canada," *Woman's Century*, October 1915.]

Constance Rudyard Boulton was national education secretary for the IODE in 1918–19. In 1919 she carried out an extensive tour of "foreign schools" in western Ontario that emphasized the bravery of Canadian soldiers during the war.

Constance Rudyard Boulton
Our Imperial Obligations (1915)

Today, with civilization, as we understand it, threatened to its very foundations, we have got to do some hard and accurate thinking. We can no longer afford to temporize and shift the issues.

Life has suddenly become so tragic that we must repudiate our favorite theories unless they can be logically sustained in the fierce light of uncompromising facts. We are challenged to say to whom and what we declare our loyalty.

We have got to make a glorious stand, neither turning to the right nor the left.

In the days gone by, separated from the present by a hideous orgy of horror and despair, careless thinkers glibly talked of Internationalism while refusing to consider the more practical and intimate problem of Nationalism and Imperialism. It is modestly suggested that this curious attitude of mind is akin to putting the cart before the horse.

If we are incapable of grappling with the lesser problem, we are utterly unable to appreciate the vastness of the issues contained in the greater proposition. However, as events have shown, we have got to accept the fact that the whole beautiful, nebulous ideal is smashed.

The facts are these: Nationalism has arisen once more with all its amazing vitality and we stand humbled before its magnificent enthusiasm, which proudly courts annihilation rather than surrender the right of the weak to exist as well as the strong.

The patriot has given the lie to the scoffer. The patriot lives, proving himself a creature of flesh and blood and soul; a creature of vitality inspired by that illusive and intangible thing, love of country. The "glittering ideal" of universal brotherly love is still wrapt in a mist of dreams and we have to acknowledge that our methods so far have been unsuccessful in reducing those dreams to practical politics. Only by realizing the unquenchable fire of patriotism, the right of each existent nation to work out its own salvation through its own idealism, can we hope to reach the ever-retreating goal of a peaceful world.

It is not by unity, but by recognizing fundamental dissimilarity, that we may hope to attain harmony in our struggle towards the light.

Canadian Nationalism is subservient to a more splendid heritage which has been victorious over time and space. British Imperialism, in which today Canada is one of the dominating factors, has been growing, slowly and painfully, through the centuries, and today has matured in a splendour of united thought and purpose, which transcends imagination.

To Canadians, Nationalism and Imperialism are synonymous. One is the essence of the other. By descent, by historic fact, by our British struggles within our national life to attain a clearer understanding of the meaning of licensed freedom, by the duty which must be begotten of gratitude, and above all by the free and joyous love which her sons and daughters give to the Motherland, we have the right and the desire to merge our Nationalism into a more magnificent whole.

It is an inspiring thought that there are women in Canada who did not need a great war to grip their souls with the British Imperial ideal. For fifteen years the "Imperial Order Daughters of the Empire" have hitched their wagon to a star, and that star was British unity. Their whole educational propaganda has been moulded to that end. From coast to coast, Chapters to the number of four hundred odd, in song and story, year in and year out, despite ridicule and discouragement, have striven to preserve a rich heritage of tradition and instill in the youth of our country a sane and practical Imperialism.

Their educational work has emphasized the principle that equal opportunity means equal responsibility, and everywhere military service for the preservation of our country and Empire has been encouraged. Thousands of prizes have been distributed for all the various military exercises wherever regiments and cadet corps were organized, and twenty-two military Chapters are definitely attached to as many regiments, the welfare of families of the soldiers being their special interest.

The hearty approval of this work by the officers and the increased esprit-de-corps in the regiments as a result is sufficient testimony to the good influence of the Daughters towards the establishment of an efficient and complete national service system.

The people and organs of the press who in the past have been slighting in their criticism of military men, and have thundered against the iniquity of military training; who in the insolence of their ignorance refused to heed the warnings of our great men of vision, today are largely responsible for the price our country is paying in suffering and sacrifice.

The pernicious teaching of these pacifists-at-any-price has tended to deprive many of our thoughtless, carefree, prosperous Canadians of a deep sense of national responsibility, and, though a lamentable fact, it is not surprising that recruiting amongst our Canadian-born has not been as keen as it should be.

We as a nation owe a heavy debt of gratitude to the women who have the courage to inculcate a robust sentiment amongst our men which has done much to save us from the stigma of cowardice, and the shirking of our Imperial obligations.

[Source: Constance Rudyard Boulton, "Our Imperial Obligations," *Woman's Century*, November 1915.]

Anonymous
Nationalism or Racialism? (1918)

In our history books we learnt of the Stone Age, when each man lived alone, or with a mate in his own cave, and warred with all other cavemen. Then because man was not an animal, but had a soul and reason, the more intelligent men were strong minded enough to drop some of their own prejudices, and unite with others to combat wild beasts, and raise crops. So the world grew full of tiny clans, and central Africa to-day is still in the independent village age; but Europe, Asia and America have long since learned that union of races and communities as well as individuals means strength; and that for better or worse, *nations* will rule the world.

Putting the Race before the Nation

It is odd that the so-called Nationalism, both in Ireland and Quebec, is really Anti-nationalism, or Racialism – the putting of the race before the nation. A South African leader defined the airs of the Sinn Feiners as "Egotistical isolation."

Victor Hugo, poet and socialist, and passionate adorer of liberty, wrote in his "Ninety-Three" (one of the few perfectly written books in the world) of Brittany, and the revolt of la Vendee. The Bretons were of another race to the rest of France, they clung to their own dialect and customs, and rebelled against the first Republic of France, because they believed in the sacredness of a race rather than a nation.

The River versus the Stagnant Pool

Victor Hugo thus defines the differences between *true* Nationalism and Racialism – "The first fights for an ideal, the other for a prejudice. The one combats for humanity, the other for solitude. The one loves his country, the other his village. The one is the man of an on-sweeping, ever-widening river, the other is of stagnant pools where pestilence lurks. The revolt of la Vendee was of the local idea against the universal; of the peasant against the patriot."

This exactly describes our so-called Nationalism to-day; its teaching would break up every nation, and divide it among the races that have blended to make it. Then would probably follow the splitting up of the races into rival villages, and as the Egotistical spirit grew, the villages might well become cavemen.

[Source: Anonymous, "Nationalism or Racialism," *Woman's Century*, June 1918.]

Henrietta Muir Edwards (1849–1931), born to a wealthy Montreal family, spent much her adult life in the Northwest and later Alberta. In 1875 she created the Montreal Working Women's Association, aimed at providing vocational training, and with her sister edited the journal *Women's Work in Canada*, which publicized evangelical Christian women's activities. She assisted in the formation of the NCWC and the Victorian Order of Nurses, and was an executive member of the Ontario WCTU. She served as the long-time convener of the law committee of the NCWC, and published several works on women's legal status. From the First World War period onward she began to advocate for additional legal protections for Aboriginal women.

Henrietta Muir Edwards
Imperial or National? (1918)

The action of the Executive of the IODE in withdrawing the whole Order from affiliation with the National Council of Women, is viewed by many daughters of the Order with surprise.

The reason given does not seem satisfactory in view of the resolution passed at the Annual meeting of the National Council of Women [see below], in which assurance was given to the IODE that, the National Council of Women of Canada (representing every class of Canadian women) would act in this matter in unison with the other National Councils representing the rest of the women of the Empire.

The resolution of the IODE was passed, presumably without the knowledge that the National Council of Women of Germany, soon after the war began, sent to the President of the International, a notice of their withdrawal from the federation. No action on this communication could be taken, as the International has practically been in abeyance, no meeting of the Executive being held. As the German women have withdrawn, as far as it is in their power to do so, from association with the International, sending notice to that effect and paying no fee, what reason could the Canadian Council give for following their example? A very large percentage of the members of the National Council are Daughters of the Empire and to many of those present at the annual meeting at Brantford, it seemed unnecessary to take any action after the present position of the German Council was understood.

The answer to the second request of the IODE resolution, namely, that the National Council of Women would pledge itself to a certain line of action after the war, was thought to be in perfect accord with the aim of the IODE. Not Canadian, but Imperial, has been the broad vision of this splendid Order, organized to further patriotism for the Empire rather than for any one section of the British Dominions The assurance, therefore, that the Canadian Council would not act as a separate unit, but with the other Councils of the Empire in the reconstruction of the International after the war, ought to be most satisfactory to the Daughters of the Empire. Surely we do not want to give up the proud title of Daughters of the Empire, of Imperialists! for the more circumscribed one of Daughters of Canada. No matter how dearly we love the latter, not "Canada First" but "Union in the Empire" should be our thought.

If, on the other hand, the Daughters of the Empire refuse to act in harmony with the rest of the women of the British Dominions are they not withdrawing from the idea of an Imperial Order and becoming in thought only National? I do not think that the thousands of our chapters organized all over the Dominion have so lost their first vision that they will endorse the action of their sub-executive in withdrawing them from the National Council of Women of Canada because it refused to take a National rather than an Imperial action on the relation of its women to the women of Germany.

When this dreadful war is over and the whole British Empire has decided on its policy and attitude toward Germany and her allies, then – and not till then – is the right time for the Daughters of the Empire to decide how they can best express their patriotism. That Canadian women should decide now independent of the rest of the women of the Empire, what they shall or shall not do after the war, does not appeal to the patriotism of

A Daughter of the Empire,
HENRIETTA MUIR EDWARDS

Resolution –

Moved by Dr Patterson, seconded by Dr Stowe Gullen, that the following be sent to the IODE:

That the work of women in internationally organized associations (with the exception of the Red Cross) has since the beginning of the war been in abeyance. The National Council of Women is in exactly the same position with regard to its international affiliations as the Young Men's Christian Association, the Women's Christian Temperance Union, the Young Women's Christian Association, the International Council of Nurses, the International Suffrage Alliance, and like these international associations, The National Council of Women is waiting until the war is won before pronouncing upon its policy.

One fact is certain, that the National Council of Women will act in harmony with the other National Councils of Women of the British Empire.

[Source: "Imperial or National," *Woman's Century*, August 1918.]

British Commonwealth League

Resolutions Passed at the Conference on Citizen Rights of Women within the British Empire, July 9th and 10th, 1925 (1925)

Political Equality

This Conference notes the pledge of the Government to deal with equal franchise and calls upon the Government to introduce and pass through all its
stages a Bill establishing equal voting rights at the same age and on the same
qualification for men and women in the next session of Parliament. This Conference would strongly deprecate attempts to link up the question of Equal
Franchise with any controversial change in the existing system which would
inevitably prejudice its chances of success.

This Conference calls upon the British Government to amend the Government of India Act (1919) in such a way that women may be made eligible
for election or nomination as members of the Indian Legislature or Provincial
Councils by the passing of a Resolution to that effect in the Chambers and
Councils.

This Conference calls upon the British Government when granting or amending a Constitution in any British Possession to include equal voting rights for
men and women: and further it calls upon the Legislatures of all such Colonies
as have a measure of self-government to take immediate steps to grant such
equal rights where they do not already exist.

This Conference expresses its sympathy with the women of Bermuda on the
failure of the equal suffrage bill in the Legislature and calls upon that Legislature to re-introduce and pass into law a similar bill without delay.

This Conference protests against the loss of status and rights of citizenship
on entering South Africa, and urges upon the British Government the importance of the South African position being brought into line with the rest of the
Dominions, in order to remove a grave disability upon British subjects.

This Conference protests against the loss of status and rights of citizenship
suffered by women from other parts of the Commonwealth on entering the
Province of Quebec in Canada, and calls upon the Government of Quebec to
follow the example of 28 countries of the civilised world and grant to women
the full provincial suffrage.

This Conference extends its heartiest congratulations to the women of Newfoundland on obtaining suffrage and eligibility and earnestly hopes for their
co-operation in our common tasks.

Equal Moral Standard

This Conference while recognizing the advance which has been made in many
parts of the British Commonwealth towards an equal moral standard in law
and its administration, calls upon the British Governments, at home and in the

Overseas Dominions, to extend this principle of moral equality throughout all their legislation and particularly in regard to the laws governing marriage and divorce, illegitimacy, prostitution, street order, and venereal disease.

This Conference urges upon all women the importance of examining the *administration* of law and guarding against "Measures of exception" being applied to women under pretext of morals.

This Conference calls upon the British Home Government to take all the necessary steps to ensure the speedy permanent abolition of all measures of regulation and of all recognized brothels in the British Crown Colonies.

Some Legislative Inequalities

Nationality

This Conference welcomes the adoption without a division by the British House of Commons the following Resolution: "That in the opinion of this House a British woman shall not lose or be deemed to lose her nationality by the mere act of marriage with an alien, but that it should be open to her to make a declaration of alienage," and calls upon the Legislatures of the self-governing Dominions to pass similar Resolutions with a view to the early promotion and adoption of legislation on these lines throughout the British Empire.

Economic Equality

This Conference holds that the economic position of women within the British Empire is far from satisfactory and believing in the principle of equality declares:

1 Equal pay for equal work must be established.
2 The existing division and sub-division of labour into "man's" and "women's" work must be replaced by a free field.
3 No obstacle must be placed in the way of the employment of the married woman.
4 Protective legislation other than maternity legislation in industry must be based upon the nature of the work and not on the sex of the worker.
5 The economic value of the work of women in the home must be recognized.

and calls upon the societies represented to take action along these lines.

Slavery

This Conference regrets very much the omission of women from the Commission appointed under the League of Nations to enquire into the whole question of slavery, and in view of the suffering entailed upon womanhood by conditions of slavery, calls upon the Sixth Assembly of the League to request the Council of the League to appoint at least one woman to the Commission.

[Source: "Resolutions Passed at the Conference on Citizen Rights of Women within the British Empire, July 9th and 10th 1925," *Report of the British Commonwealth League Conference, 1925*, 11–12.]

Florence Custance (1881–1929) was a schoolteacher who immigrated from England and became active in Canadian socialist politics before the First World War. A founding member of the Communist Party of Canada in 1921, Custance became the secretary of the party's Women's Department the next year. In 1924 she founded the Canadian Federation of Women's Labor Leagues, which was aimed at the political self-education of working-class women as well as providing support for the labour movement and left politics. Custance also edited *The Woman Worker*, the official organ of the federation.

Florence Custance

The Imperial Order of the Daughters of the Empire Discuss Weighty Problems (1926)

The National Chapter of the Imperial Order of the Daughters of the Empire are, at the moment of writing, in session in St Johns, N.B. Among the weighty problems under their consideration are: Immigration, Combatting Communist Propaganda, especially in the schools, the Support of Militia and Defense, and the Publication of a Text Book explaining the significance and use of the Union Jack.

A truly patriotic agenda, and no doubt one which gives joy to the heart of the militarist! But the Golden Rule, so often preached by our patriotic women, is never applied by themselves. They take it for granted they have special rights, and raise great objection when they discover that there are others who consider they have rights also.

We need only to take, as an example, the fact that in the schools there hang pictures which depict war. These show the wholesale slaughter of human beings and soldier heroes. These pictures are the gift of the IODE to the schools. Was this gift without motive or purpose? Quite to the contrary. The motive is propaganda. These pictures are intended to instill in the minds of our children, the children of the workers, that war is glorious, to die in battle is heroic, to kill in battle is a duty, even if those who kill each other haven't the faintest idea "what 'twas all about." The propaganda of the imperialist war lovers is dominating at this time the minds of the children of the workers.

We have not been able to discover if the communists have been successful in getting their kind of pictures into the schools. But we have an idea that the kind of pictures they would place in the schools would be vastly different. One of their pictures would show how the workers toil in field, factory, mill and mine. By the side of that picture would be one showing the kind of people who fatten at the expense of those toilers, the kind of homes they live in, and the luxuries with which they are surrounded. Another would show the children of the workers playing amid the dangers of the street, while those of the leisure class play in spacious grounds with amusements of every kind. Another would show how simple, trusting people, who want but the right to live decent lives, are enticed into spending their few hard-earned savings on steamship passages in order to emigrate to a foreign country. Another would show how the militia is used to shoot down workers when they ask for a living wage. Another would depict the spirit and the bond of international brotherhood, symbolized in the Red Flag.

But are these pictures in the schools? We have yet to hear that they are. Why are the IODE complaining? It can be said quite truly that the teachers are teaching only those things that please the IODE. The school syllabus makes no provision for communist theories.

However, it may be, that the IODE have at last realized that the whole environment surrounding the lives of the workers is a living picture, and they are fearing they cannot cope with the workers' interpretation of that living picture. But this thought can be left with our patriotic women: That if big differences did not exist between people, that if there were not poor and rich, if poverty and luxury did not exist side by side, then there would not exist a force which seeks to bring about happiness for human beings, which is possible, but which does not at this time prevail.

[Source: Florence Custance, "The Imperial Order of the Daughters of the Empire Discuss Weighty Problems," *Woman Worker*, July 1926.]

Cairine Mackay Wilson (1885–1962) was the first woman appointed to the Senate in 1930 following the ruling of the British Privy Council that were persons and hence qualified to sit in the Senate. Born in Montreal to a wealthy family she married the federal Liberal politician, Norman Wilson, with whom she had eight children. Before her appointment to the Senate she was involved in a number of women's reform groups including the YWCA and NCWC as well as being strongly committed to expanding women's power and influence within the Liberal Party. During the 1930s she focused especially on women's peace initiatives and in supporting refugees.

Cairine Wilson

Address to the Annual Meeting of the Women's Teacher's Federation, Windsor, Ontario, 29 February 1940

You probably know, I have been much interested in the plight of the refugees and we have been doing our utmost to alleviate the distress of some who have suffered under the Nazi regime, and hope to bring a few children to our land. According to our provincial regulations any children brought here must be placed in foster homes of the religion of their parents, but it has also been drawn to my attention that these children would naturally only know what was taught to them by parents or teachers, and that there was nothing to prevent a Roman Catholic child becoming a Protestant, in Protestant surroundings, or vice versa. This thought will give us a realization of the responsibilities which rest upon [us] as parents or teachers. Our intense nationalism is but a develop-ment from the original clans where each man swore to be faithful to his Chief no matter what the cost. I fancy many of us all recall in Sir Walter Scott's "Fair Maid of Perth" where the only man who survived was the man who ran away.

In place of dwelling always on our differences, the one hope for the future lies in the endeavour to share beliefs and treasures which we have in common. We may all take pride in the works of art, of music and of literature of other lands and in this way encourage our mental and spiritual growth. It is an argu-ment against intense nationalism that musicians, in particular, have considered it necessary to adopt foreign names in order to acquire fame, even in their own lands. I saw recently a fine bust of the leader of the Scottish Philharmonic Orchestra and was told he bore an Italian name, he was still a native son. Only after he acquired such fame did his countrymen regret that he was not called MacTavish, Stewart or Scott.

We are all familiar with the popular music hall skit of the English woman in China who, when accused of being a foreigner, replied, "But I'm not a for-eigner, I'm English." Perhaps Canadians are inclined to adopt this attitude. Recently a friend of mine spoke at a church gathering where one would have expected sympathy and asked that the Women's Guild do something on behalf of refugees. On the way out, one of the faithful members of the Guild said to her, "But you know I don't like foreigners." In order to bring about a better world we must all learn that people are not necessarily inferior because they are different, and the best place for this to be learned is in the school room. The present doctrines of Hitler surely should teach us the utter absurdity of any racial theory and in the words of Dr A.W. Nelson, former President of Smith College, "Let us remember we are all aliens once."

During these last two years I have felt it a great honour to be invited to attend the conference on the Committee on the Cause and Cure of War, at Washington, and was delighted to observe the cordiality with which the visitors were welcomed. The Canadians were treated as honoured guests, and with the Americans we were pleased to hear from Kamaladevi, a writer and lecturer and General Secretary of the All-India Women's Conference who told us that Indian women are active in the nationalist movement and hoped by non-violence to gain their freedom. Mrs Amnu Swaminadhan, member of the Madras City Council, also brought us some wonderful thoughts, and said: "We from the East give you a message. War cannot be stopped by war. Why cannot the women of the West come at the plague of the war by non-violent means?" It was both interesting and enlightening to hear these women talk of the policy of non-resistance. Certainly it is far from a supine policy and involves untold suffering and faithfulness to a cause. From China there was Huang Sin Chi, Graduate of the American Institute, who said "the world of the Nationalist Group of China is coming nearer and nearer to the goal of peace through democratic principles. What I would like to say at this time is that for 5000 years China has contributed to the culture of the world. She will continue, and the means now will be through democratic movements."

I felt ashamed when I asked Kamaladevi if she were coming to Canada, and she replied, "You know the difficulties of even a visit to your country." Why must we make it impossible for the women of sister Dominions to come to us?

[Source: LAC, MG27-IIIC6, vol. 13, file 2, Cairine Wilson, "Address to the Annual Meeting of Women's Teachers," 27 February 1940.]

PART TWO
Internationalism

Cross-border collaborations and connections were a key feature of first wave feminism in Canada from the outset and intensified over time. Women reformers here were enmeshed within and deeply influenced by an international network of activists in which ideas and organizational initiatives constantly circulated, albeit one in which feminists from Britain and the United States continued to dominate. Many also perceived themselves as part of a "global sisterhood" then being constituted, which as Leila Rupp and other scholars have noted espoused the principle of inclusiveness, but which in practice often perpetuated exclusiveness on the basis of race, class, religion, and colonial status.[1] Moreover, national, imperial, and international interests at times converged within the Canadian women's movement, and in other instances were points of tension and even conflict.

While the "origin stories" of first wave feminism in Canada have yet to be thoroughly examined, without doubt involvement in the international movement to abolish slavery was a major impetus. By the early nineteenth century a select number of women reformers in British North America were increasingly enmeshed in a transatlantic network of anti-slavery activists who decried the perpetuation of human bondage. The Toronto Ladies' Association for the Relief of Destitute Colored Refugees (TLA) formed in 1851, for example, not only provided material assistance to American black immigrants (their numbers having increased markedly since the passage of the US Fugitive Slave Law in 1850), but actively campaigned against "Negro slavery" in the United States. They organized, as Karen Leroux has noted, "consciously and exclusively as women to exert moral and political pressure which they and their supporters believed was well within the legitimate province of women to carry out into practical action."[2] Connected by imperial ties, the TLA participated in a British petition to American women in 1852, and embarked on its own autonomous appeal the next year: "The Affectionate Address of Thousands of Women of Canada to Their Sisters of the United States of America." Arguing from a position of living in close geographic proximity to slavery, "and coming daily into contact with its bitter fruits," The TLA maintained that American women should and could play a vital role in abolishing human bondage. This address brought attention to the cause of anti-slavery at the same time as it sought to legitimate a collective political culture among women reformers in the colony.[3]

A subsequent attempt by the TLA to enhance its international stature, however, highlighted how efforts aimed at cross-border cooperation could at times conflict with local interests, and what problems might arise when a group of privileged white women purported to be speaking and acting on behalf of all women. In this specific instance the TLA co-sponsored a fundraising bazaar with the Rochester (NY) Ladies' Anti-slavery Society in Toronto in 1854 for Frederick Douglass's newspaper *The North Star*. Mary Ann Shadd Cary, the editor of *The Provincial Freeman* responded at length. A free black from Wilmington, Delaware, Shadd Cary had moved to Canada West in 1850 in the wake of the Fugitive Slave Act and soon after founded her own newspaper.[4] Shadd Cary roundly criticized the TLA and more generally the actions of white abolitionists for providing financial support to anti-slavery advocates in the United States during a time when the immediate material needs of blacks in Canada were so great. She admonished white reformers for not taking into account the financial and political interests of black refugees. Moreover, the piece on the Toronto bazaar, in originating from a prominent black female commentator, directly challenged the claims of a group such as the TLA to represent all women.

The link between anti-slavery and women's rights, which was well established among reformers in Britain and the United States by the 1850s, appears to have been making inroads in British North America as well. In other contexts activists not only made connections between the conditions of slaves and of women, but early feminists also built on the existing transnational network of abolitionists in their initial organizational efforts.[5] Mary Ann Shadd Cary's coverage of two Toronto lectures in March 1855 – one on American slavery, the other on women's rights – reinforced that such links were starting to be made in the colony. Depicting the lectures as representing "the leading reforms now becoming popular elsewhere," Shadd Cary underscored that the speakers were important sources of "practical wisdom." The second speaker in particular, Lucy Stone, who was a feminist abolitionist from the United States, embodied the melding of these two causes. So too did Shadd Cary of course, and in her support of equating woman's rights with human rights, as she did in this column, one could characterize her as part of a transatlantic group of mid-century universalists who recognized that multiple forms of oppression existed and were intertwined.[6]

Awareness of the deleterious consequences of colonialism on indigenous peoples was also a part of the "global vision" of some of this generation of reformers as well, and at least in the case of the United States, indigenous women from specific tribes served as a form of inspiration for early feminists. As Delores Janiewski has argued, US feminists "used the example of Native American women to criticize the patriarchal nature of their own society, to construct an interpretation of the origins of women's subordination, and to demonstrate the contingent, historical, and man-made creation of patriarchy through law and social custom."[7] The matriarchal heritage of the Iroquois in which women held key decision-making responsibilities was accorded special prominence. Given the fact that the Iroquois occupied lands that traversed the international boundary between the American republic and the United Province of Canada, and cross-border contacts were then relatively commonplace among female reformers, one could expect to find some evidence that a parallel process occurred in British North America. No primary document has yet been located that addresses this issue, which is more likely a reflection of the paucity of scholarly work completed thus far on the initial years of the first wave, rather than an indication that representations of and interactions with Iroquois women necessarily failed to influence feminism on this side of the border.

Yet as already noted in the previous chapter, the specific imperial context in which Canadian feminism originated and developed resulted in Aboriginal women being largely ignored as a subject of commentary or even object of concern. And thus while other organizational ventures originating in the United States were adopted by Canadian women reformers, it is noteworthy that the Women's National Indian Association (WNIA), which was formed in 1879 to address "the Indian problem" as a "woman question," did not spur the creation of a similar group in this country. Admittedly, this organization was not without serious limitations despite its stated intention of elevating the status of indigenous women. Reflective of the racial origins of first wave feminism more broadly, the white middle-class women active in this organization sought to inflict a restrictive form of domesticity on these "primitives" that they themselves were seeking to escape.[8] The non-action of women reformers in Canada should not be viewed as somehow less deleterious, however, as this form of "purposeful overlooking" also maintained structures of oppression.[9]

An organization first formed in the United States that did receive an enthusiastic response in Canada was the Women's Christian Temperance Union (WCTU). In an excerpt from her memoir, *Campaign Echoes*, Letitia Youmans recounted her experience of attending the Chautauqua Assembly, a Methodist educational summer camp in upper New York state, in 1874. It was there that she encountered a large group of female temperance advocates and for the first time heard a lecture delivered by a woman. Emboldened by what she heard and saw, Youmans returned home to found what turned out to be the second local WCTU in Canada. She proved to be a fervent proponent of international reform work, and as the rest of her memoir attests, developed close ties with both American and British temperance supporters.

The founding of the World's Women's Christian Temperance Union (WWC-TU) in 1884 solidified relationships that had long existed among temperance reformers and marked the first of many designated "international" feminist organizations from the late nineteenth century onward. Canadian reformers not only participated in conferences and organizational efforts of the WWCTU, but also sponsored temperance advocates in foreign countries, as explained in the pamphlet *What Is a Light Line Union?* (188?). That Christian conversion was a fundamental part of this reform project was made explicit in the pamphlet in terms of the financial support sought from local women's missionary groups and in the depiction of the Light Line unions as a foreign missionary endeavour. The sacred was to be combined with social reform: "The gospel message and temperance education go hand in hand." As Ian Tyrell has pointed out, such an initiative represented a form of cultural imperialism whereby Euro-American feminists sought to impose the "gifts" of Christianity and temperance on non-Western countries.[10] In the specific case of Canada, British imperial connections and sentiments were also reinforced, as the money raised went to temperance work in India.

Illustrative of the increasingly cross-national character of feminism in the late nineteenth century, reformers in Canada sought inspiration and guidance from external sources on a wide range of issues. With regard to access to higher education, for example, feminists repeatedly cited the successes of women in other national contexts to bolster their demand to attend university and, later, to attain specific degrees. In an 1895 article in *La Patrie*, Quebecois journalist Robertine Barry employed this tactic to contend that francophone Catholic women should be permitted a university education. While she referenced various foreign universities, she also quite pointedly cited one local institution, McGill University, which was a bastion of anglophone Protestant education. On this latter point she wished to infer that women who were among the francophone minority in Quebec should have the same educational opportunities as the anglophone majority. Barry thus constructed her argument for women's higher education against a backdrop of international advances and within a nationalist politics of furthering the interests of francophone Quebecois.

The relationship between internationalism and nationalism invoked by Barry obviously did not coincide with that advocated by the Anglo-Celtic (and mostly Protestant) women who dominated the women's movement in Canada, especially outside of Quebec. For many of these women, engagement in international debates, and most notably international organizations, often allowed for a positive expression of nationalism that during this period was encoded as English Canadian nationalism and, as explored in greater detail in the previous chapter, enhanced by a commitment to British imperialism. Such was the case with the speech given by Harriet Boomer at the 1899 conference of the International Council of Women (ICW) in London, England. Boomer expressed national pride in Canada being among the first countries to join the ICW and in the subsequent accomplishments of the National Council of Women of Canada (NCWC). She also took pains to delineate women's reform efforts in Canada from the dominant presence of the US feminist movement. Just as significantly, Boomer ended her presentation with a tribute to the wife of the British-appointed governor general of Canada, Lady Aberdeen, who had founded the NCWC and become the first president of the ICW.

Improving international and imperial connections simultaneously proved to be a marked characteristic of various Canadian transnational efforts. A member of the Imperial Order Daughters of the Empire (IODE), which originated in the midst of the Boer War, recounted in a 1913 article the group's overtures to establish a tangible presence in India. The piece noted that Canadian women involved in the IODE expressed a degree of initial reluctance, and needed to be "roused from their time-honoured prejudices and conservative aloofness," but the group eventually succeeded in the inauguration of several IODE chapters and educational programs for girls in India. However, it is possible to discern within the report a glaring contradiction in this Canadian-initiated venture – the strengthening of bonds among a select group of women within the empire while keeping firmly in place intersecting hierarchies of white settler dominion and colony, West and East, white women and "other." With other initiatives such as the one outlined by Una Saunders in a 1915 *Woman's Century* article, imperial goals were not so explicit. In this instance, Saunders endorsed the work of the Young Women's Christian Association (YWCA) in Japan, which was being greatly aided by Canadian personnel and resources. By this juncture the YWCA (along with the WCTU) had shifted away from an earlier approach that combined social reform and Christian proselytizing, although the focus was now on the attainment of "enlightened" (coded as Western) secular knowledge.

The promotion of international connections outside the borders of Canada, moreover, did not always directly equate with support for them within the country. With specific regard to designated "international" populations, namely non-British immigrants, mainstream women's organizations often sought to minimize and in some instances eliminate altogether "foreign" or "alien" influences. The YWCA-sponsored International Institute in Winnipeg discussed in Kate Foster's *The Canadian Mosaic* (1926) was representative of many Canadian feminist organizational ventures aimed at the foreign-born during this era. Taken together, the institute's activities constituted a wide-ranging program of Canadianization for non-British immigrant girls and women. Foster, who was then national field secretary of the YWCA, lauded such work, yet as with Ukrainian-speaking Miss Higginbotham, whose observations of North End Winnipeg were included in this extract, she perceived some value in immigrants retaining at least certain aspects of their ethnic culture. Elsewhere in this monograph, Foster repeatedly employed the metaphor of a mosaic "to allow some signs of difference to remain."[11]

Another important facet of internationalism involved socialist and, later, communist feminists. Activists in Canada as elsewhere saw themselves as engaged in a struggle against class exploitation and for female emancipation that went well beyond national borders. Although aspects of the "woman question" remained a contentious issue on the political left, equal rights for women was a consistent demand from the early years of the Second Socialist International from the 1880s onwards. A 1928 editorial in the *Women Worker* celebrated the long-standing tradition of International Women's Day. Noting its formal adoption at an International Socialist Women's Conference several decades previous, the editorial underscored the importance of IWD for building solidarity and highlighting the plight of working-class women across the globe. Transnational collaborations and organizational ties were further reinforced in the wake of the Russian Revolution as the Soviet Union emerged as the progenitor for international communism and as an important emblem of the advances that could be secured for women and workers. A number of women from Canada even joined the sizeable contingent of feminists who visited the Soviet Union during the interwar period with a view to witnessing the positive changes that had purportedly occurred in the lives of women. Communist party activist Becky Buhay spearheaded one such trip to the Soviet Union in the summer of 1930 that was reported on in the *Daily Worker*. Of additional significance, this trip entailed one of the very few instances in which a group of working-class women travelled abroad for expressly educational and activist purposes to learn about the social conditions and political situation of women elsewhere.

Immigrant women such as Anna Mokry, whose reminiscences cover the period from the 1910s to the 1930s, did not necessarily need to travel from

Canada to gain a broader or more in-depth international perspective. As an immigrant from the Ukraine, Mokry brought with her knowledge of peasant life in Eastern Europe and of ongoing political struggles there, knowledge that shaped her burgeoning political consciousness as a left-wing feminist. And thus, for example, the Edmonton branch of the women's section of the Ukrainian Labour-Farmer Temple Association (ULFTA), which she became involved in during the early 1920s, established the attainment of literacy skills for its female members as a priority, as so few Ukrainian women arrived from their homeland with the ability to read or write. Such skills and the further attainment of confidence were necessary, she believed, because "it was only when women themselves became aware of their role in society and of their community responsibility that they began to consider themselves full-fledged citizens." Through involvement in the women's section of the UFLTA and other ethnic immigrant organizations, women such as Mokry often pursued simultaneously local, national, and international issues.

Overall, the interwar period was one of rapid expansion in terms of cross-border feminist dialogue and engagement. The further development of international networks resulted in the growth of pre-existing women's organizations and the formation of new ones. For most in the mainstream women's movement Geneva, Switzerland, became the main locus of international feminism. Drawn by the presence of the League of Nations and the International Labour Organization, women's groups such as ICW, International Alliance of Women (IAW), and Women's International League for Peace and Freedom (WILPF) located their headquarters in the city, as did many others.[12] As has been argued elsewhere, and as the rest of this anthology will demonstrate, Canadian reformers were profoundly influenced by transnational activities and discourses during this era on a wide range of issues. However, their involvement in the leading international groups was relatively limited,[13] and Canadian feminists were only a sporadic presence in Geneva. Nonetheless, there were a number of notable exceptions, with Mary McGeachy being one of them. McGeachy took a position with the League of Nations in 1928 and as this organization began to pay greater attention to women's issues in the early 1930s, was made responsible for coordinating efforts between international feminist groups and the League. In a 1931 letter McGeachy wrote to Saskatchewan feminist Violet McNaughton, she noted that an initial consultation process was taking place in recognition of women activists' influence "in the forming of public opinion on international questions and to the fostering of international understanding." She wanted input from a range of national organizations in Canada, but in writing to McNaughton she expressed specific interest in organized farm women in the West. As a Canadian, McGeachy recognized the unique collective activism of such women. She was subsequently entrusted with administering the newly created Liaison Committee of International Women's Organizations.

One of the smaller organizations that located its main headquarters in Geneva was the newly formed International Federation of Business and Professional Women (IFBPW). Dorothy Heneker, a Montreal-trained lawyer who had been president of the Canadian federation, was made the first director of the international organization from 1930 to 1936, and was vice-president for a number of years thereafter. By the time she wrote "What Women's Organizations Are Sponsoring Today in Geneva" in 1939, she had an extensive understanding of collaborations within and between international women's groups. In this report she conveyed a belief in international cooperation and, more specifically, in the role of the League of Nations (and the affiliated ILO) working in conjunction with feminist organizations to redress gender inequalities and oppression. For Heneker, one of the key accomplishments of such alliances was the establishment of international principles or regulations that could then be applied at the national level in countries such as Canada. Tensions that had long existed in feminist circles between internationalism and nationalism and had greatly intensified by this time in the late 1930s are not evident in this document, in all likelihood a reflection of Heneker's lengthy tenure in Geneva and a deep commitment to the transnational women's community created there.

Other Canadian feminists dedicated to strengthening international ties focused their attention away from Europe during the interwar period. The inauguration of the Pan-Pacific Women's Association in 1928 aimed at promoting cross-cultural understanding between women in the East and West marked a decisive departure. Canadian contributions were initially rather modest, but by the 1930s a growing number of women were staunch supporters, and in 1937 the city of Vancouver was host to the association's international meeting. In a cartoon that appeared in the *Vancouver Sun* that year, "Miss Vancouver" is depicted as greeting conference participants at the end of a bridge of goodwill linking women from East and West.

And finally, over eighty years after a humanitarian crisis directly contributed to the beginnings of Canadian transnational engagement, another would usher in the temporary cessation of many organizational endeavours and the ending of some forms of international collaborations altogether. On this occasion the crisis involved the plight of Jewish refugees that was part of the rapidly escalating geopolitical conflict leading up to the Second World War. There were a number of feminist organizations, especially the Women's International League for Peace and Freedom (WILPF), who were vocal proponents of the federal government admitting larger numbers of Jewish refugees from Europe and alongside other voluntary organizations assisted those who were permitted to enter Canada. Not all women's groups though were so supportive or responsive. When Senator Cairine Wilson, who was among the most prominent political figures advocating for Jewish refugees, embarked on a national lobbying and educational campaign in the latter 1930s she made specifically targeted appeals to various women's groups. Such was the case with her 1938 newsletter message to Canadian business and professional women. Wilson not only noted the woefully inadequate Canadian response in comparison to other countries, but in effect reminded her fellow members of CFBPW of their ongoing global responsibilities.

NOTES

1 Leila Rupp, *Worlds of Women* (Princeton: Princeton UP, 1997), 225.
2 Karen Leroux, "Making a Claim on the Public Sphere: Toronto Women's Antislavery Activism, 1851–1854," M.A. thesis, University of British Columbia (1996), 34.
3 Ibid.
4 For a detailed discussion of Shadd Cary's life and politics, see Jane Rhodes, *The Black Press and Protest in the Nineteenth Century* (Bloomington: Indiana University Press, 1998).
5 Bonnie Anderson, *Joyous Greetings* (Oxford, New York: Oxford UP, 2000); Clare Midgley, *Women against Slavery* (New York: Routledge, 1992).
6 Nancy Hewitt, "Origin Stories: : Remapping First Wave Feminism," Sisterhood and Slavery: Transatlantic Antislavery and Women's Rights, Proceedings of the Third Annual Gilder Lehrman Center International Conference at Yale University, 25–28 October 2001, http://www.yale.edu/glc/conference/index.htm; see also Nancy Hewitt, "Re-Rooting American Women's Activism: Global Perspectives on 1848," in *Women's Rights and Human Rights: International Historical Perspectives*, ed. Patricia Grimshaw, Katie Holmes, and Marilyn Lake (London: Palgrave, 2001), 123–37.
7 Dolores Janiewski, "Gender Colonialism: The 'Woman Question' in Settler Society," in *Nation, Empire, Colony: Historicizing Gender and Race*, ed. Ruth Roach Pierson and Nupur Chaudhur (Bloomington: Indiana University Press, 1998), 70. See also Gail Landsman, "The 'Other' as Political Symbol: Images of Indians in the Woman Suffrage Movement," *Ethnohistory* 39, no. 3 (Summer 1992), 247–84.
8 Louise Michele Newman, *White Women's Rights: The Racial Origins of Feminism in the United States* (New York: Oxford University Press, 1999), 119.
9 Ibid., 20.
10 Ian Tyrell, *Woman's World, Woman's Empire: The Woman's Christian Temperance*

Union in International Perspective, 1880–1930 (Chapel Hill: University of North Carolina Press, 1991), 27–30.

11 Richard Day, "Constructing the Official Canadian: A Geneology of the Mosaic Metaphor in State Policy Discourse," *Topia*, no. 2 (Spring 1998), 55.

12 Carol Miller, "'Geneva – Key to Equality': Interwar Feminism and the League of Nations," *Women's History Review* 3, no. 2 (Summer 1994), 219–45.

13 Nancy Forestell, "Transnational Citizenship in a Post-Suffrage Era?: Canadian First Wave Feminism, 1919–1939," paper presented at the annual meeting of the Canadian Historical Association, University of Saskatchewan, June 2007.

The Toronto Ladies' Association for the Relief of Destitute Colored Refugees was formed in 1851 in the wake of large numbers of fugitive slaves fleeing north over the border with the United States. The passage of the Fugitive Slave Act by the American Congress in 1850, which required law-enforcement officials to capture all blacks who were suspected to be slaves, resulted in significant numbers of black refugees escaping to British North America. The association implemented a relief program assisting more than one hundred families during its first year alone.

Toronto Ladies Association for the Relief of Destitute Colored Fugitives
American Slavery (1853)

The following address to the Women of the United States has been prepared by the Toronto Ladies Association for the Relief of Destitute Colored Fugitives. It is written in a good spirit, and contains suggestions which it is the legitimate province of women to carry out into practical action. Much may be effected by female influence, especially in family arrangements, and in the education of those who are to be the future legislators and the wives of legislators. There is about this address also what will commend it the more to the people of the United States – a plainness of speech which they like. It expresses the truth in courteous terms, and seeks not to sweeten the unpalatable fact that slavery is a sin which ought to be abolished at once by every Christian nation:

The Affectionate Address of Thousands of Women of Canada to Their Sisters, the Women of the United States of America

"While the women of England, with whom we in this Colony are identified, propose to address you on the subject of Negro Slavery, it may not seem an unfitting occasion for us to add, in the same Christian spirit, our suggestions and entreaties. Living so near to the scene of Slavery, and coming daily into contact with its bitter fruits, in the persons of those unhappy fugitives who have been compelled by law to seek an asylum in our country, we cannot but deeply deplore its continuance in the world, and especially in your mighty nation – a nation whose influences for good might be coextensive with the civilized world, were it not for this foul blot, which mars its glory and paralyzes its power.

"We would then ask you, in the spirit of Christian love, to use that influence which, as sisters, as daughters, and as mothers, you possess, for the *abolition* of a system which deprives the victims of the fruits of their labour; which substitutes concubinage for the sacred institution of marriage; which abrogates the relation of parent and child, tearing children from the arms of their parents, and parents from each other; which shrouds the intellect of rational beings in the dark gloom of ignorance, and forbids the souls of immortal beings from holding communion with their Maker; and which degrades man, created in the Divine image, to the level of a beast. We repeat not this dark catalogue of crimes, needlessly to wound your feelings, or in a spirit of self-complacency, as if we and our fathers were free from all guilt, but with the view of deepening your sympathies on behalf of the sufferers. We ask you to ponder seriously and dispassionately the fact that the system which generates such evils, is becoming daily more deeply rooted in your soil, and hence more difficult to be culled or eradicated. We presume not to dictate to you the mode of action to which your sympathies should lead, but would affectionately suggest the following as peculiarly suited to your sex – to soften the harsh and cruel – to remonstrate with the unfeeling and unjust – to confirm the wavering and encourage the timid. We do not forget that there are many masters of slaves, who like Patrick Henry, confess their guilt, and so far pay 'their devoirs to virtue as to own the excellence and rectitude of her precepts, and lament their want of conformity to them.' In the case of each, use your influence to win them into the path of 'virtue.' We believe that there are many who, like your celebrated Pinckney, declare 'that by the eternal principles of natural justice, no master in the State has a right to hold his slave in bondage a single hour but who are yet timid in their notion.' Encourage and determine such by your counsel and approbation in the quiet seclusion of domestic privacy, warn those who desire to extend the area of slavery, of the difficulties that surround its present limits, and beseech them to think of the final results. Above all, let mothers prayerfully imbue the youthful hearts of their children with those important scripture truths which declare 'That God hath made of one blood all nations of men to dwell on all the face of the earth.' 'There is no respect of persons with God.' 'Forbear threatening, for both your and their master is in heaven.' 'Give unto your servants (slaves) that which is *just* and *equal*.' 'Do unto others as you would that they should do unto you'; and we venture to predict that ere another generation pass away, every bond shall be broken, and the oppressed will go free; and your great Republic, freed from its heavy incubus, will then truly be a land in which 'all men are equal, and have a right to life, *liberty*, and the pursuit of happiness.' Women of America, your power for good is great, and great are your responsibilities. Many of you by your talents, your advocacy of the rights and liberties of mankind, and your self-denying labours on behalf of the injured African race, command the admiration of mankind. To encourage such in their works of love, and to arouse others to use more energetically the means with which Nature hath endowed them for similar purposes, we now venture to address you, and earnestly pray that to you, the women of the United States, may belong the imperishable honour of removing from your soil the Iniquitous system of Slavery, which that noble spirit – the ornament of your country – Judge Jay, has described as 'a sin of crimson dye.' And the 'abolition of which in your land was among the *first* wishes' of the immortal Washington."

[Source: "American Slavery," *The Globe* (Toronto), 11 January 1853.]

Mary Ann Shadd Cary (1823–1893) was born to free blacks in Wilmington Delaware, but moved to British North America in 1850 after the passage of the Fugitive Slave Act. Settling in Windsor, Shadd Cary made waves in the black community by championing integration, eventually establishing the first integrated school in Canada, and becoming the first female newspaper editor in Canada. *The Provincial Freeman* was one of the longest running black newspapers before the Civil War, and addressed such issues as moral reform, civil rights, and racism.

Mary Ann Shadd Cary

A Bazaar in Toronto for Frederick Douglass' Paper, &c. (1854)

Since writing the remarks to be found in another column, proposing a Bazaar for the *Provincial Freeman*, we see it announced that Miss Julia Griffiths, an English lady, Secretary to the Rochester Female Anti-Slavery Society, and assistant in the office of *Frederick Douglass' Paper*, will open a Bazaar in Toronto, about the middle of this month, under the patronage of the Toronto Anti-Slavery Society, to dispose of the unsold English and Irish goods of the Rochester Fair!

A lucky paper, that! The Rochester Bazaar is held every year for its support. It has, we are informed, a paying subscription list, numbering thousands. The first installment of the UNCLE TOM FUND, was given by MRS STOWE for its support. It has private patronage incredible, besides, very recently, an addition to its coffers has been made, called the "Thousand Dollar Fund" – a sum contributed by one hundred persons, and gotten up, mainly, we are told, by a great effort on the part of Miss Griffiths, and now, Toronto must pay her golden tribute, by solicitation of the same untiring Miss Griffiths.

Barnum is distanced, and no mistake, in this succession of brilliant efforts to get the "tin!" But how is it that the wire-workers of a paper opposed to emigration to Canada, are making arrangements to hold a Bazaar for its support in the country? Are the abolitionists of Canada, or, rather of the Toronto Society, opposed to free colored people coming into the Province to settle? And are these the initiatory steps to a public endorsement of Anti-emigration views?

We know that such is the opinion of a portion of the citizens here, but may they not be mistaken? We do not wish to be liable to a silent imputation of mis-representing the *great* people engaged in this movement – humble as we are, we would like to know more of the facts, as well to satisfy our minds, as to enlighten the public. We have had many inquiries made of us, recently, as to the movements of the Toronto Anti-Slavery Society, not one of which we could answer, of course, not knowing where to find it, to get any information. We think, however, that as there is a prospect of its being found about the "middle of June," anxious inquirers will then be able to see and hear to their satisfaction. Should they conclude not to lose a moment in the search, we would suggest an application to the parent Society, in New York City, U.S., through Lewis Tappan, Esq., the great embodiment of Anti-Slavery Society tactics for the States and the Canadas.

The Toronto Anti-Slavery Society have had Rev. Samuel R. Ward in England and other parts of Britain, collecting funds for newly arrived fugitives – because the necessary amount was difficult to raise here in a reasonable time for those needy ones. Now in the name of honor and humanity, what is the state of the case? Are those funds to be lavished on favorites in Yankeedom, because Mr Ward has unfortunately fallen into disgrace with Lewis Tappan, Esq., and the right wing of the Toronto Society, for his devotion to the interests of colored Canadians, and his manly determination not to bow down sufficient-low, to please this one or that, who may have the shadow, but not the substance of anti-slavery? Poor fugitives! We trust that you may not have to content yourselves in the coming and future winters with only the crumbs that may be left from the £1500 ($6,000) raised by Mr Ward for you. And poor people of another class, who blow the trumpet for, and "prostrate yourselves" at the feet of other people!

Well after all this array of facts and opinions, it may be well to look at the bright side: the coming "elephant" may be but a precursor of the "good time," when the "distinguished organ" of Anti-Emigration in the U.S., will cease its opposition to colored freemen who wish to settle in Canada – will emigrate hither instead of simply coming over to take away the money before our "hard" winter sets in, and pour forth its "clarion notes" as the organ of the Toronto Anti-Slavery Society, until the *globe* shall be shaken by the "awful sound."

But will not Miss Griffiths leave a few coppers behind? The Underground emigrants come on in great numbers, and may "need" a little of something in the cold weather, *besides*, we know that the friends of Mr Ward, and of the *Provincial Freeman*, talk about holding a Huzza for this paper about the same time!

[Source: Mary Ann Shadd Cary, "A Bazaar in Toronto for Frederick Douglass' Paper, &c." *Provincial Freeman* (Toronto), 3 June 1854.]

Mary Ann Shadd Cary
Lectures (1855)

The citizens of Toronto have had, during the past week, more than ordinary opportunities to become indoctrinated in the leading reforms now become popular elsewhere. The Rev. Mr Naurey held forth to a numerous congregation on Monday evening, on the condition and prospects of aliened Americans. The lecture throughout was a sensible *expose* of the workings of American despotism against the colored man of this continent, and a faithful delineation of the characteristics of those affected by it.

The apathy, jealousies, cross-purposes, general want of harmony, and determined stand in direct opposition to what is clearly their true interests, were dwelt upon in so faithful, unpretending, though decided a manner, as to secure the appreciation if not the approval of all present. One great subject of regret is, that the colored citizens should so seldom attend lectures, whether the meetings are called by their own number, or other. It would be well for them to meet oftener, to look in the face the cause of present discords and former antagonisms, and endeavor to do away with the just imputation of "division, ignorance, love of menial occupations, and the like," that however much we may regret it, can be and is brought against them with so much force every day. Why with the abundant opportunities surrounding us – the schools, churches, associations and lectures – the sad spectacle our people here present be persisted in by them. Now, it is folly to take offence; the condition of things here is well known by others and lamented over, and wisdom will be shown more certainly by working to bring about a change than by indifference. In the course of his remarks, allusion was made to prejudice in Canada, and we did wish that our anti-emigration friends could have availed themselves of the many unmistakable cases enumerated, if only to have an excuse for their theory beyond bare assertions, unsupported by positive facts. The speaker had a supply on hand, but though deprecating their existence, very properly concluded not to be driven from *home* by such trifles.

Besides the lecture alluded to, and other meetings of a reformatory character during the week, Miss Lucy Stone, of the United States has, as will be seen by extracts from other papers, held forth to crowded audiences on the subject of "WOMAN's RIGHTS," or as very successfully shown by Miss Stone, Human Rights. It would be presumption in us to attempt an opinion on these lectures, apart from the intrinsic importance of the subject considered. Miss Stone's reputation, as a talented woman and an orator, is too well known. Her numerous admirers will take hope, however, in the certainty that in Toronto, with the strong attachment to antiquated position respecting woman and her sphere so prevalent, she was applauded abundantly, and patronized extensively – the St Lawrence Hall being literally packed; and better, the cry of "brigadier," "virago," and other soft epithets which invited her approach, were "heard no more for ever." All we were disappointed at was, that then too, so few of the colored people seized upon the occasion to learn lessons of practical wisdom.

[Source: Mary Ann Shadd Cary, "Lectures," *Provincial Freeman*, 17 March 1855.]

Margaret C. Munns
What Is a Light Line Union? A Catechism (188?)

What Is a Light Line Union?

It is a union that gives five dollars to the work of the World's WCTU and sends fifty cents to pay for a subscription to *The Tidings* for a missionary or someone else in a foreign country.

May a Union Have More than One "Light"?

There is no limit to the number of lights a union may have. Some are double, some triple and some quadruple Light Line unions.

How Is the Money Obtained?

Each union is urged to hold a meeting to which all the missionary societies in the community are invited. A good program is prepared, giving a word picture of the work of the WCTU in various countries. This may be presented in short addresses or in a demonstration. A collection is taken and a candle may be lighted if the collection amount to $5.50 or two candles if $11.00 is received, etc. If the amount received is not sufficient, it may be supplemented by personal contributions.

Why Invite the Missionary Societies?

Because many women interested in missions do not know that the WCTU is a foreign missionary as well as a home missionary society, sending the temperance light around the world. The church missionaries in many countries are the leaders in the WCTU work because they realize that this phase of Christian service is necessary to the up-building of a Christian life and to combat the evils that are found in every land. The gospel message and temperance education go hand in hand. This idea we must put over to the missionary groups. Practically all WCTU women belong to the missionary society and likewise all members of the missionary society should be members of the WCTU.

Where Can the Material for the Program Be Secured?

The World's WCTU Report (25 cents per copy) contains reports from all the countries. Interesting facts can be obtained from these reports. If those representing the countries that have an unusual native costume can be dressed in native style, it gives variety and color to the program. *The Tidings* (subscription 50 cents per year) has space devoted to temperance items from other countries. This gives opportunity to get the latest facts. The pageant given at the Boston convention may be secured in mimeograph form from the Canadian WCTU Depository at 15 cents per copy. This may be adapted for Provincial or county conventions.

Is the Light Line Union Idea Gaining Favor?

The first year the U.S. National WCTU promoted Light Line unions, approximately 428 unions participated, the following year 980 unions, although in both cases unions that were double and triple Light lines and even greater multiples were included. More unions are being interested and this philanthropy will eventually be a regular part of the local union program.

What Is Done with the Money from Light Line Unions?

The World's WCTU has a budget of appropriation for countries that need help in carrying on their work. Missionaries are supported in Argentina, Brazil, West Indies and one for Europe, while workers in Burma, Korea, China, Uruguay and Chile are taking the gospel temperance light to their own people. Germany employs teachers to give instruction concerning the production of unfermented fruit juice. France, Austria, Belgium, Mexico, Ceylon, Latvia, Cuba, Egypt and India are assisted and encouraged by the small amounts received from the World's treasury. Canadian contributions at present go to workers in India. The Light Line union money helps to make this assistance possible.

Where Should the Money Be Spent?

Plans will be sent out by the Canadian Superintendent of Temperance and Missions and should be carefully followed by the local union. In order that the country also may have credit, money raised for Light Line unions should pass through the country treasury. Notice of the payment of 50 cents for a subscription to WRT should accompany the $5.00 as both requirements must be met to become a Light Line Union.

[Source: Margaret Munn, *What Is a Light Line Union? A Catechism* (London: Printed by the Canadian WCTU Literature Depository, 188?)]

Letitia Creighton Youmans, 1827–96, was educated at the newly founded Burlington Ladies' Academy, which offered an advanced secondary education for girls. After graduation in 1847, Youmans taught at that school before going on to become preceptress at the Picton Ladies' Academy until her marriage in 1850. Inspired by American temperance advocates after attending the Chautauqua Assembly, a Methodist educational summer camp in upper New York state, Youmans founded the second Canadian WCTU in Picton, Ontario, in 1874. She was instrumental in the growth of WCTU groups across Canada and served as president of the Dominion WCTU after it was formed in 1885. She published an autobiography, *Campaign Echoes*, in 1893.

Letitia Youmans
Organized Women's Temperance Comes to Canada – 1874 (1893)

[...] But most memorable to me among the varied exercises was the woman's temperance meeting announced for each afternoon at four o'clock. A tent, seating some two or three hundred was the place of resort. The meeting was for women only, to be conducted by themselves. It was understood that St Paul's order was reversed, and that a man would not be suffered to speak in the church. Nevertheless, the brethren flocked in large numbers to be silent spectators of the proceedings, and stood in respectful silence outside.

The canvas sides were rolled up for ventilation, so that the outside worshippers could see and hear to very good advantage. The first meeting was conducted by Mrs (Dr) Knox, of New York State.

The earnest prayers and testimonies which constituted the programme soon revealed to me the fact that I was in the midst of the Crusaders. They were evidently women of mental culture, good social position and deep piety, not by any means belonging to the class I had supposed. They referred with gratitude to blessings received while praying in saloons, to perishing ones rescued and sorrowful homes made happy. While they spoke and prayed, hearty responses came from many masculine voices outside, and tears streaming down manly cheeks could be perceived on every side.

During one of these meetings, an opportunity was given for requests for prayer. A pale, sad-looking woman in widow's attire arose, and with choked utterance asked prayers for her son. She said, "He is my only child, my sole dependence. Up to the present time he has not known the taste of alcoholic liquor, for there has been none sold in our village. Recently they have opened a saloon opposite the store in which he is a clerk. I am so afraid that he will be led astray." This request met with a hearty response from the company. The leader said, "Let us kneel right down and take this request to the throne of grace." No one was named to lead in prayer, but a clear, earnest voice took up the petition, and carried every heart with it to the mercy-seat. It was not a stereotypical prayer, but an importune pleading for needed answer to a request. It was really conversing with One who she believed heard and would reply. She referred to the Saviour's work on earth; to His sympathy and help to the widow of Nain. She recognized Him as the same yesterday, to-day and forever, claiming that the widow's son should be the special object of his care.

My mind went back to my Canadian home and our ruined young men; to the nine places of legalized temptation and so much apathy and indifference by even the Christian people. I resolved more firmly than ever that something must be done to rescue the perishing of Picton. One afternoon public exercises in the Auditorium were given exclusively to temperance. Mrs Jennie Fowler Willing was the principal speaker. This was the first lecture I had ever heard delivered by a woman. It was an eloquent appeal for total abstinence and prohibition. Its glowing sentiments found a deep lodgment in my heart. Dr Fowler, now Bishop Fowler, of the Methodist Episcopal Church, brother of Mrs Willing, next told us what he had seen of the Women's Crusade in Cincinnati, when stationed there as pastor of the church.

He stated that the Crusaders had visited the saloons, and aroused public sentiment, so that the traffic was beginning to suffer from its effects. The liquor sellers had influenced the mayor to issue a proclamation that there should be no more obstructing sidewalks nor praying at business places.

But the women chose to obey God rather than man. They came out as before; paused in front of a saloon, ranging themselves so as to leave room for the passersby as they sang, "Jesus Lover of my soul." A policeman approached the leader, laying his hand upon her should as she sang, and said: "Madam, you are under arrest." She looked up at this face and continued the strain, "Let me to thy bosom fly," then pausing said: "We were never arrested before; what do you wish us to do?" He looked perplexed, as if driven to his wit's end. She continued, "We women begin our proceedings with prayer. Shall we pray now?" He nodded his assent, and the company was instantly on their knees praying earnestly for the saloonkeeper, the policeman and all victims of intemperance. When they arose from their knees, the policeman led the way to the courtroom. A crowd had assembled, attracted by the unusual trial that was about to take place. The accused were seated in front of the judge's bench, while gathered around them were ministers, lawyers, doctors, wealthy merchants and leading citizens, in many cases the husbands and brothers of the arrested women, naturally deeply interested in the proceedings.

The presiding judge magistrate, evidently much embarrassed, read the indictment. His position was anything but enviable, but he must go through the formula. So, after eulogizing the criminals on their high standing in society, and their adherence to law and order, expressing a hope that there would be no recurrence of that day's proceedings, he dismissed them on suspended sentence; and, added Dr Fowler, it was well that he did, for had he committed them for even one hour, there was not sufficient cement in the city to keep the walls of the lock-up together.

The Assembly was now drawing to a close, the temperance women met together for the last time. A different programme was arranged for the afternoon. After singing and prayer, the lady presiding pronounced to take steps towards the formation of a Woman's National Temperance Association. She requested the women to arrange themselves in groups according to the states they represented. This matter was soon adjusted, and I was surprised to find the different states were so well represented. I alone was left in the cold being the only Canadian woman. My husband standing very near the enclosure or tent, addressed the lady presiding, "Mrs Willing, could you take in Canada?" She responded smilingly, "Certainly, we will make it international."

There was a moment's pause to see what Canada would do; but I, fearing to take too much responsibility without consulting my sisters at home hesitated to join the ranks, resolving at the same time that Canada would not be neglected.

The preliminary steps for the organization were now taken, and the following officers *pro tem* were elected; Mrs Jennie Fowler Willing, President, and Mrs Emily Huntington Millar, Secretary.

The closing day of the Assembly was set apart from a review of the subjects studied during the session, and the awarding of diplomas. I had studied diligently the topics assigned us, and felt quite prepared for successful examination; but a previous engagement at home induced me to leave the preceding day. Thus I was deprived of the honor of being a Chautauquan graduate.

We now journeyed homeward, highly gratified with what we had seen and heard. We crossed the national boundary lines freighted with a stock more precious to me, than silver or gold, and yet we escaped the tariff, for my merchandise was not dutiable.

I had now fresh material for both Bible-class and Band of Hope, and the germ at least of a Woman's Temperance Union. The latter sprang into existence a month or two later, but not until a similar Union had been formed in Owen Sound, which deprived Picton of the distinction of forming the first WCTU in Canada, but she stands second on the list [...]

[Source: Letitia Youmans, *Campaign Echoes* (Toronto: William Briggs, 1893), 100–4.]

Robertine Barry, 1863–1910, was born in L'île-Verte, Quebec. She embarked on a lifelong career as a journalist when she joined the Montreal newspaper *La Patrie* in 1891. Writing under the pen name Françoise, Barry wrote a weekly column and later founded a women's page at that newspaper, the first francophone Canadian publication to do so. From 1902 to 1909 she published the bimonthly *Le Journal de Françoise*, which was aimed primarily at women readers. An outspoken advocate of women's rights, Barry supported vocational training for girls and improved access for females at all educational levels as well as better living conditions for women and children. In recognition of her prominent stature as a feminist in Quebec, she was appointed along with a number of others to represent Canadian women at the universal exposition in Paris in 1900.

Robertine Barry

When Will We See [Women in Universities]? (1895)

The other day a young woman got me to thinking, as we passed in front of that superb building called the University, about when we will see women admitted to take courses aimed at increasing their education and gaining them access to their rightful place in society.

Half a century ago, such a proposal would have been considered complete nonsense; today, glancing around us, it is possible to recognize that the female sex has gained considerable knowledge in a few years.

It is no longer a surprise that we wish to extend our aspirations beyond the limits of blessed ignorance that people have been pleased to set for us. It is time to have done with absurdly inadequate methods of education, the narrow perspectives and restricted knowledge that prepare us so little for the great struggle of life.

Even though many – and often the worst opponents of the struggle for women's rights are women – even though many opposed our admission to classical studies, there have nonetheless been those who understood that woman has need of the complete development of her intellectual faculties, of the kind of deep and extensive education regarded as indispensable for the other sex, and that she needs this education both for herself and for the sake of humanity.

It has been so well understood that foreign universities have almost all opened their doors to women. In Switzerland and Sweden, in Denmark, Finland, Holland and Italy, women have the privilege of taking the courses available at the universities of these different countries.

In the great Republic of France, the Collège de France and the Sorbonne recruit a number of students, often very assiduous ones, from among young women. Just recently I was reading that Miss Jeanne Beneben, after a very difficult exam, had been admitted to the faculty of law, and that she had taken first place in a competition in which all the other participants wore goatees.

In England there are several universities exclusively reserved for women. At the University of Bombay, attention has been drawn to the very rigorous research work undertaken by the members of the female sex who are taking courses there.

It seems almost superfluous to speak of the extraordinary development that the instruction of girls has undergone in the last few years in the United States, and – it is encouraging to note – in all the public schools where the two sexes struggle for intellectual predominance, it is the women who are victorious. They are at the head of the classes and first in the competitions. So it shouldn't surprise us that some men are hostile to the system of higher education that we are claiming as our right.

In Montreal, McGill University offers these advantages to the two sexes that frequent it. When will Laval University do as much? We could invoke, as precedent, the Catholic University of Washington, that has just admitted women among its students. A professor at Laval was telling me recently how much the modesty and dignity of the young women of McGill had charmed him; yet, in the same interview he announced that he had just refused a young woman who had asked permission to take some courses at his university.

Speak of the logic of men! It is remarkable, sometimes.

Let us be patient, though; it will come. I dream, better still, I dream quietly that future generations will see one day, in the twentieth century that has already been called "the women's century," university chairs occupied by women. And that will not be the first time, by the way.

The universities of Bologna and Padua have had and continue to have several women among the doctors of philosophy. At the University of Bologna, the daughter of a celebrated specialist in ecclesiastical law, Jehan Audry, replaced her father, when necessary, as chair of theology. Christine de Pisan – herself a poet, ethicist, and historian – said, on this subject, that beautiful Novelty veiled herself in such circumstances "so that her beauty would not prevent the thought of the costs." Helene Cornaro, luminary of the University of Padua, was at once philologist, poet and woman of letters, spoke Spanish, French, Latin, Greek, Hebrew, Arabic, discussed theology, astronomy, mathematics, and solemnly took the title of doctor of philosophy in the cathedral in Padua.

These universities, having appreciated all of woman's intellectual excellence, have carried on the good tradition of granting chairs to other women who are currently, deservedly, regarded as the glory and honour of our sex. Even before the founding of universities, one can read while paging through our history that in the middle ages, the monasteries of England, Ireland and France were the nurseries of erudite women. Abbesses especially figure among them. Bertile, St Gertrude, Lioba, Roswintha, Hilda, participated in the deliberations of the bishops in synod.

I don't know how our Lords the bishops would have responded to a female deputation asking to participate in the council that has just concluded at Montreal!

It would have been even more difficult for our abbesses to present their request in the languages of Homer and Virgil, as did their illustrious predecessors in times past. When will we see once again women of knowledge and classical education? One is almost tempted to believe, by comparing those centuries and ours, that we have regressed in civilization.

It is right to add that encouragement has always been lacking. Most men, poets, men of letters and writers, expended their energy on satires, jokes or criticisms of women who wanted to get out of the rut of ignorance they were assigned as their lot. What might one say of this sentiment of Aristotle's that one reads in one of his works: "The Mityleneans honour Sappho, even though she's a woman." Does that not indicate the extent of bearded prejudice?

But God willing, as they said in the time of Henri IV, there will come a day when the gentlemen are compelled to honour us, *even though we are women.*

[Source: Robertine Barry, "When Will We See [Women in Universities]?" *La Patrie*, 14 October 1895 (trans. Maureen Moynagh).]

Harriet Mills Boomer (1835–1921) was born in Somerset, England, and immigrated in 1851 with her widowed mother, who took a position as a teacher in the Red River settlement. Boomer left for England five years later but returned to live in London, Ontario, in 1878 with her second husband, Michael Boomer. She helped to found the National Council of Women in 1893 and the Local Council of Women in London that same year. She later served as president of the Victorian Order of Nurses and was a member of the Imperial Order Daughters of the Empire.

Harriet Boomer

Address to the Conference of the International Council of Women (1899)

Mrs Boomer, as substitute for Lady Aberdeen, President of the Canadian National Council of Women, said in acknowledging the greetings extended to the Canadian branch of the International Council of Women, that she was proud of the honoured position it held as second only upon the list of National Councils, that very position being a token that the women of Canada had been quick to recognize the power for good which must naturally result from organized and united effort, "the union of all for the good of all, and God over all," a motto which best conveyed the true meaning of what is called the Council idea.

The previous speaker had said she represented the women of America, giving statistics to prove their almost overwhelming numbers, but she had added, as if it were only an afterthought, that in those numbers she included the women of Canada. "Now," said Mrs Boomer, "whilst we women of Canada are glad to fall into line with our sisters of the United States, to follow as best we can their usually most excellent example, and to recognize in them their many admirable qualities, individually and nationally, still *Canada is Canada*, and not a mere promontory jutting out from the United States, nor are the women of Canada likely to rest content with a mere *post scriptum* mention as being amongst 'the women of America.' I am sure," she added, "that this little explanation will be taken in good part and my motive in making it not misunderstood."

Mrs Boomer said that the secretary's report would in due course give details of the success which had crowned many efforts of the Canadian National Council, so she would not occupy precious moments, now fast slipping away, in more than the barest allusion to a very few of them.

The Canadian National Council had, by appeals to its Provincial and Dominion Parliaments, and to its several local municipal authorities, obtained many concessions which must bear valuable fruit now and hereafter. It had obtained the introduction of a training manual in many centres where it had not been hitherto included in the school curriculum; and in the same way the appointment of women school trustees; it had wrought home reading unions, taken steps for the protection of women and children, instituted inquiries into the conditions of working women, had obtained the appointment of women factory inspectors with a view to the remedy of existing evils, is co-operating with medical authorities in spreading valuable knowledge on the subject of the treatment of consumption, and has amongst other educational efforts, promoted systematic instruction in art design adaptable to industries and manufactures which could open any field for the self-supporting occupation of women. Above and beyond this, the formation of the National Council of Women in Canada had, to use the words of its President, "tended to increase unity and mutual understanding, to bring together and blend in common work the most earnest women of every place, irrespective of creed, class, political party or race," and in so doing had happily not only been enabled to live down nearly all the misconceptions formed of its aims and objects when it first was founded, but it had won the hearty support and actual co-operation of some of the most intelligent and influential men in Canada. "But," asked the speaker, "for how much the realization of our hopes and the reward which has crowned our efforts are we not indebted not only to our beloved President, Lady Aberdeen, but also to Lord Aberdeen, so lately the honoured Governor-General of Canada? They were both, by example, and precept, the very life and soul of the National Council of the Women of Canada. Lady Aberdeen, as President of the International Council, welcomes "her own" to England. She is still "our President," and in thanking her for greeting on behalf of her fellow workers and her own, I would say, that the seed she planted in our hearts being a righteous seed, a seed blessed by many prayers, we may surely rest assured that the harvest field of Canada, with its women sowers and reapers will yet bear golden fruit to her rejoicing, and to God's honour and glory."

[Source: International Council of Women, *Report of Transactions of the Second Quinquennial Meeting of the International Council of Women Held at London, July 1899* (London: T. Fisher Unwin, 1899), 64–5.]

Imperial Order Daughters of the Empire
The Indian Committee (1913)

In the early days it was a much desired ambition on the part of the National Chapter to gain a foothold in India, and with that in view, a Committee was formed in 1902 with the following ladies as members: Mrs Percival Ridout, Convener; Mrs Walter Brown, Hon. Secretary; Lady Meredith, Mrs Homer Dickson, Mrs Edwin Baldwin, Mrs Stratford, Mrs Harris, Mrs Thompson, Miss Florence Dickson, Miss Carty. The work was naturally very difficult and somewhat discouraging owing to the fact that it had to be carried out entirely by correspondence, always the slowest and most arduous method of organization.

The first step was to evolve a scheme by which the women would be roused from their time-honoured prejudices and conservative aloofness. It was suggested that a School of Domestic Science would be the first move towards breaking down the barriers against a wider sympathy and understanding. A number of chapters fell in with the proposition and a fund of $500.00 was subsequently forwarded to Mrs Anderson at Bombay to build and furnish rooms for this purpose. The arrangements, however, were much delayed. The ravages of the plague stopped the work entirely for a time. A great deal of preliminary teaching and explanation had to be done. Finally, Miss Sorabji, a Christian Parsee lady, was passing through Canada and spoke to the Daughters of the Empire in Toronto on conditions amongst women of India. This lady possessed all the alluring fascination of the Oriental, and presented her subject with a symbolic and mystical eloquence which produced a rare impression. Miss Sorabji became deeply interested in the Daughters of the Empire and returned to her country filled with the desire to make the cause known to her own people. A letter in the following picturesque terms was received from her:

As soon as ever I am settled, I shall call a meeting to consider the forming of a

Chapter of the IODE. I feel and know it will draw the ends of Empire together in closest friendship. You will hear from me, dear friends. The lingering place of golden memories in the days to come will be a visit to Toronto and my meeting with my Canadian sisters, the Daughters of Empire. I sign myself.

Yours in closest bonds,

(signed) Susie Sorabji.

Eventually Mrs Anderson and Miss Kinnard formed a Chapter of the Order amongst the girls of the Girgaum High School, India which was called the Princess of Wales' Chapter, with thirty-one members.

Later a Chapter was formed by Lady Jahangir at St Helen's School, Poona, and several beds are supported by Chapters in Canada at the Hospital in Nasik. English ladies are working in the School of Medicine for Women in Ludheana, Punjab, India, at the Lady Muir Industrial Home, Jaunpur, N.P., India, at Lahore, and other places are much interested in the idea of forming the high caste ladies who have come from behind the Purdah, the Parsee women who are studying to become physicians to their country women, into chapters of the Daughters of the Empire. And so the circle gradually widens, first one and then another takes it up, inspired by the ideals which are the basic influence of the Imperial Order.

Miss McKinnery, in India, and Miss Florence Dickson and Miss O'Brien in Canada, are the ladies largely instrumental in widening the knowledge of the Order in the far away Indian Empire. Miss McKinnery writes were it possible she would wish to see hundreds of Chapters organized amongst the women of India and spread the message of enlightenment which follows in the pathway blazed by Imperialism.

[Source: LAC, MG 28, series I17, vol. 22, file 3, "Report in Special Edition of *Echoes*, June 1913: The Indian Committee."]

Una Saunders was born in England and a graduate of Somerville College, Oxford University. She became involved in an organization affiliated with the British YWCA for "leisured women" that encouraged service, especially service abroad. In 1896 Saunders travelled to Bombay, India, to assist with a missionary settlement started by British university graduates for educated Parsee women. She served as national executive director of the Canadian YWCA from 1912–20.

Una Saunders, ed.
Canada and Japan in Combination (1915)

The words "Travellers' Aid" recall to many Canadian travelers now the vision of a friendly looking woman at some railroad station, wearing a badge to show what her work is, and perhaps a ribbon to show whether she is attached to the staff of the YWCA or of some other body.

This same brand of protection work is to be found also in Japan under YWCA auspices, and the following quotations from a Japanese newspaper show how vital a part this work plays in the modern life of Japan:

"During June there has been opened at the Tokyo Central Station a rest room and headquarters for the YWCA Travellers' Aid matron, through the courtesy of the Imperial Government railways. This branch of the work is of comparatively recent establishment, but although it was begun less than two years ago it has already made a firm place for itself in the 'uplift' field and now requires the services of three matrons ... Signs giving the telephone number of the matron and telling of the work are placed in all city and many outlying stations."

"The diary of Mrs Hayashi, matron in charge at the Central Station, reveals many tragic stories and shows the need for the work. Numerous cases of young girls arriving from the country without the address of friends or relatives, and who found no one to meet them, are cited ... The young woman, twenty years old, who had been working in a Tokyo household, left because her employer was so cruel to her that she lost her mind. Wandering into the station, the matron took charge of her, gave her a ticket and finally sent her to her home near Sendai ... Another young girl came to the city looking for a 'man who lived back of the station.' She had forgotten the name and address, knew only that he was a carpenter and lived back of the station. Several hours' search discovered him."

"It is not alone helpless country girls who apply for aid to the matron, but many foreign tourists, overjoyed at finding her able to speak English and direct them to town or unfamiliar districts."

"The spread of the Travellers' Aid Branch of the Association work has been rapid in the past five years, so that it now stretches nearly round the globe. Through its agency thousands of girls are yearly saved from perilous paths and annoying difficulties and deposited safely at their destinations."

"In Tokyo the work has received the warm co-operation of the railway officials and the police, and is each month becoming a better established factor in the work of women for women."

The Canadian YWCA has a special sense of participation in this work now growing up in Japan, for the National Secretary over the whole YWCA work in that country (including the Travellers' Aid) is a Canadian woman, Miss Caroline Macdonald from London, Ont., and the support for her work comes from

Canadian YWCA branches. Yet another Canadian is giving her services and Association work in Tokyo, Miss Kaufmann, of Berlin, Ont. The latter has been specially interested in the development under the YWCA of a Neighborhood House of the "Garden of Good Friends," as it is called in Japanese. Classes and meetings of various kinds for men, women and children are held regularly, and recently a playground was opened with Japanese volunteer workers present each day to supervise the games and to teach the children and do "team work" play.

Canadian subscriptions have already built one Student Hostel under the YWCA in Tokyo, and in September the Tokyo Central Building will be opened; for this, part of the money came from the cities of Toronto and Montreal.

For a time also two other Canadian women were working in the Association in Japan, for Miss Dalton and Miss Agatha Cassels took charge of a "pension," or hostel, where foreigners visiting Tokyo could stay.

Ere this magazine reaches its readers, Miss Caroline Macdonald should be back again in this country cementing by her presence here the many links already formed between Canada and Japan, countries allied now in the great fight for ideals of liberty.

[Source: Una Saunders, ed., "Canada and Japan in Combination," *Woman's Century*, August 1915.]

Kate Patullo Foster, 1878–1959, was born and raised in Woodstock, Ontario. She married Percival Foster in 1904, but after he was killed in the early stages of the First World War, she moved to Toronto, where she organized one of the first YWCA hostess centres for Canadian soldiers. She later became national field secretary for the Dominion YWCA. In that capacity she published *The Canadian Mosaic* in 1926, which included information on a diverse array of immigrant ethnic groups in Canada and discussed Canadian immigration policy. In 1933 Foster founded the Council of Friendship, which promoted the arts and cultures of ethnic groups in Canada.

Kate A. Foster
From *The Canadian Mosaic* (1926)

Friendship House in Winnipeg

Last year a new venture was launched by the Winnipeg YWCA known as the

International Institute. The securing of a large building in the northern part of the city to be used as an educational, recreational and social centre for Foreign-Born girls from the country who came to Winnipeg to work in restaurants, factories or laundries was a long-cherished dream of the Winnipeg Association, but it was not until last Spring (1925) that 770 Flora Ave. was finally secured for the purpose. While it is very far from being the type of building dreamt of – it is but a modest house – still it is splendidly situated right in the heart of the foreign section; and it is already meeting a real need in the community.

Before we proceed with its activities let us glance back a few years and see how this work was begun. The work of the YWCA among the Foreign-Born in Winnipeg had its genesis in a Club known as the Friendship Club which was started in Robertson House (Presbyterian Social Centre) in October 1922 with five girls from one district in the country where Miss Higginbotham, who is now in charge of the work, had previously taught. The Club grew steadily and closed in May 1923 with a membership of 45. Through the efforts of Mrs W.J. Rose of Krakav, Poland, now of Winnipeg, and with the co-operation of the YWCA and other women's organizations the work was properly organized in December 1923. In 1924 the membership grew to 75. The members of this Friendship Club were Foreign-Born girls in domestic service in the city and later a second club called the Comrades' Club for waitresses was formed. Some educational work was begun and there were many social gatherings, and during the summer months several points of interest in and about Winnipeg were visited. In all these activities Miss Higginbotham received splendid co-operation from the staff at Robertson House as well as from a group of volunteer workers who gradually became deeply interested in the girls.

A description of conditions in this practically solid "foreign" district will be of interest. It is on the north side of the CPR tracks that the Ukrainians, Poles and other foreign people live and in certain cases at least, their homes – especially those that are dubbed "backyard homes" – are the merest shacks. Here is a picture of one described by Miss Higginbotham. "Annie and Mary, born in this country and educated in our Schools. Father has learned some English at work. Mother still foreign, doesn't speak English; wears a head shawl, knows only Old World customs and cooking which are especially emphasized at Christmas and Easter. These circumstances make it very difficult for Annie and Mary to entertain their English-speaking friends. Nothing is sadder than the Old World mother and the Canadianized daughters who seem to have no place in each other's lives. Can we not in some way help the mother to became Canadianized without losing her 'foreign' culture and try to get her to see Annie's and Mary's viewpoint; also teach the girls to honour and respect their mother instead of being ashamed of her?"

In the following sketchy sentences Miss Higginbotham gives us a glimpse of life in the North End. "There are: a huge Ukrainian Labour Temple with meetings and plays during the week and a concert every Sunday night, an Ukrainian Narodny Dim (People's Home), a community centre serving as a Social Club; a co-operative Society and school combined; Ukrainian Church halls where plays, picture shows, concerts and dances are held during the week and on Sundays; Steiman's large dance hall on Selkirk Ave., and Minak's less pretentious one on Dufferin Ave.; smaller halls and many homes, which are crowded every Sunday with people attending weddings and dances; and Polish community and Church halls where similar activities are indulged in seven days a week. There are, too, Greek Catholic churches, Russian Orthodox, Greek Orthodox, Ukrainian Orthodox, Polish Roman Catholic and Polish Independent Catholic churches, as well as Ukrainian schools, Polish schools and thousands of homes where people speak a different language from what we do."

Miss Higginbotham understands and speaks the Ukrainian tongue and she has one assistant, Mrs Cornish, who works faithfully with her in her efforts to be of service to the families in the vicinity of Flora Avenue. The following are some of the things accomplished during the past year at the "International Institute," the name of which has been changed recently to "Friendship House."

1 **Cooking Classes** – A course of eight lessons was given during the winter, 4 lessons before and 4 after Christmas. Manitoba Agricultural College did the demonstrating and at the close, certificates were awarded. The average attendance was from 20 to 25 and over 100 attended during the season.
2 **Friendship Club** – Well over a hundred girls were reached through this club last year, there being twenty present the night I was there. Miss Higginbotham has 5 volunteer workers to assist her with this group.
3 **Young Women's Bible Classes** – Two university women have given excellent assistance with the Bible classes.
4 **Mothers' Clubs** – Miss Higginbotham got her first contact with the mothers through the clinics conducted by the Victorian Order of Nurses. Over eighty families were called on and invitations sent to the mothers. One woman said to Miss Higginbotham, "You will have to *train* our people to come." Most of those who responded were Ukrainians or Poles, most of the former coming from the Province of Galicia.

In February of this year (1926) a jolly party for boys and girls was held at 770 Flora Avenue which was a huge success according to a kindly write-up of the event which appeared in the next week's issue of the "Robertson House Broadcaster."

A Club has recently been started for mothers which appears to be their one and only outing. At any rate the meetings are eagerly looked forward to by these busy, hardworking women. Cards were sent out to school teachers, and others through the country telling them about the Institute and already many girls have been referred to Friendship House giving evidence of co-operation from outlying districts.

A flourishing night school class is also conducted by Miss Higginbotham in the YMCA building (North End). Mr Miller, the general secretary, is keenly interested in the Foreign-Born and heartily co-operates with the YWCA secretary in trying to meet the needs of the young people in this district. The nationalities represented in this small night school are: Russian, Polish, Jews and Ukrainians. There are men, women and girls in the class and the work ranges from just learning the language to the regular Grade VIII work. There are four distinct grades and "the beginners need so much attention" declares Miss Higginbotham.

A most encouraging feature about the Foreign-Born work in Winnipeg is the co-operation and support that the YWCA receives from the Women's organizations, the Churches and the community, as well as from individuals.

[Source: Kate A. Foster, *Our Canadian Mosaic* (Toronto: Dominion Council YWCA, 1926), 118–20.]

Editorial, *Woman Worker*
International Women's Day Celebrations of To-day (1928)

For twenty years, March 8th, International Women's Day, has been celebrated by women the world over, and this for the purpose of demonstrating international unity and giving voice to those things which would help along that social process known as the emancipation of womanhood. For the first few years only small groups of women met in their annual celebrations. Now these celebrations are mass demonstrations in many countries.

International Women's Day owes its origin to a conference of Socialist and Labor Women which was held in Switzerland in 1907. While its founders could not possibly foretell the outcome of their decision, yet at that time its purpose was to provide a means of educating women to look at the world as a whole, to break through narrow national boundaries, and in this way to fight the War Danger as well as to strengthen their forces for the struggle of sex equality.

The event which brought this day to the fore and made it one of history was the action of the women of Petrograd (Leningrad) who, during the height of the war fever in 1914–1918, demonstrated against the war and the miseries it brought to the people of Russia.

It was on March 8th, 1917, that they joined forces with the workers of mill and factory and demanded PEACE and BREAD. This action started the revolt movement in Russia, a movement which did not cease until the workers and peasants of Russia came to the top, thus paving the way for the ending of class oppression and the beginning of a new order of things.

Since this year one class of womanhood in particular has claimed March 8th as their "special" day; these are the women of the working class. The lesson that has been learned by them is that freedom cannot come to women so long as one thing in particular remains, and this is a system which permits oppression and exploitation of man by man, and which allows the few to rule the many because these few possess the wealth. And, also, as this condition was that which began with the dawn of civilization and which caused the enslavement of women in the first place, this condition must go before women can be truly free. The system which is at the root of all the misery in the world to-day is capitalism, or, as it is called in terms of its latest development, imperialism.

At our celebrations we shall find ourselves compelled to denounce imperialism as the breeder of greater hatreds than existed in the past; as the cause of the strife and slaughter in China; as the cause of the filled prisons in Europe; as the cause of the oppression which the workers of all lands are enduring.

But words are not enough. We must prepare ourselves so that we can take active part in the struggle against imperialism. This means more organization, more enlightenment. Let this be our resolve on March 8th, 1928.

[Source: Editorial, "International Women's Day Celebrations of To-day," *Woman Worker* (Toronto), March 1928, 1–2.]

The Canadian Working Women's Delegation to the Soviet Union included Beckie Buhay, Annie Whitfield, Bessie Schachter, Annie Zen, Pearl Wedro, and Elsa Tynjala. Buhay was the main organizer and leader of the delegation. Rebecca "Beckie" Buhay (1896–1953) was born in England and in 1912 immigrated to Montreal, where she became involved in socialist politics. An early member of the Communist Party of Canada, Buhay travelled extensively throughout Canada in support of various educational and activist aims of the party in the 1920s and 1930s. She succeeded Florence Custance as head of the Women's Department in 1929.

Canadian Working Women's Delegation
Soviet Union Inspires Canadian Working Women (1930)

We working women from Canada coming from factory and mine districts, after having spent a few days in the Soviet Union and having seen for ourselves already a number of the features of the new life the working and peasant masses of the Soviet Union are building up (rest homes, nurseries, factories, co-operatives, trade schools, etc.), have no doubt in our minds whatever about the great success of the workers revolution.

Though we know full well that the task of the Soviet workers is no easy one, that there are many hardships they are going through and must yet go through in order to build the Socialist Society, we see in each of their achievements, in the happy faces of the youth, in the life that abounds all around, the great future that awaits them in this building of a socialist society.

This is in direct contrast to the hopelessness and despair that capitalist Canada offers her workers for their future under capitalism rooted economic crisis, with thousands out of work, with intense speedup in the shops, with wages continually lowering, with hours of labor lengthening, and with no outlook except the worsening of even these conditions.

We have talked to many of the workers of the Soviet Union and nothing has impressed us more than the loyalty and love they feel for their revolution and its achievements.

Particularly are we impressed by the change the revolution has brought to the women. We have seen many of the efforts that have and are being made to release her from the drudgery of the kitchen, everywhere she takes her place side by side with her brother-worker in the building of the new society. We have been amazed and truly gratified to see the important post that woman is occupying everywhere, and now it is perfectly clear to us that her emancipation can only come through the proletarian dictatorship.

We will travel throughout the Soviet Union to see the achievements in all fields, for us it is as if a new world has been opened up, a world that through its growing pains will emerge into the highest form of society.

We wish to declare to both the workers and peasants of the Soviet Union and the workers and poor farmers of Canada, that we have made a pledge that on our return we will tell thousands of the Canadian masses of these wonderful things that the proletarian revolution is accomplishing, we will make it clear to our workers that it is their revolution as well as that of the Russian workers and that we shall do all in our power to mobilize our workers against the planned attacks of the imperialists and for the defense of the fatherland of our class, the Soviet Union.

Long live the Soviet Union.

Hasten the day for the overthrow of Capitalism in Canada!

Long live the World Revolution.

Signed – Beckie Bubay, Annie Whitfield, Bessie Schachter, Annie Zen, Pearl Wedro, Elsa Tynjala

[Source: Beckie Buhay et al., "Soviet Union Inspires Canadian Working Women," *The Worker* (Toronto), 20 September 1930.]

Anna Tsytsak Mokry was born in 1893, one of twelve children in a peasant family, in the village of Rozhniz, Ukraine. She received no formal education and worked as a young adult for rich landowners. She immigrated to Canada in 1912, living first in Winnipeg and later in Edmonton, where she married in 1916. Mokry became active in the Ukrainian Farmer Labour Temple Association, which created a women's section in 1922.

Anna Mokry
Excerpt from *Reminiscences* (c. 1910s–1930s)

[…] I was nineteen years of age when I came to Canada in 1912, in the company of other people from our village. I had no relatives in Canada. My father didn't have the money to pay for my steamship ticket, so he had to borrow the necessary amount from a Jewish moneylender … It was hoped that I would earn the money in Canada and send it to my father to repay the debt. My father had to put up our house and garden as security for the loan. [Mokry travelled by steamship to Halifax, then on to Winnipeg and finally to Edmonton.] I have lived in Edmonton ever since and have been employed in various kinds of work – in restaurants, in a laundry and in a cigar factory.

I met Michael Mokry in 1914. He was already a member of the Ukrainian Social Democratic Party and on one occasion, he invited me to an organization banquet. I met two very fine people at this banquet, John Klebanowsky and Michale Iliuk. John Klebanowsky spoke at this banquet. His speech went right to my heart. Everything that he said in some way related to my own experiences. I realized that my place was with these people and I have been one of them ever since.

The Ukrainian Social Democratic Party group presented plays on stage and I played in different roles. The first dramatic work that I took part in bore the title *Strike in Galicia*. Then the play *Verkhovyntsi* was performed. It may be surprising that I was able to memorize my parts without knowing how to read. What actually happened was that Michael Mokry read the parts to me and I memorized what he read. I had a good memory.

I became a member of the Society for Self-Enlightenment when it was formed in 1915. I began to learn to read and write as soon as I joined the society. It was thanks to the organization that I acquired the learning that I did. Among the many members, men and women of the Society for Self-Enlightenment, there were such wonderful people as John Klebanowsky, Matthew Shatulsky, Michael Mokry and John Sokolow.

When the Ukrainian Labour-Farmer Temple Association was formed we in the Society for Self-Enlightenment joined its ranks and our own society ceased to exist.

Michael Mokry and I were married in 1916. We moved to Cardiff in 1918, where Michael began to work in the mine. He was a member of the miners' union. Every time he left for work in the mine, I was worried lest something happen to him. He had suffered a serious injury in the mine when he was still single.

We stayed in Cardiff until 1921 and then returned to Edmonton. Later on, when my husband was working Bush Mine, near Edmonton, Michael Bohatchuk, who was from the village of Rozhniz, was involved in a fatal accident at the mine.

A branch of the Women's Section of the Ukrainian Labour-Farmer Temple Association was formed in Edmonton in 1922. I attended the founding meeting and was elected financial secretary of the branch. Mary Yuriychuk became the recording secretary. As time passed, I carried out various functions, whatever was given to me to do by the organization, and was head for a long time. Of course, I can't remember all of the duties and responsibilities entrusted to me by the organization after all these years.

Our work demanded more of our time when we organized the Women's Section of the UFLTA. We began to observe International Women's Day, held public meetings, conducted campaigns, and had well known speakers deliver lectures. We had to provide leadership to other women when we ourselves were limited in our knowledge of such things. We also organized a school for the liquidation of illiteracy. The teachers were John Sembay and Nick Dranuta.

It was difficult in the beginning because our women were timid in so far as public activities were concerned and they had no organizational experience. It was no easy matter for women to get up at [a] meeting where men were present and express her opinion. It took quite some effort to overcome such reticence and feelings of inferiority. This is one of the main reasons why the Women's Section was organized – to encourage the women to do organizational work and acquire confidence. It was only when women themselves became aware of their role in society and of their community responsibility that they began to consider themselves full-fledged citizens. Only a progressive organization could provide such guidance, one of these organizations was the Ukrainian Labour Temple Association which was later renamed the Ukrainian Labour-Farmer Association and latterly, the Association of United Ukrainian Canadians.

Of course, it would be inadequate to say that the women only worked in the Women's Section. The fact is that they worked in all the progressive organizations that came into being in the twenties and thirties. Take, for example, the Workers' Benevolent Association and, especially the Association to Aid the Liberation Movement in the Western Ukraine. Who was it, if not mainly the women, who did such humanitarian work as visiting the sick? Who was it, in the main, who collected aid for political prisoners and their families in those parts of Ukraine which, before the Second World War, suffered under various bourgeois occupations? Once again, it was the women for the most part. Besides, our Women's Section of the ULFTA was born during the campaign to collect aid for the starving people in the Volga Region and Ukraine in 1921–1922.

For some time I was one of the members of the Provincial Committee of the ULFTA. I frequently went on organizational tours in Alberta. I delivered public addresses in various localities in the province on the occasion of International Women's Day and May Day festivities.

I have been talking about the progressive Ukrainian organizations so far. But we must bear in mind that our Ukrainian women have been working in Canadian workers' organizations right along and have been fighting for democratic rights, for peace and against war. Much could be said in praise of Ukrainian women and their work in the Canadian progressive movement as a whole.

Can we omit mentioning how much the women members suffered at the hands of the police, how they were beaten with clubs when the unemployed were trying to get work and something to eat for their families? Is it worth recalling the Hunger Trek of the unemployed to Edmonton in 1932? The members of the Women's Section of the ULFTA walked in the front ranks of the march and many of us were beaten by the police, especially by the Royal Canadian Mounted Police. I was one of those who were beaten during this trek, in which twenty thousand people took part. The savage enraged police charged into our ranks with their horses, they beat us and trampled us underfoot. It seemed that the police, in their viciousness, would crush the unfortunate people who only asked for work or bread.

I have always, as much as I have been able, taken part in various organizational campaigns. I have been especially active in the press campaigns. I have always received a prize for my work for the press [...]

[Source: Anna Mokry, *Reminiscences of Courage and Hope: Stories of Ukrainian Canadian Women Pioneers*, comp. and intro. Peter Krachuck, trans. Michael Ukas (Toronto: Kobzar, 1991), 151–5.]

Mary McGeachy (1901–91), the daughter of a gospel hall preacher from Sarnia, Ontario, graduated from the University of Toronto in 1924. Active in the student Christian movement while at the university, McGeachy continued her involvement during the several years when she taught high school in Hamilton, Ontario. In 1927 she moved to Geneva to become editor of the World Student Christian Federation journal, *Vox Studentium*. A year later she secured a position in the information section of the League of Nations. During the early 1930s as women's issues assumed greater importance within the League, McGeachy was made responsible for coordinating the efforts of the leading feminist groups through the Liaison Committee of the Women's International Organizations.

Mary McGeachy
Letter from Mary McGeachy to Violet McNaughton (1931)

League of Nations
Geneva, November 25, 1931

My Dear Mrs McNaughton,

I am sending you for your information a memorandum on the closer collaboration of women in the work of the League of Nations. It is being sent out by the Secretary-General this week. We have been sending this memorandum to all the international organizations of women, to the chief national organizations which are not organized internationally, and to a certain number of individuals who will be interested in this matter. I have just been sending a copy to Mrs Chambers of the Federated Women's Institutes of Canada, and I should be very glad to know from you what further steps we should take to get this memorandum to all the organizations of women in the West.

Perhaps I might say a few words of explanation of this document. During recent years women's organizations have contributed greatly to the forming of public opinion on international questions and to the fostering of international understanding. The resolution contained in this memorandum indicates that the States Members of the League recognise what women have done in this regard. They have asked the Secretariat to present a report on the means of increasing the existing cooperation of women in the work of the League.

To draw up this report it is desirable that the Secretary-General should have information as to what has already been done by women's organizations and to what extent their studies and actions have already influenced public opinion within their particular circles and in their countries at large. The form of reply will necessarily vary with each organization. We hope, however, to have a description of any study of the work of the League (political, economic, financial, social or that relating to public health, scientific research or the development of the intellectual and artistic life in various countries) which women's organizations have made and a statement of any action which they have taken or are contemplating taking as a result of such study.

The Secretary-General would further be glad to have suggestions as to the means by which work of the women's organizations might be more effectively linked to the general work of the organization of peace and the promotion of international understanding, which is the aim of the League of Nations.

A good many of the organizations of women in Canada have international affiliations and may be sending their replies through their own international headquarters. One feels, however, that the organizations of farm women in the West, because of their peculiarly Canadian origin and their distinctive method of working, will have something particularly interesting to offer. I should be glad for any suggestions for you about approaching them, and I am sure that they on their part will want to consult you about the form and content of their reply.

> With kindest regards,
> Yours sincerely,
> Mary A. Craig McGeachy

[Source: Saskatchewan Archives Board (SAB), McNaughton Papers, file A1E 52(1), Letter from Mary McGeachy to McNaughton, 25 November 1931.]

Goodwill (1937)

[Source: *Vancouver Sun* (Vancouver, British Columbia), 15 July 1937.]

Dorothy Heneker (1886–1968) was born in Montreal, the daughter of a prominent lawyer, Richard Heneker. She graduated with a law degree from McGill
University in 1925 and after several years of handling women's investments
joined her father's law firm. She was elected president of the Montreal Business and Professional Women's Club in 1929 and became national president
the next year. She served as Canadian representative at the founding 1930 meet-

ing of the International Federation of Business and Professional Women. She then became director of IFBPW at its headquarters in Geneva, Switzerland, from 1930–6 and served as vice-president until the outbreak of the Second World War. In the late 1930s she was also involved in efforts by international women's groups to stem the outbreak of war, acting as secretary of the Peace and Disarmament Committee of the International Women's Organizations, and worked alongside other Canadian feminists on the Committee on the Cause and Cure of War.

Dorothy Heneker
What Women's Organizations Are Sponsoring Today in Geneva (1939)

A brilliant day of autumn sunshine at Geneva – a crowded Committee room in the new League buildings where a packed gallery of men and women, representative of organizations throughout the world, follows with eager interest the long discussion on the question of the "Status of Women" – below at two long tables sit official representatives and delegates from the Governments of many nations including women whose names have become world known.

The discussion opens quietly – then gradually the interest quickens and the Chairman's list of speakers increases. Miss Kerstin Nesselgren of Sweden rises and in her own wise and sagacious fashion presents the subject to the meeting, – a charming Chinese woman lawyer argues a subtle point, – spectators drift in from other Committees and the floor of the room becomes crowded, – the gallery watches with keener attention. Then comes the decision, and spectators and delegates stream out into the sunny morning with Lac Leman sparkling below them and Mt Blanc shining far above the blue waters of the lake.

Such was the setting when in September 1937, the First Committee of the Assembly of the League of Nations passed a resolution asking that the League should publish a comprehensive survey of the legal status of women in the various countries of the world. This resolution was adopted by the Assembly which not only provided for the appointment of a Committee of experts to superintend the work but also voted funds towards the carrying out of the work itself.

Legal Status of Women Survey

Today this question is one upon which the attention of *all* the women's organizations is focused. The Committee of Experts appointed by the League, held its second meeting in Geneva this winter and on January 10th, 1939 issued a Report on the progress of the Survey, which makes interesting reading.

Furthermore Professor Gutteridge, Professor of Comparative Law in the University of Cambridge, who is Chairman of the Committee, arranged two meetings of the Committee with representatives of the women's international organizations. At these meetings the Committee asked for further help from the women's *organizations in obtaining examples of the application of current legislation* in the various countries in which the organizations had national branches.

In response to this appeal the Liaison Committee of the Women's International Organizations, a co-ordinating committee made up of representatives from a large number of the International organizations including the International Council of Women, the International Federation of University Women, the International Suffrage Alliance of Women, our own International Federation of Business and Professional Women and many others, immediately asked these representatives to urge their national organizations throughout the world to co-operate in obtaining this information for the Committee of Experts which must be sent in before December 1939. The Liaison Committee furthermore drafted a circular letter containing full details of the points to be covered and this letter has been generally used by the various international organizations in order to avoid overlapping and to obtain a uniform type of material.

Other Aspects of the Work of the League Sponsored by Women's Organizations

Today when the peace of the world is so precarious and the menace of war seems to draw daily nearer, it is well to realize that the men and women who year after year and month after month have been representing their countries at Geneva, are still steadily engaged upon a whole series of constructive activities for the promotion of co-operation between nations upon matters which affect the day to day life of the people of each nation, such as public health, prevention of crime and, what especially interests our own International Federation, employment and labor conditions.

This task is far from easy. It has little spectacular appeal. It means a constant patient adjustment of the policies of nations, all of whom have very different histories and social systems, and most of whom have hardly begun to practice the technique of co-operation. But, as it has been pointed out "it has deep significance for it enlists the help of experts from all countries who stand outside and above the strange intoxication of politics," and it serves the ordinary people: the workers in factories and offices, the homeless and the hungry and the sick.

It is especially this aspect of the work of the League of Nations and of the International Labor Office which has attracted the interest and co-operation of the women's international organizations, and year by year their various Committees study the subjects placed for discussion on the agendas of the Assembly of the League and of the Conference of the International Labour Organization, while year by year many of their individual members come regularly to Geneva either as official delegates of their respective Governments or as experts in some official capacity.

Of latter years the women's international organizations have found it advisable to consult and take action from time to time together, and have accordingly created certain co-ordinating committees composed of two or more representatives from each of the international organizations which desires to co-operate in this manner.

Chief amongst these is the LIAISON COMMITTEE OF THE WOMEN's INTERNATIONAL ORGANIZATIONS referred to above, which is composed of two representatives and two proxies from each of its affiliated organizations. This Committee meets at least four times a year and often monthly if occasion demands. The Chair is taken in rotation by one of the representatives of its affiliated organizations and the Honorary Secretary is Miss Elsie Zimmern of London, England, so well known for her work in connection with the International Association of Women's Institutes and sister of Sir Alfred Zimmern of Oxford. Meetings are held either in London or Geneva and sometimes in Paris and on each Agenda are placed subjects of special interest to the women's organizations which will be brought up either at the League Assembly or at the Labor Organization Conference. Action is either taken jointly in the name of the LIAISON COMMITTEE or separately under the names of the respective organizations. The Geneva Meetings of the Committee are held in June and September at the times of the International Labor Conference and the Assembly of the League of Nations. This enables the Committee to follow closely subjects of interest and also to consult the women who come to these Conferences either as official delegates or experts.

Certain of these co-ordinating Committees have been created in order to allow the representatives of the international organizations to consult and act together on *some definite subject*. Examples of this type of Committee are the COMMITTEE ON NATIONALITY created to deal with the subject of the nationality of women when this subject was before the League, and the PEACE AND DISARMAMENT COMMITTEE OF THE WOMEN's INTERNATIONAL ORGANIZATIONS created to forward the aims of the *Conference for the Reduction and Limitation of Armaments* which opened in Geneva in September 1931. This latter Committee now maintains a central office at Geneva and has undertaken an extensive programme of education and propaganda. The President of this Committee is Miss Mary Dingman so well known for her work on industrial problems for the World's Y.W.C.A. and the Committee is this year engaged in the preparation for an INTERCONTINENTAL CONFERENCE OF WOMEN LEADERS to be held at Washington D.C. in January 1940 in conjunction with the Conference on the Cause and Cure of War.

The International Federation of Business and Professional Women is represented on both the LIAISON COMMITTEE and also on the PEACE AND DISARMAMENT COMMITTEE of which their Geneva representative Miss Dorothy Heneker is the Honorary Secretary. Thus the Federation is kept closely in touch with current matters of importance to its members upon which action or consultation is required.

It is interesting to realize that until the formation of the International Federation of Business and Professional Women and the establishment of their office in Geneva in 1931, there was no separate recognition of the special claims and interests of business and professional women as a class when conventions dealing with employment or wages were agreed to between the various Governments.

The Federation first won prestige for its membership when it took the initiative in 1934 in presenting a Memorandum to the International Labor Organization pointing out that the work of certain of its members such as women engineers was being seriously interfered with by a Convention passed in 1931 whereby women were prohibited from working at night between certain hours and asking that executive and professional women should be exempt from this prohibition. For the first time in history this Memorandum was signed by the great international organizations of women gainfully employed, such as the International Council of Nurses, the International Federation of Women Lawyers, Judges and Magistrates and many others.

This Memorandum was most favorably received by the various Government and other delegates to the Conference of the International Labor Organization in June 1934, when the Convention was revised and the exemptions asked for were granted.

Through this initiative the Federation gained international recognition and prestige as an organization which would take a clear and business like stand upon problems concerning which its membership was especially qualified to express an opinion.

The Advisory Committee on Social Questions of the League of Nations

In addition to its representation on the above mentioned Liaison Committee and the Peace and Disarmament Committee, the International Federation of

Business and Professional Women has been made a corresponding member of the Advisory Committee on Social Questions.

This Committee deals with various types of social matters including prostitution, child welfare, family desertion and related subjects.

So far the matters brought up for discussion at the yearly meetings of this Committee have been outside the framework of the programme of the International Federation and therefore the Federation has been unable to take an active part on this Committee.

During an interview this winter with Dr Ekstrand, the Director of the Committee, Miss Heneker the Geneva representative of the Federation pointed out that the federation, while keenly interested in the excellent work done by this Committee, felt unable to undertake work in connection with questions which were being already dealt with by women's organizations specially created for the purpose. Upon an examination of the Agenda for this Spring Meeting of the Committee, with Dr Ekstrand, it was felt that practically none of the questions being dealt with this year fell within the framework of the Federation with the possible exception of Item 7, "Training of Persons engaged in social work." Even this subject was somewhat aside from the special problems of business and professional women though related to some of them.

It is quite possible, however, that during 1939 and 1940 matters may come before this Committee affecting the special interests of the membership of the International Federation, in which case notice of such matters will at once be sent to its National sections in all countries for comment and suggestions.

It is disquieting to learn, that during the past few months the drastic budget reductions made by the Finance Committee of the League have necessitated certain reductions in the staff of the sections engaged in social and welfare work.

This matter was taken up by the members of the Liaison Committee and a special article on the matter was sent to all the National Sections of the International Federation of Business and Professional Women by Miss Heneker in January, 1939.

Questions of Urgent Importance Today

In addition to the question of the *Survey on the Legal Status of Women* discussed above, another matter of vital importance to business and professional women will be discussed at the coming June Conference at Geneva of the International Labor Organization.

This is the question of TECHNICAL AND VOCATIONAL EDUCATION AND APPRENTICESHIP. This matter was already discussed at the last Con-

ference in June 1938, and as a result of the discussions Governments have
again been consulted on a number of points, *three* of which are of special interest to our own membership namely:

a. Do you consider that workers of both sexes should have equal rights of admission to all vocational and technical schools, provided that women and
   girls are not required to undertake work which they are prohibited by law
   from performing on grounds of health?
b. Do you consider that persons of both sexes should have equal rights to obtain the same certificates and diplomas on completion of the same studies?
c. Do you consider it desirable to recommend that a sufficient number of
   schools for domestic science should be established for the occupations in
   which women and girls are mainly employed?

Last November, 1938, Miss Heneker sent an urgent letter on behalf of the
International Federation to all its National Sections advising them of this matter and urging each country to secure the appointment of Government and
other delegates to this Conference whose answers to these questions would be
favourable.

It is interesting to read in the Blue Report just issued by the International
Labor Office that replies in the affirmative have already been received from
the following countries – Australia, Belgium, Canada (Provinces of British
Columbia, Manitoba, Ontario and Saskatchewan), Estonia, Finland, France,
Great Britain, Ireland, Latvia, Lithuania, Mexico, the Netherlands, Norway,
Poland, Spain, Sweden, Switzerland, Turkey, Union of South Africa, United
States of America and Yugoslavia.

At the coming Conference Governments will be asked to adopt two Recommendations on these matters which will in due course be confirmed by the
respective countries and which will thus lead to National legislation on these
subjects.

In Conclusion

It is quite impossible within the compass of the present article to deal adequately, or at all, with *all* the matters which are constantly coming before the
women's organizations from their Geneva representatives, but perhaps enough
has been said to show how this type of co-operative work is carried on by the
international organizations and what subjects are of especial interest today.

An interesting comment has been made on the special part played at these
Geneva Conferences by the individual women who constantly represent their
various Governments which says "These women play a somewhat special

part. Not because the subjects (dealt with) are all womanly; there is nothing particularly feminine in criminal law. Their significance lies, or should lie, in the degree to which they may *modify the common standards of values*. There are things to which women attach more importance than men; all the intimate homely incidents of existence, of which they have an acute awareness. There are others to which they attach much less importance; among them the obsession of precedent and authority. When they are told that international action in some matter is impossible because it has always been reserved to national sovereignty, they are totally unimpressed. And the best of them care, above all else, for life itself. They reject ideas which harm it, they work ardently for causes which help it. That is their measure of values, and it lends them influence out of all proportion to their small numbers."

It is this broader conception of women's influence that is ever increasing today, when it is more and more realized that in addition to fighting their own battles they must fight for the general good of mankind, as there can be no liberty for women, when liberty ceases to be a recognized right for all.

[Source: LAC, MG 30, C128, vol. 2, file 2-4, Dorothy Heneker, "What Women's Organisations Are Sponsoring at Geneva," April 1939.]

A detailed biography of Cairine Mackay Wilson (1885–1962) may be found above, on page 62–3.

Cairine Wilson

Message for the Newsletter of the Canadian Federation of Business and Professional Women's Clubs (1938)

Each day the problem of the refugee becomes more acute and I am grateful for the opportunity of bringing some of the facts before my fellow members of the Canadian Federation of Business and Professional Women's Clubs.

Canada, although one of the most sparsely settled countries in the world, has given practically no assistance to these unfortunate people and I cannot but feel the greatest admiration for the generous spirit shown by France, which has not refused the right of asylum to any refugee who has been proved to be a victim of political persecution. Not only did she receive thousands of White Russians fleeing from the Bolshevist Revolution, but with each successive upheaval in Europe, she has continued to take the unfortunate into her country. At the present time France is giving hospitality to thousands of Spaniards and even now 1,500 homes are ready to receive other Spanish children.

Anti-Semitism has been part of the Nazi propaganda everywhere and it is now quite plainly visible in Czechoslovakia and steadily forcing itself amongst other democratic places of Europe. Recently, I heard of a woman physician in Denmark with a slight percentage of Jewish blood, who stated that her arrangements were in order that when conditions became intolerable she could leave that country.

Despite all the troubles of their own race, the work of Jewish organizations has been remarkable and in his report, Sir John Hope Simpson states that they have actually done more for Christian refugees than the Christians themselves. The doctrine has been prevalent in some quarters that if a new man is brought into a company the amount of labour will be reduced by the amount that the newcomer would take. These ideas are now being questioned for it is estimated that in Belgium, there are 3,000 Belgian citizens employed by refugees and in Holland 12,000 citizens of that country have been given employment by 3,000 German refugees. It has been difficult to estimate the conditions in Great Britain but we know that although Leipzig was formerly the leading fur market in the world, this enviable position has now been taken by London due to the improved processes of dying and treatment of furs brought by the refugees. In the past we know that Great Britain has never suffered when she has shown humanity towards the unfortunate and it is to them she owes her long superiority in the weaving trade. Canada's own history teaches us that had more settlers been permitted to enter the country in the years of French occupation, there would have been a flourishing colony in place of the few inhabitants on the shores of St Lawrence in 1759.

Business and Professional women should be particularly interested in the plight of their sisters in Nazi and Fascist countries where all efforts of women over a long period of years have been in vain and where the women have been relegated to a position of absolute subordination.

[Source: LAC, MG27 IIIC6, vol. 5, no. 2, Cairine Wilson, "Message for the Newsletter of the Canadian Federation of Business and Professional Women's Clubs," 16 November 1938.]

PART THREE
Suffrage

The struggle to win the vote for women in Canada was especially protracted, taking place over the better part of a century. Years of intense agitation were followed by periods of quiescence and then the revitalization of organizational efforts under new leadership. Despite sustained opposition from a broad spectrum of male leaders and even some women, female activists sought to lay claim to full political citizenship. Feminists engaged in the campaign devised a plethora of arguments to garner support for their cause, but a central theme was the important role women could and should play in nation building. They contended that if granted the right to democratic political participation, women would help to shape the "nation" in beneficial ways. However, hierarchies of race, and class, along with the ongoing legacies of colonialism, directly informed how different women reformers imagined the nation, and the role of selected female citizens within it. Pro-suffrage women sought out support not only within the country but beyond national borders as well. They drew inspiration from the ideas and practices of feminists elsewhere, and increasingly engaged in the transnational networks that were consolidated among committed suffragists at the turn of the century.[1]

As women activists began to make public demands for the vote, the petition was employed as a key technique to sway political leaders such as the one devised by the Hantsport, Nova Scotia, WCTU in 1878. Among the points raised by this women's group, they demanded political enfranchisement "as an act of justice, and as means for promoting the prosperity of the State, the Home, and the Individual." In other words, they requested the vote as an important goal in and of itself for women to secure equality with men, but also as a means to achieve various social reforms. This petition also thus illustrated that, as Caroline Daley and Melanie Nolan have asserted, "early suffragists did not espouse just one idea of democratic practice but were politically sophisticated and used different models of citizenship."[2]

The WCTU was among the first feminist organizations to publicly promote female enfranchisement. While single-issue suffrage groups remained relatively small and confined to the largest urban centres until the Dominion Woman's Enfranchisement Association emerged at the end of the century, the WCTU continued to be the most prominent pro-suffrage women's group in the country. A representative from the WCTU, Mary McDonnell, presented the Canadian case for suffrage at the 1893 World's Congress of Representative Women in Chicago. Most notably, she presented the attainment of the vote as a further development in the inevitable advance of women. That McDonnell was speaking about a specific category of females when she suggested women were well qualified to participate in the political process was assumed by at least some other participants at the congress. In a follow-up to the McDonnell speech, Emily Cummings stated, "We have other women in Canada besides white women," and went on to present her views of the condition of Aboriginal women across the country. Cummings implied that Aboriginal women who had reached a certain level of "civilization" were capable of voting responsibly, although at the same time she made clear that at present such women represented only a fraction of the entire indigenous population. Nonetheless, given that the federal government had previously banned Aboriginal men in the west from voting, and would soon effectively extend this restriction to Aboriginal men in the east, it is unlikely Cummings thought Aboriginal women might receive the franchise in the near future.

The presence of a large national contingent that included McDonnell and Cummings at the 1893 World's Congress signalled an intensification of Canadian engagement in transnational feminist networks during this period, with the campaign for suffrage eliciting particular interest. From early on in the first wave many Canadian suffragists perceived themselves as being part of an international movement to secure full political rights for women. Canada formed a national auxiliary of the International Woman Suffrage Alliance (IWSA) soon after its formation in 1904 and sent Flora MacDonald Denison as a delegate to the IWSA conference in Copenhagen two years later. In her account of the conference, Denison called attention to the set of universal principles guiding the international suffrage movement while also expressing particular inspiration from continental ties to US efforts and connections with British imperial campaigns. The influence of organizational initiatives and accomplishments in the United States and the British Empire continued to loom large among Canadian suffragists, as further illustrated in the pamphlet by Sonia Leathes, *What Equal Suffrage Has Accomplished* (1911/12). In this work, Leathes offered numerous examples of what she considered to be positive changes in the condition of women and children in jurisdictions where women had received the vote, giving special attention to American western states and white settler societies such as those of Australia and New Zealand.

Women's roles and responsibilities as mothers served as a powerful rationale for gaining the franchise in Canada, as it did in other countries. Maternalism, far more complex and diverse than historians once recognized, promoted the ideal of an actively engaged female citizenry, and in some instances was utilized "to justify quite radical departures from conventional behaviour for women."[3] The members of the Victoria Political Equality League who met in 1913 to discuss "Fundamental Reasons for the Enfranchisement of Women" addressed in various ways how women's experiences as mothers qualified them to receive the vote and necessitated greater involvement in social reform efforts. Yet the key cultural and political symbol of "mother of the race" referred to repeatedly reaffirmed the race and class privilege of the Anglo-Celtic middle-class women who attended such a gathering as it simultaneously motivated them into action. As Amanda Glasbeek has suggested, maternalism often signified a politics of dominant race and class relations.[4]

Although the suffrage movement was dominated for the most part by Anglo-Celtic bourgeois reformers, other groups of women actively participated in the struggle for the vote. And in the midst of doing so, many demonstrated that they were not necessarily reliant upon nor directly following Anglo-Celtic middle-class women in terms of either support or direction. Women immigrants from Iceland were among the most prominent. Situated almost entirely in Manitoba, Icelandic women were vocal proponents of suffrage from the early 1880s onward. In 1898 Margrét Benedictsson, co-publisher of the feminist magazine *Freyja (Woman)*, urged greater unity among Icelandic women in their efforts to secure the vote and other political rights by following the positive example of women in their homeland. Furthermore, Benedictsson constructed her feminism almost entirely in the language of equal rights at a time when many women activists in Canada highlighted maternal feminist arguments. Women from various other immigrant ethnic groups were also well represented among those advocating for the right to vote. Many Finnish immigrant women, for example, supported suffrage "almost as a matter of course," most especially after Finland granted women the vote in 1906.[5]

Working-class and socialist women, a large proportion of whom were immigrants, did not form distinct class-based suffrage organizations, as occurred in countries such as Britain and Germany, but sizeable numbers were champions of female suffrage by the early twentieth century. They framed their arguments most often in overt class terms as in the case of Lena Mortimer, who addressed her comrades in the Socialist Party of Canada on "the woman question" in 1911. Mortimer asserted that the vote would provide much-needed and long-overdue recognition of the many contributions made by working-class women, and the means to engage more directly in the struggle against class inequality. By taking up the cause for the franchise, Mortimer and other working-class women challenged the notion, if only at times indirectly, that suffrage was entirely a bourgeois movement that would benefit only the economically privileged.

Divisions that had long existed within the women's movement over conflicting claims to political citizenship became especially apparent in the debate that took place over the "partial franchise" in the midst of the First World War. In the fall of 1916 Nellie McClung suggested to the prime minister, Robert Borden, that "as a war measure" the federal franchise be granted to British and Canadian-born women, but not foreign-born women. Although this recommendation had widespread support among many Anglo-Celtic feminists, others such as the journalist Marion Francis Beynon were highly critical. In a column that appeared in the *Grain Growers Guide*, Beynon argued that such a measure would be undemocratic and discriminatory, a situation all the more egregious since some groups of European immigrant women had been more avid supporters of suffrage than many British women. McClung subsequently withdrew her suggestion, but she still maintained that in the context of the war the right to vote had become "indisputable and imperative" for English-speaking women. Janice Fiamengo has argued persuasively that McClung "was more concerned about racial injustice than many of her white contemporaries," yet in this instance her allegiance to Anglo-Celtic women clearly outweighed consideration for the interests of immigrants.[6]

A partial franchise was subsequently introduced by the federal government in the form of the 1917 Wartime Election Act, which granted the vote to the female relatives of Canadian soldiers, most of whom were of British ancestry, and denied the vote to any immigrant citizen from enemy countries who had been naturalized after 1902. The provisions in this legislation meant not only that a sizeable proportion of non-British immigrants were left out entirely, but also that French Canadians were greatly under-represented among the women who were enfranchised. The international response to this legislation by suffrage organizations such as the IASW was decidedly negative. As expressed in an editorial in its journal, *Jus Suffragii*, its criticism was premised on the fact that a select group of women had been granted the vote on the basis of their relationship to particular men. No mention was made, though, about the implications for the country's French Canadian population or the prohibition placed on immigrants. Various Canadian feminists replied to this editorial to explain, and mostly defend, the actions of the federal government to the international feminist community. Constance Hamilton, for example, refuted the premise that certain women were enfranchised as a form of reward; instead, she noted, it was about restricting the vote "owing to war perils." The federal government heralded the extension of "universal adult suffrage" with new legislation in 1918, yet even then select population groups, men and women, were left disenfranchised: Aboriginals and Chinese, Japanese, and "Hindu" immigrants.

The campaign for the vote faced far greater opposition and thus, not surprisingly, was far more protracted in the province of Quebec. The combined hostility of francophone nationalist leaders and Catholic church authorities hampered the efforts of Quebec suffragists long after feminists in other provincial jurisdictions were victorious. Their efforts were not aided, however, by interventions such as the one by anglophone suffragist Florence Trenholme Cole in 1913. Despite maintaining that this was not her position, Cole in effect contended that most francophone women were ill qualified to vote because of the relative backwardness of the Quebec countryside. By making such an argument she certainly confirmed the views of many francophone nationalist politicians that feminism, especially as espoused by anglophone activists, was hostile to the cultural and political interests of French Canadians. In the process, she also undermined her subsequent argument that female suffrage should appeal to Catholics and Protestants as well as French and English. In a radio address almost two decades later, Idola Saint-Jean demonstrated that feminism and nationalism were not inherently antithetical political projects in Quebec. Saint-Jean premised her appeal for the vote in part on the historical accomplishments of women in creating a French Canadian presence on the continent.

Debates over female suffrage and women's participation in electoral politics did not cease after women were enfranchised in most political jurisdictions. In the late 1920s Harriet Prenter wrote "The Failure of the Suffrage Movement to Bring Freedom to Woman," in the *Woman Worker.* Prenter joined an increasing number of other feminist commentators in questioning the degree to which the attainment of the vote had altered the political, social, or economic status of women. She maintained that in the specific case of working-class women the franchise had been of little benefit. But as Prenter herself noted, for women in Canada, securing the vote "was not the end but only a very small beginning" in the struggle for full political citizenship.

NOTES

1 Caroline Daley and Melanie Nolan, "Introduction," in *Suffrage and Beyond: International Feminist Perspective*, ed. Caroline Daley and Melanie Nolan (New York: New York UP, 1994).

2 Ibid.
3 Janice Fiamengo, "A Legacy of Ambivalence," in *Rethinking Canada*, ed. Veronica Strong-Boag, Mona Gleason, and Adele Perry (Toronto: Oxford UP, 2002) 151–63.
4 Amanda Glasbeek, *Feminist Justice: The Toronto Women's Court, 1913–1934*," (Vancouver: UBC Press, 2009), 8.
5 Linda Kealey, *Enlisting Women for the Cause: Women, Labour, and the Left in Canada, 1890–1920* (Toronto: U of Toronto P, 1998), 120.
6 Janice Fiamengo, "Rediscovering Our Foremothers Again: The Racial Ideas of Canada's Early Feminists, 1885–1945," *Essays in Canadian Writing* 75 (Winter 2002), 100–1.

Women's Christian Temperance Union, Hantsport, Nova Scotia
Petition for the Enfranchisement of Women (1878)

To the House of Assembly of the Province of Nova Scotia in Parliament assembled:

May it please your Honorable Body: The Petition of the WOMEN's CHRISTIAN TEMPERANCE UNION and the undersigned residents of the Province of Nova Scotia, hereby sheweth:

THAT WHEREAS, The Women of Nova Scotia compose, at least, one-half of the adult population, and in many cases have the required qualification, also contribute to the public revenue by direct and indirect taxation;

AND WHEREAS, Women, equally with men, promote the growth and prosperity of the Commonwealth, and in mental, moral and educational endowments, and all that pertains to good citizenship, the average woman is not below the average man;

AND WHEREAS, Municipal and school suffrage, as exercized by various sections of our Dominion, has been attended with naught but good results, and ever inclines to the side of morality and true progress;

AND WHEREAS, The political equality of the sexes is among the foremost questions of the leading nations of the world, and the enfranchisement of women is endorsed by many of the best and most advanced men in political and religious circles;

THEREFORE, We the undersigned Petitioners, residents of the Province of Nova Scotia declare our belief that the need, as well as the spirit of the times, demand the political enfranchisement of women as an act of justice, and as a means for promoting the prosperity of the State, the Home, and the Individual.

THEREFORE, Your petitioners humbly pray your Honorable Body to enact a law providing that full Parliamentary Suffrage be conferred on women, on the same terms and under the same conditions as that now accorded to men. And your petitioners, as in duty bound, will every pray.

[Source: Provincial Archives of Nova Scotia (PANS), RG 5, series P, vol. 16, no. 98, Women's Christian Temperance Association, Hantsport, "Petition for the Enfranchisement of Women," 13 March 1878.]

Mary McDonnell was a member of one of the earliest feminist organizations in Canada, the Toronto Women's Literary Society. She also helped to form the

Toronto WCTU and headed the Dominion WCTU for several years. McDonnell was also one of three women to contest seats on the Toronto School Board
in 1892 and was elected along with Augusta Stowe-Gullen.

Mary McDonnell
A Century of Progress for Women in Canada (1893)

It is difficult to realize the steady onward march of women of Canada during
the last quarter century. Before that time women entered very few remunerative
occupations, but now, with the progress of the modern industrial system, there
appears to be no limit to their opportunities. The active interest women are taking in all the great questions of the day is in marked contrast to the apathy and
indifference of twenty-five years ago.

Our women have organized missionary, philanthropic, temperance, educational, and political associations on a scale of great magnitude, without much
"blowing of trumpets or unseemly boasting." The Canadian woman's development has been aided very materially by the provincial enactments, which
secured to her increased educational advantages, municipal and school suffrage, most just and humane property rights, as well as a right to enter the professions. In securing to women enlarged opportunities, provincial law-makers
have placed our young nation on a higher plane, for it is a well-known fact that
the civilization of a nation may be ascertained to-day more truly by the economic and social status of its women than by its consumption of coal, lumber,
or pig-iron.

Therefore, while under heavy obligations to our provincial Parliament for
past favors, we feel that the time has come when the question of women's
further advancement should receive its thoughtful consideration. The woman
suffrage question is now world-wide, and the women who have led the Canadian contingent have had the moral support of the best men of Canada. Thus
encouraged, we are proud to say that we have kept pace with the women of
other countries.

But the steps of progress already achieved were not gained without a struggle, as the pioneers are ready to attest. From the married women's property
act of 1872 down to the latest conquest, the right of women to practice law,
every right claimed has been contested: ridicule, malice, indifference and conservatism have in turn been met and surmounted, until now the question of
women's complete political enfranchisement stands before every legislative
body in Canada, and challenges final consideration.

In its progress it has benefited all and injured none. The right to earn, hold, enjoy and devise property are proud and notable gains. The doors to colleges and universities no longer creak their dismay at the approach of women. New avenues of self-support have been found and profitably entered upon. In public affairs Canadian women receive large recognition; at the present time we have women on high and public school boards; and in the management of business affairs women have demonstrated to the public that they have heads as well as hearts.

Every step thus far taken to enlarge the sphere of women has been a benefit to her, to man, and to society. We can see no good reason for stopping here. Just at this point it would be quite in order to consider a few objections met with by the advocates of women's enfranchisement.

Objectors urge disability to perform military service as fatal to full citizenship, but would not consent to resign their own rights, even when they have passed the age of conscription, nor question those of Quakers who will not fight, or of professional men or civic officials who, like mothers, are regarded as of more value to the nation at home. They cite the physical superiority of man, but would not agree to disfranchise the halt, the lame, the blind, or the sick.

Since questions of peace, of arbitration, and of reconciliation have superseded those of war and conquest, physical force is at a discount. Reason and justice applied to human affairs mark the spirit of the nineteenth century; and, as has been demonstrated recently, wars may be avoided with safety and honor to a nation. Many of us might be diverted into more useful channels.

Men regard the manly head of the family as its proper representative, but would not exclude the adult sons.

They are dismayed by a vision of women in attendance at caucuses at late hours of the night, but enjoy their presence at entertainments and balls until early dawn. They are shocked at the thought of women at political meetings, but in Canada women have attended such meetings for years at the earnest solicitation of those in charge, and the influence of their presence has been for good.

The often-urged fear that only the degraded would vote, while the intelligent and the virtuous would stand aloof, is fully answered by the fact that the former class have never asked for the ballot, while the women who ask for full suffrage are among the most-honored women in Canada. Again, it is said that only the strong-minded would vote. We can see no objection to this provided the line be drawn irrespective of sex.

Men would not like to see women exposed to the grossness and vulgarity of public life, they tell us, or have her encounter the rough element one meets at the polls. When we have mingled among men and women in every walk of life hear men talk of sheltering women from the rough winds and revolting scenes of real life, we pause to wonder if they know whereof they speak, for it seems to us that whatever the man may be, he is known to the woman. She is the companion not only of the accomplished statesman, the orator, and the scholar, but of the vile, the vulgar, yes, and the brutal; all these classes are bound by the ties of family to some women, and if a man shows out what he is anywhere, it is at his own hearthstone; besides, the women who have voted for years in municipal and school elections attest that even the most degraded are a little more manly at the polls than elsewhere. This is quite natural, for in the eyes of men women voters rank much higher than the disenfranchised class.

Those in power always manifest nervous unrest whenever new claims are made by those out of power, even though the request of the claimants may be just and reasonable. They imagine that if the request for the claimant be granted, they must of necessity sacrifice something that they already possess; they can not divest themselves of stocks, bonds, and mortgages, and that if every new claimant is satisfied the supply must in time run out, forgetting the fact that in this case it is individual rights, and that though thousands of women may be deprived of the ballot their poverty in this respect does not add to the man's wealth.

We are told that the right of suffrage inheres in the people; women are people. Again, it is said law to bind all should be assented to be all; for that reason women should have a voice in selecting those who make the law.

Men claimed the right of the governed and the taxed to a voice in determining by whom they shall be governed, and to what extent taxed. What justification can be offered for the exclusion of women? Women work in the home but it does not follow that their place is solely in the home, any more that the farmer should never leave his farm, the mechanic his shop, the teacher his desk, the clergyman his study, or the professional man his office for the purpose of expressing his views at the ballot-box.

It is not enough that men assert the superiority of Canadian women in intelligence and virtue. We want them to consider the gain to country in their further advancement.

I think that most of us have come to feel that a voice in law is indispensable. Experience has fully proved to me that the influence which we are said to possess is vague and somewhat powerless until coined into law, and that without the direct voice in legislation women's influence is eventually lost. If we have, as is claimed, influence, we should also share the responsibility, even as we now share with man in his education, his amusements, his work, and his religion. When we are told that politics are unclean, as a remedy we would suggest cleaner politicians. We do not share in the fears of our opponents that politics will degrade women: on the contrary, we believe that women will purify politics. When women vote, the character of candidates will be more closely scrutinized and better officers will be chosen to administer the laws. The polls too will be freed from the vulgarity and coarseness which now too often surround them, and the polling booths, instead of being in stables and kindred places (now thought good enough for the electorate) would be located in more attractive centers.

We believe that when woman takes her place in the body politic, politics will be invested with a dignity and seriousness worthy of the science of government.

Man has done well in his onward march, but man alone can not grasp the needs of the whole of humanity.

Political questions do not mean merely questions of finance, of currency, of tariffs, and of railways. The great questions of the future will be economic and social ones. Moral questions are also involved, and deeply involved, in politics.

We often hear it asserted that the voice of the people is the voice of God. If that be true the voice of God has never yet been heard in human governments, for half the race is silent.

[Source: Mary McDonnell, "A Century of Progress for Women in Canada," in *An Historical Resumé for Popular Circulation of the World's Congress of Representative Women, Convened on May 15, and Adjourned on May 22, 1893, Under the Auspices of the Women's Branch of the World's Congress Auxiliary,* vol. 1, ed. Anonymous (Chicago: Rand McNally, 1894), 682–6.]

Emily Shortt Cummings (1851–1930), the daughter of an Anglican minister and his wife, in 1871 married the lawyer Willoughby Cummings. She helped to found the Woman's Auxiliary to the Missionary Society of the Anglican Church in Canada in 1885. Cummings became the corresponding secretary of the newly formed NCWC, a position she held until 1910.

Emily Cummings
A Century of Progress: Discussion Continued (1893)

We have other women in Canada besides white women, and I am going to tell you something about the Indian women. I visited some Indians two years ago who are now in the same condition that the Ontario Indians were one hundred years ago. I visited several tribes of Indians who in dress and habits were thorough savages.

The women are intensely fond of their children, and if the children die they cut their legs in long gashes, and go around uttering piercing cries of sorrow. To appease the great spirit of the sun they chop off their fingers sometimes. I saw many women with their fingers chopped off for this purpose.

I saw other Indians who had been in contact with white people only a very few years. Something like ten years ago they were taken in charge by the government, and others have been in contact with civilization for about forty years. They live in neat homes and have nice little farms. A great many of them can read and write, and they are wonderfully advanced when you think it is only forty years since they were like the others I have spoken of.

Coming down to Ontario, let me tell you with pride that we have there an Indian woman who is a noted poetess, who stands high in literature, whose contributions to literature you have often read, I am sure – Pauline Johnson by name. She is a great elocutionist, and is welcomed by large audiences wherever she may appear. Her sister, also, though not a poetess or an orator, is highly thought of in literature, and has contributed to a great many magazines. To show that these women are not the only ones who are advanced, I might say that at our last year's missionary meeting two delegates came from an Indian women's missionary society, and although they could not understand a word of what was said, a lady interpreted for them, and they discussed all the questions and voted just as intelligently as any white woman in the audience.

[Source: Emily Cummings, "Discussion Continued," in *An Historical Resumé for Popular Circulation of the World's Congress of Representative Women, Convened on May 15, and Adjourned on May 22, 1893, Under the Auspices of the Women's Branch of the World's Congress Auxiliary*, vol.1, ed. Anonymous (Chicago: Rand McNally, 1894), 689–90.]

Margrét Jŏnsdŏttir Benedictsson (1866–1956) immigrated from Iceland to Canada in 1887. She moved to Winnipeg around 1892 and several years later married Sigfŭs Benedictsson, a poet and plant scientist. Between 1898 and 1910, Margrét and her husband published *Freyja*, an Icelandic-language journal whose purpose was to promote women's rights, especially female suffrage. Benedictsson travelled extensively giving lectures in Icelandic to immigrants in the United States and Canada in order to garner greater support for women's issues. In 1908 she founded an Icelandic suffrage association in Winnipeg that worked closely with similar groups elsewhere in Manitoba.

Margrét Benedictsson
Women's Rights and Women's Equal Rights (1898)

Women's Rights

Are women fit to receive equal rights, if they were immediately to be placed in their hands?

Not as a whole, because women have collectively done very little to prepare themselves for that great change in their circumstances which undoubtedly will occur sooner or later. Hopefully it will not be decades before equal rights become not only the ideal property of a few individuals, but rather the real property of everyone – property which all know the value of and use sensibly and conscientiously.

Those who have fought and struggled most and best for the rights of women have been men rather than women, and in the future it will be men who will win the victory in this struggle. On the whole the women are passive, and little interested in how change goes. Still, there are many women who reach out with both hands towards those rights which they have the opportunity to obtain. A few stand at the forefront, and are proceeding to work zealously side by side with their brothers towards the education of women. But when they are compared with the large numbers who passively cross their arms across their chests and say "It wasn't that way when I was growing up, and I have still made it to this day, thanks be to God," progressive women are relatively few. But at the same time, they are numerous enough to guarantee that women will, with time, learn to value and use their rights.

Women do not have citizenship rights – that is, they have no right to vote in elections, and they may not sit in the parliament as representatives. But they could have untold influence in all such elections, if they would only be willing to sacrifice something for it. They do have FREEDOM OF THE PRESS and FREEDOM OF SPEECH. These privileges are so extensive, so magnificent that it is impossible to see how other new privileges could rightly be made use of, as long as these are left unused. Through them individual voices can be heard, but what does that matter?

Women must first learn that in UNITY is POWER; such power is obtained only through associations and those associations, and the individuals who form them, can only thrive when the "principle" is believed and something is sacrificed for it. But jealousy and suspicion, which the men say is the characteristic of women, must be laid to the side. How much truth there is in this statement each woman must answer for herself.

Western and Eastern Icelanders have often been compared. In Iceland there is a women's political association, which is concerned with the most serious issues which the nation and the parliament have on the agenda. This association is said to be very well supported, which can be demonstrated by the fact that it had the means to gather nearly 7,000 women's names on one petition which it sent to the Alþing in spite of all the obstacles that there were with transportation. Have Western Icelandic women exhibited any such interest in the various issues which are on the agenda here? No, no such associations have been established. There are actually in existence many women's associations, but what are they doing? With very few exceptions they work for the church – which is perhaps not blameworthy – but they could do more. What if all these women's associations united into one whole to work toward some universal issue, such as the protection of the working class in relation to capitalism, that terrible power which the entire world quakes and trembles before; the truly awful blood-sucking force which feeds off the living flesh of the national body, sucking the blood out of its heart, and extracting all resources out from under the poorest of the working masses. What if those associations united their strength to struggle towards the observance of the holiness of Sunday? That is to say, a Sabbath which restrains the right of the individual, either in his religious observances or some other way, which hinders communication by banning people from traveling on their bicycles or by halting street cars on Sundays.

UNITY is POWER. Women could in a few years obtain equal rights, if they only wanted to. They could do it with organizations and with petitions, which their friends, women's liberationists and philanthropists, would, with most satisfaction, lend all their support to as the supporters of women's emancipation are numerous. They can also do it in other ways – in those places where they have voting rights for school matters and can, in that quarter, select men and women on the school board and for school teachers. In schools there is the opportunity to sow the seeds of liberation, not only to lay the foundation for women's equal rights, but also for the general growth of the intellectual development of girls in complete equality with boys. By sowing these seeds, the interest of children, whether boy or girl, in the welfare of their homeland and the individuals of which it is composed (the nation in general) could and should be awakened. Then might the innocent boys learn effortlessly, before selfishness and the old superstitions have obtained power over their feelings, that which seems so obvious: that their sisters should take part in the politics. If children learned political science together in the same way as various other subjects, the youth would obtain knowledge of the serious issues relating to the welfare of the nation, and the nation would thus be doubly prepared for the approaching times. Such preparation would ensure that the nation has many to select from for its service. The sooner that issues relating to the welfare of the nation can come into the understanding and feelings of children, the purer the enthusiasm for it, and the cleaner, brighter and better workers which she (the nation) will be likely to produce.

Women's Equal Rights

It is equal rights which women are seeking, equal rights with men, equal rights in lines of work, equal rights in the protection of the law and equal rights in citizenship. That women have not received the right to vote is the biggest evil. As long as they do not get this right, they cannot exert their influence on legislation. Women must get into parliament, get into public leadership – then it will be possible to talk about their value to civil society. Women are born with these rights, of this there is no doubt; that they are suitable for these rights, was long ago established. That they improve all associations which they are in is acknowledged. That morality is placed on the highest plane where women are most influential is recognized by those nations which stand at the highest level of culture. The belief that women ought not to attend election meetings has only one argument in its defence: men might possibly lose their old privilege to curse and to get shamefully drunk. To say that it is unwomanly to pay attention to elections is like saying that it is manly to fall down drunk in the muddy ditch on the way home from the election campaign.

If men cherish moral improvement, then there is no danger in letting women take part. If women are not threatened by the boorish customs of men, then it is safe to let them participate. And the truth is that the longer the general public moves slowly forward on the road of civilization, and the value of temperance becomes recognized, the sooner it will be that women can take part.

It is obvious to everyone that it is a scandalous evil to deny women those rights which would make them free citizens. That women are not generally with the movement for women's emancipation, does not establish that these rights should not be granted to them. This lack of support is caused by ignorance and because the consciousness of equal rights is not sufficiently aroused in them. It ought not to require their request to obtain citizenship rights; men ought to grant them without it. If women get the same education as men, they are as qualified as them, whether to vote alone or more.

If women do not have a desire to vote, then they can sit at home. If they find it their vocation to vote, they must be able to do that. If a woman has such a love of her native country that she wants to enter parliament so as to be useful there, then she ought to be allowed to do that. Or if she would go only because of the pay alone, then she ought to be allowed to in the same manner as a man.

To reduce the freedoms and rights of individuals is called wrong; must it then not be wrong to impair the rights of half of mankind?

And one thing which people ought never to forget when they discuss the rights of women is that women are the mothers of mankind. How much influence does the mother have on her children? They would be bettered, as she is bettered. They would be more educated, as she is more educated. She can teach more about justice, the more justice that she knows. They would be better indoctrinated into free and easy generosity of opinion, the more independent that she is – the stronger that the consciousness of liberty is with her.

Freedom is a sun which shines into the window of the soul of mankind. The brighter the beam which is allowed to shine in, the more beautiful will be the picture which reflects itself in the calm-blue still-waters of civilization. Slavery makes people into a mob, but freedom turns the mob into civilized human beings.

Women must awaken and ready themselves to fully believe that they are needed to take part in the struggle of life, the struggle for better laws, better government, better conditions, and better human beings.

A FRIEND OF LIBERTY

[Source: Margrét Benedictsson, "Women's Rights" (Réttindi Kvenna) and "Women's Equal Rights" (Jafnrétti Kvenna), *Freyja* 1, no. 2 (March 1898), 4–5 (trans. Ryan Eyford).]

Flora MacDonald Merrill Denison (1867–1921) held a number of different jobs before she settled in Toronto in 1893 and entered the dressmaking trade. She combined this occupation with other forms of employment to support herself, her daughter, and perhaps even her spouse. She took an increasing interest in the women's movement from the turn of the century onward and in 1906 became secretary of the Dominion Women's Enfranchisement Association, which soon after became the Canadian Suffrage Association. She also began writing a regular column in the *Toronto World* on women's rights. Denison attended a later convention of the International Woman Suffrage Alliance in Budapest in 1913.

Flora MacDonald Denison

Report on Attendance at the International Woman Suffrage Alliance Conference (1906)

I would like to speak tonight, about some Canadian women. I would like to tell you that we have had in Canada such splendid women as Dr Emily Stowe, Mary MacDonald, and Dr Stowe-Gullen, who have devoted much time and money to the cause, but as the President distinctly gave me to understand that my work tonight was to be a report of the International Woman Suffrage Alliance held in Copenhagen in August, I therefore take great pleasure in presenting it to you, especially so at this time when the press of Toronto has been so busy with adverse criticisms and cartoons in reference to the action of some women in England who are fighting for what they consider their rights.

Most progressive thinkers are evolutionists, but history shows that in many cases the evolutionary process has been so extravagant in its use of time, that reformers got tired and resorted to revolution.

Many of the women of England are possibly getting tired, and are anxious to bring about reforms by a quick process. However, having heard Mrs Montifiore, the English delegate for the Woman's Social and Political Union in England, I am inclined to think that the Press has woefully exaggerated the behavior of the women who are not lunatics or fanatics, but earnest women, anxious and willing to sacrifice themselves that the race may be benefited and moved nearer an ideal civilization of co-operative brotherhood and sisterhood.

Since many may not know the platform of the organization called the International Suffrage Alliance, I am going to read the Declaration of Principles.

1 That men and women are born equally free and independent members of the human race; equally endowed with intelligence and ability, and equally entitled to the free exercise of their individual rights and liberties.
2 That the natural relation of the sexes is that of interdependence and co-operation, and that the repression of the fights and liberties of one sex, inevitably works injury to the other, and hence to the whole race.
3 That in all lands, those laws, creeds, and customs which have tended to restrict women to a position of dependence; to discourage their education; to impede the development of their natural gifts, and to subordinate their individuality, have been based upon false theories, and have produced an artificial and unjust relation of the sexes in modern society.
4 That self-government in the home and the state is the inalienable right of every normal adult, and the refusal of this right to women has resulted in social, legal and economic injustice to them, and has also intensified the existing economic disturbances throughout the world.
5 That governments that impose taxes and laws upon their women citizens without giving them the right of consent or dissent which is granted to men citizens, exercise a tyranny inconsistent with just government.
6 That the ballot is the only legal and permanent means of defending the rights

to, "Life, liberty and the pursuit of happiness," pronounced inalienable by the American Declaration of Independence, and accepted as inalienable by all civilized nations. In any representative form of government, therefore, women should be vested with all political rights and privileges of electors.

The International Suffrage Alliance I attended was the third conference held by that body, and must have been a source of joy and satisfaction to every women interested in its cause.

Mrs Chapman Catt, Pres. of the Alliance was in the chair at every meeting. Meetings were held for five days, and generally three meetings a day. Each day found the interest increasing, especially noticeable by the large number of men who attended the last few.

A personal word about Mrs Chapman Catt must here be said. She is among the most eminent of the many able women of the United States, and is widely known as a speaker and writer. While still very young her attention was called to the terrible wrongs suffered by wage earning women, and this led her to investigate the condition of women in general. She found not only in the domain of work, but everywhere, they were at great disadvantage, and that the laws, customs and public sentiment discriminated against them.

The more deeply she studied the question, the more fully she was convinced that the root of this injustice lay in their disfranchisement, and that *the most important service which could be rendered women, was to secure the ballot for them.*

It was indeed a privilege to listen to any word Mrs Chapman Catt might utter. She is clear, logical and forceful, converting the most skeptical to a belief in the justice of her cause. Her beauty as well as her sweet womanly dignity does much to enhance the power of her eloquent words, while her tact and graciousness in dealing with both men and women, fit her admirably for the position of leader.

To those who have had the privilege of visiting in her beautiful and well managed home, she is convincing proof that public life does not impair the domestic qualities. Mrs Catt was received by the Queen of Denmark, and hospitably entertained for over an hour, which placed the conference under Royal Patronage.

Beside and supporting Mrs Chapman Catt were the officers of the association and I may say I was amazed by the expedition and able manner in which the work of the Alliance was dispatched.

The Secretary, Mrs Kramer, took the minutes in three languages. The interpreters seemed to speak any language required of them. There were present delegates and alternatives from ten countries, besides fraternal delegates from twelve associations.

The meetings were held in the Oddfellows Palais which was beautifully decorated with the flags of Denmark. A shield with the name of each country represented was placed beside the respective delegations, while each delegate's seat was marked by a banner with her National Flag.

In view of the course pursued by the National Council of Canada, in convention at Hamilton, a few weeks ago, it gives me great pleasure in being able to show the sincere sympathy existing between the International Council of Woman and the International Woman's Suffrage Alliance.

Five of the fraternal delegates were sent to Copenhagen by the International Council, and each one made it clear that she considered political equality the most important plank in the platform of any woman's organization, and the International Council of Woman has itself established a standing committee for Woman Suffrage.

It would take too long to even give a summary of what was said by the different speakers, but I must not omit saying something of the attitude of both factions in England.

Mrs Millicent Fawcett rejoiced all hearts by saying there should be no disunion between factions of women who work for Woman Suffrage. She showed by examples from history, how every extension of the suffrage had been obtained not only by philosophical and scientific argument, but by revolution as well, and although rough methods were not for her, she had no reason to cry shame upon the women who might accomplish more for the cause than she was able to.

It was plain to be seen that interest centered around Mrs Montifiore, and what she herself might say with regard to the situation in England as she represented the society of rough methods, and at that time three of its members were in jail. There must be some truth in the saying: "Saxon and Norman and Dane are we," for surely a drop of Viking blood is needed to keep up such a valiant struggle for the suffrage, against the authority of the government, and the opinion of the public, as these women have done.

Years before Mrs Montifiore had started the first Woman's Suffrage Association in Australia, and afterwards joined the Woman Social and Political Union, founded in London to facilitate the collection of funds to defray the expenses of labor representation in Parliament. It seems that among the trades' unions which contributed, many were composed of women, so in some cases 60% of the necessary sum was paid by women. Who then should wonder at the fact that at length those women wanted a member of parliament to really represent them in their claims.

Mrs Montifiore does not seem to doubt, since the battle has been won in Australia, that we shall soon see women politically enfranchised, in England, if the English woman of the working classes remain as unflinching and true to their purpose as hitherto.

A resolution of congratulation to Finland is too important to pass by: "We rejoice in the granting to the woman of Finland of the full suffrage and the right to sit in Parliament, and we commend to the men of all nations, that sense of justice which impelled the men of Finland to make the woman who shared with them the degradation of disfranchisement, equal sharers in the honor of enfranchisement."

I may be pardoned if I tell with what favor and enthusiasm the report from Canada was received. It was written by our esteemed President, Dr Stowe Gullen, who so ably stands for all that progressive womanhood means, and though in it, she could not tell of much advancement of the cause, for the past few years, it was probably owing to the favorable impression made by this very able report, that the delegate from Canada received so much kindness and consideration, both from subsequent audiences, the press, and the people of Copenhagen.

Possibly the most important of all reports was the message from Australia, where political equality is enjoyed. It has been found that women have not neglected homes because they have occasionally gone to a political meeting, where before, they might have been to afternoon tea or to the theatre.

Experience has falsified every objection raised against woman suffrage. The state is only an enlarged home, and women are in the state what they are in their homes. Australia's experience should cast to the four winds of heaven any fears of domestic, social or political disaster.

Personally, I was most interested in the Russian delegates, since the strife for women's rights there was of a peculiar character compared with that of other countries, and the terrible social conditions existing in Russia has enlisted the world's sympathy. The women in Russia are almost equal to men, and both are conspicuous in their absence of "rights." These beautiful, scholarly and cultured women who talked to us in good English had the history of centuries of oppression written on their faces, which told the tragedy of their nation.

With gratitude and pleasure, they received the hearty greetings and friendship of women made their sisters, by this great international gathering, and although they risked much by coming to such a meeting, they added hope to their courage while there [...]

Today, one country secures political equality, tomorrow, another. Time will bring it everywhere. We ask the boon of suffrage, not from our enemies, but from our dearest friends – our husbands, brothers, sons. We cannot therefore feel any bitterness, since this right is not ours, for it is our own who withhold it.

We trust in the spirit of justice and enlightenment, which in time will conquer all. It is significant that those countries which have suffered the greatest oppression are the first to give women the full rights of citizenship. Here in peaceful Denmark, which has never taken anything by force, our Danish sculptress has drawn a woman who stands quietly, with the scale of Justice in her hand. This woman has been accepted for our badge, and is the real emblem of our cause.

Know you, all men and women who are not yet standing with us, it is only justice we demand.

We would help to build better homes and better institutions, and for those reasons, we ask the right to partake in the privileges of the general suffrage. I think you must all agree that political equality has for its champions women who will compare favorably in intellect and dignity, with any body of either men or women.

Mr Chairman and Madame President, I will close this report by reading a paragraph from Mrs Chapman Catt's message: "We can certainly find much encouragement in the events of the past two years, and may well feel that our Alliance came into existence at the exact moment to be of use to our cause. In the period of 1848, there was a very general enfranchisement of men, now, after half a century, we are apparently in the midst of another movement which will end only when it has affected many changes in the suffrage of women.

"One man, one vote" is the war cry of the new movement. It is important that women should be alive to the opportunity this time may afford. Whatever may be the plan of the future, adopted by the Conference, I feel that we must not neglect to extend every encouragement to agitate for educational organization in every land.

"The enfranchisement of women upon the same terms as men, is as certain to come as the sun is sure to rise tomorrow. The time must depend upon political conditions and the energy and intelligence with which the movement is conducted. The future belongs to us."

[Source: University of Toronto, Fisher Rare Books, Flora McDonald Denison, 15, box 2, file 14, "Report on the Woman Suffrage Alliance held in Copenhagen, Denmark, August 1906."]

_____

Lena Cameron Mortimer (?–?) was born into a farming family in St Vincent,

Minnesota. She became a Socialist Party activist and married the journeyman tailor and union leader John Mortimer in Winnpeg in 1901. They had several children before he drowned in an accident in 1910.

Lena Mortimer
One Woman's Way of Thinking (1911)

As I passed out through the crowd as it was dispersing on Sunday evening after the meeting at which Comrades Pettipiece and Fitzgerald were speaking on the Woman question, I chanced to hear a few remarks from some of the men that had been present at the meeting which struck me as rather amusing. One of the worthy bunch said in a rather sneering way: "What! Give the women a vote? Not much, their place is to stay at home and mind their business, let us men do all the voting."

To me, of course, it was the same old yarn. I have heard it so often that I cannot keep silent any longer. Some of the men do not stop long enough to think just what a very important part a woman does fill in this life. If we women are fit to be the mothers of their children; fit to teach those same children in the schools, and fit to fill most every position in life, then by all that's good and holy we are able to stand shoulder to shoulder with our noble brothers and cast our vote along with them for the one great cause for which we are both fighting, the only cause that will benefit the working men and women of today.

Men say that we women do not have sense enough to vote the right way. Ditto my brother. Could we possibly make it any worse than you have made it by your way of voting? Give the woman a chance. Let her once grasp the situation and see if she won't vote right. Treat her as an equal and try to help her get hold of a few socialistic ideals. Help her to see what it all means. Give her as fair a chance as you would give a man, and you will find that she can grasp the truth just as quick as any man.

I believe it is up to every woman in Vancouver or any other place on top of this old earth, to get busy, and dig down and find out for herself just where she is at and if some of the men turn up their noses at our feeble efforts, go to it with more heart than ever. Prove to them that if given a chance we can at least use our vote to as good advantage as they have in the past. We cannot make matters any worse than they are making them right now. So go to it, my sisters. Show them if we are fit to be the mothers of the coming generation of Socialists we are fit to march to the ballot-box and vote the right way just as soon as you men give us a chance. And fit to share equally with you all the comforts that

Socialism will bring when the men as well as the women get into their heads sense enough to vote the right way to hasten its coming.

[Source: Lena Mortimer, "One Woman's Way of Thinking," *Western Clarion* (Vancouver, BC), 27 May 1911.]

A member of NCWC, Sonia Leathes wrote a number of pamphlets advocating women's suffrage including the one below and *Where and How May Canadian Women Vote* (1911).

Sonia Leathes
What Equal Suffrage Has Accomplished (1911/1912)

The Age of Consent has been raised to 18 in all states and countries where women obtained the parliamentary franchise, and mostly within the first legislature following upon their enfranchisement, i.e., New Zealand, all the States of Australia, Wyoming, Colorado, Utah, Idaho, Finland and Norway. Bills are already pending in the newly enfranchised States of Washington and California to raise the age of consent from 16 to 18.

Where women do not possess the power to directly control legislation the age of consent varies between 10 and 16 years. The only exceptions are Kansas, which possesses a very wide municipal franchise for women and where the age of 18 was secured by them, without the parliamentary vote, and New York, where the age 18 was established as the age of consent after twenty-five years of struggle, not however, without a considerable reduction in the penalty provided, and it is difficult to obtain convictions.

In Canada, the legal age of protection is 16. A considerable difference is made, however, in the punishment of offences committed against girls of over or under 14, treating the former in the nature of a misdemeanour only.

Equal Guardianship of Father and Mother over Their Legitimate Children

In countries where women have the vote the mother has been made equal co-guardian with the father of her own children. Such legislation was enacted in most cases at once after women obtained the ballot.

It took the unenfranchised women of Massachusetts fifty-five years to secure such a law, which the enfranchised women of Colorado obtained in the very next Legislature following upon their enfranchisement. The women of New York obtained this right in 1860 after ten years of persistent effort, and it was quietly repealed in 1862. After another thirty years of agitation it was again granted to them in 1893. In Canada the father is the only recognized legal parent of his legitimate children to the exclusion of the mother. This right extends even to the "infant at the breast." He has absolute control over their religion and secular education, place of residence, etc., and his consent alone is necessary for the marriage of his minor sons or daughters.

Children

The school age in Colorado is from 8 to 16. In New Zealand and Australia there is compulsory attendance at continuation schools for children between 14–16 years. It is a criminal offence punishable by the imprisonment to employ children under 14 in any trade or industry in Colorado. A special law in Wyoming forbids the employment of children under 14 in any public exhibitions. There are free State-supported kindergartens in Wyoming. In Wyoming, Colorado, Utah, New Zealand and Australia there is a State provision made for the care and custody of deserted or orphan children; also for children of infirm, indigent or incompetent persons. There is a State Industrial Home for Girls in Colorado, and State provisions for the care of the feeble-minded. In New Zealand and in Australia the State pays a subsidy to widows who have to support children under 16, so as to enable them to remain at home and so look after their families.

A system of municipal nursing is also established in Finland. A system of State-paid nurses spread all over the country has helped to reduce infant mortality in New Zealand and Australia to 61.6 and 67.3 per 1,000. The infant mortality in Ontario in 1910 was 125 per 1,000.

Illegitimate Children

In Norway the father of an illegitimate child has equal responsibility with the mother for its education and maintenance.

In Australia the father of an expected illegitimate child can be prevented from leaving the country without making adequate provision for its support.

There are State-supported maternity homes in Australia and New Zealand.

The Maintenance Act in New Zealand makes provision for enforcing the maintenance not only of wife and family, but it also applies to a father's illegitimate children, and maintenance orders can be enforced in adjacent colonies.

Patriotism and Imperialism

Australia and New Zealand are the only two parts of the British Empire which have adopted compulsory military training for their men, and these measures were passed after half the electorate came to consist of women.

At the last Imperial Conference it was the representatives of these two Dominions who alone urged seriously the establishment of Imperial Councils and Imperial Appeal Courts, and both Australia and New Zealand have contributed Dreadnoughts to the British Navy.

Crime

Legislation and administration directly controlled by women has succeeded in diminishing the proportion of crime in the respective States by raising the age of protection for girls, by insisting on adequate punishment for all sexual offences, by better measures for the protection of neglected children, of the feeble-minded, and by the extension of the school age. The proportion of female delinquency, especially, has been reduced and practically abolished in some of the States.

In Colorado it has been made a criminal offence to contribute to the delinquency of a child.

The United States census prison statistics of 1904 state that of all the prisoners in the States of California only 3 per cent, in Colorado and Utah 2 per cent, in Washington four-fifths of 1 per cent, and in Wyoming and Idaho none were women.

Gambling

Is illegal in Colorado, Idaho, Wyoming, and there are strictly enforced laws dealing with gambling in Australia, New Zealand and Tasmania.

Equal Pay for Equal Work

In the suffrage States of Wyoming, Utah, California, New Zealand, Australia, Norway and Finland there is equal pay for male and female teachers of the same grade and qualification. In New Zealand and Australia there is equal pay and an eight-hour day for male and female factory workers who do the same grade of work. In New Zealand there is a minimum wage of £1 5s 0d. a week for female workers in factories or workshops, and all "sweating" has become illegal.

On November 17th, 1910, the Senate and Commonwealth of Australia passed the following resolution:

1. That this Senate is of the opinion that the extension of Suffrage to the women of Australia for States and Commonwealth Parliament has had the most beneficial results. It has led to the more orderly conduct of elections and at the last Federal elections the women's vote in a majority of the States showed a greater proportional increase than that cast by men. It has given a greater prominence to legislation particularly affecting women and children, although the women have not taken up such questions to the exclusion of others of wider significance. In matters of defence and Imperial concern they have proved themselves as far seeing and as discriminating as men. Because the reform has brought nothing but good although disaster was freely prophesied, we respectfully urge that all nations enjoying representative government would be well advised in granting votes to women.

Resolution passed by the House of Representatives of Wyoming:

"Be it Resolved: – That the possession and exercise of Suffrage by the women of Wyoming for the past quarter of a century has wrought no harm and has done much good in many ways; That it has largely aided in banishing crime and pauperism and vice from this State and that without any violent or oppressive legislation; That is has secured peaceful and orderly elections, good government and remarkable degree of civilization and public order; and we point with pride to the facts that after nearly twenty-five years of Woman's Suffrage not one county in Wyoming has a poorhouse, that our jails are nearly empty, and crime except that committed by strangers in the State, [is] almost unknown; and as a result of experience we urge every civilized community on earth to enfranchise its women without delay."

On May 5, 1911, in the British House of Commons the second reading of the Conciliation (Women's Franchise) Bill was carried with a majority of 165 in its favour.

Mr Balfour, the Conservative leader, said on that occasion:

"My view is that democracy properly understood is government by consent broadly speaking. When you get to the point that a class feels itself as a class excluded and outraged by being excluded, then those who believe as I do, that democracy properly understood is the only possible government for any nation at the stage of political evolution which we have reached must consider whether it is not their business to try and see if a government which is a hypothesis not a government by consent can be turned into a government by consent ... when women, or any section of women have begun to feel they suffer under an hereditary disability it is your business to see if you cannot remedy that grievance."

The Chief Justice and all the Judges of the Supreme Court of Idaho have published a statement saying in part: "Woman suffrage in this State is a success; none of the evils predicted have come to pass, and it has gained much in popularity since its adoption by our people."

[Source: Sonia Leathes, *What Equal Suffrage Has Accomplished* (Toronto: Equal Franchise League, 1911 or 1912).]

Political Equality League, Victoria, British Columbia
The Study Club (1912)

A very interesting meeting of the Study Club was held at the home of Mrs Baer, Vancouver Street, on Thursday afternoon, October 1. It was the first of a series to be held through the winter season, at which free and full discussion of various topics of interest to the "new woman" is being arranged for.

The initial subject chosen for discussion was "Fundamental Reasons for the Enfranchisement of Women," and everyone was requested to come primed with a "reason," the meeting was of a very general, interesting and varied character, and as one lady expressed it, "We had to stop long before we got through."

Mrs Baer, chairman of the club, said in introducing the subject: "Today we are discussing fundamental reasons for the enfranchisement of women. This is a large subject and may be studied from many viewpoints. Primarily there is a theoretical side and a practical side. We may study the scientific, philosophical and religious aspect or we may turn to the social and economic significance of the movement. Some women are with us because they are laboring and see others laboring under the disabilities of existing conditions, other women as idealists see that the political equality of the sexes is the basis of a more desirable state.

This afternoon we meet to express our different viewpoints on the question of woman's enfranchisement.

The Mother of the Race

The particular reason I want to emphasize is this. By the very nature of motherhood, racial progress and development is largely in the hands of women, and the rights and privileges of citizenship should be hers, in order that she may have liberty to serve and care for her children more adequately.

Look at the people as you go down the street and ask, Isn't there room for improvement in the human specimens you meet? What is the reason for the manifest imperfections? What is woman going to do about it? What can she do while her sex means her subjection? I think, first of all, before she can do anything, she must wake up to the responsibilities of her position, and become conscious of her own ignorance and lack of development. How little we know, for instance, of all that is involved in motherhood, and what is there for us more important? (This is a subject for study, to which some of our meetings will be devoted.) How negative we are, tamely accepting, as we do conditions against which we should struggle with might and main – as for instance, a double standard of morality, drink and disease, enforced maternity, sickly and imperfect children, sweated labor, man-made standards for women. How calmly we are detailed to take care of home and babies in much the same way that you give dolls and toys to children to amuse them, keep them quiet and occupied. When are we going to fully realize that instead of being a condition imposed, motherhood should bear the royal insignia of freedom? The result of making one-half an adjunction to the other half is producing such dire results that women are being aroused to the need of sterner, more positive and potent ideals of womanhood and a restatement of her relative position. Standards for women must be set by women, not by men.

We must go forward as women or racial progression must cease, for we are the mould in which the future race is cast. And while hitherto man, with his physical strength has dictated the terms, and woman in her weakness has submitted – a perfectly natural result – in the course of evolution and with increasing knowledge, the subtler forces of mental and spiritual power are superseding material and physical force, and the necessity for the awakening of that latent woman power is felt in every department of human society today. We women have got to take the broader view – the step forward. We are the Mother of the Race, not the subject of the man.

So long as woman regards herself as the subject of the man, she needs no vote; she is looked after according to his will. But when she awakes to the fact that she is the mother of the race, she does need a vote in order to more adequately attend to her own business. As women come to recognize this larger aspect of their glorious calling so shall their influence be more potent and for good."

Mrs Mitchell as next speaker made a very thoughtful plea for woman's liberty to serve in the larger life of the world as well as in the home and emphasized the inherent right and duty of the individual to self-expression in service, no matter whether man or woman.

Miss Ralph thought the high death rate of infants in Canada should be a call to arms to all women and open their eyes to the need of enfranchisement and pointed to the results as shown by government statistics in this particular, in the countries where women had the vote. She also took up the educational view of the question from the standpoint of a teacher.

Perhaps one of the most interesting talks of the afternoon, because of the personal touch, was given by Mrs Saunders, who told of the loss of her baby girl in Vancouver two years ago. The milk she had been feeding to her sick baby was analyzed by the doctor and found to contain no milk whatever, a purely chemical production. That winter 300 children had died in four months in Vancouver and she and some of the other mothers had tried to get a public investigation into the matter and prosecution of the vendors of the impure milk.

She spoke of the tremendous difficulties that faced the women and the way was blocked because certain authorities feared that public investigation would injure the tourist traffic. This experience, Mrs Sanders said, opened her eyes to the need of the woman's viewpoint in the realm of government. Man was so liable to place commercial and private interests before the consideration of human life.

She also cited the unequal divorce laws as a potent reason for woman's enfranchisement, and gave instances of women having to put up with a life of unbearable insult, but no suit for divorce in order because the husband had not used personal violence, the only redress being to run away, as one lawyer advised.

Mrs Elkin thought the laws regarding the guardianship of children were enough to arouse any woman to a sense of the degradation of her present position under existing law and thought immediate action should be taken to have them changed.

Mrs Pethick, Mrs Savile and Mrs Foxall took part in the general discussion which followed and Mrs Christie's excellent paper we reproduce on another page.

Mrs Gordon Grant in summing up the discussion emphasized the growing need of "woman power" in every department of public work. She called attention to the work of the League, the paper, the meetings and petition, which all were invited to sign. The serving of afternoon tea brought to a close a most interesting meeting.

In connection with the Study Club, the Rev. W. Stevenson will deliver an address on "Women, Past and Present," at the home of Mrs Mitchell, 641 Superior Street, on Wednesday evening at 8:15, November 13th.

[Source: "The Study Club," *The Champion* (Victoria, BC) 1, no. 4 (November 1912), 6–8.]

Florence Trenholme Cole (1871–1940) was the wife of Lt. F. Col. Minden Cole, insurance executive and commanding officer of the Montreal Garrison during the First World War. She was a member of the IODE and the Montreal Suffrage Association, which included both francophone and anglophone women.

Florence Trenholme Cole
Concerning Suffrage (1913)

To the Editor of *Le Devoir*

Dear Sir,

You will permit me, I am sure, to elaborate a little on my remarks about female suffrage, remarks that served as the basis for your eloquent article of Monday last. To say that I accused the French women of this province of ignorance is to translate my thoughts in too crude a manner. I have far too much admiration and respect for my French sisters to express myself in that way. What I said was that our province is ruled by the countryside, and that the rural districts are so lacking in educational resources that it is doubtful democracy will win out there if women who have no opportunity to educate themselves are given the right to vote. I firmly believe that the innate intelligence of the French-Canadian woman is so great that, if she wins the right to vote, she will soon be capable of using it intelligently.

No-one can deny, I think, that education is not what it should be in this province. A little book that the *Times* of London has just published about Canada states: "There may be no doubt that such a prolonged neglect of education in the province of Québec has considerably disadvantaged its population." The one who wrote these lines has studied Canadian affairs with interest and without prejudice. But the situation is improving: more is being spent on education; a greater number of men and women are concerned about the need for a better education.

Now, let me address, for a few minutes, the remarks Mr Bourassa made about women's suffrage in general. First of all, what he says about the English women who break windows, burn houses and throw hatchets is entirely beside the point. These women only constitute a very small minority. The great majority of women deplore these tactics, tactics which will never take root here among Canadian women. Is Christianity discredited because a few Christians do things contrary to its spirit? Must the cause of women's suffrage suffer because certain women, in one single country in the world, commit acts that are not approved of by the vast majority?

I completely endorse Mr Bourassa's remarks about the spirit of sacrifice of many mothers, women and sisters, and about the wonderful charitable works performed by the nuns both in and out of the convents toward the relief of the poor, the ill and the afflicted. I also agree with him when he says that marriage and maternity constitute the normal womanly state. But female suffrage will not interfere in any way with these functions. Where women do have the right to suffrage, it has produced none of the terrible consequences that were predicted. Women continue to marry, to be loving wives and mothers, to devote themselves to their homes and families. What, then, has happened? Just this: families have become happier; men and women have become better friends; women have become better mothers because they are treated like intelligent human beings, capable of taking part in the governance of their countries. Something else has happened: the laws governing women, children and families have improved. These positive facts demonstrate that where women vote, they use their votes to combat the traffic in liquor. The subject of alcohol is equally of interest to the French and the English. In New Zealand, where women have been voting for twenty years, the white slave trade has disappeared. Those who are opposed to female suffrage should not forget that the only organized opposition to female suffrage in the United States comes from liquor merchants and those who profit from the degradation of women. This fact alone should incline Catholics and Protestants to support women's suffrage.

Mr Bourassa says that men and women are created different, and that suffragists want to make them the same. Not at all. It is precisely because women are different that we want the vote. Laws govern women as much as they do men, and if women are different, could they not say better than men what laws they need? Should one social class legislate for a different class?

Mr Bourassa observes that suffrage is only one step in the emancipation of women. That is true. Those who believe in suffrage believe that it will open several doors currently closed to women. If God has given women certain aptitudes, is it just that men prevent women from realizing them? A woman should be allowed to do what she is capable of doing. This freedom would never interfere with the duties of wife and mother that nature has made the principal vocation of women. But not all women are wives and mothers; should access to certain careers be closed to those categories of women? In conclusion, Mr Bourassa anticipates a social revolution if women were to win the right to vote, but history shows definitively that such a revolution will not occur.

His late Eminence, Cardinal Moran of Australia once launched an appeal in favour of women's suffrage, declaring that "in voting woman quite simply makes use of a just privilege that democracy gave her ... The woman who fears losing her essential quality in voting is a silly creature."

Other eminent ecclesiastics have expressed similar opinions. The Archbishop of Illinois declares – and his words could just as well apply to our province – "that women constitute the most religious, most moral, and most sober among the American people, and it is not difficult to understand why their influence in public life is so feared."

I do not want to take up more space in your newspaper, but I would like this topic to be treated more thoroughly.

> I remain, sir,
> Florence Trenholme Cole

[Source: Florence Trenholme Cole, "Concerning Suffrage (À propos de suffragisme)," *Le Devoir*, 5 April 1913; repr. in *La pensée féministe au Québec: Anthologie, 1900–1945,* ed. Micheline Dumont and Louise Toupin (Montreal: Les Éditions du remue-ménage, 2003), 157–9 (trans. Maureen Moynagh).]

Marion Francis Beynon (1884–1951) first worked in advertising and later as a journalist in Winnipeg. Along with her sister, Lillian Beynon Thomas, she advocated a broad reform program for women. A co-founder of the Political Equality League of Manitoba, Beynon wrote a regular column and was editor of the woman's page of the *Grain Growers' Guide* from 1912–17. She was an outspoken critic of the ethnocentric and anti-immigrant attitudes of many of her fellow feminists. Her pacifist stance in the midst of the First World War resulted in a forced resignation from the newspaper in 1917, after which she left Winnipeg for the United States. She subsequently published a novel, *Aleta Day* (1919), which well captured her feminist and pacifist politics.

Francis Marion Beynon
The Foreign Woman's Franchise (1916)

When a coincidence of engagements brought Sir Robert Borden and Mrs Nellie L. McClung to Winnipeg together recently Mrs McClung made use of the opportunity to ask the Premier to grant the federal franchise to all British and Canadian born women, excluding the foreign born women.

In this Mrs McClung was speaking for herself alone and not for the organized women of the suffrage provinces, and its seems to me regrettable that she should have spoken at all in this vein without first having the request endorsed by the leading suffrage workers. Many of our women would probably believe, as Mrs McClung does, that it would be unwise to extend this privilege today to foreign born women, but we hope that the majority of the women who fought and won the suffrage fight on the ground that democracy is right still believe in democracy.

Personally if I had a religious faith or a political conviction which wouldn't stand the test of a great crisis, and which had to be discarded whenever an emergency arose I would rise up and take it out and bury it in a nice deep grave, and pray that it might have no resurrection day.

So it seems to me that if democracy is good when applied to ourselves it is good when applied to the Icelandic women who worked so hard to get the vote, and to the Polish and Ruthenian and other women who took a keener interest in the suffrage petition than many of our British women.

Mrs McClung also overlooked the fact that unless a discrimination is to be made between provinces it would mean disenfranchising the foreign born women in Manitoba and British Columbia, always a difficult thing to do and a thankless task for any government to undertake.

I am sorry to have to disagree unalterably in the matter with Mrs McClung who has done and is still doing such splendid work for women, but having pointed out from the public platform, time and again the tyranny of unrepresentative government and the injustice of debarring any portion of the people from the franchise because of an accident of birth I cannot subscribe to that injustice being meted out to another woman of any nationality whatsoever.

The foreign born women are here largely as the result of the colonization program of the Dominion Government. They have come at our own urgent invitation and they will suffer just as great an injustice as we have done in the past if their point of view does not find expression in the government of the country.

For my own part I believe in democracy just as invincibly today as I did in the yesterday of my own political minority, and if a serious attempt is made to exclude these new women citizens from the franchise my tongue and pen will do their little best by way of protest.

[Source: Francis Marion Beynon, "The Foreign Woman's Franchise," *Grain Growers' Guide*, 27 December 1917.]

Nellie Mooney McClung, 1873–1951, was born in the Souris Valley, Manitoba, and worked as a teacher before marrying in 1896. She became a prominent member of the Women's Christian Temperance Union and in the midst of the First World War played a leading role in the fight for female suffrage in Manitoba, and after she moved there in 1915, in Alberta. She later served as Liberal MLA for Edmonton from 1921 to 1926 and was appointed as a delegate to the United Nations in 1938. McClung was author of 16 books including *Sewing Seeds in Danny* (1908) and an autobiography, *Clearing in the West: My Own Story* (1935), as well as of numerous newspaper articles and magazine columns.

Nellie McClung
Mrs McClung's Reply (1917)

Dear Miss Beynon: – I have read your editorial of December 27, and I am sorry to see that you stated my conclusion without stating my reason, but I have your kind letter inviting me to make reply, which I am glad to do.

The going away of so many of our best and most public spirited men has changed the moral tone of our electorate. There are districts where almost all of the English speaking men have enlisted, leaving the Austrians and Germans in full numbers, and the indifferent ones of other nationalities. Now, I believe the German and Austrian women in these districts are entitled to the full franchise because they are responsible human beings, but their claim on the franchise is no greater (and no less) that it was before the war, but the right of the English speaking women whose men-folk have gone to fight, has become indisputable and imperative.

What I suggested to the Prime Minister was that, as a war measure, and to offset this abnormal condition caused by the war, that Canadian and English women be given full voting privileges at once. I reminded him that Manitoba and British Columbia women had already achieved this, and that therefore my suggestion did not concern them.

I have not tried to influence public sentiment toward this measure. Neither is it my intention to try to make it the policy of any society. It is merely my own opinion, and when I spoke to the Prime Minister I stated this.

I have not in any way departed from my opinion that all women are entitled to a part in government, and I did not in any way regard this as a settlement of the franchise question, but merely as a war measure. A partial franchise seems to me better than none, and opens the way for the full measure. But I am not advocating this as a policy. I quite realize that our forces must not divide, for the cause we stand for has in it the whole wellbeing of humanity and as such cannot be jeopardized by a difference of opinion over the method of procedure.

Because I place woman suffrage above all personal considerations, and because I know that any one person's judgment is quite liable to be faulty, I will withdraw the suggestion of a partial franchise.

Sincerely,
Nellie McClung

[Editorial comment by Francis Beynon follows:] I have great pleasure in giving space to this letter from Mrs McClung. While Mrs McClung's stand would not have altered my high regard for her as a woman, I am glad that we shall still be able to work together as we have done in the past with so much pleasure and profit.

I must confess that the fear that the foreign born citizens of this country would ever combine on any issue seems to be fantastic, since they differ from each other at least as widely as they do from us.

I am sure, also, that Mrs McClung had not given sufficient thought to the difficulty these foreign born women would experience in getting this privilege if once they were left behind, or she would have said, "We'll wait a little longer, if necessary, and all go in together," for Mrs McClung is a generous woman.

[Source: Nellie McClung, "Mrs McClung's Reply," *Grain Growers' Guide*, 24 January 1917.]

Editorial, *Jus Suffragii*

International Response to Women Gaining Federal Franchise in 1917 (1918)

The promised Canadian Federal Franchise Bill is disappointing, limiting Woman Suffrage to relations of soldiers. It is meeting with considerable opposition, and attempts are being made to widen it in the direction of universal Suffrage.

The vicious principle of according a right which is based on justice and freedom for the individual, and should be given to women on the same terms as men, to a selected group of women, and on the ground of their male relations having performed some service to the State, is one that cannot be too strongly condemned, and whose very absurdity should surely be self-evident.

Strangely enough, even democratic Australia witnesses another exhibition, though not such a flagrant one, of the same impertinence. Soldiers' women relatives are to receive medals! Women have had reason to complain that in their case State service did not meet with the recognition given to men in the bestowal of honours, but this topsy-turvy award to women on account of their men relations' service has no basis in common sense or fairness, one only has to imagine the boot on the other leg, and *men* given enfranchisement or medals if their *women* are deserving to see how that would strike the public.

[Source: Editorial, "Features of the Month," *Jus Suffragii* 12, no. 1, October 1917, 1.]

Constance Easton Hamilton (1862–1945) was born in Yorkshire, England, and immigrated to Canada with her family in 1881. A devoted supporter of women's suffrage, she was first president of the Toronto Equal Franchise League and at the outset of the First World War became president of the National Equal Franchise Union. At the request of Prime Minister William Borden, Hamilton sent a telegram along with the presidents of the NCW, IODE, and WCTU which queried: "Would the granting of the Federal franchise to women make conscription assured in the general election, if such is inevitable, taking into consideration the vote of foreign women." Along with these other women she subsequently released a statement in support of the Wartime Election Act.

Constance Hamilton
Letter to the Editor of *Jus Suffragii* (1918)

To the Editor of the *International Suffrage News* (*Jus Suffragii*)

Madam:

I note the leading article in the *International Suffrage News* of October 1st, in which you take exception to the War-time Election Act recently passed by Canada by the late Government.

Suffragists in Canada are by no means unanimous in their objections to the Bill, many feeling it is not only fair and just, but eminently safe under prevailing conditions.

To a full understanding of the Bill it is necessary to know something of the political situation existing at the time of its enactment.

The country has just been passing through a difficult and chaotic period, now happily resolving itself into comparative harmony and into which outstanding men of both parties are now rapidly swinging, and which will go before the electors in December. Some months ago Sir Robert Borden had made an abortive attempt to bring about a fusion of parties, and at the time the Election Act was passed a Union Government seemed very doubtful. The enforcement of Conscription was receiving severe opposition from followers of Sir Wilfrid Laurier, though a number of Conscription Liberals had support the Military Service Act.

Sir Robert Borden subsequently begged for an extension of term for his Government, but this was defeated, and as a result Conscription and Canada's continued participation in the war hung in the balance.

It must be well understood that the Enfranchisement Act [Wartime Election Act] is a war-time measure, framed to meet war conditions; the Bill in no sense gives enfranchisement as a reward, but restricts it owing to war perils and war necessity.

The Union Government, if returned, has pledged itself to an extension of the franchise to women, a measure with which all concur once the war necessities are safeguarded by a national unity made possible by a fusion of all Win-the-war forces.

Yours, etc.

Constance Hamilton, L.A.

[Source: Constance Hamilton, "Letter to Editor," *Jus Suffragii* 12, no. 4, 1 January 1918, 48.]

Harriet Prenter was one of four female candidates to run for federal Parliament in 1921, the first election in which women were eligible as candidates. In the decade previous to this election Prenter had been a vocal proponent of women's suffrage, serving as president of the Political Equality League in Toronto. Her political affiliation shifted, though, from the Liberal Party to the Independent Labour Party as she came to identify herself as a socialist and concerned with the struggles of working-class women and men. Although Prenter did not win a seat in the 1921 election, she remained active in left-wing politics in both Canada and the United States in the 1920s.

Harriet Prenter

The Failure of the Suffrage Movement to Bring Freedom to Woman (1928)

The great activity shown when occasion demands by political parties in their efforts to get the woman vote, brings to mind many of the promises and prophesies which were made by friends and foes in those not distant days when it required a little courage to wear a "votes for women" button.

Of course the "Antis" sounded their usual alarm – the home would be destroyed – and one admits that many suffragists also showed their ignorance of the "world process" by their optimistic arguments along opposite lines. And after it was all over what happened?

In the first place, the anti-suffragists who were loudest in proclaiming that "woman's place is the home" were the very first to step out and seek political and other offices. And of all the others who fought so well for this right of self-expression, only one or two, here and there over the whole country, saw that this was not the end of the struggle, but only a very small beginning.

To be sure, it was not a working class movement. The majority in it were middle class and fairly satisfied with conditions – as one well known club woman said to me, "It seems so absurd that my gardener can vote and I can't." It was just a matter of status with her.

They were the sort who used to get up in meetings and enquire anxiously – "but who will do the menial work," when one was trying to picture a better social order. Evidently, if it meant work and responsibility for all, they were not going to stand for it. But they were mostly nice, kind ladies, and they often meant well, as on the occasion when one of them undertook to investigate conditions in a certain workshop, she brought back an excellent report, and when asked from whom she got her information, she said, "Oh, I went right to the manager!" And how they wanted to supervise the spending of working class housewives at the beginning of the war. It seems that some of these wasteful creatures were discovered buying oranges and pickles – and later on it was gramophones and pianos!

But when election time came these same fine ladies were very busy calling on women in various working class districts, and acting so "perfectly lovely," that many a foolish woman voted against her own interests and against her family and her class, because she was so flattered she was easily deceived.

In the USA a group of influential ones, called "The Women's National Party," are now going before Congress – supported by members of the employer's association – and opposing legislation that would aid great numbers of women to an approach to economic equality with men. They call it, asking for "equal rights." If, for instance, men are working ten hours a day in certain places, women employed there must also have the "right" to work ten hours a day. If successful, they will nullify the work of years done by trade unions and labor groups for the betterment and relief of working women. It may be that they do not grasp the serious problems of the woman worker, but, anyway, they are proving again that the business of fair play for all who work for wages is the worker's own task.

Another reason why the vote has been of so little use to us is the fact that hundreds of thousands are always disenfranchised.

The law requires certain conditions and the worker following his job or moving about in search of employment is thus automatically off the voters' list.

And the working class generally is suffering today in "mind, body, and estate" because we've been too confiding, too good natured, too patient. We have failed to see that whatever value there was in the vote was lost entirely unless used for ourselves. And if this be intelligent selfishness there's little to argue about.

Certainly the so-called "dignity of labor" is only an election phrase, but there are enough workers to give it real meaning. We could very well take a lesson from the conduct of those in authority over us. They realize what class loyalty means, even though they may not like or in any way approve of each other individually. Yet they are rarely so silly as to be caught voting or acting in any way against their class interests. They stick together.

And since we have in Canada such a high class paper as "The Woman Worker" it must be now much easier to get together in great numbers with one common denominator – working class freedom.

If we meet just as working women, with no handicaps because of race, creed or color, it will speed up the day when voting will not be the farce it now is, when governments will not be something remote and threatening, when the ruling of peoples will give place to the administration of things "for the well-being of all."

[Source: Harriet Prenter, "The Failure of the Suffrage Movement to Bring Freedom to Woman," *Woman Worker*, December 1928, 12–14.]

Idola Saint-Jean, 1880–1945, was born in Montreal, Quebec, the daughter of a prominent lawyer. After studying in Paris, Saint-Jean supported herself by teaching elocution in Montreal schools and French at McGill University, and also worked as a journalist from the 1920s onward. She formally became involved in women's rights in 1922 after joining the recently created Provincial Suffrage Committee, and in 1928 founded the Alliance canadienne pour le vote des femme du Québec. Along with Thérèse Casgrain of the Ligue des droits de la femme, Saint-Jean made numerous overtures to the provincial government to grant women the vote. In order to promote women's issues to a wider audience, she wrote a column in the *Montreal Herald* and from 1933 published the magazine *La Sphère feminine*. She also had a bilingual radio program throughout the 1930s.

Idola Saint-Jean

Radio Address on Granting the Vote to Women in Quebec (1931)

Ladies, Gentlemen,

Tomorrow the Legislature will for the fifth time receive a bill demanding suffrage for the women of this province. A just and legitimate demand which, if it is finally realized, will put the women of Quebec on an equal footing with their sisters in the other eight provinces of Canada.

The women of Quebec were the first on the scene and as one looks back to the early pages of our history, we find them working with ardour at the admirable work of colonization.

In all aspects of social life, they have been the valiant companions of men, always at work, giving the best of themselves to build a country destined to play a great role in the history of the world.

Let our legislators, when they are called tomorrow to vote yes or no on whether we will be admitted to full participation in our political life, remember that, in 1705, the first cloth manufactory in Canada was founded by a woman, Madame de Repentigny; let them recall the work of Marie Rollet, the great mistress of our Canadian farmers, who brought to our country the first plough. Then there was Jeanne Mance who set herself up as the municipal treasurer of Ville-Marie and found the necessary money to bring in a regiment charged with the defence of the colonists against the devastating attacks of the Iroquois. The founders of the first hospitals, the founders of the first schools, were they not, these women, whom we have the honour of calling our ancestors, the equivalent of Ministers of Commerce, Ministers of Social Welfare, Ministers of Education, and, I dare say, Ministers of Finance, filling these offices, in such a way, thanks to their organizational and economizing skills, as to even give pointers to a large number of men?

No man, witness to what our pioneers accomplished at the dawn of our history, would have refused them access to Parliament, if there had been one, at the time. They were consulted on all questions, those intelligent and wise women and, thanks to the cooperation between the men and women of that time, we enjoy today the progress and development of our Canada.

Moreover, this right that we are claiming, did we not possess it until 1834? and did we not exercise it with conscience and dignity? To convince ourselves of the scrupulous fashion with which our grandmothers accomplished their duty as voters, it is sufficient to recall the speech that the mother of Louis Joseph Papineau made in casting her vote: "I vote," she said, "for Louis Joseph Papineau, my son, not because he is my son, but because I think him to be qualified to represent with dignity our race." That's intelligent and sane politics!

We women have not lost our abilities, it seems to me, ladies and gentlemen, one finds us today in all the areas of charity and work. Economic conditions throw us into industry, into commerce, into education, in a word into all spheres of activity. As we have to work to live, then, why are we condemned to occupy only the subordinate positions? Why not allow us access to the professions and also the parliaments which make the laws that affect the woman as much as the man? Why, I ask you, Gentlemen, should we not bring to bear our qualities as teachers when a law concerning our schools is being discussed? Why should mothers not have the right to vote when the House studies a law concerning the welfare of the child, of the family, etc.? Are those not the problems that a woman will always understand better than a man?

In all sincerity, Gentlemen, tell us, are there questions that your mothers, your wives, your daughters could not understand, even if they had a very rudimentary education? And tell us, divested of your egotism, that brings you less happiness than you seem to think – tell us if you would be satisfied if, one day, a woman declared herself your arbitrary ruler, took upon herself, as you did sanctimoniously centuries ago, to dictate totally your way of life, making herself the only judge of your destiny. You would protest with good reason against such a state of affairs, wouldn't you? Well! inspire yourselves with the words of the Lord, "Do unto others as you would that they would do unto you." Let us elect our legislators. We are responsible human beings when treated as such. If a woman is guilty of an offense, your laws punish her, it is not her husband who mounts the scaffold, it is she who atones for her sin; therefore does it not seem to you to be unjust in the extreme that under statute law a good mother, a good wife does not have the right to conclude a transaction without having previously obtained her husband's signature whether it be good or bad? Do you realize that under your law a mother, separated from her husband and to whom the court has given custody of their children, does not even have the right to consent to their marriage, that that right is reserved exclusively for the father, even if he is unworthy of the title? Are those the laws of a country that calls itself Christian?

The happiness of a man, Victor Hugo said a long time ago, cannot be made of the sufferings of a woman. Egotism is the cause of all the ills humanity suffers. Contribute to the establishment of our society on the basis of justice, that's the best way to work for its well-being.

Dream of the great evangelical truths, Gentlemen, our legislators, when tomorrow you are asked to grant the admission of women to the political realm and to establish women's right to unrestricted work – because the draft legislation for the admission of women to the bar will also be discussed tomorrow.

Instead of treating us as dangerous rivals, let us become your companions in all spheres of activity. Be proud of our aptitudes and let us apply our talents to the service of our province. The national pride in the hearts of all real Canadians should be flattered by the success brought by our own, whether they be men or women. In 1914, McGill University awarded the first law degree to a Canadian woman, Mrs Langstaff who placed first in criminal law and business law, the two most difficult subjects at the faculty. Miss Marthe Pelland, who died last year, won the first place in the faculty of Medicine at the University of Montreal. Happily that profession is not closed to us. How many other courageous and brilliant women could I not cite here? Born in another province, women can aspire to higher positions, but Quebec holds hers in tutelage and does not let them give their productivity to society.

Think about all these women, Gentlemen, and let your vote tomorrow be liberating. In the interests of all of us rather than that of all men, generously open the door of the political and professional arena to women who will learn to stay in public life, as they are in private life, the descendents of the Jeanne Mances, the Marguerite Bourgeoises, the Madeleine des Verchères and all of the others who contributed to the development of our country. Since all the professional women and the legion of women who work are unanimous in reclaiming their political rights and their right to unrestricted work, do not take responsibility any longer, Gentlemen, for keeping them on the sidelines of the political and professional life of their province that they love and the welfare of which they want to serve.

Idola Saint-Jean

[Source : Transcription of radio broadcast by Idola Saint-Jean, reprinted in *Mon héroine: Les lundis de l'histoire des femmes, an I, Conférences du Théâtre expérimental des femmes, Montréal 1980–81*, ed. Michael Jean (Montreal: Les Éditions du remue-ménage, 1981), 139–41.]

PART FOUR
Citizenship

In a pamphlet produced by the Political Equality League of Manitoba in 1912, Nellie McClung declared, "No longer is the ideal woman the one who never lifts her eyes higher than the top pantry shelf nor allows her sympathy to extend past her own family. Women who believed they must sit down and be resigned are now rising up and being indignant. The new womanhood is the new citizenship."[1] The new womanhood heralded by Nellie McClung and other Canadian first wave feminists referred to a more publicly engaged female population for whom citizenship represented "a sustained field of contest."[2] Women activists challenged the very meaning of and rights attendant with citizenship as they attempted to expand their "sphere of influence." Yet their claims making was by no means uniform nor was it premised on a single vision of citizenship. Moreover, many of their efforts were directly and indirectly influenced by the consequences of imperial conquest and ongoing political ties to Britain as well as by international feminist campaigns related to female citizenship rights. Subsequent sections will examine specific areas of citizenship-related agitation and organization such as moral reform, work and economic status, and peace activism. Documents in this section will address in somewhat broader terms efforts to alter women's relationship to the state and to nation building while also considering a number of key struggles over legal rights and citizenship status.

Female reformers asserted entitlement to an increasing number and range of rights for women – civil, political, and economic – from the mid-nineteenth century onward. But they did so within a colonial and later national context that continued to refuse many of these same rights to Aboriginal peoples, male and female. The legal framework for Indian status constructed by government authorities, as Sarah Carter has noted, meant that Aboriginal people had "none of the rights and powers of British subjects."[3] In England to protest the dispossession of Anishinabe lands in 1860, Nahnebahwequa (Catherine Sutton) challenged the regime of colonial governance that relegated indigenous people to the inferior position of the "poor Indian." She pointed to the ongoing discriminatory treatment of Aboriginals over land and the far higher standards they had to meet than people of European ancestry to be designated "civilized." Aboriginal men and women prior to and following Nahnebahwequa made appeals to state authorities to attain or retain certain rights and possessions, but they occurred largely alongside, and rarely if at all intersected with, the claims making of Euro-Canadian feminists.

Annie Parker endeavoured to further the cause of female citizenship rights, in an article published in 1890, by arguing that women were not marginal to but in fact played a crucial part in nation building and the well-being of the Canadian state. Furthermore, she maintained, such contributions qualified women for "just title to rank as citizens." Indeed, Parker advocated that citizenship be reconceptualized so as to include women on an equitable basis with men. In her view the expanded role then accorded women would be of widespread benefit to the state and the nation because of the unique qualities that they possessed. Representative of other feminist treatises of this period, though, Parker's article referenced the religious and cultural values of Anglo-Celtic Christian women as especially suited to "reconstructing the social life of the nation." Moreover, she formulated her argument in support of improved citizenship rights in Canada in terms of the inevitable advance of a "civilized" nation as distinguished from "savage" ones.

In a memoir written several decades later, Emily Murphy, aka Janey Canuck, did not hesitate to assert herself as a citizen, although, as she also noted, one still lacking full political rights. In the excerpt included here, which recalled her encounter with a group of Aboriginal families who had travelled from their reserve to a small-town fair, Murphy explicitly demarcated citizenship in racial and colonial terms. As a self-identified white person she automatically assumed the title of citizen in direct contrast to the non-citizens in her midst – the Aboriginals. Of additional significance, Murphy depicted the identity of citizen as inherently a marker of modernity vested not only with selected rights but also with certain responsibilities and even burdens. She juxtaposed this identity with that of the premodern Aboriginals who she suggested were not beset with worries about such things as electoral politics or paying taxes.

Aboriginal people were not the only ones designated by women reformers as "other" in feminist discussions over citizenship. As the number of non-British migrants rapidly increased at the end of the nineteenth century, "foreigners" assumed ever greater prominence as cultural and political referents against whom many Euro-Canadian women viewed themselves as superior. Such a stance contributed to reformers seeking to limit or deny rights to non-British immigrants as it simultaneously provided them a platform for a more publicly engaged citizenship. Reaction towards Chinese immigrants represents a particularly important instance. Amidst escalating racial fears of Chinese immigrants on the west coast, Chinese women became the object of ongoing activism. More specifically, under the widespread belief that Chinese women were being brought to Canada for prostitution and slavery, various women's organizations lobbied the federal government to restrict their arrival or to expel them after entry. The Methodist Women's Missionary Society was especially prominent; not only did this group repeatedly appeal to the dominion government to enforce immigration controls, it also established a home in 1887 for the "rescue" of Chinese women in Victoria, whose activities are outlined in a 1892–3 report. In effect, the MWMS advocated what historical sociologist Renisa Mawania has referred to as restrictive "spatial governance" alongside efforts aimed at moral suasion and protection.[4]

The fault lines of gender, race, and citizenship status also directly informed the struggle over homesteading rights on the prairies, part of the broader and more extended campaign related to women's property rights that originated in the mid-nineteenth century. In this western region women began to agitate for access to free title to frontier lands at the turn of the century, a legal right that single and married women were then denied. The influx of scores of immigrants from continental Europe to Canada during this period further inflamed the issue as large numbers of male "foreigners" – non-British immigrants – were granted free homesteads while most women who were British subjects were officially prohibited. A vocal supporter of the female homestead-rights movement, as evidenced in her much celebrated *Wheat and Women* (1914), Georgina Binnie-Clark echoed the sentiments of many when she stated that the land laws "whilst seeking to secure the prosperity of the country in enriching the stranger, ignores the claim of the sex which bore the brunt of the battle in those early and difficult days." The position adopted by Binnie-Clark and her allies that legislative reforms should initially apply to women of British birth alone did not go uncontested, however, as Sarah Carter has pointed out. If alterations were to be made to the homestead laws, it was argued, "they should benefit all, not just British women."[5] In a column for the *Grain Growers' Guide*, Marion Francis Beynon critiqued more generally the racist attitudes of many Euro-Canadians towards foreigners, noting that despite being treated "as if they were the very dust beneath our feet … they become good citizens of our country." Beynon's document serves as an important reminder that while white supremacist beliefs predominated in feminist citizenship debates at the turn of the century, there were "statements of empathy and solidarity with non-white people," as Janice Fiamengo has cogently argued.[6]

The homestead-rights movement was by no means an isolated occurrence in which Anglo-Celtic women asserted entitlement to legal and political rights ahead of female non-British immigrants, for the latter proved capable of defending the interests of their ethnic/racial community and establishing the groundwork for full citizenship on their own terms. The organizational activities of Chinese immigrant women in the early twentieth century are just beginning to be uncovered, but the 1903 photograph of the Victoria chapter of the Chinese Empire Ladies' Reform Association (CELRA) represents key visual evidence of female group engagement. CELRA, which was affiliated with the all-male Chinese Empire Reform Association, or Baoghuarghui, constituted the first time that Chinese women in North America formed their own organization. It would appear that the general aim of this group was to support progressive political reform in China and attempts by Chinese citizens to persuade federal authorities in Canada and the United States to alter their restrictive immigration policies.[7]

Elsewhere, the Local Council of Jewish Women was formed in large cities such as Toronto and Montreal at the turn of the century as a vehicle for self-improvement and social reform among the European Jewish population in these centres. In its report of 1915, the Toronto local council highlighted in particular its work among recent female Jewish immigrants "by putting them in touch with the best of Canadian life." Composed primarily of middle-class and elite women, in many respects the council resembled that of other maternal feminist groups with members exercising noticeable class privilege in their determination of appropriate activities for the working-class Jewish women whom they sought to educate and protect. Yet this local council also demonstrated that not just Christian women had the requisite abilities or values to act on behalf of the public good and, by extension, the well-being of the country.

Other immigrant and racialized groups of women also made claims in terms their fitness for citizenship. Such was the case with the Ladies of the African United Baptist Association who gathered in Halifax in 1920. Their meeting was touted as "the first congress of colored women" in the country. While African Canadians did not experience the denial of formal citizenship rights that African Americans did in the United States, they still encountered various forms of de facto segregation as well as occupational and educational restrictions. The Halifax event focused less on these forms of discrimination and instead emphasized the expanding opportunities that did exist for African Canadian women. The women in attendance were encouraged not only to work alongside white women in improving the nation, but also to engage in the "uplift" of African Canadians.

Canadian feminists participated in a number of international campaigns relating to citizenship rights. One of the most protracted initiatives, albeit one with widespread support, pertained to married women's nationality rights. As legally stipulated in many countries, a woman automatically assumed the nationality of her husband upon marriage. If her husband was an alien (i.e., was not a naturalized citizen) the woman also became an alien, and thus, in effect, lost her nationality and the rights and privileges that went along with it. In a speech to the House of Commons in 1927, Agnes Macphail joined a chorus of national women's groups in conjunction with the leading international organizations in the decades-long protest against such legislation that resulted in numerous women being "citizens of no country, unable to claim the protection of any government." In the case of Canada, nationality remained an imperial matter, with all citizens designated as British subjects. By necessity, Macphail placed the issue of women's nationality in the broader context of imperial politics, but unlike many other feminists in the Commonwealth during this period, she did not frame the issue explicitly in terms of remaining "within the British imperial family."[8] She made the case for legislative reform principally on the basis of equality and justice.

Neither Macphail nor her contemporaries in Canada, however, drew any kind of parallel to another group of women who lost rights and privileges upon marriage – namely, Aboriginal women who married non-status men. Such silences did not pertain to this issue alone. Attempts to launch an international campaign in support of Six Nations women's political and civil rights in the 1920s do not appear to have elicited either organizational assistance or comment from Euro-Canadian feminists. On this occasion, the International Alliance of Women and the International Council of Women were each alerted to the decision of the Canadian federal government to impose an elected system of band governance that granted voting rights to males only and did away with the centuries-long tradition of Mohawk women nominating chiefs to a central council. In both instances, these large international organizations were asked to protest against the injustices suffered by the "Pays des Iroquois." These requests, however, did not originate from women reformers inside Canada, but from female members of the British and Foreign Anti-Slavery Society and Aborigines Protection Society, which had its headquarters in London. Women from this organization such as Sarah Robertson Matheson and Rica Flemyng Gyll developed close ties with residents of Six Nations, including the teacher, Emily General. A 1925 letter to Gyll from General noted the difficulties that had resulted from the recent inauguration of a "mock council" and, more broadly, from the enforcement of different elements of the Indian Act, despite ongoing objections on the reserve.

One of the most prominent citizenship contests during the interwar period involved the effort to admit women to the Canadian senate. By the end of the First World War, women had gained the right to vote and to hold elected office at the federal level, but they could not be appointed to the upper chamber of the Canadian parliament as they did not meet the legal requirement of "qualified persons" as specified in the British North America Act. A group of well-known female social reformers spearheaded by Emily Murphy launched a constitutional challenge, as evidenced by their August 1927 letter to the Governor General to have women legally declared persons. After the Supreme Court of Canada ruled in the negative, the "famous five" pressed for an appeal of that decision by the Judicial Committee of the Privy Council in England, which in that era acted as the final court of appeal for Canadian constitutional law. An illustration that appeared in *Chatelaine* in the midst of this litigation visually depicted the feminist position underlying the Persons Case – that women were interested in and capable of acting as equitable partners in the affairs of the Canadian state. The subsequent successful decision of the Privy Council not only allowed women to serve in the senate, but as Robert Sharpe and Patricia McMahon have noted, enshrined the principle of "full citizenship and personhood for women."[9] The significance of this legal victory was recognized and celebrated well beyond the borders of Canada in other Commonwealth countries and by various international women's organizations. Yet at the same time it would take over another decade for women in Quebec to gain the provincial franchise, while select groups of women on the basis of race, indigenous status, or nationality continued to be denied in one way or another certain citizenship rights.

The much-belated achievement of women's right to vote in Quebec afforded long-time activist Thérèse Casgrain the opportunity to reflect on women's place in a liberal democratic state. Casgrain revisited an argument long held by feminists in Canada, but which had particular cultural resonance and political significance among French-speaking Québécois: the necessity for women to participate in what she called "the entire social body" in order to better protect the interests of the family. Casgrain's conception of the family, though, was not of an autonomous privatized entity but as interdependent with all facets of society. Women's energies were thus not to be relegated primarily to the home; instead, Casgrain called on women to engage in an ambitious program of political and social action. As with many first wave feminists, she did not conceive of citizenship as an abstract status, but as an active practice involving simultaneous engagement in the family, local community, and the state.[10]

NOTES

1 Nellie McClung, *The New Citizenship* (Winnipeg: Political Equality League of Manitoba, c. 1912), 1.
2 Kathleen Canning and Sonya Rose, "Introduction," in *Gender, Citizenship and Subjectivities*, ed. Kathleen Canning and Sonya Rose (London: Blackwell, 2001), 2.
3 Sarah Carter, "Aboriginal People in Canada," in *Canada and the British Empire*, ed. Phillip Buckner (Toronto: Oxford, 2008), 208.
4 Renisa Mawani, *Colonial Proximities: Crossracial Encounters and Juridical Truths in British Columbia, 1871–1921* (Vancouver: UBC P, 2009), 121.
5 Sarah Carter, "Introduction," in *Wheat and Women* by Georgina Binnie-Clark (Toronto: U of Toronto P, 1914; repr. 2007), xix.
6 Janice Fiamengo, "Rediscovering Our Foremothers Again: The Racial Ideas of Canada's Early Feminists, 1885–1945," *Essays in Canadian Writing* 75 (Winter 2002), 86.
7 http://www.cinarc.org/Women.html.
8 M. Page Baldwin, "Subject to Empire: Married Women and the British Nationality and Status of Aliens Act," *Journal of British Studies* 40 (October 2001), 523.
9 Robert J. Sharpe and Patricia I. McMahon, *The Persons Case: The Origins and Legacy of the Fight for Legal Personhood* (Toronto: U of Toronto P, 2007), 7.
10. Laura Mayhall makes this point with reference to suffragists in Britain, but it is equally applicable to Canada. See Laura Mayhall, *The Militant Suffrage Movement: Citizenship and Resistance in Britain, 1860–1930* (Toronto: Oxford UP, 2003), 6.

A detailed biography of Nahnebahwequa – Catherine Sonego Sutton (1824–65) may be found on page 28.

Nahnebahwequa – Catherine Sutton

Speech to the Aborigines' Protection Society of London (1860)

"I felt rather a little cast down when I heard that in this large place, when you have a public meeting of this kind, a very few went; but I am glad to see with my own eyes there are such a number; and I am glad to find that there are friends to the poor Indians, to those that can't help themselves – that people will rise and be the friend of the poor Indian, the poor destitute people that can't help themselves. May God bless you. When I was first chosen by the council, my people thought that I had better dress in an Indian style; and they talked it over amongst themselves, and thought it was best I should come as a fully dressed Indian. But I told them, if they had chosen me to go, I was not going to go back to paganism after the Missionary had tried to civilize the Indians, and to make us like white people: and was I to go back and dress like pagan Indians, and come over here to shew myself? I told them I was not going to do that; and some said, 'It is best to let her go in her simple Christian dress and the Queen will know that we are civilized.' And I have been asked by different people why didn't I fetch my Indian dress. I tell them I had not, this was my dress; this is the way we dress. I tell them we are not pagan, that we try to be like white people – to be clean and decent, and do what we can to be like the civilized people. Well can I remember the time they could not speak a word of English; but the Missionaries have tried to civilize our little Indian children, and have even them under their own roofs. For many a time Father Cook, who was the first Missionary to come among the Indians – I think he came from the States – and he brought with him a school mistress, her name was Sophia Cook; she was the first one who taught us to say the ABC. She taught me the first English words I learned and she has prayed for me. And now I was once a little poor pagan child, but see what Christianity will do, and civilization will do, for the poor heathen children. And now I stand before you, that you may see what the Gospel has done for the poor Indian; and whilst the Missionary is working, the great head, the Indian Department, is striving to do their best to make the Indian civilized. But how can the poor Indian be civilized? As soon as he makes his land valuable then he is driven further back, and the poor Indian has to begin now again. It is said that the Indian is lazy; but he is lazy because he has also to go further back; he is only clearing the land for the white men, and making it valuable for the Indian Department; and so he has to go further back. And they know that the work they put on their land, that their children won't see the benefit of it; and since I have been over here I have made known what my people wished to have make known, and God has blessed me with great friends; he has opened the way, and I have found that there are many who stand up for the poor Indian; and I hope, by the blessing of God, they will not give it up, although I am now in my own home. But the interest they have taken may still grow, though the poor Indian has nothing to give in return but look there (pointing to the inscription on the wall), 'Do good and lend, hoping for nothing again, and ye shall be the children of the Highest.' Now my Christian friends, I hope that whilst the poor Indians are away off in their native country, that those who have taken up an interest in the poor Indian will not let it drop, but that many will be stood by and do what they can. Though since I have been here and made known our grievances to our dear Mother, the Queen, and she has been very kind, and received me very kindly, and have listened to the poor Indian that has been sent to her; and whilst all this is very good, and the Queen herself has promised her aid and protection; but still what can she do if all is against us? No; we want the people to help us, that know more than we know; we want people to help the poor Indian because they have been driven from one place to another. But now we are getting to the end of the peninsula, and where to go next we do not know. Since I have been in this country I have been told the Indian can purchase the land of that country, like the white people, and before I left home we could not purchase land; but since I have been here I have had a letter from my husband saying that we can purchase land – but on what conditions? Why, the Indian must be civilized; he must talk English, talk French, read and write and be well qualified for every thing before he can purchase land. Why, the poor Indians, none of them can go there. Poor things, how are they to get their education? And is that the way they do with your own people? Why, I can tell you something. I have seen some people in our country that came from your country that neither read nor write; and they came to buy Indian land. But the poor Indian must be so well qualified before he can have a house of his own! No, we want people to stand up for the poor Indian, and may God help us do what is right and do what is good, and we should do to others as we should others do to us. May God bless you, and may God bless my poor people, who are now merely a handful. These people they call monkeys: I know them well, and I think very few men that can stand equal with them. They are many of them noble-looking men; well, you would be surprised at what they can carry, and you would be surprised how many fish they will kill in an hour. If they were monkeys they would not do this." The speaker then resumed her seat amidst applause, with which she had also been frequently interrupted in the course of her address which she delivered with considerable force.

[Source: Nahnebahwequa (Catherine Sutton) in *The Colonial Intelligencer and Aborigines' Friend, 1859–1866*, vol. 2, new series (London: W. Tweedie), 156–7.]

Annie Parker was a member of the WCTU and Dominion Women's Enfranchisement Association. In 1891 she was named the superintendent of franchise for the Dominion WCTU.

Annie Parker
Women in Nation Building (1890)

[...] There are two features in nation-building which are peculiarly the work of woman, but which we are convinced have never yet received their just need of recognition, viz., the physical and the social. What is to be the physical character of the nation? Shall our sons and daughters be weak and nervous and puny of constitution, or, shall they have strength of bone and muscle and sinew, and vigor of brain? For answer we must look chiefly to the mothers. Whether we shall be a strong, pure, intellectual people depends most of all upon our women, and their just apprehension of all the possibilities attaching to the holy office of motherhood. As this subject is closely allied to "The Physical Culture of Women," which is to be treated in another chapter, we pass on to notice what we may designate the social up building of the nation. The savage nations give no evidence of culture, refinement or education. Their policy or custom of retaining their women in a state of degradation, has re-acted upon them with fearful retribution. They are themselves degraded, and exert no influence on the great stage of the world. They have no social life. Christianity which elevated woman is the force which has given to the world the measure of social organization we now possess, and it is safe to say, when the world reinstates woman, in the place which God originally assigned her as the equal of man, the first step will be taken to introduce the millennium. What we understand by the term society in its broadest sense, is no doubt under the domain of woman, and to her we must look for its maintenance in purity and its advances to the truest standard embodied in the teachings of God's word. A modern writer gives the following pen-picture of society: "The rich eating up the poor; the poor stabbing at the rich; fashion playing in the halls of gilded sensualism; folly dancing to the tune of ignorant mirth; intemperance gloating over its roast beef, or whiskey-jug, brandy-punch, champagne-bottle, bearing thousands upon thousands down to the grave of ignominy, sensualism and drunkenness." Does this picture portray a phase of Canadian society? We cannot say nay. Where is the remedy? Not in increasing wealth, for we have all seen wealth prostituted to just such uses. Not in education, for some of the best educated men are victims of drink and licentiousness. Not in culture or refinement for these have been known to be handmaidens of debauchery. Where then? The remedy is in the hands of Christian womanhood, through the application to society's laws and customs, of that cleansing element, the Gospel of our Lord Jesus Christ, which, as a personal force regenerates the individual. This is the key to the solution of all our social problems. To our bright young Canadian women, just stepping on the sphere of life's possibilities, we appeal. Give your allegiance to reconstructing the social life of the nation, on the line of one standard of virtue for the sexes, that you may command the purity that is exacted of you; the entire abolition of every form of alcoholic beverage that the fathers of your children may be sober men; the substitution of amusements requiring the exercise of brains instead of heels; the recognition of true worth wherever found, though it walk in fustian; and the knowing of God, His Sabbath, and His teaching. Surely here are aims worthy your best endeavor.

Thus we have indicated how, the basis of this superstructure of the State, lies the initial important work of woman and we claim that as no building can stand without a firm foundation, so no civilized nation can endure without this work of woman. Its necessity to our growth and stability stamps it with a dignity which demands a just recognition at the hands of the State.

It has been said by some distinguished writer that people carry their minds, much as they do their watches, content that they go, but indifferent as to the plan or quality of their mechanism. Just so, many people live from day to day and year to year accepting conditions as they find them, receiving standards as they are, without any thought of the why or how, the causes or effects, the good or evil. It is however well for the world, that there are also many who are possessed with the spirit of questioning; or reforming, or reconstructing; of righting old wrongs; and exploding old theories; leaving the old narrow trail, and hewing out a broader pathway for the march of human progress. The women of to-day have left the narrow trail. It was so narrow they had not room to grow. They have been toiling for ages in the great work of nation-building. In the home, the school, the great field of philanthropy, in social, moral and religious effort; in art, literature, commerce, medicine, missions: indeed in all departments of the nation's activities, with energy, fidelity, and success. And surely have earned a just title to rank as citizens, and be no longer classed by law with *infants* and *idiots*. Every advance of the cause of woman has been made through opposition; but in common with every righteous cause advances have been made, and the result has been fraught with abounding good to the nation. As reforms never go backward; the greatest reform, that which contains the germs of all true reforms; the political equality of women with men, will we trust at no very distant day be accomplished. But to this hour the boasted enlightenment of the nineteenth century takes us no further in the work of nation-building. It is ours only to deal with conditions resulting from certain evil legislation without power to improve it, though in every sense our "qualification" meets the standard which gives to men the voting power. Women may not protect themselves. Every intelligent person to-day knows that the ballot is the standard of value to the legislator. Electors secure their ends by the ballot. But not all the logic, for which the male sex are so wonderfully distinguished above the female, can convince our legislators that the woman has trained a band of boys up to honorable citizenship; who has led them from the cradle to the polls, and who moreover pays taxes in her own right; has as much interest in her country as the bloated whiskey sot who sells his franchise for fifty cents!

We read that the fundamental idea of the State is justice. "For what is the State," says Cicero, "if not a Society of Justice?" More pithily, Cousin says, "Justice personified – that is the State." But the State has reversed the plan of God. God made man and woman equal. "He said unto *them*" – "have dominion." The State has made woman inferior. As a flash of light in darkness, and even as a sure work of prophecy, it is borne in upon us: "How apt the personification of justice!" A WOMAN blindfolded holding balances, and a sword, denoting that she is no respecter of persons, but weighs and decides according to law; and impartially executes its decisions! Passing through that wonderful structure known as Brooklyn bridge, which a woman's brain so helped to construct, we look upon the figure of "Liberty enlightening the world." Is it not an impressive fact, that it is a *woman's* hand that holds the light? Liberty and justice! The battle-cry of ages, personified by woman! May we not accept this fact as emblematic of the future, when both Liberty and Justice shall be given to woman?

The question is often asked, why do women desire political equality? We may say, first, as a matter of simple justice, that they may have the right to defend themselves, and secondly, because the ballot is the point at which public opinion takes hold on public action. It is the point where sentiment crystallizes into law. It is the instrument by which we may infuse into the corporate body of the State that Christianity which, as a personal force in the individual, renews the nature, and puts him in harmony with the designs and will of God. Though, as we have seen, women are neither idlers nor a burden to the State, but perform all the functions of useful citizens, they are yet debarred from impressing their God-given characteristics upon the nation, by the very power that admits to the full franchise, the vicious, the drunken and the illiterate.

It is therefore little wonder that politics, the science of government, highest of all sciences, has degenerated into that "soiled thing," our virtuous statesmen "fear to have women touch." But, as Henry Ward Beecher said, "Woman dawned into literature and changed the spirit of letters. When she became a reader, men no longer wrote as if for men. She enforced purity and higher decorum." It is not then, that woman will sink to the "low level of politics," but rather that she will lift politics to their proper sphere.

The "womanizing of society," or the reconstruction of the State upon the broader basis involving the principle of political equality, means the introduction of elements that in their very nature tend to consolidate and perpetuate the nation.

The qualities in womanhood which revere purity and chastity, embodied in the national laws, would rid us of evils under which we groan; and snap the fetters these evils are now forging, with which to bind the yet unborn. That quality of womanhood which shrinks from the spilling of blood, woven into national law, will make for that triumph of conscience, intellect and humanity, over the mere brute force which men call war, and hasten the day when "swords shall be beaten into plough-shares and spears into pruning-hooks." That quality of womanhood which instinctively guards the innocence and purity of youth, woven into national law, will accord to the young of the State the highest protection from destruction; and licensed sins, either of liquor selling or prostitution, will be blotted from the Nation's Statute Books. To the mind of woman the presence of an evil demands a wherefore. It demands also a removal. And the problem "how to do it?" is sure to be demonstrated. "Ah" said that school janitor, "they have put women on our school board, and for the first time in my life, I'm ordered to clean and air the cellar."

In every true Canadian woman's heart there is a strong aspiration after the ideal nation, built on the best foundation: God, Freedom, Righteousness, Love, exhaustless fisheries, illimitable forests and mineral wealth, of boundless extent; with a territory large enough for the homes of 40,000,000; free from the blighting evils that affect and torment older lands; with the opportunity to graft upon our young national stock the best elements of the four or five nationalities that claim kinship with us; why should not Canada lead the world today, in all that makes for human progress? "May we not hope in shaping our nation life to avoid the mistakes of older nations?" Is it too much to expect, that with the records of all peoples open before us, we may learn lessons of wisdom and dealing with our problems, make precedents to suit ourselves?

Is this fair land to be cursed with the vile and degrading liquor traffic, whose destructive influences flow on from generation to generation?

Is our country to lift up its voice against the command of the God of Heaven, and secularise His holy day?

Are we Canadians to yield ourselves and our children's children to be yoked in the bondage of priest craft and Romish oppression?

Shall we ever, in servile truculence to partisanship, forgetting our manhood, and our god-given convictions, compromise with unrighteousness? We trust not! Great is our heritage of light and liberty and Christian teaching! Great things will God require of us!

What if we have no landed aristocracy, if every man and woman bears the stamp of Nature's nobility, honest industry?

What if we have no great tenanted estates, if every man be his own landlord?

What if we have no princely palaces absorbing treasure, if the riches of the nation flow out to bless all the people? What if we have no inherited royalty, if we are the children and servants of the King of kings?

Women of Canada, around whose board sit the statesmen of the future, the lawyers, judges, physicians, the legislators, ministers, mechanics, and perchance the inventors of the next generation, how important is our work! "No man liveth to himself!" The principles of righteousness must be implanted by us. It must be "precept upon precept, line upon line, here a little and there a little." We want to grow patriotism of that holy type which shall harmonize with all the claims the God of nations makes! We want every man and woman, every boy and girl, inspired with the ambition to do their best for their country.

Let Canadians respect themselves! Let us respect our laws and institutions! Let us speak proudly of *our* country, and God grant that Canada, under His divine guidance, may yet give the world the highest ideal it has ever known.

"And it shall be to me a name of joy, praise and an honor before all the nations of the earth, which shall hear all the good that I do unto them and they shall fear and tremble for all the goodness and for all the prosperity that I procure unto it."

[Source: (Mrs Dr) Annie Parker, "Women in Nation Building," in *Woman, Her Character, Culture and Calling*, ed. B.F. Austin (1890), 462–6.]

The Methodist Women's Missionary Society assumed responsibility for the "rescue" of Chinese girls and women from prostitution and slavery in Victoria, BC, in 1887. That year the organization opened the Chinese Rescue Home (later renamed the Oriental Home and School). The MWMS provided funds to hire a succession of women, including Elizabeth Cantwell, who was the first to speak Cantonese, to act as matron of the home.

Elizabeth Cantwell, Methodist Women's Missionary Society
Report of Chinese Rescue Home, Victoria, BC (1892–1893)

Report of Chinese Rescue Home, Victoria, BC

| | Names of inmates | | Ages | Time since rescue | |
No.	Chinese	English	Years	Years	Months
1	San Kam	Gertrude	16	6	5
2	Kam Ho	Mary	17	4	6
3	Don Choy	Daisy	17	4	5
4	Loi Hoi	Jessie	13	4	2
5	Yuen Kee	Edith	13	2	10
6	Ah Kui	Emma	10	2	10
7	Wong Ah Hor	Martha	16	1	10
8	Chong Lin	Rose	21	1	5
9	Sun Hang	Sarah	28		11
10	Ah Quai	Laura	15		7
11	Mon Yeo		24		1
12	Yuet Lin		6		1

The time having come for the annual report, I recall the many mercies of the past year with devout gratitude to our heavenly Father.

The case most requiring medical aid has been that of our bright little Jessie, who, we feared, was not only going to lose the sight of one eye, but that the eye itself would have to be removed; but I am thankful that, although the sight is impaired, it has recovered. Dr McKecknie most kindly gave her daily attendance for three or four weeks, and performed two operations. In the last he was assisted by Dr Jones, and we looked to the Divine Healer, whose power is now not less than in the days of His humanity. Gertrude also had an operation performed on her eyelids by Drs Hall and McKecknie, which was a great benefit to her sight. Some of the girls had slight attacks of influenza last winter, but we had not other serious illness.

It has been a year of contest with the iniquitous traffic in Chinese women and girls. One was rescued from the destroyer and brought to the Home two weeks after she arrived from China. Another was prevented from landing, and after being taken from port to port for some weeks was finally shipped back to China, thus helping to make the trade unprofitable to those engaged in it.

Another that we made a great effort to reach and hope to save is still in evil surroundings, but the time may soon come for her deliverance. The twelve persons named in the list are all now in the Home except Gertie, who is at present at New Westminster, but may return very soon. The woman Nun Yeo came voluntarily to escape the ill-usage of a first wife. She brought with her a bright little girl of about 6. I will give the circumstances more fully elsewhere. She seems very willing to learn and teachable. It is our hearts' desire and prayer that while they are here they may find the way of salvation, the peace of great price.

Our Friday afternoon prayer-meetings are now very well attended, and great interest appears to be taken in the scripture lesson by the married girls and a few others who have been in the habit of attending occasionally. No altogether new ones come. We have had as many as twenty-six Chinese women and children at one time. We trust that these meetings are times of spiritual help and refreshing.

Messrs Hall and Ross still continue their generous donation of rice for the girls in the Home. Our thanks are due to them and the other friends who take an interest in "The Home" and manifest it by gifts and prayers.

Elizabeth Cantwell

[Source: Methodist Women's Missionary Society, *Twelfth Annual Report*, 1892–3, xl–xli.]

The first Canadian branch of the Chinese Empire Ladies Reform Association was formed in Victoria in 1903. This organization was affiliated with the all-male Chinese Empire Reform Association or Baohuanghui. The Victoria branch's first president was Kang Tongbi, the daughter of Kang Youwei, who formed the all-male Chinese Empire Reform Association in 1899. Tongbi was a vocal supporter of the women's movement in China and after her arrival in North America pursued a university education at Barnard College. Another branch was formed in Vancouver in 1904 and was composed primarily of the wives and daughters of the more affluent members of the Chinese community.

Chinese Empire Ladies Reform Association, Vancouver (1904)

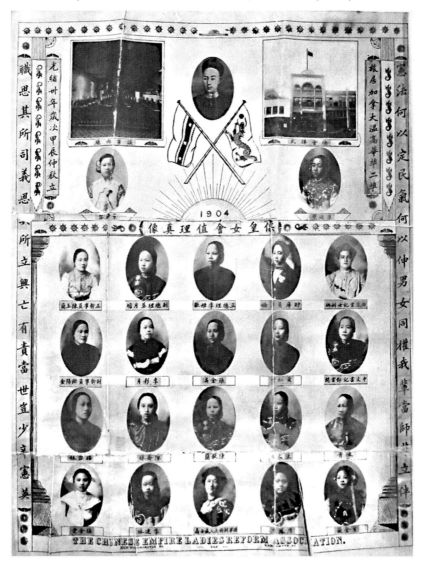

[Source: Vancouver City Archives, Chinese Empire Ladies Reform Association, Vancouver, 1904.]

Emily Murphy Ferguson, aka Janey Canuck (1868–1933), was born to a prominent Ontario family whose father was a wealthy landowner. Later married to an Anglican minister, she combined family life, writing, and engagement in a wide range of women's reform activities. Living first in Manitoba and later Alberta, she published four books of personal reflections including *Open Trails* (1912). She spearheaded the campaign to secure dower rights for widows in Alberta and played an active role in numerous women's groups including the Canadian Women's Press Club and the Federated Women's Institutes of Canada. Appointed as a police magistrate in 1916, Murphy later led the effort to have women legally designated as "persons."

Emily Murphy
From *Open Trails* (1912)

> There is a world outside the one you know,
> To which for curiousness, 'ell can't compare
>   KIPLING

There is no good and sufficient reason why I should not ride out and meet the Indians. They are to be the guests of the citizens during Fair Week, and I am a citizen even if I may not vote as to how I shall be taxed, or how I shall be hanged. Yes! I shall ride out, and say "Good welcome to this place!"

There are seventy-five wagon loads of Indians in the procession, and I have the distinction of being the only citizen. I feel guiltily white. I ride ahead with the young men and the chiefs, up the hills, down the hills, through the streets, across the river, down the golf-links, and out to the camping-grounds under the shadow of the old Hudson's Bay Fort. My esquires have been three days coming in from the Reserve. They are not talkative till I offer to trade horses; then it is my turn to take refuge in silence. Did I understand you to say the Indian has no genius for grasping essentials? Did I?

It only took four minutes to hoist the tepee poles and shroud on the canvas. It would probably have been done in three if I had not turned the poles wrong end up.

The girls are brightly good-humoured and intelligent. Marie Louise has a mouth the colour of blood-lilies. God told her to laugh with it, and He has inclined her heart to keep this law. The men-folk tether the ponies – stealthy-footed ponies, with absurd, knitted garters tied round their necks – cut the wood, light fires, and amuse the papooses.

The only problems here are those of bread and butter. They do not even worry about elective affinities. I warn you they are a commonplace lot.

The bucks unlace the moss-bags, cocoons, or whatever the casings may be called, and free the babies' hands. Soul o' me! but a Cree brave may have a soft, wheedling tongue. The old women sit around and smoke. Their faces bear the imprint of monotony. This tottering beldame, with skin like a wrinkled prune, is the very sybil who had already lived seven hundred years when Aeneas went to Italy. She gave Aeneas instructions, you remember, how to find his father in the infernal regions, and even conducted him to the very entrance of hell.

While the meal is being cooked, sundry of the young men play cards. There be philosophers who say the cheerful loser is winner. This has no application to poker. All the cheerful loser gets is experience. These youths have a good method in that they do not hold a post-mortem inquest on each hand, as white folk do. The game's the thing!

What are these Indians eating? I do not know. It is some part of the insides of animals with which I am not familiar. It looks tough. But, after all, what the Indian eats does not matter so much as what he digests; and then he can eat what he wants to in Lent.

Some of the men have long hair and wear their blankets toga fashion, just as the lawyers do in the Royal Courts of Justice, in the Strand. One old, old man is particularly mark worthy. He has a gaunt old head that might have been mod-elled with a tomahawk, and a chest like a draught horse. His eyes are bright bronze, and look out from under his brows like Q-F guns from their portholes. He and his old mate-woman are pitiably poor. I hope they are chums. How else could they live on? If I had the dictatorship of creation, men and women would be born thirty and remain thirty. Babies would be a separate race of beings – just as angels are – and should exist merely for purposes of discipline.

In one tent a white man of thirty or up lives with a squaw. He may be unhap-py but, be it said to his credit, he lives out his mistake gamely. All teachers and literary critics are agreed that the hero of "Locksley Hall" is a most romantic fellow with a praiseworthy philosophy of life. Yet at one time he seriously considered the desirability of being "mated with a squalid savage," of rearing an iron-jointed, supple-sinewed brood who would whistle back the parrot's call and hurl their lances in the sun. He greatly desired this, but, in the end, he was a coward, and ranted and canted about "the Christian child." He made a virtue out of his impotence, this philosopher with the covetous eyes, and was not big enough to break the conventions that stood in his way.

It is so easy to be good; it requires no effort at all. Only strong people may sin with impunity; only greater ones may live up to their sins. Those who fail are outcasts. There is only a finger's fillip between a hero and a rogue. For my part, I think this philosopher was a prig and weakling, and that Cousin Amy did well "to sympathise with clay."

While there are positive disadvantages in the Indian's method of living – such as the unaesthetic intimacies of wedded life in an 8 by 12 tent – on the other hand there are superlative compensations. They have no perpetual arrears of unfinished work, and they know nothing of transcendentalism, microbes, or Mrs. Eddy. They do not pay taxes, have no "at home" days, do not have to re-bind their skirts, and get no offensive yellow bills intimating that their water supply will be cut off at the main unless promptly paid for. They need not serve on a jury, or in the militia. They need not Fletcherise their food, need not shave, and never heard of a financial stringency. They keep their appendixes inside, where they properly belong, and their children know nothing of a punctual, pitiless school-bell. Of what other blessed race can this be said? Not even of the early Christians!

The Persians taught their children three things – riding, truthfulness, and archery. Even so the Indians. There are quite a few of us who think we might imitate them with advantage.

So far as I am able to deduce from the conversations I have heard, the Indian's deadly and unpardonable sin lies in the fact that he has not made money. And how, pray tell me, can a man make money when his blood is mixed with the sap of trees?

[...]

[Source: Emily Murphy, *Open Trails* (London: Casell, 1912), 77–82.]

Georgina Binnie-Clark (1871–1947) was born in Dorset, England. A journalist, she travelled to Canada in 1905 with the intention of writing a travel account of her experiences. Visiting her brother who was farming in the Qu'Appelle Valley, Binnie-Clark decided to remain and purchased land nearby. In 1914 she published *Wheat and Women*, which documented her experiences as a woman farmer on the prairies and criticized existing homestead legislation that restricted single women from receiving free land. She became a public proponent in the feminist campaign to reform homestead laws.

Georgina Binnie-Clark
From *Wheat and Women* (1914)

[...] The faithful chronicle of one's own difficulties may at first though appear but a poor foundation for one's hope and firm belief that agriculture will prove to be the high-road and foundation of wealth and independence for Woman, but the strength of a chain is in its weakest link. To command complete and uninterrupted success for an agricultural experiment on the Canadian prairie or anywhere else, a certain amount of training in the theory and practice of agriculture is necessary, and also some knowledge of stock-raising, capital in adequate relation to one's proposition whether it is to be worked out on five or five hundred acres of land, a commercial instinct and a true vocation for life on the land, an innate love and understanding of animal and vegetable life. I had no training, inadequate capital and my commercial instinct, thought strong in theory, is weak in practice – I fail to hold my own in buying or selling, and should never discuss price except on paper. But in spite of this, and the fact that I am still behind my conviction that three hundred and twenty acres of good land in Canada can be worked to produce a net profit of £500 per annum to its owner, my weak link is very much stronger than at the time I sent out for Ottawa to claim the right of women to their share of homestead land of Canada.

On my way from the West I gathered news and considerable encouragement from the press-women of Winnipeg and Fort William. At Winnipeg I met Miss Cora Hind, who is the editor of the commercial page of the most powerful organ of Western Canada – the *Manitoba Free Press*. To her is entrusted the responsibility of first voice in the opinion, and report and publication of information which concerns the agricultural side of the industrial development of that section of the British Empire which attracts the interest of the world. It is hardly necessary to add that she has no parliamentary vote. The strongest weapon that she holds in her professional equipment is her instinct for the weak link in the chain, and this is backed by excellent mental balance, wide experience, and impregnable honesty. I found her enthusiastic about everything connected with the expansion of resource for women, and kindly and deeply interested in the prospect of agriculture, in which she was theoretically well up.

From her and Mrs Lilian Graham, and Mrs Sherk of Fort William, I learned that Canadian women had already taken up the matter of Homesteads for Women with a deep sense of injustice of a law which, whilst seeking to secure the prosperity of the country in enriching the stranger, ignores the claim of the sex which bore the brunt of the battle in those early and difficult days when every inch of our great wheat-garden of the North-West had to be won with courage and held with endurance. No pen can depict the fine part that Woman played in the spade work of expansion in Canada, although history throws many a search-light over the past, which discovers her claim to an equal share in the land which over a hundred years ago she helped to win by travail and hold by toil.

It is still among the pleasing traits of Canada that 'men in great places' are easy of access; throughout the Dominion there rules between man and man a common respect for Time. When I reached Ottawa Mr Scott, the Commissioner of Immigration, received me at once, told me his full mind on some facts and conditions of immigrants and immigration, and listened to all that I had to say about women-farmers and homestead land. I learned with regret that Hon. Frank Oliver had left Ottawa that day for the Christmas recess, but Mr Scott advised me to see the Deputy-Minister – Mr Cory, with whom he fixed an appointment for the following morning.

Mr Cory was kind and wore the anxious-to-please air of the professional politician which is always soothing, but I think he knew rather less of the practical side of agriculture than I of Blue books, and, just as I had anticipated, firstly, lastly, and all the time the argument, 'she can't.' However, there was a promise to place the matter before the Minister of Interior on his return. But I never discussed the matter with Mr Oliver. Not long before the fall of the Liberal party I heard that Miss Cora Hind had seen him on the matter, and that he had arrived at a decision to refuse to recommend the expansion of home-steading law in order to permit women to homestead because he considered it would be against the main interest of the country. He argued that the object of granting the land-gift to men is to induce them to take home on the prairie – home in the centre of their agricultural pursuit. He held the first requirement of the genuine home-maker to be a wife: he marries, he has a family, etc., etc. Women, he assumes, are already averse to marriage, and he considered that to admit them to the opportunities of the land-grant would be to make them more independent of marriage than ever. The reason was at least flattering to the Woman-Framer if it was unpromising to the race; but the birth rate of Canada is not nearly as high as it should be, so perhaps Maeterlinck's 'Blue Bird' has warned the myriad of 'winged thoughts' eagerly awaiting their human moment against the trap of the 'homesteader's requirement.'

Since there was not the smallest hope of official encouragement, the only way of going on seemed to lie in refusing to give up, so I did what I could alone and very imperfectly. I have neither sufficient capital nor experience to carry out my 'women and wheat' experiment in any way other than by teaching my would-be women-farmers what to avoid and to give them the opportunity of learning by actually working with the horses and implements on the land. The double responsibility naturally needed even more knowledge and training and patience and endurance than the chronicled end of my experiment, but over and over again I recognized the splendid qualities I had always believed to be in women, and I don't think a woman ever worked on my wheatland without discovering a finer energy and stronger and more independent Self than she dreamed she possessed [...]

[Source: Georgina Binnie-Clark, *Wheat and Women*, intro. Sarah Carter (Toronto: U of Toronto P, 1914; repr. 2007), 306–8.]

A detailed biography of Marion Francis Beynon (1884–1951) may be found on page 144.

Marion Francis Beynon
The Foreigner (1914)

In a recent issue of a certain daily paper there appeared a letter criticizing some of the pictures in the Winnipeg Art Gallery. To the writer's opinion of art in general and the moral effect of this exhibit in particular we are utterly indifferent, but that any reputable newspaper should have allowed a certain sentence in that letter to pass censorship in this supposedly enlightened age is a matter of comment.

The sentence to which we take very indignant exception is this: "It is also painful to think that the portraits of two negresses possibly late attendants in disorderly houses, should be allowed to besmirch the walls."

The pictures referred to are merely two very excellent and respectably portraits of negresses and the only reason for the base insinuation against the originals is the writer's race hatred.

That there are those mean and cowardly enough to cast such an unfair aspersion on a people not strong enough in the community, either numerically or financially, to make an effective protest is conceivable, but that a paper with any standing in the community should lend its columns to so contemptible an end gives one a shock of surprise.

Because we of the Anglo-Saxon race have been able to bully less militant and aggressive peoples into handing over their territory to us is a poor basis for the assumption that we as a race are the anointed of God and the one and only righteous and virtuous people.

Even if we would draw the curtain of forgetfulness over certain dark and unbeautiful passages of our history, ancient and modern, and believe ourselves to be all that we ought to be, it would hardly justify us in denying the claims of any other race to those same virtues. Certainly nothing could excuse the brutality of such wholesale condemnation of another race merely because it does not happen to be born of the same color as ourselves.

The pity is that this base innuendo that any and all of the women of the African race are apt to be immoral is all of a piece with a too common attitude on the part of our race towards foreigners. We throw the doors of our country wide open to them and when they enter we treat them as if they were the very dust beneath our feet. The wonder is that they submit so patiently to this unchristian treatment and struggle as hard as many of them do to become good citizens of our country.

[Source: Marion Francis Beynon, "The Foreigner," *Grain Growers' Guide,* 11 February 1914.]

The Local Council of Jewish Women (LCJW) was first established in the United States in 1893 to assist Jewish immigrants. A Toronto branch was founded in 1897 and others subsequently followed in other Canadian urban centres such as Montreal and Winnipeg. A voluntary organization, the LCJW aided Jewish women and their families in the areas of education and social service.

Lily B. Levetus
Local Council of Jewish Women (in Toronto) (1915)

Another year has been added to the life of our Toronto Council of Jewish Women, and we feel we are not only striving to make our Society a power for good in our own community, but eager, as a body, to work for the good of our city.

It is gratifying to report that twenty-one members have been added to our membership list during the year, making a total of 115. Our Program Committee has helped to build up Council interest by inviting to our bi-monthly meetings, men and women of distinction and authority, who have given their wisest thought and best talent to our Council audiences. So far this year we have had addresses from Prof. Squair of Toronto University, Dr Stephan Wise of New York, Mrs Willoughby Cummings, Mrs Grant Needham, Rabbi Jacobs and others.

In the department of Immigrant Aid, no work is more important and none more far-reaching, nor does any give any greater opportunity for the expression of true womanly service. Every year hundreds of foreign girls come to our city to earn a livelihood, many leaving other countries on account of conditions there. The immigrant is given much misinformation in regard to Canada, and on arrival is apt to get false impressions of Canadian ideals, standards and ways. We must correct this misinformation and help them, by putting them into touch with the best of Canadian life.

Our Jewish Working Girls' Club, at 254 McCaul Street, was organized to protect, educate and uplift the Jewish working girls. This Club now has 200 members. Last year three thousand attendances were registered. So far this year we have 3,376. Besides classes in English, instructions are given in dress-making, fancywork, calisthenics and dancing. During this winter on Saturday evenings we have converted our Assembly Room into a dance hall. At these social affairs, special invitations are extended to any boyfriend a girl may wish to invite. Supplying the girls with this recreation has been a successful feature of our work, as it has weaned them from the allurements of the public dance halls, and awakens in them a feeling of social responsibility. A close touch is kept with our girls by personal talks and friendly visiting.

The Junior Council of Women has looked after the unemployed girl this winter. Work has been procured wherever possible, and assistance given to those boarding with strangers. We have forty ladies assist in making the work a success.

The Children's Sewing School has done splendid work. Little girls between the ages of seven and fourteen years are taught every Tuesday afternoon, from 4 to 6 o'clock, all branches of sewing, from the simplest stitches to the more advanced stages of apron and underwear making. We have enrolled 290 girls this year – 24 ladies each week assist with the work.

After the outbreak of war, our President, Mrs Kahn, called a meeting, not only for our members, but all women interested in furnishing money and supplies for the comforts of soldiers. The Montefore Patriotic League was formed, from which has been sent numerous supplies to the British regiments on the firing line.

Respectfully submitted,
Lily B. Levetus, Corresponding Secretary.

[Source: *Report of the Local Council of Women of Toronto*, issue 22 (1915), 55–6.]

Mrs Donald Shaw

African United Baptist Association an Organization Nova Scotia Should Be Proud of (1920)

The First Congress of Colored Women to Be Held in All Canada Assembles in Halifax. The Aims and Ambitions of This Splendid Band of Women Representing Nearly 40,000 Colored People in Nova Scotia.

Halifax, which has already been the scene of many events that have been recorded in the history of the British Empire has added yet another page to her annals. On Thursday last, at the Cornwallis Street Baptist Church, took place the first congress of colored women which has been held, not only in Nova Scotia, but in the Dominion of Canada. Fifty delegates, representative women of the great movement which is now in progress towards the general uplift of the colored population of Canada, attended the convention which was remarkably successful in every way. The ladies, all at first a little strange and self-conscious at taking their first step into public life, were full of interest and enthusiasm, and the promoters of the movement have every reason to be proud and gratified with the result of their initial effort to organize the women of their race as a great auxiliary force to the work of their church in Canada, and also of the sincerity and earnestness and intelligence with which the whole affair was carried out from start to finish.

At this first convention of the Ladies of the African United Baptist Association of Nova Scotia, the proceedings opened at eleven o'clock in the morning with a service of prayer and hymns, followed by the roll-call of the officers, after which the photographer claimed the undivided attention of the entire body of delegates and organizers. Owing to the fact that the little church had not suitable ground for the photographs to be taken on its precincts, an adjournment was necessary to the nearest cleared place which happened to be at the site of St George's church on Brunswick Street and the needful procession thence occasioned quite a bit of interest in the neighbourhood.

The afternoon meeting was of a strictly business nature and opened as in the morning with a short service and hymns. The Rev. W.A. White then welcomed delegates to the Cornwallis church, Rev. W.E. Thompson replying and there followed addresses by Rev. W.A. Wyse, Mr J.A.R. Kinney, Rev. W.N. States, Bro. T. Johnson, Dea. J.A. Thomas, Rev. M.P. Montgomery and short general discussion of the work, in the course of which, the women were appealed to to unite in a determined effort to raise the status of the colored race, and the following ladies pledge themselves as willing to make any sacrifice they might be called upon to undertake in the interests of the cause: Mrs W.A. Wise, Mrs Maggie M. Upshaw, Mrs W.N. States, Mrs Louisa Bundy, Mrs Maggie Walsh, Mrs Sophie Williams. Mrs J.A.R. Kinney, Mrs Annie Thompson, Mrs Sarah Clayton and Mrs Ida Harris. It was decided that their first effort should be devoted to the sale of 1,000 good-will tickets at 25 cents each; an excursion; the sale of 4,000 single tickets for the benefit of the Home for Colored Children at 25 cents each and a fair.

The Meeting held at 8:15 in the evening was open to the public, and the church was filled to its utmost capacity. A well-balanced program of addresses, solos and choir singing was presented, followed by the passing of votes of thanks to the executive of the Ladies' Auxiliaries of the African Baptist Association of Nova Scotia, to the members of the Cornwallis Street Baptist Church for placing it at the disposal of the convention, and to the pastor, Rev. W. White and Mrs White, who as choral-master was responsible for the excellent music rendered, to Miss Mary Symonds, organist, and members of the choir, also to those who had entertained the visiting delegates, and to the ladies who had prepared and read papers. The whole affair wound up with a banquet of the delegates.

Probably there may be many people who are unaware of the very important factor which the colored people of Nova Scotia form in the province. Numbering between 35,000 and 40,000, fully 90% of them are members of the Baptist Church and Nova Scotia has twenty churches of that denomination entirely supported by the colored people. A large number of these people are descendents of those of their race who threw their lot in with the families they served in the States and came to Canada when the Revolution in that country drove the United Empire Loyalists to seek fresh homes under the British flag – others are descendants of those who were sent out in the early days of the development of the province, and hence all are a component part of the actual people of Nova Scotia, and their interests are as much bound up in her growth and prosperity as those of any of the white brethren. Therefore, this new effort to organize the women on identically the same basis as those followed by the promoters of women's development amongst the white races, and to train them and instruct them in the laws of citizenship and participation in the nation's welfare is of as much importance to every man or woman interested in Canada's progress as it is to the promotion of the movement and the members of the Convention.

It marks an epoch, small in itself perhaps, but nonetheless a vital and important one, and one that is fraught with great possibilities in the future if maintained and carried on sound and practical lines.

Mr Kinney's eloquent address in which he gave many interesting statistics regarding the work and its objective, touched on this particular point, vis. the ultimate union of the colored and white races for the general betterment of the world, and quoted the words written by a white man which are touchingly true and significant:

Again I slept, I seemed to climb a hard ascending track;
And just behind me labored one whose patient face was black;
I pitied him, but hour by hour he gained upon the path,
He stood beside me, stood upright – and then turned in wrath
"Go back," he cried, "What right have you to walk beside me hence?
For you are black and I am white" – I paused struck dumb with fear
For lo the black man was not there, but Christ stood in his place.
And oh! the pain, the pain, the pain, that looked upon his face.

Mrs W.N. States in a short but very interesting speech sketched the history of the colored race in Nova Scotia, and made special mention of the great facilities afforded by the Province of Nova Scotia towards the population of the colored population, all doors being opened to them. Mrs A.W. Thompson dealt with the necessity for women to realize their own responsibilities in the new fields opening up to them, to the widening out of their children's prospects in education and citizenship, and to the wonderful possibilities that lie open today for the girls of the rising generation and to fit themselves for public life as teachers or nurses. Miss Marjorie Butler, President of the Dorcas Girls' Society spoke briefly on the needs of the girl who devotes her attention to domestic service, and pointed out the need for community work in organizing clubs or hostels where girls may find sympathy, help and recreation. Mrs J.A.R. Kinney gave a short concise paper on the ideals of Christian womanhood; Mrs C.M. Saunders, who holds the position of Superintendent of the Bureau of Social Service at the Cornwallis Street Church, in her paper, reviewed the various points on which the social and mission worker must be trained. Mrs Maggie Upshaw, the official organizer of the Convention, explained the need for efficient organization and the methods of carrying out the ideals which the Convention pledges itself to support and uphold and Mrs Fred A. Pelley presented a paper on education.

The reporter of the *Sunday Leader* was honored by an invitation to the banquet and presented with a delegate's badge of scarlet ribbon as a memento of the primal efforts to organize the colored women of Canada, a little trophy which may in the lifetime of the writer, come to represent the inception of a possibly world-wide movement to really raise the status of people, who, though differing in complexion, are akin in sentiment and feeling, in desires and aspirations, to those with whom they are even now beginning to work shoulder to shoulder, instead of one behind the other.

[Source: Mrs Donald Shaw, "African United Baptist Association an Organization Nova Scotia Should Be Proud of," *Sunday Leader* (Halifax, NS), 13 June 1920.]

Anonymous
The Pays Des Iroquois – The Six Nations of Grand River (1923)

The Alliance has recently been asked to take up the question of certain alleged injustices suffered by the women of the Pays des Iroquois and the following details received in a letter sent to us in answer to some inquiries will probably be of interest to our readers.

"The Six Nations are governed by the wise old laws of Hiawatha and his Chiefs, which are greatly admired. It is probably in memory of the woman who inspired Hiawatha and Dekanawideh to form (or renew) a League of Nations to preserve peace in the sixteenth century, that ever since the *women* of the six peaceful nations who responded have had the privilege of naming the Government or Chiefs who form the Council of the Six Nations, ie seven Chiefs from each nation. I understand the women watch the career of each before choosing him as worthy. These people have long had the referendum and woman suffrage and other sage laws, and are an example to all the Red Race in their lives of industry and self-support as agriculturalists. They have their annual agricultural fair, which compares favourably with any in America. The Council meets in a fine building with great ceremony always when the old wampum belts – relics of the past – are carried in. They have a Speaker and a Secretary. A certain proposal from Canada was recently addressed to 'the Chiefs and Warriors' and males of 'over 21' were asked to vote to ratify any settlement, but the Council answered wisely to the negative, including the complaint that the *women* of Grand River had been overlooked."

[Source: "The Pays Des Iroquois – The Six Nations of Grand River," *Jus Suffragii* 18, no. 3 (December 1923), 43.]

Sarah Robertson Matheson (1863–1943) was a Scottish poet and member of the Anti-Slavery and Aborigines' Protection Society which was headquartered in London, England. She wrote many letters to the Canadian government advocating on behalf of First Nations people. Among the issues she took up was the removal of women's political rights on Six Nations.

Sarah Robertson Matheson
An Appeal to "Women of the World" (1925)

May 6, 1925

Women of the World,

May I on behalf of our sisters the Iroquois or Six Nations, women of Grand River, Ontario, protest against Canada's recent deprivation of these good women's *Immemorial Rights* which they have wisely and successfully used since, or even before, the time of their forbear Hiawatha?

If this were required it would be seen what a great wrong has been done to these peaceful people – the world's *first* League of Nations as inspired by *a woman* whom they still call "the Great Mother." They have always before chosen and nominated the Chiefs for the Council, and other rights and with their laws well admired by both ancient and modern historians and I beg that the world women will now take their hand and help them in their sorrow, and fear of a threatened existence and dark future which the old happy conditions would have guarded as if ever before.

Hoping that we may have the honour of an answer, and happy to give all details.

                              S. Robertson Matheson (Mrs)
                              Ka-tsi-tsa-non-nen (adopted by the Iroquois in 1919)

Source: LAC, MG28, vol. 29, Prospective Councils, File – Canada, Letter to the International Council of Women, from Mrs S. Robertson Matheson, 6 May 1925.

Emily General

Letter to Rica Flemyng Gyll, British and Foreign Anti-Slavery Society and Aborigines' Protection Society (1925)

Extracts from letter

                                                    Caledonia, Ontario
                                                    March 19, 1925

I cannot tell you very much because I don't hear very much about my people, perhaps because I am so deeply absorbed in my studies.

As for the folks who have been abused by our Government officials, I know little about. Mr S. Isaac was put in jail, as undoubtedly you have heard, for a little while but long before his times was up, they found out that he was not guilty and let him come back home.

The mock council are working hard to accomplish something. They are going to build a road so they say through our (reserve) as they call it. There are a lot of things they are going to do, but I do not know where they are going to get their funds. It will cost a great deal and when our money is gone we cannot pay for the up-keep of the improvements and then, where will we poor, ignorant inefficient Indians go. I often think that. There are a number of us who are very inefficient to sudden changes. It will not do us a bit of good to come under new influences. It will only crush us out of existence. Truly there are a number of industrious fairly well-to-do Indians who could withstand the change perhaps for a while. But we have not a right to choose for ourselves?

You spoke in your last letter about the population remaining the same. The why of that I do not know, perhaps because we are being crowded by a superior race.

All the same we are still trying to do something. There is communication between our people here and Deskaheh who is still in [the] United States. He is trying to raise our prestige; he speaks often even on radio.

The members of the mock council threaten that if Deskaheh comes back they are going to do something to him. I don't know just what they intend to do, – sue him for treason perhaps. The mock council [is] only what you would call a figure-head. Mr Col. Cecil B. Morgan is doing the ruling. What he says is to be carried out. Some protest against the adoption of the Indian Act (that is among the councilors) and he said: "Why that is what brought you the elective system, you cannot do without it." So you see the councilors are bound and have no power to vote Mr Morgan's decisions. That is just what we have been a long time fighting against (the Indian Act) and now they have enforced it upon us regardless of the protest we made.

Sometimes I think we should have made our feelings felt more seriously and many think the same. It is pretty hard to see yourself and your people crushed out without a word to say for themselves.

I don't think I would mind so very much if we did have councilors so long as their foundation was not built upon the Indian Act which binds us so entirely to dependence upon the department. For many many years Indians have ruled themselves by chiefs and now in these enlightened days are we to be crushed under by another race.

The white race prides themselves on their modern civilization; do they never stop to think if other races are suited for a civilization to be forced upon them. It is a good thing I do not doubt it; but should they annex peoples so entirely under their power.

Well Miss Flemying Gyll I think I have said more than I intended. Thanks very much for the Xmas gifts; and for your kind sympathies for us. I thank others in your country who have tried to help us in our cause.

We are still confident but perhaps we are hoping against hope. The Almighty Power will help us too, and may his blessings be upon you.

Signed ...

[Source: LAC, MG 40, Q31, British and Foreign Anti-Slavery Society and Aborigines' Protection Society, MSS British Empire, S22 (G306), Extracts from a letter to Miss Flemying Gyll, 19 March, 1925.]

With the exception of Louise McKinney, biographical information is provided elsewhere in the book on the rest of the group who were referred at the time as "The Alberta Five" and subsequently designated as "The Famous Five." Louise Crummy McKinney (1868–1931) desired to become a doctor, but due to educational restrictions and economic limitations became a teacher instead. Increasingly involved in the temperance movement, McKinney left teaching to act as an organizer for the WCTU for several years in the mid-1890s. After she married and moved west, she assisted in the organization of the Northwest branch of the WCTU in 1903, and became president of its successor, the Alberta and Saskatchewan Union, for over twenty years. She was elected to the Alberta legislature for a four-year term in 1917.

Henrietta Muir Edwards, Nellie McClung, Louise McKinney, Emily Murphy, and Irene Parlby

Petition to the Governor General of Canada Regarding Women as Persons (1927)

August 27, 1927

To His Excellency
The Governor General in Canada
Rideau Hall
Ottawa, Ontario

Sir:

As persons interested in the admission of women to the Senate of Canada, we do hereby request that you may be graciously pleased to refer to the Supreme Court of Canada for hearing, consideration and adjudication the following constitutional questions:

1 Is power vested in the Governor-General in Council of Canada, or the Parliament of Canada or either of them, to appoint a female to the Senate of Canada?

2 Is it constitutionally possible for the Parliament of Canada under the provision of the British North America Act, or otherwise, to make provision for the appointment of a female to the Senate of Canada?

These questions are respectfully referred for your consideration pursuant to Section 60 of the Supreme Court Act, R.S.C. 1906. Cap. 139.

> We have the honour to be,
> Sir,
> Your obedient servants
> Sgd. Henrietta Muir Edwards (Macleod)
> Nellie L. McClung (Calgary)
> Louise C. McKinney (Claresholm)
> Emily Murphy (Edmonton)
> Irene Parlby (Red Deer)

[Source: LAC, RG 13, vol. 2524, file C1004, Petition from Henrietta Muir Edwards, Nellie McClung, Louise McKinney, Emily Murphy, and Irene Parlby, 27 May 1927.]

Henrietta Muir Edwards, Nellie McClung, Louise McKinney, Emily Murphy, and Irene Parlby

Request to Appeal Supreme Court of Canada Decision to British Privy Council (1928)

May ... 1928

To His Excellency
The Governor-General in Council,
Rideau Hall,
Ottawa Ontario
Reference to the admission of women to the Senate of Canada

Sir: As persons interested in the admission of women to the Senate of Canada, we do hereby earnestly request that you may be graciously pleased to refer to the Judicial Committee of the Privy council an appeal from the decision of the Supreme Court of Canada delivered on April 24, 1928, at Ottawa with reference to the following question: – "Does the word 'persons' in Section 24 of the British North American Act, 1867, include female persons?"

The question was answered in the negative by the Supreme Court.

This appeal is respectfully referred for your consideration pursuant to Section 60 of the Supreme Court Act R.S.C. 1906.

[Source: LAC, RG 13, vol. 2524, file C1004, Letter to Governor General from Henrietta Muir Edwards, Nellie McClung, Louise McKinney, Emily Murphy, and Irene Parlby, May 1928.]

Agnes Macphail (1890–1954) was a country schoolteacher who became the first woman elected to Parliament in 1921, the first year women were eligible as candidates. Representing the Progressive Party and later the Co-operative Commonwealth Federation, Macphail served as a federal politician for a rural eastern Ontario riding until 1940. While she initially entered politics to represent the interests of farmers, over time she increasingly advocated for a range of women's rights. She joined the Canadian section of WILPF and was named to the executive of the international federation in 1929.

Agnes Macphail

Speech in the House of Commons on the Naturalization of Married Women (1927)

Right Hon. W. L. MACKENZIE KING (Prime Minister) moved that the house go into committee of supply.

Miss A. MACPHAIL (Southeast Grey): Mr Speaker, there are many Canadian women who resent the injustice which women who are British subjects, but married to aliens, suffer in regard to naturalization. A woman may be a Canadian, she may be the grandchild of Canadians, but if she marries an alien she ceases to be a British subject. She may not resume her British nationality until her husband chooses to become naturalized; and if he dies or the marriage is dissolved the women remains an alien until she makes a declaration and obtains a certificate from the Secretary of State. It would seem that such treatment makes naturalization of small account. It must be of little importance if adults can be naturalized without satisfying the condition as to desirability and without being required to take the oath of allegiance, and it certainly is insulting to women to assume that their allegiance can be transferred without their own consent.

Under the present law marriage and citizenship are very much mixed up. I don't think the two should be so closely related, if related at all. There are scores of British women resident in Canada who, having married aliens, find themselves citizens of no country, unable to claim the protection of any government, unable to vote, unable to teach or to accept any civil position should the need arise, and, in the event of their husbands' death, unable to participate in the mother's allowance for the benefit of their children. Because of their statelessness they find it almost impossible to obtain a passport. I have a letter from a woman in Ontario received when the resolution in regard to this subject appeared on the order paper. She lives in Prince Edward County and pays taxes, but at the last election on December 1 not only herself but twenty-five other women in the county were prevented from voting. She tells that her great grandfather was an officer in the Revolutionary war and a British subject and she describes how loyal they had always been; yet after marriage to an American, although they live in Canada and she owns large property and pays taxes, she finds herself unable to vote in any election in this country. She writes protesting against such treatment.

Last year I tried to get a passport for an Ontario girl who was married to an alien. I could not obtain the passport and she had to cancel her trip. Many other members of this House could tell similar stories. I have heard them in private conversation and if they had the opportunity to speak I am sure they could tell of experiences such as I have described. When it is considered that, in western Canada particularly, we are receiving from many shores aliens who are marrying women of British nationality; this is a matter of vital concern to Canada.

The right of women to retain their British nationality although married to aliens was enjoyed until the year 1870. Previous to that time the common law of England contained two principles: first, that a British woman who married an alien should retain her British nationality, and secondly, that an alien woman who married a British subject remained an alien. Women were regarded as chattels; after marriage they had no right to their property, which passed into the control of their husbands. They did not possess the franchise and generally they were in a humiliating and subordinate position as compared to the status of women to-day. Yet until 1870 they had the right to retain their nationality. In that year the law was changed to provide that a married woman should be deemed to be the subject of the state of which her husband for the time being was subject. When this change was made the women of Great Britain – for this is British law – were not consulted at all, and the subject received very little debate in the House of Commons, through which it passed very hurriedly. The law was amended in 1914 to read:

That the wife of a British subject shall be deemed to be a British subject and the wife of an alien shall be deemed to be an alien.

In the amending act of 1914, however, "Women did make certain gains. In the British nationality and Status of Aliens Act, 1914, women gained the principle, excluded since 1870 that a woman might be of different nationality from her husband's. If her British husband should change his nationality, she might under the act declare that she would remain British; and a British-born woman with a foreign husband may now apply, on the dissolution of her marriage by death or divorce, for readmission to British nationality without complying with the requirements as to residence."

In 1922 Lord Danesfort brought forward a bill, which passed its second reading, containing two important principles: first, British women should have the right to retain their nationality when they married aliens; and, second, that an alien woman should not by the mere act of marriage with a British subject become a British subject. Dissolution of parliament prevented anything further being done, but in 1923 a select committee of the Lords and Commons was appointed to consider the subject. This committee, comprising five commoners and five lords, agreed that a change was necessary. But, one of the lords dissenting, no recommendations were made when the report was presented. The objection advanced by this dissenting lord was that the change would, result in trouble, in the home. Men and women, it was urged, were one. We all know that, but the thing I want to know is which one? If it is going to disturb the harmony of the home to have any change of nationality on the part of either husband or wife, let the husband take the nationality of the wife. It is as fair that way as the other. I have no great fear that the home will be disrupted if women are given the vote, or if they go to work, or if they retain their nationality. Every advance made by woman has been frowned upon because of this very fear of the home being disrupted, men are always worried about this consequence, but it does not happen, for the simple reason that the real home is a community of interests so strong that it will take more than any change of nationality, more than the vote or any of these things to disrupt it. We need not worry about the home on that account.

The matter was brought forward again in the British House of Commons in 1925, when Major Harvey introduced a resolution, which was carried, to the following effect:

"That in the opinion of this House a British woman should not lose or be deemed to lose her nationality by mere act of marriage with an alien, but that it should be open to her to make declaration of alienage."

During the course of the debate on the resolution the Under Secretary of State informed the House that after the meeting of the joint committee of the

House of Lords and Commons to which I have referred, no agreement having been reached, the matter had been raised at the imperial conference of 1923. It was referred to a sub-committee of the conference. The suggestions of the sub-committee of the conference as well as those of the joint committee of the Lords and Commons were submitted to the dominions in the autumn of 1924, but up to the point when Major Harvey was taking part in the debate in the resolution I have quoted only one of the dominions had expressed itself on the subject. I wonder why Canada did not reply. I believe that public opinion in this country favours a change. I have no doubt it is the desire of the people of this Dominion that a British woman married to an alien shall have a right to retain her British nationality. Mr Hurst speaking to Major Harvey's resolution in 1925 said:

"I do not believe we ought to wait until the principle adopted in this resolution has been accepted by all self-governing dominions. On July 14, 1921, I put a question to the then Prime Minister on this subject and I was told that no decision could be arrived at until the dominions had been consulted with. That is four years ago and we are not one inch further along the road to legislation than we were then."

From the beginning we can conclude that the British House of Commons on various occasions has wanted to do something about the matter. As I have pointed out, they referred the question to the dominions, from only one of which they received any reply. I cannot see why they did not hear from our Dominion, and I think it is time the parliament of this country do whatever steps are necessary to make it possible for British women married to aliens to retain their own nationality.

The United States tried the law which we now have for the period from 1907 to 1922 when, by the Cable act, the law was changed to read:

"A woman citizen of the United States shall not cease to be a citizen by reason of her marriage unless she makes a formal renunciation of her citizenship before a court having jurisdiction over naturalization of aliens."

It was further enacted that:

"Any woman who marries a citizen of the United States shall not become a citizen by reasons of such marriage."

By this law an American girl who marries a Canadian becomes a British subject while still remaining a citizen of the United States, but a Canadian who marries an American ceases to be a British subject and does not become a citizen of the United States, and is therefore a citizen of no country. There are many practical examples of this, and I am sure every member of this House is aware of some of them. The republics of Argentina, Brazil, and Chile have similar naturalization laws to those of the United States. Belgium in 1922 gave women the right to retain their nationality after marriage if they so desired. In 1924 Sweden gave women the same right, so long as they remained in Sweden, and other Scandinavian countries have followed the same procedure.

Resolutions asking for this change have been passed by women's organizations in Canada for many years past, among those outstanding being the National Council of Women, who have time and again asked that women be naturalized of their own right, and that marriage to an alien should not affect them in anyway. The Canadian Council of Agriculture have presented this question to the cabinet almost times without number. The Women's Institutes of Canada, have taken a firm stand upon it, together with the Social Service Council of Canada. The Alberta legislature on two occasions adopted resolutions with this problem, one of which was introduced last session by Hon. Irene Parlby and seconded by Mrs Nellie McClung, but no action was taken in this House. As I have already pointed out, Great Britain adopted Major Harvey's resolution in 1924, and I do not see why the parliament in Canada has not taken some stand on this question.

I realize that this is an international matter, but after all it will not be dealt with in an international way until the countries affected deal with it first, and I appeal to the members of this House, in the name of the womanhood of this country to see that this injustice is removed and that women have the same right of citizenship accorded to men. I think women love their country as much as men, and since women are not to-day property as they were thought to be in days gone by, but thinking individuals, I appeal to the House of Commons to take the first opportunity to do all that can be done in this matter. Let it be taken up by the League of Nations or the next Imperial conference; let us do anything that can be done in order to remove this injustice.

[Source: Canada, *Debates of the House of Commons*, 6 April 1927, 1983–5.]

Ship of State: Are Women Wanted in Public Life? (1928)

Illustrated by
J. S. HALLAM

Are Women Wanted in Public Life?

Source: *Chatelaine* 1, no. 7 (September 1928), 1.

Thérèse Forget Casgrain (1896–1981) was born in Montreal to a wealthy French Québécois family. Later married to the federal Liberal politician Pierre Caisgrain, she played a leading role in the fight for women's suffrage in Quebec. In 1921 she co-founded the "Comité provincial pour le suffrage féminin," later renamed "La Ligue des droits de la femme." Casgrain served as president of this feminist organization for 14 years from 1928 to 1942. Through the radio program that she hosted in the 1930s, "Femina," she reached a large audience of French and English women in the province.

Thérèse Casgrain
Woman's Place in a Democracy (1941)

Ladies:
    The usual words of welcome seem too weak to express the joy and comfort

that your presence brings me. You bear active witness to the degree to which the problems of the moment interest and move you. With all the sociologists – and, my God, even without them – we know that the primordial role of women is that of guardian of the family. Alas, an arbitrary and artificial conception of the family has gained credence among many souls, even if for them the home immediately evokes not a living reality, not a human institution, but the puerile image of four walls and a roof. I know of no misconception more widespread or dangerous, since it substitutes a symbol, which is the house, for the only essential thing, which is the family itself. There is nothing less original than to compare the family to a cell in the social body; Christian sociology long ago introduced this metaphor into its lexicon. A cell, yes; the first cell, but a cell that all others emanate from, the cell around which an infinite number of institutions are grouped for which the cell is both origin and home; a cell that is in numerous ways linked to the entire society which it feeds and from which, in turn, it draws its life. And if we put the family back into its proper framework (did Barrès not say that the nation is a large family of families?), would we not see that woman must participate in the workings of the entire social body to protect the cell of the family for which she is responsible? The man who undertakes a job or a profession outside the home, the child who spends long hours at school, the woman who devotes herself to charitable works or hospitalization: do these human beings, even outside of the home, not constitute a family? Must we understand that the family dismembers itself each morning, when offices and schools open, only to reconstitute itself around the dining table in the evening? Or is it not more sensible to say that the family remains the family in all of its ramifications, all its extensions, just as the tree is itself in its roots, its branches, its leafy boughs.

I am not talking here about the evolution in social and political mores that, in the eyes of some, would justify woman's emancipation for her alone. I am merely describing the inevitable interdependence that exists and always has existed between the family and the society. An iniquitous law, passed by a parliamentary assembly very far from the family, reaches the family as directly as a particular injustice perpetrated against one of its members. This, ladies, is why the woman who takes good care of her family also protects it from outside enemies. These enemies of the family wear the most diverse faces these days: some slip into the school to reach the child; others are introduced into the economy to reach the head of the family and take from him his right to work, to a good salary, his property rights. And it is in fulfilling one's primordial role with intelligence, courage and especially with concern for others that one may combat these destructive forces wherever they are found.

When the woman insists on having her most elementary rights recognized, she dreams without fail of weapons for protecting her family against whatever threatens it. One of these weapons, and not the least necessary, is suffrage. We won that right a year ago today, after an apparently fruitless struggle that lasted many years. At the moment of this victory, we were told in several quarters: "Now that you have gotten what you asked for, you can forget your labour; you can rest." These words make me think of the conclusions of sentimental novels, in which the hero always marries the heroine. What one forgets is that the real story begins only *after* the wedding. Isn't that right, ladies? This invitation to rest is doubtless well-intentioned, but it shows, alas, how some people have misunderstood the reasons and the goals of our labour. The right to suffrage is not an end in itself, could never be an end in itself; it is a means, and, I have just been saying, a defensive weapon.

Now that we possess some of the means of action we were once deprived of, our real task is becoming apparent, our responsibilities are taking shape, our duties becoming more clear. It is in order to better inform ourselves about the nature and importance of our task that we have called this conference. We have chosen three major themes: education, work and social well-being. There is a vast program of political and social action in these areas.

The close correlation I spoke of a moment ago between the family and other social institutions is particularly evident when it comes to education. Does it not strike you that the family and the school, the one extending the other, are tied to the point where neglect of the first will weaken the teaching of the second, and that one cannot do without the other without compromising the well-being of the child? It is generally accepted that a great many economic and social problems are fundamentally problems of an educational nature. The dangerous direction pursued by totalitarian states regarding child development should rouse us to redouble our efforts to train our children, not for the bloody tasks of war or the brutal techniques of invasion, but for the freely accepted responsibilities they will assume in the future. We should collaborate closely with schools to cultivate a love for the family and the nation in our children's hearts. Tracing borders on maps is like praising a country with empty rhetoric and conventional phrases. You will never create a homeland this way; you will only do it by drawing the borders of the nation in the hearts and minds of your children! Patriotism is not and never has been a question of rhetoric or convention; it is an indefinable emotion that grips the heart when a foreigner pronounces the name of your country, a tremendous happiness that wells up when you tread your native soil, when you breathe in the scent of it, when its lines and contours seem extensions of yourself. Familial and scholarly education will inculcate this understanding of a true homeland, a living homeland in our youth.

In the general uncertainty of our time, a sound education is the only legacy we can be sure to pass on to our children. The post-war world – and I am not trying to predict the future here, just to examine the facts coolly and calmly – the post-war world will have no tolerance for the weak, the misshapen, the indecisive. It will be a world where only intellectual and physical qualities will triumph. Will our children have the tools necessary for their success and happiness?

The second problem this conference proposes to study is that of work and, particularly, women's work. Modern life has established women's work outside of the home, in the workshop, the office, the store, in business and industry. What are the working conditions to which women are subjected in our society? The exploitation of women's labour is not a theory; it is a sad reality too often demonstrated by the facts. We should concern ourselves with this problem. Equal pay for equal work. Nothing in the world justifies treating female manpower and male manpower differently, everything else being equal. For the rest, has it not been proven, most notably by the report of the inquiry on the textile industry, that the depreciation of women's salaries entails the proportional depreciation of men's salaries? To claim just remuneration for women's work is therefore to safeguard a sacred right, but it is also to protect the security of the family. As for working conditions, in order to grasp their importance it suffices to have a Christian spirit or simple respect for human dignity.

The concern for safeguarding human dignity will also give rise to our discussions of social well-being. We will consider three aspects of this vast problem: urbanism, hospitalisation, and child protection. What vices, for instance, the shameful existence of slums give rise to in the city! What dens of physical and moral contagion are created every day in these dark, dirty shelters where one never finds a ray of sunshine or a whiff of fresh air? Is it necessary to repeat that slums are the greatest source of juvenile delinquency and that most men and women who fill our prisons today lived, as children, in these sunless holes? How can woman, the guardian of the home, not be interested in the problem of the slums, a cancer that gnaws away at the social tissue and attacks the very life of the family?

Hospitalisation and child protection will also be taken up in our meetings, but I don't think it useful to pursue these subjects for the moment.

This address, which I had hoped would be brief, has somehow come to resemble a speech. I apologise. We recognize today, more than ever before, the extent of our collective task. This first conference marks for us an anniversary; it will also be a point of departure if it is true that our work really begins today.

I am certain, and your presence confirms it, that we will all bring to the accomplishment of our new duties the ardour and patience that we found within ourselves to have the old rights recognized.

[Source: Thérèse Casgrain, "A Woman's Place in a Democracy," in *Québécoises du 20e siècle*, ed. Michèle Jean (Saint-Léonard, QC: Quinze, 1977), 243–7 (trans. Maureen Moynagh).]

PART FIVE
Moral Reform, Sexuality, and Birth Control

Over the course of the second half of the nineteenth century and the early decades of the twentieth century, the women's movement engaged in an extended campaign to elevate the moral tone of Canadian society. Feminists were by no means alone in this battle, and if anything male clergy, physicians, and civic leaders were more prominent, but far more than others they raised concerns specific to the situation of women and with a view to altering certain aspects of existing gender relations. The demand for a single moral standard was a key and for the most part unifying issue among women reformers, while others such as the legalization of birth control were fraught with tensions and division. For Anglo-Celtic middle-class reformers in particular the activist project of moral regeneration was part of a broader program of nation and empire building, albeit one in which the asymmetries of race and class were more often reinforced than subverted. At the same time, it is also possible to discern that organizational priorities and reform rhetoric were shaped by transnational connections and collaborations.

Feminist engagement in moral reform was in part an outgrowth of women's long-standing participation in the benevolent work of assisting the sick and impoverished. As female-exclusive organizations were formed in the mid-nineteenth century "to systematize charitable practices,"[1] women activists assumed a more prominent public role as moral leaders and rescuers in their communities. Moreover, religious fervour played a role in attempts to elevate the moral tone of Canadian society, with evangelical Protestant women in particular viewing such efforts as a fundamental part of fulfilling their Christian duty. The Women's Christian Association of Halifax, which originated in 1875, operated not only a night school that offered religious and moral instruction to young working-class women, but also a reformatory for delinquent women and those recently released from jail – the Women's Home. While the WCA's 1880 annual report noted numerous impediments in running the home, there had been "a reformation in morals" on the part of at least some of the inmates. A combination of social reform and spiritual impulses were also at play in other initiatives during this period such as the creation of the Crosby Girls' Home for Tsimshian adolescents in Fort Simpson, British Columbia. Emma Crosby, the wife of a Methodist missionary in the Pacific Northwest, revealed in an 1881 letter that the formation of such a residence was necessary to shield Aboriginal girls from "a life of dissipation and shame." Crosby was guided by good intensions, as Jan Hare and Jean Barman have observed, but her decisions were "informed by a colonial agenda that in all aspects of life, set Aboriginals apart from newcomers."[2] And what began as the stated mission of the home to provide moral protection soon transformed into confinement and later incarceration.

Not surprisingly given its original focus on temperance, the WCTU took up an early and leading role in moral reform. Although temperance continued to be a primary concern, this women's organization devoted a great deal of time and resources to social purity work, especially from the turn of the century onward. In general terms social purity was concerned with the improvement of sexual and moral aspects of social life, and more specifically within the WCTU, it involved the dissemination of "proper" knowledge related to sexuality, reproduction, and marriage with the goal of attaining a high moral standard for both females and males. The organization formed separate social purity departments, as evidenced by the 1898 report composed by Jessie Smith in which she emphasized the essential part Christian mothers needed to play in educating children about "the bodies in which we live." In the process, the Anglo-Celtic Protestant women involved in the WCTU sought to advance the nurturing role of mothers for larger social purposes; however, "this nurturing was perceived as involving the reproduction not of human beings in general, but of their race in particular."[3] Indeed, the WCTU often drew upon the language of race as well as imperialism in elevating the status of white women over and above racialized and non-British immigrant women.

The campaign for moral regeneration assumed a more secular orientation within the NCWC than the WCTU, with this organization concentrating for the most part on the introduction or alteration of state regulations. Age of consent was one such example. Addressing recent legal changes with regard to the crime of seduction, Lady Julia Drummond, president of the Local Council of Women of Montreal, lauded the federal government in 1896 for increasing the age of consent for girls from fourteen to sixteen. Taking British law as her point of reference, though, an ongoing common practice as it was assumed legislation in Canada should replicate as much as possible the legal traditions of the mother country, Drummond objected to the additional requirement that girls in Canada had to prove they were "of previously chaste character." In her view this clause largely abrogated the legal and moral protections that should be provided young girls at the expense of defending the interests of men. However, as Karen Dubinsky has noted, Drummond reinforced "the hierarchies of class as she attempted to deconstruct those of gender" in her assertion that "in the class of life where such offences are most frequent, girls thus defiled are not likely to be able to substantiate a good character."[4]

In Drummond's commentary and numerous other feminist discussions dealing with moral reform, males were often depicted as the principal source of sexual disorder, with female activists being disparaging of the "excessiveness" of male desire. Reformers' efforts were aimed, though, at shielding girls and women from unwanted advances rather than "lay[ing] the foundation for sexual pleasure."[5] Notable but rather rare exceptions in the Canadian context were those who identified as sex radicals. While female sex radicals in the United States and Britain gained a considerable public profile (if not notoriety) at the turn of the century, the socialist Dora Forster Kerr was among the few women reformers in this country to adopt such a stance. In her pamphlet *Sex Radicalism as Seen by an Emancipated Woman of the New Time* (1905) she portrayed relations between men and women as a "sex war" that persisted to the detriment of the latter. As part of a broader critique of monogamous relationships and the institution of marriage, Kerr argued that sexual pleasure or "sex love" should not be depicted in negative terms or narrowly confined to marital relationships, but viewed as a "power for good and a principle to regulate the conduct of men and women as equal comrades."

Although women were far less often the target of explicit criticism by female activists, blame was apportioned to "fallen women," especially those who engaged in "the social evil" of the moral reform era – prostitution. And hence, in an article discussing the problem of vice in Montreal in 1913, a member of the Fédération Nationale Saint-Jean-Baptiste (FNSJB) portrayed young women's descent into prostitution in part as their own fault. Yet this article also raised the spectre of white slavery, which the FNSJB described elsewhere as "an international scourge"[6] of young women lured into immorality. Those specifically identified as being at risk in this piece were francophone women from Quebec rural areas. In the midst of the moral panic over white slavery that took place in Canada and other countries in the early twentieth century, and despite the marginalized status of francophone Québécois, the FNSJB largely replicated the racialized discourse of many Anglo-Celtic reformers in their stated concern for young women designated as white.

At the same time, reflecting the ongoing linguistic and religious divide that existed in Quebec and elsewhere in Canada, the FNSJB promoted the work of a francophone Catholic organization to safeguard young women from moral dangers. Anglophone Protestant women preserved the purity and respectability of young women through the Young Women's Christian Association (YWCA), one of the largest feminist organizations in Canada from the late nineteenth century onwards. The YWCA offered protection and supervision to young adults during this formative time in their lives. As indicated by a report produced by its national director, Una Saunders, the YWCA did not deem it sufficient just to operate boarding homes, but sought to ensure moral and physical well-being through the provision of holiday camps and recreational facilities. The organization had even begun to turn its attention to younger female teenagers by embarking on a new program – Canadian Girls in Training – with the goal that teenagers attained a "Girls Standard." The middle-class reformers who spearheaded the YWCA promoted what has been depicted as positive solutions in the face of multiple moral threats, while simultaneously they legitimized a wide-ranging system of surveillance for the mostly working-class women in their charge.

Sex hygiene, also referred to as purity education, was widely promoted by many first wave feminists, at least through to the 1920s. Although emphasis continued to be placed on the essential informal role of mothers in this regard, more formal educational ventures were initiated, with, for example, Arthur W. Beall being hired by the Ontario WCTU as their "purity agent" for school-age children in 1905. Beall concentrated almost exclusively on male sexuality, though, which made the feminist Beatrice Brigden's educational work all the more significant. In 1913 Brigden took a position with the newly created Methodist Department of Social Service and Evangelism that entailed teaching sex education across the country, principally to girls and women. In a series of letters that described her experiences as a sex educator, she espoused the popular feminist opinion that leaving girls and women ignorant of such matters did not ensure their purity but made them vulnerable to moral ruin. Brigden's primary aim was to raise female consciousness. Advocacy for sex hygiene by feminists began to wane in the interwar period as the moral reform movement more broadly lost its momentum, and as scientific solutions aimed at stemming societal degeneration, especially eugenics, gained support.

One of the most controversial issues within the women's movement related to sexuality and morality was "family limitation." Against a backdrop in the late nineteenth century of the criminalization of contraception and abortion, combined with increasing fears over the decline of the fertility rate and "race suicide" among the Anglo-Celtic middle-class population, the key women's reform organizations largely avoided public discussions over the restriction of family size. On the political left, though, debate over the efficacy of family limitation began at the turn of the century, and by the early 1920s a growing number of socialist feminists promoted the use of birth control. These women were greatly aided, Angus McLaren and Arlene Tigar McLaren have contended, by Marie Stopes in Britain and Margaret Sanger in the United States, who acted as de facto transnational guardians for the nascent birth control movement in Canada.[7] In a 1924 column for the *One Big Union Bulletin* Florence Rowe endorsed the use of birth control to alleviate both the physical and financial burdens placed on women. Rowe even raised the spectre of scores of women dying from abortion because they could not "freely and legally obtain the information necessary" to avoid pregnancy. Of additional significance, Rowe framed the issue in class terms, noting that fertility control was a crucial means to better ensure the well-being of working-class women and their children.

While some mainstream women's groups such as NCWC adopted in effect a neutral stance on family limitation, as evidenced by Winnifred Kydd's 1934 statement, other organizations and individual activists began to call for the legalization of birth control over the course of the interwar period. Many of these endorsements, however, did not occur until after the onset of the Great Depression, when the economic and social consequences of unwanted pregnancy became especially pronounced for poor and working-class women. And there were still others, such as Dr Helen MacMurchy who remained vocal opponents. A recognized national expert on child and maternal health as well as social reformer, MacMurchy condemned the use of contraception as "unnatural" and unsafe in her widely read 1934 book *Sterilization? Birth Control?* (1934). She did not object to all forms of fertility control, though as elsewhere in this publication she unequivocally supported the practice of sterilization. MacMurchy, as with a growing number of feminists, was guided by eugenic principles that espoused "responsible motherhood" – that is, encouragement of the reproduction of the "fit" and stamping out of the "unfit" or "degenerate." The rigid bifurcation of such categories had direct and profound implications as racialized, immigrant, and working-class populations were greatly over-represented among those designated as unfit. Moreover, in this way genetic purity and moral purity were combined in efforts to construct a higher moral standard.[8]

NOTES

1 Carmen Nielson Varty, "'A Career in Christian Charity': Women's Benevolence and the Public Sphere in a Mid-Nineteenth-Century Canadian City," *Women's History Review* 14, no. 2 (2005), 245.

2 Jan Hare and Jean Barman, eds., *Good Intentions Gone Awry: Emma Crosby and the Methodist Mission on the Northwest Coast* (Vancouver: UBC Press, 2006), xxii.

3 Mariana Valverde, *The Age of Light, Soap and Water: Moral Reform in English Canada, 1885–1925* (Toronto: U of Toronto P, 2008), 61.

4 Karen Dubinsky, *Improper Advances: Rape and Heterosexual Conflict in Ontario, 1880–1929* (Chicago: U of Chicago P, 1993), 78.

5 Lucy Bland, *Banishing the Beast: English Feminism and Sexual Morality, 1885–1914* (New York: Penguin, 1995), 305.

6 Tamara Myers, *Caught: Montreal's Modern Girls and the Law, 1869–1945* (Toronto: U of Toronto P, 2006), 60.

7 Angus McLaren and Arlene Tigar McLaren, *The Bedroom and the State: The Changing Practices and Politics of Contraception in Canada,1880–1997*, 2nd ed.. (Toronto: Oxford UP, 1997), 22.

8 Bland, *Banishing the Beast*, 230.

Women's Christian Association of the City of Halifax
The Women's Home of Halifax (1880)

Although, perhaps, we would all rather forget the things which are behind and reach forward to those which are before, yet we feel that it is needful for ourselves and only just to those who have so kindly assisted us during the past year, that we take a look back at what we have been doing.

The working of the Woman's Home has never given the Committee greater satisfaction than during the past year. The regulations have been better and on the whole the management has been more complete. The inmates have earned during the year $267.10.

The Night School Committee held a session of nearly seven months. The attendance was larger and more uniform than formerly. The Committee feel that if many of the scholars refuse the moral and religions instruction given them they have the satisfaction of knowing that many have been taught reading and writing who would otherwise have remained ignorant.

The Visiting Committee feel that they have not been as useful as they might had their efforts been more united. However, the claims of the sick poor have not been wholly disregarded. Some special efforts have been made to increase the funds of the Association which has enabled us to begin the year with a balance on hand. Eight members have joined during the year and five have left the city. There is now eighty-eight names on the roll, and we earnestly hope that in the year upon which we are just entering our numbers may be greatly increased, "that we all may be of the same mind and of the same judgment," and the Master may see fit to use us for His service more than He has ever yet done.

Report of the Women's Home

In submitting their Sixth Annual Report, the Committee of the "Woman's Home" would state it has not been without many struggles that the Institution has been sustained during the past year. Times of discouragement have been experienced from lack of funds and apathy of friends, when even the most sanguine of some members have been forced to question the possibility or at least the wisdom of continuing the Home. The conclusion has invariably been that duty forbids us to lay aside the work which Providence has placed in our bands.

We have to deplore the lack of sympathy manifested by the community at large, no doubt partly owing to the little faith some persons have in the final success of the work. Still our warmest thanks are due to those who have assisted us with their means, upon solicitation and also to many others for voluntary donations.

The collectors have been treated with politeness and kindness when calling upon the yearly subscribers, and many new contributors have cheerfully placed their names upon our list.

Some special efforts have been made during the year for the purpose of increasing our funds in the form of a Musical Entertainment, a Lecture by Canon Dart, and a Fancy Sale and Tea. Each of these was an assistance, but neither was as successful as we wished.

The different branches of work have been engaged in industriously by the inmates, bringing in more for the support of the Institution than in any previous year. For the information of those who are strangers to our Home we would mention that the different branches of industries engaged in are washing, reseating cane chairs, quilting, knitting, hooking mats, and sewing. Patronage is earnestly solicited from the public in each of these departments.

Financially, we are in a much better position than at the close of last year, for which we would desire to be grateful. Another source of encouragement is that we have recently secured the services of a matron who has had eleven years' experience in similar Institutions in the United States. Adding to experience the very qualifications of true piety, kindness, good judgment, thorough knowledge of housekeeping and strict economy, we look forward to greater prosperity than has yet been attained.

Among those who have been inmates of the Home during the past year, many have expressed desires to lead Christian lives, and with some there has been a decided reformation in morals.

Religious services have been held on Thursday evening of each week by clergymen and on Sabbath afternoon by clergymen, laymen or members of our Committee. The women also attend church on Sabbath morning. Adding to this amount of religious instruction the influence of the Committee and matron, we earnestly look for a plentiful harvest to succeed the sowing.

The Committee would express their sincere thanks to the various clergymen who have kindly held services at the Home, also to Drs Cowie and Woodill for gratuitous medical attendance, and to Miss Bell for devoting one afternoon in each week to giving instruction to the women in reading and writing &c., without remuneration.

Twenty-one girls were received into the Home during the year, many of whom are giving excellent satisfaction as servants.

A.A. Shields, Sec'y

Night School

We opened on the 7th of November and closed on the 28th of May. Average attendance of scholars 43, of teachers 7.

Some of the girls who have been in the school since the first opening show marked signs of improvement, both in behaviour and in reading and writing, while others rather disturb those who come to receive benefit from instruction given. The most attentive scholars were those who lived at service, some of whom commenced their alphabet with us three winters ago, and are now able to read and write. One little girl, eleven years of age, commenced her letters at the beginning of last session and at the close was able to read and spell words of four and five letters.

The school met on Monday and Friday evenings. During the months of March, April and May, sewing was taught on one of these evenings to all who wished to learn.

The Committee are indebted to four or five ladies not belonging to the W.C. Association, who gave their services as teachers and took a warm interest in the school. Two entertainments were given to the school. At the closing one 41 girls received presents; 13 were given out of the funds of the school, 9 by the teachers and their friends, and 19 consisted of aprons and other unfinished work left over from the "sewing class."

Thanks are due to the friends of the school. To Mrs Wm. Stairs for her liberal donation to the sewing class, and also Mrs Duncan MacGregor. To the gentlemen who come forward so willingly to amuse and instruct the girls with their addresses and recitations. To the ladies who send cake and other good things. To Dr Cogswell who so kindly lends us his organ when asked. We renew our thanks to the Board of School Commissioners for our school-room, stationery, &c.

Fannie Coleman, Sec'y

Visiting Committee's Report

In a few words, we wish to say that the Visiting Committee still merits a humble position in the working of this Association. Many ladies who, at the beginning, offered their services as visitors, have continued to evince the same interest, in visiting Rockhead, the Poor House, Hospital, and last but not least, regular weekly visiting. Owing to circumstances so few meetings have been held during the year that, we cannot state in figures the extent of work accomplished, but we believe, that in a quiet way, as much work has been done this year as during any in the past; and we pray, that in God's strength, we may go forward realizing our own weakness, but pleading His promise "I will uphold Thee."

Lillie Stirling, Sec'y

[Source: PANS, Pamphlet Collection, Women's Christian Association of the City of Halifax, *Sixth Annual Report of the Women's Christian Association*, 1880.]

Emma Douse Crosby, 1849–1926, was born in Cobourg, Ontario. The daughter of a Methodist minister she received an advanced secondary education at the Wesleyan Female College. Upon graduation she became a teacher before marrying Thomas Crosby in 1874. Following their marriage the couple departed for Fort Simpson on the north coast of British Columbia, where Thomas Crosby was to serve as a Methodist missionary among the Tsimshian people. With financial assistance from the Methodist Woman's Missionary Society in Hamilton, Ontario, Crosby founded a girls' home for Tsimshian adolescents in 1880.

Emma Crosby

Letter from Emma Crosby to Mrs H.M. Leland, Secretary of the Hamilton Women's Missionary Society (1881)

Port Simpson, BC, July 28th, 1881

Dear Madam, – Your kind letter of June 20th, written on behalf of the Woman's Missionary Society of the Methodist Churches of Hamilton, reached me a few days ago. I need not tell you that it was with great pleasure and thankfulness that we read it, and with much rejoicing that we found we were remembered so kindly in the prayers and givings of the ladies of your Society, and that the Lord had put it into your hearts to help on a work that lies so near our hearts, and so heavy on our hands, as our "Girls' Home." The care of these young girls has been thrust upon us. Before we had any thought of undertaking such work in connection with the Mission, one case after another of urgent need was pressed upon us. Indeed the alternative was often coming under our roof or going to ruin, and, alas! to our grief we found in the case of two or three girls whom we felt we were not prepared to take in at the time they applied to us, ruin speedily followed. A gay life in Victoria, or other places has led away many, very many, of the young women of these tribes. There are Indian villages where scarce a young woman can be found, the whole of that class having left their homes for a life of dissipation and shame, and only to come back, in nearly every case, after a few years, to die a wretched, untimely death among their friends. The temptation to this was strong, and we found it one of the most difficult things we had to contend with: Almost from the time we entered the Mission-house we had two or three, or four girls living with us; as one would be married – very few left us until married – another would soon come to take her place, and so the number be kept up. But we felt we could well continue this, little as it was that we were doing, and as our own family increased we felt that our house was not the place for these girls. We could not abandon the work, so, after much prayerful consultation, we decided to build an addition to the Mission-house which should serve as a "Home" for the girls, and could be under our closer supervision, but entirely separate from our own family. We believed that, in doing this, we were following the direction of Providence, and that all necessary means would be provided. Two years ago next month the new building was brought into use. We began with four girls, but the number soon increased, and during the following winter we had twelve. The number has varied since that time, but during the last winter twelve were under our care, and twelve is our number now. We could easily gather in more, but have not felt ourselves in a position to do so hitherto.

Of course, as we undertook this "Home" entirely on our own responsibility, we had to move very slowly and incurred no expense that was not absolutely necessary. As yet the building is unfinished, and almost unfurnished, but we hope that the help Christian friends are now sending us will be sufficient to provide what is needed for the comfort of the girls and their training in some suitable industries. We have had difficulties and inconveniences all the way, thus far, but things look brighter now.

The care of the girls we have divided among us as best we could arrange it. Miss Lawrence, who is in charge of the day-school, gives what time she can to them, and Mr Crosby keeps a constant supervision; but we feel that for the proper care and training of so many girls there must be a thoroughly practical and competent woman to give her whole attention to the work. Hitherto, of course, we have not been in a position to employ anyone for this purpose; but now, we think, we should be justified in doing so, and it has occurred to me that the two hundred dollars your Society has voted to the "Home" would be well used if given towards the support of the Matron for the first year. I hope a suitable person may soon be found, with a heart for the work. Our plan would be to train the girls in general housework, in needlework of various kinds, in spinning, and weaving, if possible, and whatever else they might be able to turn to good account. We aim at making them capable Indian women, fitted for such a life as they are likely to be called to in after life. The most they can do is, as they leave us, to establish Christian homes for themselves where, as wives and mothers, they may show what industrious habits and a Christian spirit can do. What we desire most of all is that the heart of each girl who may enter the Home may be brought under the power of the Gospel; without this we fail, whatever else may be accomplished. It is most emphatically true among these people that "knowledge puffeth up" and is worse than useless unless true humility goes with it. How the glory of Christ and the good of man go hand in hand! Let me bespeak, dear Christian friends, your most earnest prayers, that everyone of our girls may find the Saviour, and that the Lord may graciously abide with us.

We feel that we have been blessed in this work through all its course and though we have met many difficulties and some sad disappointments, yet we feel thankful and encouraged. Most of the girls who have been with us have done well; very few have left us except to be married [...]

You ask if Indian girls will stay Christianized and civilized. As to the Christianizing, while many mistake the form for the reality and so soon fall away, those who get the real "root of the matter" are mostly steadfast. There are those among our Indians here who for some years have adored the doctrine of Christ, and among our girls there are several who have long given every evidence of being true Christians.

Of course, the ignorance and inexperience of such a people as this, and the absence of the restraints thrown round a more refined state of society, leave them an easy prey to many temptations. Still we find St Paul rebuking the churches of his time for just such sins as those poor Indians fall into. As to civilization these people are, many of them, very ambitious. Sometimes they try to take it on too fast, they want to play the organ before they know how to make bread, and a necktie is of much more importance often than an apron. Still, we can see considerable improvement throughout the village in the keeping of the houses, while the children are much better cared for than formerly. The people come to Church, almost invariably neatly dressed, and observe the strictest decorum. The girls are, as a rule, quick to learn, both in school and housework, though, of course, we find some who naturally lack all idea of order, and can never be thoroughly neat and clean. There is a girl in my kitchen now who makes bread that could scarcely be surpassed; very good butter, can do plain cooking well, and is clean and systematic about all her work. Less than two years ago she came to us from one of the most miserable houses in the village. Others have done equally well. There is a vast work, such as our Home is designed to accomplish, to be done among such a people, and we feel confident that so long as the Home is supplying this want, the means will be providentially provided, though, as yet, with the exception of two or three subscriptions, none exceeding five dollars, promised annually, the Institution has not pledged support.

You are greatly honoured in being the Pioneer Women's Missionary Society of our Church. I hope you may not long stand alone. Pray for us, especially for the Home, and with many thanks, in which Mr Crosby and Miss Lawrence most heartily join,

> Believe me, dear Madam,
> Yours most sincerely,
> E.J. Crosby

[Source: Letter from Emma Crosby to Mrs H.M. Leland, Secretary of Hamilton Women's Missionary Society, 28 July 1881, in Jan Hare and Jean Barman, eds., *Good Intentions Gone Awry: Emma Crosby and the Methodist Mission on the Northwest Coast* (Vancouver: UBC Press, 2006), 178–82.]

Julia Parker Drummond (1861–1942) was born in Montreal, and after being widowed at the age of nineteen married the prominent businessman and politician George Drummond. Involved extensively in philanthropic activities in Montreal, she became increasingly active in various women's issues at the local and national levels during the 1890s. She was the president of the Local Council of Women in Montreal from 1893–9 and helped to form the Montreal branch of the Victorian Order of Nurses in 1899. Widowed for a second time in 1910, Drummond went to London, England, during the First World War to work at the headquarters of the Canadian Red Cross.

Lady Julia Drummond
Age of Consent (1895)

Mrs Drummond (Montreal): We must all be glad that the present Minister of Justice, the Hon. Mr Dickey, is so much in sympathy with our endeavor to raise the standard of legislation regarding the most prevalent – in our estimation the most dangerous – form of evil, with which it has to deal.

But while we are thankful for any raising of the standard, the time has hardly come when we can rest content, much less rejoice, over what has been attained. I would lay stress on just one or two points, in which, to many of us, the law of our Dominion is at fault touching this matter.

We have been considering of late what is commonly called the age of consent – that is the age up to which the law affords protection to the girl against defilement, not holding the man excused even if she have given her consent. As stated in the report, there was some difference of opinion amongst us as to what is now considered the age of consent in Canada, 14 and 16, and some eminent legal authorities on being consulted had no doubt that it was 16, the same as in England.

Now we are not questioning this opinion as to what is considered the age of consent in our Dominion, and the fact is indeed patent to those who have copies of the laws of Great Britain and of Canada re "Age of Consent," that in both cases is there a law affording protection to a girl from defilement up to the age of 16 years.

This doubtless was all that was intended by the eminent legal authorities who were asked for an opinion. But our inquiry after all is not as to what is called or considered the "Age of Consent," but as to what it signifies, and as our law regarding it has been compared to the law of Great Britain, let us set the two laws side by side that the one may elucidate the other.

Our own law runs on this wise: – "Every one is guilty of an indictable offence who seduces and has illicit connection with any girl of previously chaste character of or above 14 and under 16."

By the law of Great Britain: "Every one is guilty of an indictable offence who unlawfully and carnally knows or attempts to have unlawful carnal knowledge of any girl being of or above the age of 14, and under the age of 16 years."

I need hardly point out to you that there is a difference. It is plain to you that in one case the attempt is punishable as well as the act, in the other the act must be consummated. In one case the protection is absolute, in the other it is altogether contingent upon the character of the girl. That this latter condition hardly constitutes a distinction without a difference is proved by the opposition with which the proposal to strike out this character clause has been received by our House of Commons for years past, and by the very words used by our Minister of Justice, in his reply to our request for its omission. "It is not thought wise to strike out the words of previously chaste character. It must not be forgotten that after the age of 14 a girl may acquire vicious habits, and in that case, some such protection as these words provide would seem to be necessary."

Must we not then weigh our words when we say that a law which contains this clause, and a law which does not contain it are the same, and yet are told that the omission of this clause from our law would make such a difference as can hardly be contemplated?

Yes, we believe that it does make a difference, a difference of such importance that we women who have taken up this matter should fail in our duty did we disregard it. In the class of life where such offences are most frequent, girls thus defiled are not likely to be able to substantiate a good character nor to disprove the charge of a "bad" one; and, therefore, we may say with truth, that this character clause makes almost all the difference, that in fact it qualifies away the ostensible protection afforded by this law to girls of or above 14, and under the age of 16. But our House of Commons looks at it from another standpoint. It says that this character clause is essential for the protection of the man. Is it that the man must be protected from possible physical coercion on the part of a girl of 14 or 15 who may have acquired vicious habits? (Pardon such plain speaking, but it is necessary here.) No, physical coercion is of the weaker by the stronger, a possibility which can hardly be contemplated here. Is it that he may be protected from the temptation afforded him by a girl of 14 or 15 who may be of doubtful or unchaste character? No, it is that having yielded to temptation, having finished her ruin, a ruin to which no law needs to add its penalty, he may stand before a jury whose sympathies are invariably with their sex, and plead her guilty, to cover, to condone, to justify his own.

Yes, we must understand that when men adduce, as the reason for retaining this character clause, the urgent need that they should be protected from blackmail or the extortion of money by intimidation that blackmail signifies the exposure of actual as well as of supposed wrong-doing, nor can we but believe that the blackmail which is feared is exposure of actual wrong, for the fact is notorious that false charges of this kind are of very rare occurrence, and we have also to bear in mind that whether the charge be true or false, no conviction can be obtained by the girl or woman, unless her statement is corroborated in some material particular, implicating the accused. Therefore, let a man protect himself by leading a chaste and reputable life, and let the law help him thereto by protecting him, not in, but from his follies and his sins.

It is well to have patience. It is very necessary to have patience in this cause, a cause which is especially the woman's cause, whilst the laws which relate to it being made by men, and by men alone, must in the very nature of things be partial laws, but it is hard sometimes not to lose patience, and I confess that when the old word "blackmail" is advanced as a reason for robbing the girl of 14 or 15 of adequate protection, that the man may be excused on the plea of "opportunity" or may be shielded from a very unlikely possibility of a false accusation which the law already guards against by "demanding corroboration in some material matter implicating the accused," I confess for one that my patience is hardly worthy of the name.

Let us not despise any improvement however small, let us be thankful if even the age of qualified protection be increased, but let us realize that that qualification does to a great extent abrogate the protection, and let us not rest content till the age of absolute protection, which is now in Canada 14, be at least raised to 16, as it is in England.

One other fact to which I would direct your attention. The trade of procuration, that hideous vice-traffic which is the most flagrant disgrace on our modern, our Christian civilization, goes on practically unchecked. The law does not interfere with the trade of the procurer as such. The vice-traffic, the trading and exchanging of prostitute girls is, in fact, a legal occupation. Until our laws make such trade criminal, we can do little to check the degradation of womanhood, and the wholesale demoralization of manhood.

But the responsibility does not rest entirely with the laws nor with the men who make those laws – the responsibility is also ours.

Men may laugh as they will at the "Woman's Ideal," but in their hearts they know it to be the true ideal, and that in such proportion as the woman is strong and true to that ideal, so will they realize the truth and strength of their manhood in such proportion as the woman falls below or relinquishes that ideal, so will they decline in the noblest qualities of their manhood.

If to hold this ideal in our ignorance has kept it from fading away out of men's hearts, to hold it still, when, with a courage born of the desire to save we have known and understood those facts that tell against its realization, to hold it then not as an impossible standard but as one which as God is God, and we are His children, can and must be possible of attainment, thus to hold up the standard shall surely be to lead a forlorn hope to victory.

[Source: National Council of Women of Canada, *Appendix to Women Workers of Canada: Being the Reports and Discussions on the Laws for the Protection of Women and Children, and on Pernicious Literature at the Third Annual Meeting of the National Council of Women of Canada* (Montreal, 1896), 319–22.]

Jessie C. Smith was superintendent of the WCTU Department of Social Hygiene in the province of Nova Scotia. The WCTU, whose initial focus was primarily on temperance, branched out into other reform issues such as social purity.

Jessie C. Smith
"Social Purity" (1898)

"A nation rises no higher than its mothers."

Would that these words might be printed indelibly on the mind of every woman, and burn like fire in her heart, giving her no rest day nor night, until she should recognize her own little individual responsibility before God as a factor in His work for the elevation of humanity, aye and in united work with her sisters, His most powerful agent on this earth.

Let the few of us assembled here this afternoon bring home to ourselves our responsibility as co-workers with God – and I make no apology for the use of the word "us," when addressing wives and mothers, for the painful solicitude of the old maid, for the proper bringing up of her children has become a matter of proverb and notoriety and, since the partial emancipation of woman through their admission to education and a consequent participation in a more active and public life than was formerly possible to them, the children of the desolate have become more than of her that is a married wife. So let us all, mother creatures endeavoring to realize our responsibility toward the rising generations, consider in what ways and by what means we may help to cleanse away the sins that are a shame unto this people, and – how we may help to bring in, working with God, the righteousness that healeth a nation. Here we are from many parts of Nova Scotia, every one of us, disclaim the burden as we may, distinctly conscious that, each in her own community is, must be, an influence for or against progress, a worker with or against God – and inaction counts with God for opposition. With this admission of our responsibility let us further admit that there are everywhere, many women like-minded with ourselves, and many more who would gladly join in our interest and help in our work if we wisely and lovingly tried to win them over. So enlarging our circle and extending our influence, let us look forward twenty years and say whether or not we may, by earnest loving service, help the generation that is now rising around us to a higher plane of life than is the lot of the days in which we live. A very awful thought it is that

"A partnership with God is motherhood,"
and well may we continue,
"What strength, what purity, what self-control, What love, what wisdom should belong to her Who helps God fashion an immortal soul."

That is the burden that rests on Christian Mothers, helping God fashion immortal souls, and our WCTU true to God, and Home, and Native land, sets itself to help Mothers, and Fathers too, in laying, as the hearthstone of every home, the foundation of Social Purity in Canada, let us, then, like charity, begin at home. In this department we lay hands first on the little child that is born, – for the little unborn child, with its heritage as it may be, of pure or of sinful tendencies, of weakness or of strength of body and mind, is the charge, in our work, of the Department of Health and Heredity.

What can Mothers do? What can they not do! "Give me the first five years of a child's life," says a wise man, and you may do what you like with him afterwards; he is always mine. The wise man does not mean by this a child who only plays about his house for the first five years of its life, perhaps getting a good-night or good morning kiss six days in a week, and a loafing time with the over tired father on the Sabbath day. No, he means a child who is his constant companion, modeling its early deportment on that of the admired "big man," and so growing into habits of rudeness or of courtesy; imitating his speech, refined or vulgar, foul or clean; absorbing his ideas on every subject; knowing only the books that he reads, – and the Bible may be among them, – on every side of his nature, while mind and heart are yet as "wax to receive, and marble to retain," receiving those impressions which will never pass away, because at this stage of life they form habit, and, in weaker and slower minds, even character. We sadly admit, that many Mothers do not sufficiently estimate the importance of the earliest days and years of a child's life. If they did, and in the fear of God, with a sense of responsibility for immortal souls committed to their charge, how soon, oh! how soon, would this sad world change into a great house of purity and peace, and, generation by generation grow again into the lost likeness of sons of God, dwellers on earth on that great day when angels stood in multitudinous ranks to see Gods wonders in creation.

"When, up against the white shore of their feet,
The depths of creation swelled and brake,
And the new worlds, the headed foam and flower
Of all that coil, roared outward into space."

When the morning stars sang together, and all the sons of God shouted for joy. Oh! let us, my sisters, bear witness continually, at every opportunity, in every home that we enter, to mothers and to fathers, of the eternal importance of the first five years of a child's life, and of their awful responsibility in regard thereto.

We are not sufficiently informed on these matters, some of you will say. Well be informed. Pray God to give you deep convictions in this line of WCTU work, and, take my word for it, by this time next year you will be informed, for we know that if we ask according to His will He heareth us. You will observe, you will read, you will act, for God uses not the willfully ignorant, nor the idler. The better informed we are the more respect will our work receive from those whom we approach, and the more valuable will be our help.

We will suppose that, by day and by night, while the little child has been wholly under the influence and tuition of father and mother, it has been carefully watched and guarded from every impurity of thought or of act, taught cleanliness and modesty, and most of all, has learned to pray to God – not merely to say its prayers. Now comes the launch into life, – entrance into school, and companionship with the vile. This cannot be avoided. At this time there is circulating in Ontario schools, and God knows in how many other places, an abominable doggerel verse, set to a familiar air which gives with obscene wit the whole story of ante-natal life of a child, and of its birth, and we know that there are everywhere circulating filthy slang expressions which fasten as burrs in the minds of children and cannot be got rid of. What shall we do about this? Get the help of the teachers. Ask them and they are already interested in great part, and the unawakened teachers will be stirred and helped by your interest – ask them to keep sharp ears for foul language and writings on walls of outhouses and elsewhere, keep sharp ears yourselves for what children bring home in their hitherto clean little mouths. Look out for nasty pictures that are often circulated in schools by those debased creatures whose business in life it is, for trade purposes to create a taste for filthy literature and illustrations in young minds. Look after the outhouses in connection with your schools, and, if your own schools are well provided, take the country schools to your heart. We all know what the country school house outhouse is like, – if there happens to be one. A little box of a place with one door half off its hinges, and no decencies. Boys and girls have to dodge each other, and modesty is in danger of strangulation. Here you have to confer with school commissioners. Get up a sentiment among the women – (and their husbands), before you move in this matter, then move, and your sentiment will find itself a power. Next thing, if you go so far, you will see the necessity for women being members of school boards. There are many things in school management on which young women teachers feel themselves unable to talk with men – strangers to them. A pure minded, earnest, intelligent woman on a school board would be a greater power for purity among school children than any three men have ever been – and this not by way of disparagement of our brothers, but merely as a statement of fact which they will be the last to question – for by their works, particularly in the line of outhouses for schools, do we know them.

Still your boys and girls are growing. Are they questioning? They have heard things of curious import, and a sense of shame and indecency becomes connected with what is a pure ordinance of God. "Where did I come from?" asks the child, and if Mother or Father has not already prepared the way, by suitable, delicate, loving instruction in regard to the bodies in which we live, the child is not apt to ask that question of those who have the responsibility of helping at that time. What the parent does not tell cleanly, and make sacred, as belonging to Fatherhood, to Motherhood, someone else will tell foully. Henceforth it is more than difficult to keep the heart pure – and out of it are the issues of life. Ignorance is not purity, nor ever can be, – nor is it a friend of purity, nor helpful to the cause.

I have lately received a letter from a lady interested in this subject, in which she tells me that last winter, in one place an infamous scoundrel, a music teacher, ruined the lives of thirteen young girls. Probably the great majority of these girls were absolutely ignorant of what, as women, they should have known. They were ignorant, but the world will never again call them innocent. For youth or for maiden properly instructed in regard to their bodies as temples of God, in every function, sacred to Him, I believe that knowledge concerning all functions is the safeguard of purity, health and happiness which it is the duty of every Christian parent to impart.

Now lookout for the Press. Watch for objectionable stories, for smart reports of questionable plays, and for nasty advertisements, and help your Press Superintendent in her work for the suppression of all these features in your local as well as in our Provincial news-papers. She cannot do it all alone, but if all the women in your district would combine to protest against the publication of advertisements which tell of crime and disease, and, among women lead to further sin. Your local Press Superintendent would find her hands strengthened and her work accomplished. Help her also, to watch the post office. She will or should have, a list of prohibited magazines and papers, get a copy, and if you see one of the number in possession of any one notify her of your discovery and the postmaster will, if requested at once suppress that evil.

Now your boys and girls are forming friendships, going into society, and they are yet in danger. You know of some whom they must meet socially, and you advise and warn. Do more than this: investigate the record of every man or woman your children may meet. There are not, I hope, many of those utterly abandoned men who use drugged sweets to accomplish their purposes, but I have known of two cases myself in one of which a young married man attempted unsuccessfully, the ruin of a girl of sixteen, his own cousin at that, a stranger in this country, whom he was taking home in his carriage to visit in his family. Another case I know, most pitiful, in which a young girl innocent, sweet, religious, was ruined by her lover, and quite without her knowledge or even a suspicion. Her anguish was terrible. Her family forced a marriage but the poor girl has never lived with the man who served her so, and now, with her little child, lives worse than widowed.

You are aware that, up to the age of sixteen years only our girls are protected by law against seductions. Here is a field for work in Social Purity. A girl ruined early becomes a seduction, a ruin to the young men. For the sake of the boys, if not for the sake of the girls even, let us endeavor to influence legislation to help keep our girls pure until they have reached an age at which the great majority of them at least do know the consequences of error or sin on their part.

But, above all, let us constantly endeavor to elevate the standard of Social Purity among men. Mr Stead says that the English have taught men to be brave, and women to be chaste. Let us go farther, teaching men to be chaste and women to be brave. Let us insist on a white life for two, holding the boy's chastity of as vital importance as the girl's, and let our own girls be brave in choosing only pure companionship among young men. It has been said that society's public opinion has been, and is, the safeguard of women. Why should not this be so of men? What we expect of obedience from a child we get. What we expect from courtesy of friends we get. What we expect of purity in women we get. Why not expect purity of young men? Of all men? Let us not shrink from the battle, but be vigilant watching the cradle, the home, the school, the press, our legislative bodies, ever endeavoring with the Purity Alliance, "to secure the repression of vice, the better protection of the young, the rescue of the fallen, the extension of the white cross work among men, the maintenance of the law of purity as equally binding on men and women."

Let us be practical, beginning work in our own neighborhood. Let us find out where are the disreputable houses, and get the names of the frequenters and their inmates, and let us as Christians, do personal work with both classes as we may get to know them. Christ when on earth must needs go through Samaria. His great heart sorrowed for the woman who was a sinner, and He sought her out, and got her on His side and she worked with Him and for Him, and does yet, in the story of her change of heart and life under the power of Love incarnate.

What did Christ see in this lost woman? He saw great spiritual nature which time nor sin can destroy. He saw a heart burdened with sin, longing for purity. He saw a life held down to the ruin of others. He lifted it up for the help of others. No heart is fully evil. Every soul hears the divine message and honors it. Every soul may be saved. Shall we let the women of the city go down to death and lead the young after them, when we may, like Christ, approach them in some humane office, win their confidence, awaken interest, love, and bring them, by the grace of God, again to the purity and peace that is ever for women!

[Source: Jessie C. Smith, "Social Purity," *Third Annual Report of the Nova Scotia WCTU, 1898*, 58–63.]

Dora Forster Kerr was born in England and immigrated to Canada with her spouse, R.B. Kerr, in 1893. During their time in Canada, from 1893 to 1922 they lived in a number of smaller British Columbia communities. Kerr wrote for the Chicago-based libertarian journal *Lucifer* from 1899 to 1905, and a number of articles that she published in it were reissued as *Sex Radicalism*. She also wrote for Canadian publications such as the *Western Clarion*, *Western Socialist*, *Cotton's Weekly*, and *Champion*, albeit in none of these journals did she adopt such a radical stance on issues related to sexuality.

Dora Forster (Kerr)
From *Sex Radicalism* (1905)

VI. The Sex War

The sex forces will always be liable to produce disturbance and conflict as surely as electricity in the atmosphere under certain conditions gives the explosions of thunder and lightning. Sometimes the battle is in the mind of the individual, sometimes it is in the half-conscious rivalry of persons of the same sex, but under fully developed Puritanism it is more or less open war between men and women, with the priests encouraging it, as is their wont in all strife, and taking fees here and there for drawing up a partial truce, supposed to be a lasting Peace of God, called marriage.

There is supposed to be a kind of standard of honor or fair play in all contest. If so, it is hard to say whether men or women, ranged on opposite sides in this social strife, have descended most mean when acting singly, entrapping men into marriage, and the men most ungenerous when acting in bodies, trying to starve or harass women of every profession except marriage.

The men seem actuated by pure malice, only partly excused by their ignorance. But a woman who tries to get married has in case of failure to lose some of the most obvious rights of a human being, and moreover loses usually her only chance of a career. And the women certainly have the excuse of acting by puritan principles. The marriageable woman is never allowed to lose sight of the main chance. Even in our nurseries the lesson is instilled. In the ballad of "The little man and the little maid," the maid replies to her ardent wooer, "Will your flames assist a little to boil water in the kettle?" and her scorn of love is deemed praiseworthy.

Should a girl have an ambition to cultivate the friendship of some man comrade, – "What can it lead to?" asks the puritan aunt or mother. A young Scotch lady when congratulated on her engagement to a neighboring minister, replied, politely depreciating the merits of the bargain she had secured, "Yes, it is a very nice manse, only the bedroom ceilings are rather low." She was imbued with true puritan principles. And how often is marriage in England or America as much an arrangement made by the parents as any marriage in France!

The girl who turns from this sort of bargaining and aims at independence soon finds that one has not only the sneers of men to face, but their persistent endeavors to keep her out of all but the lowest work. Men like to preach about the place of the womanly woman being in the home, when the girl who suffers from their spite not only may have no home to look forward to, but has to struggle to live and work in a garret.

Perhaps it is a good sign that the women have begun to "talk back," and many now think it spirited conversation to make little hints at the weaknesses of men, though the speakers are often without any appreciation of the working of a sex system that weighs most heavily on the best men as on all women.

Among the worst effects of the sex war are the divisions it causes among women, and the want of sympathy between the three classes, the married, the celibate and the prostitute. The contempt of the wife for the spinster is sometimes unconcealed. "It is a good thing," said one, "that there are sisterhoods in which superfluous women can do useful work." And the attitude of a past generation toward some of the saddest sides of these questions is well worth noting, that women, at least may never again fall so low as to take such an attitude. The clear-sightedness of youth would lead to some amazed questions of what? how? or why? And our grandmothers or aunts would reply: "oh, we know all about that, but *do not stir up the mud*." That the best human vitality should be forced to flow in underground courses, and be regarded as a sewer too foul to be ever cleansed, is a situation which is wholly unworthy of an age rejoicing in the dawning light of science.

I have seen a good deal of the "class war," and it was what I heard in comfortable drawing-rooms which first made me feel heart and soul with the weaker side. Such remarks as "shoot them down," which were no mere pleasantries were passed, when workmen were on strike for living wage or for decent hours of work. Yet the brutality of men upholding wage slavery is fully equaled by that of men upholding sex slavery. If they do not want to take the lives of women, they are desirous that everything should be taken from the lives of women that make life worth living. Men seem able to behave generously towards any one woman in concrete form (unless married to her), but cannot feel the simplest humanity toward women collectively.

History has not failed to record the behavior of the men who in every instance opposed the endeavor of women to obtain university education. Formerly it was the "blue" woman who was the object of ridicule; now it is the "new woman"; but the speakers always seem equally ignorant of what they are talking about.

The sex war can perhaps be best studied in England. The sex which utterly refuses to have celibacy thrust upon themselves is quite willing that it should be thrust on the opposite sex; and men of the most cultivated social class who are forever preaching maternity to women as their one great function are indifferent to the fact that fifty per cent of the women of their own class are condemned to be unmated and childless. One can scarcely avoid the conclusion that men like the presence of a number of sexually starved women to minister to their vanity and afford a large selection when it pleases them to choose a wife. The sexual starvation and coercion of an Oriental harem scarcely goes further than this.

Again, professional life, with its training, regular occupation, the social position that salaried work gives, the social variety it usually affords is so healthful as largely to counteract the evils of the sex deprivations above noticed; yet men have persistently tried to bar all professions against women.

It would be noted, however, that menial work, or work poorly paid or unpaid, is not called unwomanly. All the most trying work in the treatment of diseases, whether in public or private, is done by nurses mostly women. The clergy induce women to perform the work of curates in the parish without payment. The professional man asks his sister to keep house for him without salary and turns her off without a pension when it suits him to replace her by a wife. And the menial offices of that "great unpaid" class, the mothers of families are too numerous to mention.

It is some years over a century since women, led by Mary Wollstonecraft claimed to be human beings in their own right, and not mere appendages to men. That claim is not yet fully established, but it will be, and men will wonder how it could ever have been denied. And the greatest force to end the bitterness of the sex war will be the recognition of sex love as a power for good and a principle to regulate the conduct men and women as equal comrades; and thus will be abolished all buying and selling and coercion in sex favors.

[Source: Dora Foster, *Sex Radicalism as Seen by an Emancipated Woman of the New Time* (Chicago: M. Harman, 1905), 24–8.]

Anonymous

The White Slave Trade in Montreal (1913)

There is vice here like there is in all big cities. Many are the young women who fall victim to it, whether through their own fault, through the fault of the pimps in the employ of houses of ill repute, or through the fault of public authorities. But vice has also elicited a generous and zealous dedication from some who are working to remedy the problem.

The blame for these lamentable falls from grace belongs first of all to the young women themselves. Danger fascinates and attracts them; they go toward it like moths to the flame. The charming insect burns its wings and often dies. The child, innocent and pure up to that point, loses her modesty and reservations, that indefinable attraction that adds to her grace. Many are not only imprudent, they are flirts, girls of easy virtue. They have scarcely arrived to earn a living in the big city, when they begin to frequent the theatres, the cinemas, and the busy streets filled with crowds of idle folk. There they make acquaintances, form dangerous relationships. On a slippery slope, they slide all the way to the bottom of the abyss. Others turn to vice because they expect luxury, flashy clothes, to have ease and comfort in life.

When these young women do not turn toward vice themselves, it lies in wait and seeks them out. Panderers creep like snakes in the grass everywhere they can make off with defenceless young women. They are in the trains, on the boats, in the restaurants, at the stations. There are reports of them disguised as commercial travellers scouring our countryside in the region south of the St Lawrence. They seduce naïve village girls with enticing promises and the addresses they give these girls lead them to perdition.

Unfortunately the authorities are more or less indifferent. The guilty ones who are caught and convicted are punished, but little effort is made to apprehend them and put an end to their appalling traffic. Faced with an immense country that is developing at an almost violent rate, government finds it necessary to address so many commercial and industrial problems, finds it so crucial to multiply the lines of communication, agricultural outlets and avenues for immigration, that purely moral issues are lost from view, relegated to the back burner.

It is left to private initiatives to take up the challenge, and that has not failed to happen. The wonderful, collective work of coordinating these scattered undertakings is yet to come. Our hope is that it will. Already the work of the protection of young women has been undertaken by affiliated institutions. Le

Foyer, a Catholic association in Montreal, which aims to come to the aid of the young woman and the working woman, is at the centre of this effort in Canada. It has been engaged over the past few years in establishing contacts, both in big cities and in the countryside, who will notify it of the departure for Montreal of young women who are travelling there to work. These young women are met at the stations, directed to secure rooming houses and well-run workshops. An information bureau (60 Notre Dame Street West) has been opened and placed at the service of those arriving so that in establishing themselves in the city, these young women will not be exposed to all the dangers to which so many arriving before them have been lost. It is important to acknowledge here that the secretary of the bureau has never called on railway personnel or public officers without finding them ready and willing to carry out the interventions requested of them.

The immigration bureaus, at the head of which the diocesan authority has placed priests, also zealously track the relocation of our women workers and domestic servants.

To sum up: in the face of great dangers and considerable vice, there is a charitable and dedicated organization whose work, thus far quite fruitful, promises to become more effective in the near future.

[Source: Anonymous, "The White Slave Trade," *La Bonne Parole*, July 1913, 2 (trans. Maureen Moynagh).]

Beatrice Brigden (1888–1977) grew up on a Manitoba farm and later attended university in Brandon before receiving a degree in elocution from the Toronto Conservatory. Brigden was a member of the WCTU and the Political Equality League of Manitoba. She worked for the Methodist Department of Social Service and Evangelism from 1913 to 1919. She resigned her position in part out of disillusionment at the conservative stance of Methodist leaders during this period and being drawn to the labour church movement. She went on to play a leading role in the Women's Labour League on the prairies in the 1930s.

Beatrice Brigden

From One Woman's Campaign for Social Purity and Social Reform (1913-1920)

[…] I returned from Toronto with a maturing social concern. There I became interested in city social problems. I first glimpsed slums as I walked through the old St John's ward toward Eaton's and Simpson's. With a YWCA worker I visited factories, observed the utter lack of factory inspection, unsanitary conditions, the slavery of low wages, the indifference as to quality of product. To this day I eat chocolates with a certain distrust. Back in Brandon I became active in the Methodist Epworth League in which young people were now involving themselves in the social concerns of immigration and the city outlined by Woodsworth in his *Strangers within Our Gates* and *My Neighbor.*

Our inspiration often came from the summer schools started by the League in the West and throughout the country, where one could meet and discuss with men like William Ivens, A.E. Smith, J.S. Woodsworth, and Salem Bland. In the summer of 1913, at the Souris and Rock Lake Summer Schools, I met a Mr Clark, boys' worker for the newly organized Methodist Department of Social Service and Evangelism. In many conversations he urged me to take on a similar task among girls, to lecture and counsel on sex hygiene and social problems. It seemed both an adventurous and a chancy undertaking for a single young woman barely into her twenties, but I allowed him to mention me to Dr T. Albert Moore, Clark's superior. Moore shortly came to Brandon to interview me, and after coming to the inevitable final and solemn question, "Are you converted?" – to which I stammered some sort of answer – persuaded me to take up the work. I was embarked on a fascinating and exhausting six-year career.

I needed preparation for embarking on such a venture, of course, and was soon on my way for Lacrosse, Wisconsin, for special studies in counseling, sex education and kindred themes. Then on to Hull House, Chicago, for two months of social studies and observation which entailed some contact with Jane Addams. Later I went to Louisville, Kentucky, for a special seminar, and in Toronto there was preliminary work in connection with city missions, the YWCA, juvenile delinquents, police women, the courts, as well as first-hand examination of industrial conditions.

Then came the travel; endless travel, including five months in Newfoundland, two winters in B.C., over all of old Ontario, little in Quebec outside Montreal, but most of all across the prairies many times, east to west, north to south. Always I was in touch with Dr Moore, reporting and seeking advice. He was utterly constant in his support. Together we worked out the format of week-long appearances in communities that requested my services. The program seldom changed, and took good advantage of my training in vocal arts. There were regularly thirteen meetings per week, beginning with morning and evening sermons on Sunday and an address to Sunday School teenagers. On Monday morning came a recital of specially chosen stories and poems of social significance, interspersed with musical numbers. In the towns and villages especially, this combination of entertainment and thought-provoking content roused remarkably large audiences and evoked a moving response that carried through the week. Then on succeeding days came afternoon and evening meetings for mothers, girls, young women and mixed audiences. With Saturday came the parting from people one had become close to, a rush for the train, and arrival in a new strange town.

The pattern was only broken when summer came with its summer schools. There were still addresses, discussions, disputations, but the association was more sustained, intimate and relaxed. But the chattering of girls far into the night and the sagging cots did little to rest one. Only a month's holiday at home did that. Then the year began its cycle once more.

Nothing can better convey my experiences in those years of pioneer lecturing on sex education and social problems than excerpts from the letters I regularly sent to Dr Moore in Toronto.

Brandon, Manitoba, September 22, 1913.
Re – my sending you a lecture, I call them talks ... I very rarely write out anything ... however while preparing the last of my talks I put it on paper [for you] ... I am searching for suitable illustrations, and shall have to adapt my discussion of venereal diseases to the illustrations I am able to possess. Am not sure how you will view my introductory pages, but in teaching I have found Nature a never ending source of analogy ... Since beginning work on these talks I have resolved to use my own charts in a number of cases, drawing the desired figures or organs ...

Pilot Mound, January 23, 1915.
My days were filled with personal talks in Crystal City. Words cannot describe Heaven glimpsed through a soul, still less can they describe the despair of another, driven to that despair, that Hell shall I say, by the cruel deception of one well loved, and the mock modesty of offended society. I shall feel for many a day the clinging of those arms and the shaking of that voice saying over and over "If you had only come to me a year ago," a little fifteen year old girl.

Lumsden, Saskatchewan, May 3, 1915.
Our first mothers' meeting was largely attended but the second was most decidedly not. When a discussion was suggested they all modestly hung their heads ...

Nelson, B.C., Feb. 13, 1917.
Our week in Cranbrook proved a very interesting and successful one ... The Women's Institute made a special effort ... and attention was extraordinary ... The only

work out of the ordinary for me was a visit to "the district" back on the hill – Mrs Keyworth is an old time slum worker and wished for an opportunity to visit those houses. So we went together, of course beyond showing our interest, there was little for us to do as most of the women are older than I am – have been in "the business" too long to care about leaving – and I think on the whole were somewhat amused at my work … I have not met nor have I heard of many women who are so engaged today – of as broad a culture and refinement as one of the keepers, a young woman – a widow who claims economic pressure as the cause of her entering the life – She discussed her life very freely and was most generous in her advice.

Taber, Alta., Jan. 16, 1917.

Our week in Medicine Hat was a perfect delight … The Collegiate was opened to us and the Local Council of Women and our Socialists friends were much interested – While the Pastors attitude alone would have been sufficient to bring out the best in me.

Olds, Alta., June 2, 1916.

We had a really delightful week in Ponoka. Such crowds of girls and all so interested … so many little personal chats. Many women in the town told me they were "awfully bad girls" … The girls asked at the last meeting if a club could not grow out of our week together, but no one could be found to take charge of organization etc … People do not give young folks anything of a helpful nature, and then complain all the time of their frivolity …

Such excerpts do not tell the whole story, of course, of interesting contacts with professional people and social reformers across the country. I was particularly excited to meet and have my work heartily endorsed by Nellie McClung and Judge Emily Murphy during a notable week in Edmonton. Always I was supported by women's groups and the editors of local papers. Unfortunately, I met with no such unanimous response from the clergy, even of my own church. Many readily took up the challenge, and you could always be sure of the support of those who had come under the influence of Salem Bland at Wesley College. Some were finicky about letting me speak from the pulpit, and most were very curious about what I told their women and girls – not infrequently I became aware of an intent listener behind a curtain or partially closed study door. Many simply quietly ignored my letters, too embarrassed, perhaps, even to pass the offer on to the women of the church. Often, when I attended conferences of women's groups, local delegates would learn with high indignation of the spurned proposal – and I sometimes shuddered at the thought of the encounter that would follow their return home! […]

[Source: Beatrice Brigden, "One Woman's Campaign for Social Purity," in *The Social Gospel in Canada*, ed. Richard Allen (Ottawa: National Museums, 1975), 43–52.]

A detailed biography of Una Saunders may be found on page 91.

Una Saunders

From *The Young Women's Christian Association in Canada and Its Work* (1919)

[...] HOLIDAY CAMPS – For girls with limited means, the question of Summer Holiday is a very difficult one and many of them have been gladdened when they found the City Association to which they belonged, had a summer camp or cottage to which they could go. Calgary has one at Banff, Vancouver one at Whytecliff Beach, Montreal one in the Laurentians, to mention only a few renowned for especial beauty. Some City Associations also have a camp during the summer within car-fare distance, so that girls who cannot afford a real holiday may yet go and live out there and come in daily to their work. The Dominion council has also managed for three years a Provincial Holiday Camp near Lake Couchiching, Ontario largely for industrial workers. These camps are found to be such a source of benefit, to body, mind and soul that the Council is desirous of seeing a considerable increase of them throughout the country, and it is hoped that public-minded citizens may help to make them possible by giving land on which a camp centre could be erected.

RECREATION – While a camp provides one of the best summer recreations for a privileged few the whole vital question remains of the leisure hours of girls in cities and the many difficulties and temptations surrounding them. Commercial bodies direct their best efforts to make recreation attractive, and while some few are highly principled, the greater number pay no real attention to the moral aspect of the question and too many actually pander to the lower instincts and stimulate the very passions we would fain see kept under strict control.

As an Association, the provision of recreation has not yet gone far. The clubs and classes, the athletic meets, the physical culture departments are all, of course, the best of counter-attractions to the lower forms of amusement, but they reach far too few. The accommodation and equipment of most of the Association buildings is utterly inadequate to provide for all the wholesome fun that should be within the reach of girls living away from their own homes. It will undoubtedly require in many cities the co-operation of the churches before such provision can be made. There are Church buildings still unused certain nights of the week, as well as school buildings. Why should not an effort be made to organize recreation on a much larger scale under a regularly equipped director, perhaps attached to the YWCA staff and free to co-operate with any bodies that can provide a place suitable for social gatherings?

It will not alone be the recreation of girls that calls for this united effort. One of the pathetic sights is to see men and girls obliged to use the streets or "movies" for opportunities for perfectly legitimate friendship. The few girls boarding in the Association Home can of course, bring their men friends there to sit and talk but what is really needed is something of a centre or club, perhaps under the united guardianship of the YMCA and YWCA and backed by the churches they represent. There men and women could enjoy real fun together, could at times play and dance, could sit down to a light meal together and feel the joy of something approaching a home atmosphere. A beginning of this kind has been made by the YWCA in Halifax in two efforts, one being a Patriotic Service Battalion of women recruited from many churches and uniting to provide good recreation for the many soldiers and sailors in the city; the other a girls' club where every night girls may bring in their men friends. One sailor, in expressing his appreciation of this place described how till then he had to go to a dance hall, "a hell of a place." The question of dances under proper supervision is being discussed in many places and various small experiments have been made.

TEENAGE GIRLS' WORK – Under this title we class a wide spread and comparatively new part of our work, much of which is done in co-operation with the Sunday School leaders. The great success attending a similar work of co-operation for boys, called the "Canadian Standard Efficiency Test," led to the formation of a National Advisory Committee on co-operation in girls work some three year ago. On this Committee sit representatives of the Sunday School Boards of the Anglican, Baptist, Methodist and Presbyterian bodies, the Sunday School Association and the Young Women's Christian Association. Unitedly, they have drawn up and are propagating throughout the country an outline programme for girls work called "Canadian Girls in Training." The idea at the heart of this lies in the thought of a symmetrical four-fold development of every girl's life and is based on the words, "Jesus increased in wisdom and stature and in favour with God and man." The task of making this symmetrical development tangible to girls is a difficult one. A "Girls Standard" has therefore been worked out, showing in tabular form some of the ideals (physical, social, intellectual, religious) to which each girls' life should approximate in some degree. Such a "standard" explained practically and sympathetically by a leader at a conference or in club or class, may be the very spur needed to quicken some girl to make use of the opportunities around her and develop those qualities in which she sees herself to be lacking. Under the physical standard come such matters as health education, physical culture, sports, etc.; under the intellectual, school, home-reading, public speaking, educational trips, hobbies, etc.; under the religious; daily prayer, and Bible reading, public worship, personal dedication, systematic giving, mission study, etc.; under the social (or service) standard; personal relationships in home and church and community, training for leadership, choosing a vocation.

Plans for helping towards this development are also outlined and great stress is laid on Sunday School classes, and the midweek meeting which should be associated with the class. Programmes worked out in much detail are included in the pamphlet which is used unitedly by all the co-operating bodies and can be obtained from the headquarters of each denomination and the YWCA.

Growing out of this work has been the succession of Conferences for Teen Age girls and leaders, held throughout the Dominion, under the united auspices, with speakers from each group. The National YWCA has thrown itself whole-heartedly into this work and is giving the services of three or four national workers to cover the Dominion and work in co-operation with the churches. In some cities the mid-week meetings of the Sunday School group are held in the YWCA building, because it provides equipment for physical culture and can also accommodate the separate groups in different rooms for that part of the evening's programme which belongs to the small class alone with it own teacher. The same scheme of "Canadian Girls in Training" is of course, used by many YWCA groups and clubs. In this co-operative work, however, much attention is being given to encouraging girls to remain in or to join Sunday School classes ...

[Source: Una Saunders, *The Young Women's Christian Associations of Canada and Its Work* (1919), 8–11.]

Florence Rowe
Better and Fewer Babies (1924)

A young married woman came to me the other day and said: "I wish I knew how to avoid having babies."

I quoted: "The sky is falling I must go and tell the king." "Good gracious I thought you both liked babies?"

"So we do," said my visitor. "Teddy thinks the world of the three we have, in fact, in fact he spoils them, but we don't want any more. I don't want to spend all my life bearing children. My mother had ten and you see what she is now. She is only fifty-two, but she looks like seventy-two."

"She certainly looks old," I was obliged to agree, "but still lots of women do have a good-sized family and seem to thrive alright," I said just a little amused perhaps, for my young friend was taking it so seriously.

"Oh, yes," she said, "but not those who do the work for them, not those who bear all those children, and do the washing for them and get up at nights to give em a drink and tuck the bed clothes in and never get a full night's sleep, and then have to get up to get father's breakfast like my mother had to do, they don't 'thrive,' they look like my mother and she says she wouldn't have more than three, anyway, if she had known how to prevent it, but she was brought up a Roman Catholic and so was I, for that matter, but I don't care, I don't believe we have to let the church rule us!"

I clapped my hands and said, "Amen. Neither do I. They have ruled us through our ignorance, but as knowledge grows, the power of superstition dies."

We sat quietly for a time and then my friend remarked, "I think it is a crime that working women cannot freely and legally obtain the information necessary to avoid a large family without injuring their own health, as we know so many do now."

"That is so," I replied, "and W.J. Robinson, M.D. in his book says, 'Abortion is the most horrible evil,' is responsible for the death of thousands of (legally) unmarried women and tens of thousands of (legally) married women."

"Well," said the young married woman rather positively, "I won't have any more. I love those I've got too well. I want to bring them up decently, anyway."

"Alright," I said, "I hope you will be able to keep your vow, but mind what you do."

And after she was gone I continued to think of what a silly short-sighted affair our social system is. We had a Social Service Congress a week or two ago and many quite well-intentioned people sat and heard equally well-meaning folks deplore doubtless quite sincerely the vast numbers of "under privileged" children (not to mention the defective ones) with all that is therein implied. How much better, wiser, to prevent them coming until homes were fit for children to come to. They spoke of the amount of money and effort required to even remedy these things yet never even mentioned what would be a real social service, and that is to make possible the obtaining sufficient intelligence and love for each other and their children to desire it, the information as to how to limit the family without injuring the health or happiness of either, instead of as now, ignorance on the matter prevailing where such a knowledge would be of the greatest use. Health and business are both seriously jeopardized, to say the least, when there is a large family and little or nothing to keep them on.

Then again, I heard from a public platform of women whose husbands had been in the mental hospital, or the tubercular hospital and they, the women, wishing to avoid any more children, seeking authoritative information from one of our public agencies where it might reasonably be expected to be found, being refused because it is "against the law."

You ask me "what is this to do with working class women?"

I answer, "it has much do with them. Is it not from our children the ranks of labor are recruited? Is it not our sons who are the rank and file of the army and navy? Is it not our sons who are the great sad army of unemployed, gradually becoming, as the years roll on, the great army of the unemployable, for to be continually 'out of work' and obliged to take the quantity and quality of food decided on by someone else is one of the most demoralizing things I know of. It embitters the spirit and lowers the mentality."

"Sister women, mothers who think, turn this matter over in your minds. Refuse the undignified position that either Abraham or Paul or the later creation of man's mind, the prayer book, give you. Look at life as it really is for us of the working class."

The question of the scientific regulation of human births is not offered as the "complete solution," but it is one that has deep significance. Nothing is unrelated and when seriously studying the problems of the working class this side of life may well be considered in its relation to the ever-growing, more acute class struggle.

[Source: Florence Rowe, "Better and Fewer Babies" *One Big Union Bulletin*, 6 November 1924.]

Helen MacMurchy (1862–1953) briefly taught high school before enrolling at the Ontario Medical College for Women in Toronto, from which she graduated in 1901. She practised medicine for a short time before taking a position with the Ontario government as a medical inspector. In 1920 she was appointed director of the Division of Child Welfare within the federal Department of Health. She wrote a number of pamphlets and books including *The Canadian*

Mother's Book and *Sterilization? Birth Control? A Book for Family Welfare and Safety*. The latter publication reflected her growing interest in and public advocacy of eugenics.

Helen MacMurchy
What Are We Going to Say to Our Young People? (1934)

> It is characteristic of science and progress that they continually open new fields to our vision.
>
> Pasteur

We come back to the Canadian doctor's question – "What are we going to say to our young people?"

No wonder that he asked the question. Every member of the profession feels the pressure of demands never made before. Nor would any of us wish to deny them. Our young people have a right to know the truth. And the truth about this matter of birth control is that it is against one's better judgment. It is unnatural. It is contrary to one's higher instincts. It is repugnant to a member of the medical profession whose work and whose desire is to promote health and happiness, to prevent or cure disease and to search out new knowledge and new and better ways of doing our work. Each patient who comes to the clinic, because that is the only chance of the poor for medical consultation, has a right to the truth. We must say, too, that there is no entirely reliable method of preventing conception except the way of abstention and even in that way there are dangers. Nor are other ways of preventing conception safe. They all appear to be more or less harmful. No safe and unobjectionable method has yet been discovered.

The case of each patient must be decided on its merits, after a thorough and careful study and consideration of the patient and of all the patient says and thinks, and of all the reasons and conditions which may properly affect the doctor's decision.

There are grievous cases known to us all – cases which are shocking and intolerable. Such cases do not come till self-respecting and self-control, love and kindness, are lost or losing. These cases should be prevented. The patients should be helped. The doctor must take the responsibility of considering and advising on these.

But shall we consider birth control as a matter of course for the bridegroom and the bride? No. The love and grace and tenderness, the beauty and sanctity of life centre in the home and around the marriage that founds the home. Grace and beauty and tenderness, sanctity and affection can hardly remain if what should be revered like a sacrament is treated as a thing to be lightly esteemed.

Summary

1 Birth control or contraception is not a normal thing. It should not be undertaken or carried on except for clear, definite and grave reasons of a medical nature and under medical advice.
2 If a married couple decide to practice contraception, medical advice and supervision are always necessary to preserve the health and safety of the patient and consequently the happiness of the home. Mental health as well as physical health may be affected by carrying on the practice of birth control.
3 The effects of contraceptive practices are often serious; perhaps these effects are always serious, but so far little or no attempt has been made to study, record and follow up the medical history of patients who have practiced birth control for a long period of time. If and when such a study is made, it must be under medical scientific supervision and control in order to be satisfactory and reliable.
4 There are good reasons why those contemplating marriage should consult their family physician and request a thorough health examination, such as the periodic health examination which many people now have every year and which is usually made by the family physician. Advice as to the conduct of married life may be requested at that time. Perhaps in any case, even if the request is not made, the family physician may think it wise to inform the patient of the risk and danger of contraceptive practices. This applies to women about to be married as well as to men.
5 If and when at any time the use of contraceptive methods is suggested or considered, no decision to use any such method should be made until the family physician has been consulted, and his advice should be followed in every particular.
6 Contraceptive practices, at the best, are of an emergency nature and for use in exceptional cases only. They are probably never entirely free from risk and danger.
7 It cannot be denied that there are cases of a grievous and intolerable character in which, for example, the health of the mother has suffered from excessive child-bearing and in which the patient needs help. Some of these cases are referred to in the foregoing pages. Help in these cases is a matter of such urgent importance to the individual, to the family, to the medical profession and to the community that in some way it should be given.

[Source: Helen MacMurchy, "What Are We Going to Say to Our Young People?" in *Sterilization? Birth Control?: A Book for Family Welfare and Safety* (Toronto: Macmillan, 1934), 148–51.]

Winnifred Kydd received an MA from McGill University. She served as president of the Local Council of Women of Montreal from 1929–31 and as president of NCWC from 1931–6. Prime Minister R.B. Bennett appointed Kydd as delegate to the Disarmament Conference in Geneva in 1932. She was dean of women at Queen's University from 1934–9.

Winnifred Kydd
Miss Kydd's Statement on Birth Control (1934)

As your President I feel compelled to make the following statement.

The subject of Birth Control and Sterilization has never been passed upon by the National Council of Women of Canada, but the time has come when I honestly believe that, it is necessary for us to make our non-sectarian and non-political stand plain to our Federated Associations and the Public at Large. The proud boast of the National Council of Women has been that we are representative of the womanhood of this nation and that organizations of individuals federating with us have full political and sectarian immunity in discussion. I would urge you with all earnestness and sincerity within me to declare that we have so many problems facing us as Citizens of this great Dominion that we will not discuss these two questions in the National Council of Women of Canada.

This has been given serious consideration by reason of: 1) observation of the action taken by our own Women's Institutes and of the Federation of Women's Clubs in the USA, and 2) the careful consideration of what the unity of the womanhood of the Dominion may mean in the life of our country.

Let me request what I said in my last Annual Report: "Let us not take up questions, which if discussed and passed upon would prevent us being called representative of the womanhood of this country."

[Source: LAC, MG 28, 245, vol. 29, file – Prospective Councils, Winnifred Kydd, "Miss Kydd's Statement on Birth Control, February, 1934."]

PART SIX
Work and Economic Status

It is not any woman's part
We often hear folks say.
And it will mar our womanhood
To mingle in the fray.
I fear I will never understand or realize it quite.
How a woman's fame can suffer
In struggling for the right.[1]

The above stanza is part of a poem entitled "Only a Working Girl," by Belleville, Ontario, domestic servant and labour advocate Marie Joussaye that was published in 1886. Joussaye's poem was aimed at encouraging women to join the Knights of Labor, a union organization that had originated in the United States and crossed the border into Canada in the early 1880s. In this specific stanza she argued that a woman's femininity would not be harmed by "struggling for the right," which referred to the reform efforts under way to improve the lives of labouring women. Women's economic status and their position in the paid labour force was yet another central issue that elicited continued debate and resulted in ongoing agitation during the first wave. Although overlapping social hierarchies shaped how reform initiatives were formulated and reformulated as well as how individuals and organizations participated, there was far greater working-class representation on this women's issue. And reflecting to some degree increasing continental economic integration and the growth of "international" labour organizations situated in North America, the imperial metropole was less of a referent in debates and endeavours over female labour-force participation than with other feminist concerns.

Marie Jossaye was by no means an exception among working-class women in endorsing collective solutions to the challenges brought about by the emergence of industrial capitalism in the mid-nineteenth century. Under the pseudonym of Canadian Girl, shoe factory employee Katie McVicar wrote a series of letters to the *Palladium of Labor*, official organ of the Knights of Labor in Canada, in 1883. Calling attention to the low wages and poor working conditions of female factory operatives and of other working-class women, McVicar proposed a "new departure" – organization by the Knights. This undertaking represented the confluence of a newly emerging union willing to accept female members, one of the only organizations of its kind to do so during this period, and a generation of working women seeking to ameliorate existing labour conditions. In an era in which male workers were joining together in ever greater numbers to address workplace problems through union formation, McVicar argued that this option must be available to women as well. But she also cautioned that the traditional methods of union organization for men would not be successful with working women. McVicar sought to draw attention to the specificity of labouring women's situation, while attempting to address inequities in the workplace and in the labour movement. Unfortunately, the sharp decline of the Knights by the turn of the century left working women once again with virtually no options for union organization, a situation which prevailed until the First World War.

Protective labour legislation was also widely advocated by working-class women and by many middle-class reformers on behalf of working women. Generally speaking, protective measures were deemed necessary by the former to limit some of the most exploitative aspects of paid employment since so few female workers had recourse to unions, and by the latter to safeguard the morals and health of future mothers.[2] The introduction of factory and shop acts at the provincial level beginning in the mid-1880s, which restricted hours of employment for women and children and implemented a system of workplace inspection, did not end but actually ushered in an ongoing discussion over protective legislation. Women activists questioned the relative merits of legislative protections and what, if any, new measures should be introduced. *The Conditions of Female Labour in Ontario* (1892) by social reformer and political economist, Jean Scott, provided one of the first in-depth studies of women's paid work in the country and also assessed existing labour legislation. Scott framed her analysis in comparative terms not only with England, "the parent of factory legislation," but also with the set of recommendations devised by the first international conference on labour legislation which had been held in 1890. Scott was thus able to point to numerous loopholes as well as demonstrate that Canadian protections lagged behind other national jurisdictions and did not yet meet proposed international standards with regard to hours of employment, night work, and maternity provisions.

Protective labour legislation was not uniformly supported within the women's movement, however, as illustrated by the debate which took place within NCWC in 1895 when members considered a resolution to reduce the maximum work day for women and children in industrial employment from ten to nine hours. Of particular significance, the main opposition came from middle-class and elite women in the Local Council of Women of Montreal who maintained that the perspective of employers had to be taken into consideration and that a mandated reduction in the work day might actually be harmful to the economic interests of working women. The views of working-class women were rarely well represented in the ranks of the NCWC, but on this occasion a member of the recently affiliated Working Women's Protective Union backed the resolution. Yet even she qualified her position by noting that employers found other ways of exploiting female workers beyond the length of the work day such as the widespread practice of intensifying production through reductions in piece rates. This employer strategy meant women had to work harder in order to earn the same level of wages.

The conditions of female industrial work remained a central concern, but other forms of women's employment received considerable notice as well. The Civic Committee of the University Women's Club of Winnipeg embarked on an extensive study of department store employees in 1913, an occupation which was part of the rapid growth in clerical and retail work after the turn of the century. The study documented the "hardships" of the occupation, noting in particular the poor working conditions in department stores related to constant standing, bad air, and "nervous tension" as well as unsuitable living accommodations. However, the committee's report reflected a widespread reticence on the part of many middle-class feminists in Canada and elsewhere to explicitly name one of the greatest problems facing working women which was inadequate wages. In fact, the report noted that "efficient adult saleswomen" could earn enough for minimum standard of living. A regular contributor to *Labour World/Monde Ouvrier,* Éva Circé-Côté did not concur with such an assessment. A staunch defender of working-class interests, Circé-Côté argued in one of her columns that part of the solution to women's low wages was equal pay for equal work. She offered the department store as an example where women should be granted wages equal to higher paid male employees.

Solutions were sought with regard to still other women's employment issues. Thus, West coast feminist and labour activist, Helena Gutteridge, touted the formation of a women's employment league in Vancouver during the economic recession in the early stages of the First World War. Gutteridge noted that this league, which she helped to create, assisted women in finding work at the same time as it called for an expanded role by the state in job creation. Yet similar to many female labour activists during this period, her support for women's access to employment was not absolute as she fully embraced the family wage ideal. This ideal gave priority to work for men as the designated breadwinner who should earn a wage sufficient to maintain an entire family. Gutteridge explained that in such circumstances married women could remain at home and they would not have to enter into competition with single women.

As evidenced by a separate article which appeared in the *BC Federationist*, Gutteridge was representative of working-class opinion in another important respect – she espoused the belief that the employment needs of white women superseded those of Asian men. In this specific instance, Gutteridge argued that Chinese men working in Vancouver hotels be replaced by unemployed white women. Although no further details are provided, it may be surmised that she approved of such women being hired only when the employer was white and not Asian. This was a period of time, after all, when there were repeated efforts in urban centres across the country to ban Asian business owners from hiring white women because of the sexual danger the men posed. Female and male labour leaders did not resist these initiatives but often championed them. While the labour movement in Canada challenged other aspects of the hegemonic culture in the late nineteenth century and early twentieth century, as David Goutour has maintained, with a few notable exceptions it "consistently embraced" racism and whiteness.[3]

Racial prejudice also directly influenced how the economic interests of Aboriginal women were perceived. Racism and the legacies of colonialism in large measure meant that Aboriginal women's engagement in paid labour remained almost entirely outside of discussions of "women's work." In many instances physically isolated on remote reserves, especially on the Prairies and in the North, and typically occupied in various kinds of family-based subsistence production and home manufacturing, indigenous women were rarely the subject of commentary on female employment. Even when engaged in "modern" labour such as canning in the fishing industry or as hop pickers, Aboriginal women warranted little recognition as wage workers.[4] As evidenced by the 1912 report by Amelia Paget for the Canadian Handicrafts Guild, their involvement in home-based craft production was framed far more often in cultural than economic terms. Paget who travelled to various Cree and Saulteaux reserves in Saskatchewan accentuated the importance of perpetuating handicrafts among these peoples, even encouraging that girls in residential schools be taught arts and crafts. While Paget promoted the retention of female handicrafts during an era when many other indigenous cultural traditions were officially banned, her report only hinted at the tangible economic benefits of such work.

The economic status of Euro-Canadian farm women garnered far more attention with feminists in many rural areas campaigning for legislative changes which would allow greater financial independence and power for agrarian women. In the prairie provinces in particular most women lacked homesteading rights and thus could not access free legal title to frontier lands, and were unprotected by dower laws which left them without any control of family property. Although the struggle for homestead rights extended well into the interwar period, rural women attained dower rights during the 1910s. Their success coincided with the "agrarian revolt" which saw the formation of farm protest groups and political organizations across the country. Farm women created separate organizations which worked in close alliance with male agrarian groups. Irene Parlby reminded readers of the *Western Producer* in 1925, however, that the economic situation of married farm women remained precarious.

The end of the First World War brought renewed attempts to foster greater co-operation on international labour standards for women. While state officials had spearheaded most efforts before the war, a more combative and energized international labour movement assumed a greater role afterward. Female leaders pressed for universal standards on the length of the work day, maternity allowances, hazardous occupations, and other matters of direct relevance to working women. Such was the case with the First International Congress of Working Women (ICWW) held in Washington, D.C. in 1919 with Canada being one of twelve countries to send a delegate. This delegate, Kathleen Derry, served as a vice-president on the ICWW for the next four years. In a subsequent submission to the *ICWW Bulletin*, Derry offered her support for government measures aimed at alleviating the exploitation of female immigrant workers.

The onset of the Great Depression created significant new challenges for working women, and for socialist and communist feminists who had long been their vocal advocates. These left-wing activists viewed themselves as engaged in an international struggle to eradicate all class inequality, and at the same time, to combat the gender specific problems of labouring women and of working-class women more generally. While often critical of state intervention, they nonetheless viewed protective regulations as necessary. For many of these women, their "dreams of equality" further involved an explicit commitment to gaining equality with men.[5] A 1935 report by Annie Buller, Director of the Women's Department of the Communist Party of Canada (CPC), criticized the party's inattention to mobilizing women or addressing their concerns. Citing various instances in which women had proven effective in participating in "militant" actions, Buller called upon her comrades to take up the demands of the employed, unemployed and housewives. Priority was given to the union organization of female industrial workers, but as part of the CPC's Popular Front strategy, it was also proposed that working-class housewives work in alliance with middle-class women to address economic issues such as the high cost of living and other aspects of the politics of consumption.

Bourgeois "career" women were also buffeted by the economic crisis of the depression, but middle-class feminists defined and defended their interests differently. They defined the "female labour question" for the most part in terms of ensuring access to the professions and skilled white-collar occupations, and defended the employment status of middle-class women by seeking to establish equal job opportunities and conditions with men. A 1936 study by the Canadian Federation of University Women (CFUW) emphasized that equality could only be achieved by the removal of protective labour legislation. The CFUW concurred with the stance adopted by Open Door International, a transnational feminist group which opposed all forms of gender-specific labour regulations.

NOTES

1 Quoted in Christina Burr, *Spreading the Light: Work and Labour Reform in Late-Nineteenth-Century Toronto* (Toronto: U of Toronto P, 1999), 145.
2 Nitza Berkovitch, *From Motherhood to Citizenship: Women's Rights and International Organizations* (Baltimore: Johns Hopkins, 1999), 47.
3 David Goutor, *Guarding the Gates: The Canadian Labour Movement and Immigration, 1872–1934* (Vancouver: University of British Columbia, 2007), 5.
4 Paige Raibmon, "The Practice of Everyday Colonialism: Indigenous Women at Work in the Hop Fields and Tourist Industry of Puget Sound," *Labor: Studies in Working Class History of the Americas* 3 (2006), 23–56.
5 Joan Sangster, *Dreams of Equality: Women on the Canadian Left, 1920–1950* (Toronto: McClelland & Stewart, 1989).

Katie McVicar (1856–86) was born in Hamilton, Canada West to a Scottish immigrant father and English immigrant mother. She followed two older sisters into industrial employment as a factory operative in the 1870s. McVicar never married and hence remained in the formal labour market far longer than most other working-class women during this period McVicar is attributed with being the author of a series of letters to the Knights of Labor in 1883 calling upon this industrial union to organize working women. Female textile workers and shoe operatives were part of a Knights local assembly created in January 1884 and several months later an all-female assembly was created with McVicar as directoress.

Katie McVicar

Organization Our Only Hope (1883)

To the Editor of the Women's Own Dep't:

On the 13th of April last I wrote you what I thought and still think, a very reasonable letter referring to the wages paid sewing girls in general, and those who work for wholesale houses in particular, and which you kindly published, and until last week I thought no notice had been taken of it, but in that I was mistaken, for I have it from first-class authority that assisted by our fathers, brothers and friends, we are going to organize, and none too soon say I, for the wholesale clothing manufacturers still continue to "do" the continent, at our expense, every "splurge" to Europe, the North-West or the Pacific Coast, or a Princely Donation to such a Mission or Charity means another "grinding" of the operatives. "If you don't like the prices don't take the work, I can get plenty to take it" says the charitably inclined cloth king. Of course I know that, and I also know that organization is our only hope. Nothing else can prevent the still greater reduction of the wholesale prices, for our employers have no conscience, they are all "gall" and avarice, there is no room in their anatomy for anything else. I have seen it in print that General Crooks, of the U.S. Army, is the most successful Indian fighter in America, simply because he fights, as does his adversaries. Now why couldn't we do the same. Our employers are organized for this purpose of keeping the selling prices up and the manufacturing prices down, and we ought certainly to accept the assistance and invitation of our gentlemen Knights and organize; remain no longer strangers to each other, but combine and protect ourselves to some purpose. There is no use in occupying your valuable space with a schedule of prices, as those interested can easily learn what they are. I may, however, state that for making a sack coat, with four pockets, everything complete (excepting button holes) as high as 35 cents is paid, and mind you we have to furnish our own thread out of that, and buy it from our employer at his own prices. This may seem strange, but it is nevertheless a fact.

There is another class of girls which I hope will join the Union as soon as it is formed, i.e., the dry goods clerks, for they are if anything worse off than we are. Perhaps you noticed in the personals of the dailies a short time ago, that a certain James street dry goods dealer had returned from Europe, where he had been combining business with pleasure, etc. Now, sir, if your readers knew the magnificent wages paid by that man's firm to its girl clerks it would not only astonish them, but would also send many of them elsewhere to make their little purchases, for surely no working man's wife or daughter could be contemptible enough to patronize such vampires if they knew that the girls who so patiently wait upon them and are on their feet seventy-one hours per week, scarcely receives sufficient wages to buy butter and bread for an average appetite, saying nothing of the clothes and the thousand and one little nothings which a girl needs. I am not at liberty to give the exact figures they pay, but if you take the trouble to multiply the hours they work by three (3) you will find the answer will amount to considerably more than their average weekly remuneration. Now, sir, as the boys say, "how does that strike you," it strikes me that such extortionists are a disgrace to the community in which they live, their pretensions to Christianity a blasphemy, their attendance at divine service a mockery, their donations an advertisement, or as they would be pleased to learn it a "masterly stroke of business." Such as they have no souls to speak of, certainly none worth having the God they worship is pasted on their windows, his name in "Spot Cash," any other has no charms for them, and the woman who spends the working man's $ with them "after knowing the truth" ought to have no $ or husband to earn one. There is little sense in preaching that dealers and manufacturers have to sell so cheap, that cannot afford to pay more than they do, the fact of their booming immensely rich in a few years is sufficient proof that such reasoning is nonsense, the fact is they can make the prices what they chose. Sir John protects them from the outside and their organization from one another, so that they have nothing to fear from competition. Neither is there any argument in the musty cry that there are too many girls taken to sewing. "You would be far better off in service, my dear," says the sympathetic dowager, but the majority of us think differently, supposing we didn't, where would we find service, certainly not at home, for notwithstanding the cry for domestic help, the supply is far greater than the demand – but as this letter is already the right length, and the domestic service question one of considerable dimensions, I will leave it over till my next, when I will show your readers that the "ordinary domestic" is like the tailoress and clerk, an underpaid, and in many instances an underfed "drudge" that perhaps would be more benefited by organization than either of the others. I will not apologize for my grammar, or rather lack of it, for like Horace Greely, I believe that Lindley Murray should have been hung before he wrote that nonsensical book. Hoping you will assist us all you can in our "new departure," I remain a CANADIAN GIRL.

[Source: Katie McVicar, "Organization Our Only Hope," *Palladium of Labor*, 29 September 1883.]

Katie McVicar
Organization for Girls (1883)

To the Editor of the Palladium:

A very candid girl-friend of mine told me the other day that my letters to *The Palladium* so far did not amount to much. As they merely stated what every woman and majority of the men already knew, without showing how the situation could be bettered. Organization, she said, was all very well, but how were girls to accomplish it, were they to advertise mass meetings, mount platforms, and make speeches, if so the Canadian girls, at least, would never organize. I admit I could not solve the problem, while I was compelled to acknowledge the truth of her assertion. What is the use she said, of writing letters to a newspaper unless you can tell us how to inaugurate this Union. I told her frankly that I knew nothing more than she did of how the Union was to be accomplished, but that I understood that the Knights of Labor had invited us from a branch of their Order, that there were several in the United States and I suppose they could be formed here the same as there. From what I saw in *The Palladium* I thought the Knights had taken the necessary steps to make the Girls' Union a certainty. She said she believed the thing was all talk, or else some of the men would have something to say about it. She knew several who belonged to Trade Unions, etc. and they knew nothing about it, only what they saw in *The Palladium*. What was everybody's business was nobody's. So she thought, that unless two or three girls of sufficient nerve could be prevailed upon to wait upon the gentlemen Knights already spoken of, and confer with them, or rather receive instructions from them, how to proceed, the matter might as well be dropped for all the good it would ever do to the girls, as their houses are already twitting them with being Knights of Labor, and wanting to know how long it will be before they "*don the unmentionables, etc.*" I would therefore like to have some light thrown on the subject. If the Knights invited us who received the invitation? Was it general, or was any particular girl or girls chosen to take the initiative? All these things could be explained in *The Palladium* without mentioning any names or laying any person liable to be victimized. Many of the girls of this city have both fathers and brothers in the Knights of Labor, and how it is that they cannot find out the particulars from them is to me a mystery. I think if I had any such I would call on them for assistance in the matter and would not be put off with evasive answers, for if organization is of any benefit to the male portion of wage earners, why not the female portion as well. Hoping to see something definite on the subject in your next issue, I remain, yours truly, "Canadian Girl."

[Source: Katie McVicar, "Organization for Girls," *Palladium of Labor*, 13 October 1883.]

Jean Thomson Scott
From *The Conditions of Female Labour in Ontario* (1892)

Preface

It is appropriate that the first contribution to the University of Toronto Studies in Political Science from a lady graduate should concern itself with the labour of women and children in Ontario. It is to such careful examination by competent observers of the actual facts of industrial life, rather than to hasty and sentimental agitation, that we must look for permanent reform.

The existing Factory Acts of Ontario are in some respects more stringent, in others more lax, than those of England, the parent of factory legislation. Taking the two essential points, the *age* of permissible child labour and the *hours* of employment for women and children, the comparison may be stated as follows:

1 In Ontario the age of legal employment is for boys twelve and for girls fourteen. In England it has hitherto been for both sexes as low as ten; but by the recent Act – which will not, it is true, come into complete operation till the end of 1893 – the limit has been raised to eleven. The Berlin Labour Conference of 1890 recommended twelve. But while in Ontario boys over twelve are permitted to work as long hours as adult women, in England children between ten and thirteen (the age at which the school authority practically ceases) are only permitted to work "half-time" (and that only on passing a

certain school standard, which however the great majority of them have no difficulty in doing at about the age of ten). The English practice is in substantial agreement with the recommendation of the Berlin Conference, that children should not be employed for a longer period than six hours daily, with a minimum interval of half an hour (though this recommendation applies to children under fourteen, while the English half-time rule only applies to those under thirteen).

An Ontario Statute of 1891 does, indeed, enact that all children between eight and fourteen years of age shall attend school; but until the local authorities make a serious attempt to enforce the Act, it cannot be regarded as substantially affecting the situation.

2 With regard to the hours of labour of women and young persons the general result of the English legislation is a working week of fifty-six and a half hours in textile factories, and sixty hours in non-textile factories and workshops, while in Ontario the limit of hours is sixty.

Two minor points of contrast are also of interest:

3 Night labour for women and children has for some years been expressly prohibited in England, and the Berlin Conference recommended that this example should be generally followed. It is not yet prohibited in Ontario. Of course the cases in which night work is attempted are at present very rare.

4 The legislation of Germany, Hungary and Switzerland imposes restrictions on the employment of women for a certain period after child-bearing, and the Berlin Conference recommended their exclusion for four weeks. The recent English statute has carried out the suggestion, providing that "an occupier of a factory or workshop shall not knowingly allow a woman to be employed therein within four weeks after she has given birth to a child" (54-55 Vict. cap. 75, s. 17). The number of married women employed in factories in Ontario has hitherto been so small that no crying evils have appeared. But for the very reason that the number is small, it might be wise to introduce the rule now that it can cause but little distress or inconvenience. There are, no doubt, objections of weight to any such action; but they would seem to be outweighed by the advantages. For a discussion of the subject the reader may be referred to the article by Jevons in the *Contemporary Review* for January, 1882, reprinted in *Methods of Social Reform* [...]

Hours of Labour

Sub section 3 of section 6, of the Factory Act enacts that no child, young girl or woman shall be employed in a factory for more than *ten* hours a day or more than *sixty* hours in any one week; unless a different apportionment of the hours of labour per day has been made for the sole purpose of giving a shorter day's work on Saturday. Sub section 4 requires that every employer shall allow each child, young girl and woman not less than one hour at noon of each day for meals.

In addition to these regular hours for work, exemptions may be granted by the Inspectors, where the exigencies of certain trades demand it, for working overtime; but in such cases no child, young girl or woman shall work longer than twelve and a half hours a day or seventy two and a half in any one week; and such exemption shall not comprise more than six weeks in any one year, nor shall the time fixed for meals be diminished. During the period of such exemption, every child, young girl or woman, employed in any factory to an hour later than seven in the evening shall be allowed not less than forty-five minutes for an evening meal between five and eight o'clock in the evening. While working overtime, women are not to be employed before six in the morning, nor later than nine in the evening, except in canning factories where they may work later than nine in the evening for not more than twenty days in a year.

In those places coming under the Factories Act where women are employed, comparatively few work for the full sixty hours a week. In a list comprising eighty factories in Toronto, only ten worked for sixty hours a week; fourteen worked less than sixty but over fifty-five; thirty worked from fifty to fifty-five hours; and the remainder from forty-four to fifty. One cause of the reduction of hours in Toronto is the general adoption of the Saturday half-holiday. Outside Toronto it is not so general, and the hours of labour per week reach a higher average. It is to be hoped that fifty-five hours will be made the limit instead of sixty; and so cause the hours of labour to be nine hours a day, or else five and a half days a week.

The clause in the Act which allows a different apportionment of the hours per day in case of shorter hours on Saturday is an unfortunate one, because it would permit an average of eleven hours a day for five days in the week – far too long a period for women to work.

Those factories which work the full sixty hours are principally cotton, woollen and knitting mills, where expensive machinery is employed.

Before the Factories Act came into force many factories worked longer than ten hours a day; so that the results of inspection have been thus far beneficial.

Another loop-hole in the law is the clause concerning the noon meal hour. It reads, "the employer shall allow not less than one hour at noon," which has been interpreted to mean that the employees may take less if they choose, and in some cases this has been done, either in order to stop work earlier in the evening or to lessen the hours of work on Saturday. It need hardly be said that shortening the meal hour is poor economy in the way of preserving one's health. In this matter the girls themselves are not the best judges; for the majority of them would even prefer to take only a half hour at noon if by so doing they could stop work earlier in the evening. In some cases where girls made such a request the employers wisely advised against it; and in one case a compromise of three-quarters of an hour was effected. It would be better if the law were more absolute in the matter especially where the full ten hours a day is insisted on.

Still another matter in which the law is indefinite is that of night labour for women and children. The law *does* state that where, under the exemption women work longer than ten hours a day they are not to be employed before six in the morning nor later than nine in the evening, but it does not prohibit night labour *per se*. As a matter of fact girls in Toronto have been employed for a few months from eleven o'clock in the evening till five or six in the morning in setting up type at the central Press Agency for the cable dispatches to country newspapers. The Deputy Attorney-General was appealed to for the interpretation of the law, but it was decided that nothing in the Act prevented the night employment of women. Fortunately for the women themselves, in the case referred to they found the work too arduous, and have ceased working (since September 18th, 1891).

The Factory Law in Switzerland is more definite in this matter and states that "under no circumstance shall women work on Sunday or at night work." The law of Massachusetts is "no corporation or manufacturing establishment in this commonwealth shall employ any minor or women between the hours of ten o'clock at night and six in the morning." The Quebec Factories Act as amended states "that the day of ten hours work shall not commence before six in morning nor end after nine in the evening." According to the new English Act, the employment of women must now be brought within a specified period of twelve hours, taken between 6 a.m. and 10 p.m., with an hour and a half off for meals, except on Saturday, when the period is eight hours with half a hour off. It is to be hoped that the law in Ontario will be so amended that night labour for women will be prohibited.

Complaint has frequently been made to the Inspectors that women in millinery and dressmaking establishments are employed over ten hours a day; but of course as long as the legal limit of sixty hour per week is not exceeded by any one employee, the Inspectors cannot interfere. It seems usual during the busy season to ask part of the staff to remain after six o'clock, the usual hour for closing, one part taking turn with another. There is generally no allowance made for an evening meal in such cases, the girls preferring to work till they finish rather than go home and come back again; but to work from one till eight or nine in the evening without food is certainly not conducive to health. Legislation on the subject seems to be called for. According to the English Factory Act no women can be employed for more than four and a half hours without an interval of half an hour at least for a meal. The overtime occurs only during the busy season or on Saturdays. Employers argue that it is not always possible to foresee what work is coming in, and that in order to oblige their customers they have to promise the work at a certain time. Some establishments make it a rule never to work overtime; and when urgent work comes in, other work is put aside for a time. It would be well if all would make this the rule. A little more forethought too, on the part of customers would lessen the evil. Ladies could often wait a day or two for a bonnet or gown; or, if not, could give their order earlier. Conversation with those in the business reveals the fact that it is not orders for dresses for weddings or funerals which cause overtime – but those for balls and parties, this of course in establishments doing a trade of that kind. The general desire again on the part of many to have a new gown or bonnet for Sunday makes Saturday the busiest day for dressmakers and milliners. In England no woman can be employed in such establishments after 4 p.m. on Saturdays. It is not customary to pay for such overtime in Toronto. The matter seems to be looked on as only occasional, but there is a danger of too much of it being done if some restriction is not placed on the length of time in any one day during which a woman may be employed [...]

[Source: Jean Thomson Scott, *The Conditions of Female Labour in Ontario* (Toronto: University of Toronto, 1892), Preface, 13, 14.]

Agnes Maule Machar (1837–1927) was the daughter of a prominent Presbyterian minister and principal of Queen's University from 1846–1954. A poet, novelist, and historian, she was an early supporter of women's higher education and women's rights more broadly. Beginning in the 1870s she wrote political tracts promoting women's access to universities. The conditions of female labour in the context of an industrializing economy were also of increasing concern to Machar. In the 1890s she was on the executive of the NCWC and with the local Kingston chapter. In the document below, Machar was one of the most vocal advocates for limiting the length of working hours for women and children in factories.

National Council of Women of Canada
Length of Working Hours for Women and Children in Factories (1895)

Miss Agnes Maule Machar moved the following resolution: "That on account of the injurious consequences which naturally result from the present length of working hours, during which girls and women may be and are often employed in factories and stores, the Legislature be respectfully petitioned by the National Council of Women of Canada to limit the legal hours of such employment of women and girls and also children, to at most nine hours a day, and also to provide that a forewomen – who should always be employed to superintend female employees, should arrange for occasional rest and change of position, if not work, during each division of the working day."

Miss Machar said: A few years ago an attempt was made in Kingston to establish a Young Women's Christian Association which it was hoped would afford facilities for educational improvement and profit to the working girls of our city, more especially to those employed in the factories, of which we have a few in Kingston. We tried to establish evening classes to afford evening lectures and talks, but we found it was utterly impossible, for this chief reason, because the girls were employed there from half past six every morning, winter and summer, till half past six in the evening, every day but Saturday, when they had a half holiday. The legal enactment which limits the work of women and children was not transgressed, because the girls had a half holiday on Saturday, which they sorely needed; but the effect of those long, exhausting hours of work was such as to make them so utterly wearied out in body and mind that by the evening they were unfit for any mental exertion, and seemed indisposed to do anything except rest or lounge or perhaps take some form of amusement which did not require any exertion. We felt, therefore, that in these circumstances we must some way or other try to do something to reduce this evil. I also came in contact with a number of the girls themselves and knew their own feeling in the matter, and also with medical ladies who had an opportunity of giving their testimony to the physical effects of that course of work. The girls themselves felt it a grievous burden in most cases. There were some strong ones who did not, but I did not meet with one case in which the girl would not have gladly submitted to a decrease of pay if they had a decrease of hours, if that was obtained by opening at seven instead of at half past six. As to the physical effects, one can easily imagine what it would be to have to get to a place of labor at half past six in winter mornings. The door is shut at exactly the half hour. If a girl comes a minute or two later she loses her place. It means getting up about five, having hurried breakfast, tramping through dark streets

– our streets are often quite dark at that hour of the morning – through snow or slush or wet, standing in many cases with wet clothing till the clothing dries, then a hurried walk home, a hurried dinner, and a walk back again, then work till half past six. The physicians say that in many cases it induced anemia, the foundation of pulmonary disease and other consequences. Standing the whole day wearied them – not having a change of attitude. We know how glad we are for a few minutes' rest or change of attitude. We can imagine what it would be every day, six days a week, during the year to work without a change of attitude or occupation. We can imagine how indisposed we would be to go through the whole dreary routine again. The great King Alfred of England divided up the day into three parts, eight hours for labor, eight for sleep, and eight for recreation. I believe in the good effects of manual work; I believe most of us need more manual work than we have; but I think too much manual work kills out the mental powers just as a moderate amount stimulates them. I think after a day's work like that, a girl is not able to develop her mental powers to any extent, certainly not to the extent her Creator intended them to be developed, and I think the consequences are morally deteriorating, because if a girl cannot develop her intellectual powers she cannot reach the moral status or high ideals she was intended to reach. On the contrary, it promotes a love of sensation and amusement, a love of mere idling and anything that will not cause too much mental exertion, thus deteriorating the morals in all these ways. I speak of them not merely as individuals. Of course we should like to say to these girls what was said long ago, "Maid, arise!" to a higher level of intellectual, moral and spiritual life; but I speak of the consequences to our country, and I think the principle of legislation in such matters – which, of course, has been considered in all our factory legislation, can be fully justified by the consequences entailed on the community by such long hours, because if the mothers of our coming generation are to begin enfeebled, what can we expect the coming generation to be? I should like, therefore, to see this resolution adopted in full – of course the change only to be adopted as far as practicable in the work; but I think our girls are of more consequence than webs of cotton or wheels. I think that persons are far more valuable than things, and that in order to have the kind of mothers we want for the coming generation – strong in body and strong in mind – we should have a change of system which would make our Canadian people stronger and better fitted to cope with the new conditions of life in the new century to which we are all looking forward with so much hope. For the sake of Canada, as well as for the girls, I beg to move this resolution. (Applause.)

Mrs Talbot Macbeth (London), in seconding the motion said: I believe that at present 60 hours a week or 10 hours a day is the time allowed for women to work, and I noticed by Miss Scott's paper published in '91 or '92, when the Act was passed, that the regulations then appointing inspectors and limiting the hours did not apply to mercantile establishments; but unless I misunderstand what took place at the last session of the Ontario Parliament that law was extended so as to deal with mercantile establishments as well as with the workshops. I think that the work of the Women's Council will only begin when this law is passed. Mr Kelso, in the preface to the pamphlet of which he has sent us copies, states that many well-meaning persons suggest remedies which are already on a statute book in the laws relating to women and children, but which are not carried out, and I think that perhaps the way in which this Council will aid most will be in trying to enforce the laws which are already passed. One of our members of the Trades and Labor Council of London asked me when we were agitating for the Curfew Bell in London: "What are you going to do about children who are employed in shops?" "Oh, but," I said, "they cannot employ children in shops for more than 10 hours a day." "Yes," he says," "the law says so, but you can go to – " naming several shops in town, "and see little girls not more than thirteen years of age there in the morning at 8 o'clock and kept until 10 o'clock at night." "Well," I said, "the law does not allow it." "No," he said, "but how is the law enforced? We have worked and worked in all our meetings, and we are not able to get it enforced." Well, I think it is impossible for the industrial classes to have those laws really carried out. The attempt to enforce them very often means the loss of their position. We know that that would likely be the case. Then, another reason why they are handicapped in enforcing those laws is that they are employed from early in the morning till late at night, whereas women of leisure have a chance to enforce these laws by bringing them before the police magistrate. Now, the law provides that there should be a sufficient number of seats for all the women employed in the shop or factory, and I am sure we all know shops and factories where the seats are not provided, but do we ever try to have them put there? We could do it without the faintest loss in any way except the dislike that we have of publicly coming out on such questions, but it would be nothing for us to do it beyond that, because we would not lose our position in any way, we would not suffer in any way, and we have plenty of time and means, many of us, to get these laws enforced if we chose to do it. While I have the greatest pleasure in seconding this resolution, I do hope that the members of the Council will try to form public opinion on this matter, so that their friends may not go into shops where they see women standing and be absolutely callous about it, and that they may try also to remember when they give orders for clothing to be made up in the shortest possible time that they are undoing what we are trying to do when we have these laws passed, and also that people who do their shopping at late hours are contributing to those long hours for the working classes. (Hear, hear, and applause.) If we would only make up our minds to put into our pockets our fellow citizens, and to protect those who are unable through lack of leisure and means and the fear of losing their positions by putting these laws in force, I think it would be very beneficial fruit to be borne by this Council.

Her Excellency read the following communication received from the Women's Protective Union:

> As to the above resolution it may be observed that Ontario has two laws regulating the working hours of women, girls and children in factories, viz.: The Ontario Factories Act, 1884, Chap. 208; The Ontario Factories Amendment Act, 1889, Chap. 43, also "An Act to make further provision respecting Factories," of session of 1895. See also "An Act to regulate the closing of Shops and the hours of labor therein for Children and Young Persons," 1888, Chap. 44. These two last mentioned Acts also provide that *seats* shall be provided for female employees when not necessarily engaged in the work or duty for which they are employed in a shop.

Mrs Wood: Two years ago this subject came up before the public and was handled by the Toronto Humane Society. I am one of the deputation to visit the establishments. In every shop in Toronto seats have been provided, or will be willingly provided – in Eaton's and all the large shops. The girls have seats where they desire to do so; we have had no difficulty whatever.

Mrs Drummond (Montreal) said: Speaking for the Local Council of Women of Montreal, I would say a few words with regard to the matter brought up before us in this resolution – we do not feel ready as a Council to endorse this resolution, for these reasons: That we consider the whole question of the limits of working hours a very difficult one, involving great and far-reaching issues to both employer and employed; That we do not feel that our knowledge of the matter is such as to justify us in advancing the opinion that a further limitation of the hours is at present advisable. It may seem to us all that, speaking generally, 10 hours a day is too much, and 9 hours a day quite enough for anyone; but admitting this to be a fact, it is a fact we must consider in relation to a great many other facts, such as wages, competition, etc., and in order to do this we must consult first *the employers*, for they must know best what such a change as that proposed would imply to both themselves and those in their employment; and *next* the working women themselves; and before taking their opinion we must inform them fully as to all the probable issues of such a change in the legislation regarding their trades. Now it is extremely difficult to get all this requisite information, but till we get it we feel that we should suspend our judgment. We have made enquiry of both men and factory girls, and they are unanimous in declaring that so far as their experience goes, hardship comes oftener from slack work than from overwork. In most trades there is a slack season and a busy season, and as in the majority of factories women are paid by the piece, it is difficult to see how they can live at all unless short hours and small pay at one season are adjusted by long hours and good pay at another.

We are not questioning the need of legislation in these matters, but I would suggest that we first get our woman inspector to see that the present regulations of the law are carried out and that we then derive from her more intimate acquaintance with factory girls and their needs, knowledge to guide in ameliorating their condition, otherwise we may injure when we most mean to help.

Her Excellency: The Woman's Art Association moves an amendment to this resolution that all words after "9 hours a day" be omitted.

Mrs McMaster: It is not from any lack of sympathy we have – the idea is a beautiful one – but because of the impossibility of having it carried out, and if we committed ourselves to asking too much of the Legislature they may consider we are asking impossible things, and that is why I move the amendment.

Mrs Hoodless seconded the motion. She said: I endorse what Miss Machar has said. Being interested in the Women's Christian Association we have found a great difficulty in carrying out the work with young women on account of the long hours. I think we should make haste slowly.

Miss Shenik: The Edmonton Council have approved of the resolution.

Mrs McNaughton: I feel that this question is a very important one for women to touch upon without very thorough study of the question. We Montreal delegates represent a large industrial city where thousands of women are employed, and it might mean starvation to some of them to have such a law as this carried. Manufacturers would certainly have to discriminate in their employment of women as against men if they could not have the services of these women for longer hours during certain periods. This is felt, too, in other countries. I was interested to see in the Conference held at Glasgow, 1894, a discussion upon this very question. There an amendment to the Factory and Work-shops Act just to this effect has really resulted in throwing the women employed in the bleaching trade entirely out of employment, because they had to work at certain seasons for longer hours, and their employers not being able to use their services in that way were forced to dismiss them and employ men. This threw them into other businesses where they were not skilled, and so the labor market was upset, there was too much competition in that one direction and starvation wages resulted. I believe Mr Asquith has a Bill in England, but it has been put back until the following year. These amendments, if carried, will have a familiar effect. They relate specially to the hours of work in connection with laundry work. The competition between steam laundries and hand laundries is very severe. In the hand laundries women are employed entirely. In the steam laundries men are employed for the machinery, and one can do the work of five women. Now, in the laundry business there are times – the end of the week. Men can go on working if necessary till twelve o'clock at night, for they have the machinery. Women cannot do this, and the work would not be sent out, and the hand laundries as a consequence would have to go down. It was stated that if this amendment was carried, it would result in Glasgow alone in throwing out between 4,000 and 5,000 women who are employed in hand laundries; so that there are far reaching issues here. We must remember that when women enter into the industrial field they must accept the same conditions under which their brothers labor. While there is need of protective and restrictive legislation where women are concerned I do not think it can be carried too far under our present social conditions. In the Province of Quebec we have a very good Factory Act with good regulations for sanitation, for protecting dangerous machinery and the hours of work are fixed at 10 per day or 60 per week, but the law is not carried out well. We all know the trouble with regard to every working woman and man, too, as far as that is concerned. I think that before introducing a new issue into our work, it would be better carried out until the growth of public opinion will so change social conditions that shorter hours will be granted to both men and women. (Applause.)

Miss Hepburn, Secretary of the Women's Protective Union, said: I did not intend to say anything, but after what has been said, I feel that I would not be true to my fellow workers if I did not just try to point out the difficulties that women work under. To me this resolution is the most important of all that has come to this Convention. All who have studied economics know that wages always tend to the point of subsistence. Walter Besant speaks of the girls of the east and of London living under what he calls the law of eleven pence ha'penny – that is, that employers find that girls can live on eleven pence ha'penny a day, therefore they get only eleven pence ha'penny per day; and it is just the same all over. When we were discussing this, one lady said to me, that if we were restricting hours would not we be trenching on the liberties of the individuals who would be for making as much money as she possibly could? Well in some instances we want to do that, for the simple reason that there are some girls that have constitutions like horses and work like their machines, and they have more money than the majority do; then the employer, when her pay sheet goes down, does not ask how many hours that girl has worked, but how much money she has made. Then there is a cut down all around. I know of one girl in a corset factory in the city here who has three times been the means of the other girls being reduced. In one factory where they make dress shields for ladies' waists they get just now five cents for stitching of a gross of steels; she must stitch over 2,000 every day. I would like very much to have spoken in favor of the whole resolution, but I don't think we could get the whole resolution at all. I speak only in favour of the amendment, not because it is not necessary – for some of the girls tell us how much better it would be for some of them to have some change every day, just even from stooping over the machinery for five consecutive hours – they feel as if it would be almost a blessing to just get up and run around for a little while: but wages are so that they cannot do that, and in most factories girls work so by piece that one girl works on one part of an article and another works on another part, so that they could not possibly change their work in large factories. (Applause.) [...]

[Source: National Council of Women of Canada, *Women Workers: Being a Report of the Proceedings of the Second Annual Meeting and Conference of the National Council of Women of Canada, Toronto, 1895*, 173–80.]

Amelia McLean Paget (1867–1922) grew up in the Northwest, where her father was a factor with the Hudson's Bay Company. Of Aboriginal ancestry on her mother's side, albeit a heritage that neither she nor her family publicly acknowledged during her lifetime, Paget spoke both Cree and Ojibway. After she married a civil servant who had a position in the Department of Indians she moved to Ottawa. She later received a small commission from the federal government to document the history and customs of Aboriginal peoples, which she compiled in *The People of the Plains*, published in 1909. In 1912 the Canadian Handicrafts Guild, principally based in Montreal, asked her to report on Aboriginal crafts in the West.

Amelia Paget
Report on Mrs Paget's Trip to Indian Reserves in Saskatchewan (1912)

Leaving Ottawa on Monday, the 3rd of June, I arrived in Winnipeg on the following Wednesday.

As the object of my trip was to revive and conserve Indian handicrafts in as many places as it was possible to reach through every possible channel, my arrival was timed to be in Winnipeg before the departure of my father, Mr W.J. MacLean, to James Bay and other northern places at which the Indians of Treaty 9 were to be paid their annuities. His interest in the objects of the Guild has been most fruitful of results, and will be of much future value to those far away Indians, as the literature which he distributed for us has been the means of interesting others in the conserving and perpetuating of Indian handicrafts in those far away districts.

I was fortunate enough to meet Mr Cadzow, of Rampart House, Yukon, who trades with the Indians in that isolated part of Canada, and who was in on his annual purchasing tour. He promised to do all he could to interest the Indians in keeping up the standard of their work, which he assured me was of the best. He will endeavor to supply them with only such materials as will conform with the rules for good workmanship.

The first Agency I visited was Moose Mountain; here were many Indian women who still excel in beadwork and mocassin [sic] making, also in dressing leather for their use in these lines. Upon them was urged the necessity of teaching the younger members of the Band their handicrafts in order to perpetuate them. The work of Mrs Egg and Mrs Red Star was especially good, and they were recommended as workers for the Guild. I was also shown the work of a little girl of twelve (all Assiniboine) which was really excellent.

My next visit was to the Crooked Lakes Agency. A lack of proper material was responsible for the poor showing of work on these Reserves. When this is overcome good results will be forthcoming, as there are a number of skilled workers in the different bands, especially in Sakimay's.

As the Annuity Payments were being made at the time of my visit, I had every opportunity of speaking to each Chief and Headman of the four bands. They all seemed to appreciate the efforts of the Guild in trying to perpetuate their handicrafts, and realize how much depends upon their own efforts to attain these ends.

Through the kindness of the Indian Agent, I had an opportunity of driving to the Roman Catholic Boarding School in the Valley north of the Agency. I spoke to the school children in their own language, and impressed upon them the necessity of their learning from the older women of the bands all forms of the handicrafts for which the Crees and Saulteaux have been noted in the past. The Sisters of Charity, who were in charge of the children, will do all they can in future to encourage them along these lines, which have been sadly neglected in this school.

From the Crooked Lakes Agency, I went on to the Assiniboine Reserve. Here were seen samples of very fine Indian work. Unfortunately, most of the Indians were away at the time of my visit, so none were spoken to personally, but Miss Lilian Grant, a daughter of the late Agent, has taken the matter up, and will be sure of doing even more good than could be accomplished by a comparative stranger.

It was at this Agency, I happened to find out the name of a wholesale firm in St Paul, Minn., who carry a splendid stock of seed beads, and this firm supplies these Indians with material for their excellent work.

Returning to Winnipeg from here, I next visited the Qu'Appelle Industrial School at Lebret. Many Indians from Reserves north of the Qu'Appelle Valley were at the School at the time, bringing their children back after their summer holiday. To these I explained the objects of my mission, and the desire of the Canadian Handicrafts Guild to help them revive and perpetuate their hand-work. They were made to understand thoroughly how much depended upon their co-operation to bring lasting results.

From the School I went on to the Qu'Appelle Reserves. Here were found many really good workers, who will teach their children all they know, and impress upon them the benefits they will reap from the best work and use of proper materials.

My recommendation to the officers of the Guild to have Indian handicrafts taught in the Industrial School at Lebret, has been placed before the Department of Indian Affairs at Ottawa, and I understand the Department has agreed to pay a small salary to the person whose name was suggested as being in every way competent to teach these arts and crafts. It is not necessary to comment upon the lasting good which will surely come of this teaching, and the great pleasure it will bring to the Indian children at this School. Prizes for the best work produced by the pupils should be given once a year at least.

Before closing my report, I wish to mention the interest taken in the Canadian Handicrafts Guild by Mr Inspector Conroy, of the Department of Indian Affairs, by his efforts to revive and encourage quillwork and other fine arts among the Indians of his Inspectorate in the Peace and Mackenzie River Districts. His work in this connection is very much appreciated by all members of the Guild.

Thanks are due to the Indian Department at Ottawa and to the officials at the different Agencies and Schools visited during my trip, for kindness and help received, and for the interest shown in the work of the Canadian Handicrafts Guild.

Respectfully submitted,
AMELIA M. PAGET

[Source: Amelia Paget, "Report of Mrs Paget's Trip to Indian Reserves in Saskatchewan," *Annual Report of the Canadian Handicrafts Guild, 1912*, 15–17.]

Helena Gutteridge (1879 or 1880–1960) was born in London, England, and immigrated to Vancouver, British Columbia, in 1911. Active in feminist politics before her departure from England, Gutteridge founded the BC Women's Suffrage League soon after her arrival. Increasingly interested in the plight of working-class women, Gutteridge also assumed a prominent role in the Vancouver Trades and Labour Council. During the First World War period she organized the Women's Employment League and was chairman of the Women's Minimum Wage League. She was the first woman to be elected as an Vancouver alderman in 1937.

Helena Gutteridge

Women Organize an Employment League (1913)

A few weeks ago Sir Richard McBride, premier of British Columbia invited a number of representatives from various organizations and associations throughout the province to a conference with the executive council and himself to consider the situation brought about by the war, insofar as it affected financial conditions throughout the province. After earnest consideration and deliberation the conclusion arrived at and advised by Sir Richard McBride, was that "we must have courage and confidence."

That the possession of courage and confidence does not prove to be a talisman whereby to obtain food, clothing and shelter is easily seen, by the number of women who are seeking, in addition to courage and confidence, employment, or rather the money earned by labor to obtain the bare necessities of existence.

Since the Women's Employment League came into existence a week ago hundreds of women have registered their names as seeking employment. Stenographers, saleswomen, garment workers, tailoresses, domestic employees, all saying, "I will take anything," "Father is out of work," or "I have no friends here and must get work or I don't know what I shall do."

Courage indeed! The courage of so many mothers who are striving to keep the bodies and souls of their children together and maintain the self-respect which shrinks from charity to enough to make angels weep.

The many entries on the list of the Women's Employment League, when the name is followed by "husband out of work," in some cases, two, three, four or five children to support and the one word "urgent," in the corner are evidence enough that something more than "courage and confidence" is needed to feed a family on.

The Women's Employment League formed for the purpose of devising ways and means of dealing with the problem of finding employment for women has passed a resolution calling on the provincial government to provide employment pointing out that although many offers of hospitality for the unemployed women have been received something more is required, and must be provided by the government, namely work.

Sir Richard, a short time ago, expressed his opinion that if a certain measure were passed by the legislature, it would tend in the direction of making women neglect their homes and the children would suffer.

Now is the time for Sir Richard to protect the homes and the children. Give *work* to the fathers of families and the mothers will not have to neglect the home and children, when trying to get food for the family by doing washing, sewing and for those who are in theory so very anxious to protect family life.

With men working, mothers can remain at home, and the single woman does not have to enter into competition with the mother, who in sheer desperation for the children's sake will work for so very little.

"Government of the people, for the people, by the people." What is the representative of the people going to do?

[Source: Helena Gutteridge, "Women Organize an Employment League," *BC Federationist*, 9 October 1913.]

Civic Committee of the University Women's Club of Winnipeg

The Work of Women and Girls in the Department Stores of Winnipeg **(1914)**

The Civic Committee of the Women's University Club beg to report on their work for the season 1913–14. In response to a circular sent out by the Executive of the Club, fifteen members volunteered for service on this committee, and the organization meeting was held on November 6th, 1913. The only instructions received from the Club were that this committee should proceed to make a study of some form of women's work. Realizing that the committee included no trained social workers, and no members who were free to give a large amount of time to this study, it was decided to narrow the field for the first year's work: After thorough discussion as to various alternative fields of work, the committee determined upon the department stores of Winnipeg as the subject of this inquiry. It should be understood clearly that in the first place the work of only women and girls is considered, and, in the second place, only the work of those women and girls engaged in the four department stores, T. Eaton Co., Robinson & Co., Ltd., Hudson Bay Co. and Carsley & Co. which employ altogether from 2,432 women and girls to 3,200, according to the season.

In undertaking this inquiry, the object of your committee was two-fold, economic and educational. In the first place, it was felt that accurate information as to conditions in Winnipeg would be of great value, it being now the opinion of experts in social science that too great emphasis cannot be placed on the dissemination of the facts in relation to any industry.

Secondly, your committee have tried to ascertain what opportunities are offered to women in these stores, and what training, if any, would better fit them to take advantage of such opportunities.

Before actually commencing our work, your chairman corresponded with social workers in other large centres where this work had already been done, and your committee was much discouraged by the unanimous opinion of these experts that such a study could not be undertaken with any hope of success by volunteer workers. However, your committee felt that not only was it desirable to obtain facts, but that the training involved for those who sought them was an equally valuable object of this work; and it was determined to proceed. The field work in this study was carried out by ten members, the other five members acting in an advisory capacity [...]

Hardships of the Occupation

There are three principal ways in which the work of department stores bears heavily upon the women and girls employed therein: first, the constant standing; second, the bad air; the third; the nervous tension.

With regard to the first which is by far the greatest hardship, we have already given the provisions of the excellent law of the province. Were the provisions enforced, and could the customers be educated to the point of being sometimes served by a clerk who was seated, this hardship would practically disappear from Winnipeg stores.

The second hardship is one which is found in many public buildings other than the department store, and will probably not disappear until our methods of ventilation are completely revolutionized. This hardship generally bears with most severity on the cashiers of the tube system, who, as a rule in large stores, work in the basement. Only one store here has girls so working, and an effort is made to help relieve this strain by having them work week about in the basement and in an upstairs office.

This particular group suffer an additional strain from the glitter of the brass tubes and the constant noise. Your committee suggest that this strain might be relieved by painting the tubes, and that some system of periodic rest, such as is afforded telephone operators, should be arranged.

The ordinary shopper probably does not appreciate the extent of the nervous strain under which saleswomen suffer. To begin with, they must work at high pressure to keep up their sales because their wage and their promotion generally bear a fairly direct relation to the amount of sales. The saleswomen must be able to turn readily from one form of sale to another and to make out quickly the requisite sale slips. There are pay and take, COD, deposit account, transfer and charge sales, all requiring different methods. Moreover, in each sale several operations are involved. There is the handling and measuring of the goods, the clerical work and the return of money or parcel or both to the shopper. In all these things speed and accuracy are the first consideration. This hardship is incidental to the business, and can only, your committee think, be lessened by the thoughtfulness of the individual shopper who too often does not realize all that is involved in a seemingly simple operation, and so increases the tension by displaying irritation.

To these hardships may be added the lack of a rest room in these stores which do not maintain one.

Your committee have interviewed a number of employees in each store, most of them being those who had spent some time in the service of the firm, and have found, on the whole, the details of life in the stores as given by the managers corroborated from this different viewpoint. They have also found a general loyalty to the firm which speaks well for conditions in the stores, this loyalty existing even where suggestions for improvement of conditions were freely made. With one exception the women interviewed expressed the opinion that some training preliminary to entering the store would greatly benefit those who enter this part of the industrial world. There was a general feeling also that the opportunities for advancement were continually offering for the woman who had made herself thoroughly efficient. In fact, the belief appears general that the advancement is limited only by the limitations of the individual, and that the department store offers a big field for women. It is a feature of the stores in Winnipeg that very rapid advancement may be hoped for owing to the frequency of marriages in this western country.

Another difficulty encountered by women employed in the department stores, as, indeed, by all women working in Winnipeg, is the difficulty of finding suitable rooming or boarding houses. It would be impossible to overstate this difficulty, and stories so appalling as to be almost unbelievable have been told by different women of their experience in the search of a home.

One or two general considerations arising out of conversations with both employers and employed should be noted. The first is the relation between the general wage and the cost of living. A wage to be considered as adequate minimum should provide for the adequate minimum of food, proper lodging, car fare, clothes, recreation and possible sickness. Your committee have not attempted to make a thorough investigation into the cost of living, and there are no accurate figures available for the cost to the women under consideration. Social workers in the city place the minimum from eight to nine dollars. If this is correct, it will be seen that the efficient adult saleswomen in Winnipeg are earning this minimum. It might be added that what information we have been able to gather goes to show that the minimum is nine dollars rather than the lower figure.

The second consideration, your committee feel, must be referred to out of justice to the women employed in the stores. This is the charge made with great frequency and equal carelessness that much immorality exists among them. Your committee have made careful inquiry in various directions, and can positively state that every effort is made by the general management and the department heads to keep the stores free from women whose conduct is in the least questionable. Grave injustice is done a large body of women working in one store against whom this accusation is particularly made. In this case, as in all the others, your committee, after investigation, beg to state that these careless statements have no foundation in fact.

Out of the difficulties of the present situation, as expressed by both employees and employers, have come two suggestions which your committee beg to offer in concluding this report.

First we heartily recommend to the school board that some attempt should be made first in the night schools, and later amplified into a department in trade schools, to evolve some course which would fit the girls who intend to enter department stores to begin at a higher point than they can now do and also to make more rapid progress once they begin. It seems clear to your committee that the opportunities in this business are many, but equally clear from the point of view of the management as well as from the saleswomen themselves that not many are equipped to take advantage of them. A knowledge of general department store methods, of ways of keeping stock, of the various routine operations in selling, of the principles which make for good salesmanship, a training in mental arithmetic, in the courtesy due to customers, in the advantage of proper dress and manner, and a working knowledge of the various kinds of goods they may expect to sell would in the opinion of those who may be termed experts, greatly facilitate the progress of women in department stores. One of the stores has made a beginning in this work and teaches its new employees the routine of salesmanship and some of its psychology. It is now undertaking to give its younger employees who lack it, some necessary training in the rudiments of primary education. Admirable as this effort is, it cannot from the nature of things be made as thoroughgoing as a course in the schools. When it is remembered that as many as 3500 women and girls work in these four stores alone in the course of a year, it will be seen that there is a pressing need of such training.

The second suggestion arises out of the dearth of proper boarding houses for the business women of the city. In this situation your committee believe lies a real danger to the community. We have heard with great satisfaction of plans which have been made by another women's organization for the erection of hostels and hope that the fulfillment of the project will not be long delayed. But we beg to suggest that in the meantime a great service would be rendered if some body of women interested in community service in Winnipeg would compile and maintain a list of boarding houses to which business women might with safety be recommended. The existing situation is one not peculiar to Winnipeg. One of the largest stores in Philadelphia maintains a woman official whose duty it is to keep a watchful eye on the boarding houses which shelter employees of this firm. The results obtained from this inspection have so impressed the manager of one of our large stores that he is considering introducing it here. It seems to your committee that if the Local Council of Women which from the large number of women it could reach would have special facilities for doing this work, could be induced to prepare a list of proper boarding houses of varying standards and place that list at the disposal of the business women, it might accomplish much good for the community pending the erection of proper hostels.

This report has been submitted to the managers of the four stores under consideration and the figures herein contained as they concern his particular store have been approved by each manager.

WINIFRED L. COPELAND, Convener

[Source: Civic Committee of the University Women's Club of Winnipeg, *The Work of Women and Girls in the Department Stores of Winnipeg* (Winnipeg, 1914), 1, 18–21.]

Anonymous

Orientals in Hotels Displace White Labor (1915)

"I have no color prejudice, but I think in this case and in the interest of efficient white female labor in this city the board might put a white labor clause in the granting of hotel licenses, so that work being done by Chinese help to-day may be done by white women who are now out of employment." In these words Miss Gutteridge, appearing on behalf of the Women's Employment League before the license commissioners at the city hall last Wednesday afternoon, made her application. The board decided after some discussion, to hear the hotel point of view at their next regular meeting. Miss Gutteridge appeared also as did Mr Graham on behalf of the cooks and waiters' union. There were she said, between 400 and 500 Orientals employed in the city hotels whose places could be satisfactorily filled by white women. Mr Ireland had told her that there were 18 cooks, six waitresses and 50 hotel helps receiving city relief. That meant that the city was keeping them. In addition there were on the books of the Women's Employment League 125 women used to general house work and who could do chamber work in hotels. There were also cooks and chamber maids, housekeepers and waiters numbering 244, all out of employment and suited for such work as was being done by Orientals and particularly the bedroom work.

[Source: Anonymous, "Orientals in Hotels Displace White Labor," *BC Federationist*, 12 March 1915.]

Éva Circé-Côté, 1871–1949, was born in Montreal and pursued a number of occupations before becoming a journalist in 1899. In a career spanning over 40 years, she wrote on a wide array of subjects. Writing often under the male pseudonym Julien Saint-Michel, among others, Circé-Côté was a staunch defender of women's rights. She decried deficiencies in access to higher education for Catholic francophone women and inequalities in the Civil Code, and promoted women's right to vote. In the midst of the First World War, Circé-Côté wrote extensively on the necessity to improve women's wage employment.

Éva Circé-Côté
Equal Pay–Equal Work (1917)

Why are women who perform work that is as difficult as that of men not as well paid?

The feminist question has become an economic question. Woman today is no longer claiming the right to work and it is foreseeable that before long she will be loudly demanding the right to rest. What she should demand is equal pay for equal work. One thing is certain and that is that if more women are being employed everywhere, they are not being paid as well as they once were, and they are still being paid less than men. The female cook receives treatment inferior to that of the male cook, the housekeeper inferior to the butler. Why is the compensation unequal if they are both performing the same service?

Such examples of injustice cannot leave those interested in the economic uplift of women indifferent. It is just that an imbalance in the task should translate into an imbalance in salary. But when the woman's work is just as long, just as tedious, just as productive as that of the man, why are the woman and man not equally well remunerated?

Reason and equality make it a duty for the boss to equalize the salaries of the two sexes. Because to pay the woman less than the man is to violate the most elementary laws of humanity; it is to subordinate, without justification, the weaker sex to the stronger. To replace the male worker with the female in the workshop, because she is paid less, eventually hurts the man because positions will be harder to come by for him; it is also to stir up competition between female and male labour power, and to divide forces made to help and understand one another. When you enter our department stores you are immediately struck by an anomaly over which it is worth pausing and analysing.

Young women dominate the personnel in terms of numbers, but not in terms of importance. There are ten salesclerks as compared with two shop assistants. There is one personage who immediately grabs your attention, since all respectable stores must have one of these swells – pomaded, curly-haired, with a heart-shaped mouth, obsequious and evasive – whose mission it is to greet the ladies with an engaging smile, and to guide them to the departments where they will find the items they desire, all the while making insipid pleasantries: compliments about how pretty they are, or observations on the weather, if they are no longer spring chickens. The floor walker is a decorative object, if you will, but as necessary as the swing mirror and the mannequins, and he enjoys the consideration once accorded the gold-bedecked concierge of Notre-Dame. Precisely because he is useless he enjoys an immense prestige. Only for the classy clientele will he deign to offer his opinion and unfold the corset to emphasize its harmonious lines with a ribald look. Since this position is honorary and regarded as of capital importance, why should it not be filled by a woman?

You will tell me that it is for peacocks to strut about, especially in front of all the "birds" … that hundreds would not come to "haggle" if they were not attracted, silly little geese, by honeyed lips and the muscular arm of that working-class Apollo, six feet tall, not an inch less, and with the neck of a bull, gentleness allied with strength, the one who is stereotyped in the heads of the scatterbrains. But after all, what if all the store owners agreed that this position, which comes with a salary of twelve thousand dollars or more, should be opened to women, the most senior women employees for whom it would be a promotion ... Morality would certainly improve, because this rooster among the chickens does not give me a good feeling. I believe him capable, if not of abusing his influence over the bosses to place suspicion on one of the young female clerks who resists his sidelong glances, at least of breaking shy hearts, or creating rivalries [...]

[Source: "Equal Pay–Equal Work," *Labour World/Le Monde Ouvrier* (Montreal), 25 August 1917 (trans. Maureen Moynagh).]

Kathleen Derry, a member of the Boot and Shoes Union in London, Ontario, was selected by the Dominion Trades and Labour Congress to represent Canada at the First International Congress of Working Women in Washington in 1919. Derry was named a vice-president of the International Congress, a position she held for three years. In 1921 she attended a summer school for working women at Bryn Mawr that was sponsored by the US Women's Trade Union League where she undertook a study of Canadian minimum-wage laws. This research was subsequently published in the *Journal of Political Economy*.

Kathleen Derry
Government Regulation of Female Migration (1920)

Washington, D.C.
Bulletin – No. 7
Nov. 25, 1920

This newsletter, published each month, is primarily intended to be of assistance to the delegates and visitors to the First International Congress of Working Women, enabling them to keep in closer touch with each other.

Canada – Government Regulates Migration of Women

From Mrs Kathleen Derry, our Canadian correspondent, comes a letter, dated Oct. 25, telling of the efforts which the Canadian Government has been making to regulate the migration of women. She says:

"I am forwarding to you a copy of a 'Memorandum on the Migration of Women,' which is of particular interest as it is a recent Law established for the protection of the women emigrants coming to Canada, and is the result of the investigation of various cases of the exploitation of certain manufacturers of the women and girls from the Old Country.

"They have been engaging women and also men to come to work in Canada, promising them certain conditions upon their arrival, but failing to keep those promises when they have them safely in their power. One favourite way is to advance the fare to the persons engaged, which they agree to pay back out of their wages upon their arrival, and this is a hold upon them by the manufacturers, and there have been many cases where the immigrants have found, on getting to their job, that there is a strike in progress and that they must either act as strike-breakers or they are out of employment and at the same time they owe the employer the passage money that he has advanced them.

"Only the other day, I read of a case where two men were brought out like this, only to find they were to act as strike-breakers, and upon their refusing to go in to work as such, the employer had them arrested, for, I think, breach of contract, and the last I saw of it was the Lawyer for the Trades and Labour Congress had been engaged to defend them. The case, I believe, is still proceeding.

"The Trades and Labour Congress had repeatedly made protests against this practice, and also the Canadian Council of Immigration, and this law seems to be one of the results of these protests of organized labor.

"Other results have been obtained such as the notifying of agents of Britain by the Dominion government that certain lines of workers were not needed at the particular times, in times of slackness in some trades, one case of recent date being the bringing out of a considerable number of Boot and Shoe Workers when the trade was slack, and though the immigrants had promise of work in different factories in Toronto, when they came there was nothing for them, and they were in a bad plight, as they had sold up their homes in Leicester, England, to come and had been compelled to spend the money on the way and so had neither homes or money."

The Memorandum to which Mrs Derry refers reads as follows:

"During the past season, the Dominion Government has been giving special attention to protection for women immigrants coming to Canada. They have now temporary officers at the ports of London, Liverpool, and Glasgow, engaged in this work. By order in council, it has been decided to make these positions permanent, and also to provide for women officers to assist the general immigration staff at the ocean ports in Canada. In addition, conductoresses will be engaged to travel with parties of unaccompanied women from the ports of landing in Canada to their destination. A woman officer will also be added to the permanent staff at Ottawa to co-ordinate the work of these special women officers, and to undertake special duties for the department where women immigrants are concerned. Arrangements have also been made by the Dominion Government through the immigration department for the steamship companies to provide conductoresses on their vessels carrying women immigrants, who will act in conjunction with the immigration department. The object of these measures is twofold. First, to give assistance and protection to women unaccustomed to travel, from the time they leave their homes in Great Britain to the time of their arrival at their destination in Canada, and secondly to more effectively check the entry into Canada of unsuitable and undesirable types of women.

[Source: Papers of the Women's Trade Union League, reel 20, *International Congress of Working Women Bulletin,* no. 7, 20 November 1920, 1–2.]

Irene Marryat Parlby (1868–1965) was born in London, England, and spent part of her childhood in India and Ireland. On an extended trip to the Northwest in 1897, she met and married Walter Parlby, an Oxford-educated English immigrant who wanted to farm. As president of the newly formed Alberta Farm Women from 1916–19, Parlby promoted the economic and political interests of farming families generally and farm women more specifically. She was elected as a member of the United Farmers of Alberta to the provincial legislature in 1921 and remained in office until 1934.

Irene Parlby

The Economic Status of the Married Woman (1925)

Leading feminists in Europe many years ago recognized the fact that the economic position of the married woman had a very distinct bearing on the economic position of women who worked outside the home, whether at manual or intellectual labor.

Because the work of the married woman in caring for her household was supposed to be a labor of love, and of no economic value, women had bred into them the idea that their labor was of inferior economic value to that of men; and when modern conditions forced them out of the home to make a living by the labor of their hands or brain, they were at first content to sell their work at far below its real value, and thus depress the wage-scale for all workers.

Today women have proved themselves capable of entering many fields of labor manual and intellectual in which men work; and their demand for equal opportunity and equal pay for equal work is being more and more recognized. Until it is fully recognized, women's work will always have a tendency to hold down the standard of wages, and displace men. Not only because under present conditions women are often content to take a lower wage, but because they have been proved in some lines of work to be more efficient.

Meanwhile, the married woman who has been looking on at the gradual economic emancipation of the woman outside the home has been doing considerable thinking on her own account. She is not only less fond of her home and family, but she has been educated; she no longer accepts a thing as right and just because it happens to be, and has been for a long period of time. She weighs things in the balance, and analyzes and questions. That is, of course, the thinking woman, but even the unthinking woman has intuitions at times which often lead to the same conclusion.

Again, a very large percentage of women today have been employed before marriage, in positions where they drew good salaries and enjoyed full independence. When they marry, they may find and frequently do that the husband is not earning more than they themselves were doing, and that amount has now to go to maintenance of a household. Hence we see people living in little flats where children are not wanted; we see the natural decay of home life, and many marriages which end in disaster.

Where there was, before marriage, a weekly or monthly cheque to draw upon, the wife has now to depend on her husband's generosity, every postage stamp has to come from him. Where the marriage condition is ideal, and love does not fly out of the window with the disillusionment that many marriages bring after the first flush of romance is over, things may carry on in a perfectly harmonious and happy manner. But the majority of marriages though are by no means ideal, and the economic condition of the wife becomes humiliating beyond words.

***

Perhaps no group of women have suffered more from this condition of affairs than farm women. Certainly, no group of women has labored so hard or ungrudgingly and so unselfishly. And yet we know for a fact that in many instances not even the produce they raise by their own labor, can be sold and classed as their own.

I have a letter in my desk from a farm woman, telling the story of various farm women she knows, who while working like slaves for their husbands, are never allowed to handle one dollar of the cash that comes in; one who is not even allowed to sell the eggs from the chickens she raises unless she steals them, although her husband is well-fixed with a half-section farm.

Can such a humiliating condition be conducive to a happy married life or a right environment in which to bring up children? And it is not so uncommon a condition as might be supposed.

Moreover, it is a condition which will continue until the economic value of a wife's work is legally recognized. There is a great deal of resistance standing in the way of this being done, and strangely enough it is the finest men who in their own married lives carry out the principles of partnership, financial and otherwise in marriage, are often the most opposed to such a principle being enacted into law. They seem to have some fear that the idea of a true marriage is being decorated by insistence on the fact that the law should recognize and demand a just return for the work the wife does in the home.

***

I wonder did the Swedish women have the same sentiment to combat when they passed their famous marriage act. The Swedish people, however, are very practical. Their women have always been in the fore front of the battle for the emancipation of women.

In ancient times, too, "The Swedish marriage ceremony ended with a speech declaring the bride to be legally married to the keys and locks of the house, thus acknowledging her as the right and lawful guardian and mistress of her new home, and giving her the same authority as her husband as far as family matters were concerned." The gradual subordination of the wife and the assumption of all authority to the husband, finally led to the elimination of this old clause from the marriage law, which had for so many years insured the independence and rights of the married woman; and it is only since the passing of the new Marriage Act of 1921 that their former liberty and independence has been restored.

If I may be allowed, I would like to quote from the speech of the Swedish delegate to the International Conference of Women in Washington in May. She said: "The full independence of the married woman is now legally recognized, not only as her right, but also as absolutely necessary if we are to have good and happy homes. The wife's work in the home has now an economic value, and she herself is no longer dependent on her husband's generosity; she needs no longer to beg for money, which may be more or less grudgingly given.

"We owe to the Scandinavian lawmakers, and in this case, to the gifted and forceful women who helped to draft the new marriage law, that this law has legally recognized woman's equal work for home and family, and has estimated it at its economic value. By giving it the same value as the work of the husband, the law emphasizes the fact that the working woman, who has no income of her own but is not SUPPORTED by her husband but by her household work, is considered as having fulfilled her part of maintaining the family. The wife now has full right to claim her allowance, and to manage independently, and without interference from her husband the money that is her due.

In the space of a short article, it is not possible to deal fully with the Swedish act; it has worked satisfactorily for four years; a similar act has now passed in Denmark, and will probably be passed in Norway before very long.

It took time in Sweden for public opinion to adjust itself to the new conception of a legal partnership in marriage, and common ownership of the family property; but this clause of the act has already proved its usefulness, and is now being accepted as quite right and proper.

**

Why should we, in this young and progressive country, lag so far behind Scandinavia? Our law is little or no protection to the married woman; the Dower Act is of little value, and women in the west have long been groping for a solution.

The Community Property Act, introduced at the last session of the Alberta legislature, was the embryo from which some satisfactory legislation may result. The act as drafted has served a useful purpose, been criticized by lawyers and women's organizations and has served a good purpose in focusing public attention on an important matter which needs good brains to work out a really satisfactory legislation.

Meanwhile, it would be well for all those who are freely criticizing the decline of home life, lamenting the growing tendency of successful business and professional women to refuse marriage and prefer a bachelor existence, the growing looseness of the marriage bond as shown in the largely increasing number of divorces year by year, to seek the cause of these things. If modern life is to be happy and contented, if children are be brought up in the right environment of a good home and parents that they cannot only love but respect, then certain conditions must be faced, and the farm wife not be placed in an inferior economic position to the unmarried woman because she gives herself to the valuable and important work of caring for home and family.

[Source: Irene Parlby, "The Economic Status of the Married Woman," *Western Producer*, 1 October 1925.]

Annie Buller (1895–1973) immigrated with her Jewish parents from the Ukraine to Montreal when she was a child. In the midst of the First World War she became involved in the Socialist Youth Movement and joined the Communist Party of Canada in 1922. Throughout the 1920s and 1930s she devoted herself full-time to party activities, including taking over editorship of the *Woman Worker* in 1927 and organizing the communist-led Industrial Needles Trades Workers Union in the 1930s.

Annie Buller
The Need for Mass Work among Women (1935)

Comrades:

I whole heartily agree with Comrade Smith's report. Three of the basic points which standout very closely to me and which I have followed with particular interest are:

1. The question of the People's Party; 2. Trade union unity; 3. The fight against political reaction and for the legality of the Communist party.

To carry into life recommendations of the report presented to us we will certainly have to mobilize the women as never before. We will not be able to carry out the decisions of the Seventh Congress of the C.I. [Communist International] and the decision of our last congress held in July, 1934, unless we critically analyze our work among the women and ask ourselves the question: "Have we brought our congress decisions to the party membership? Have we mobilized the entire party membership to carry out our decisions?" It must be agreed that with the exception of one or two districts, the work among women got very little attention. Had our convention decisions been put into life we would not come to the plenum and report to you that only 12 percent of our members are women of which 8 percent are housewives. Here we see a tremendous gap between our political following and our organizational strength. It is necessary to refresh our memory as to what were the decisions of our Party Congress in 1934.

Decisions of Last Congress

The following quotation is from the resolution of the last congress: "The party must immediately commence mass work among women. This work must be directed towards quickly drawing the mass of women workers into the revolutionary trade unions, building the women's auxiliaries of the revolutionary unions, strengthening the women's mass of organizations, ensuring mass recruiting among women by all workers' mass organizations, and quickly recruiting a large number of women into the party.

"The party must take up the struggle for the demands of the women in the factories and the special demands of unemployed women, and the unemployed demands which particularly concern the housewives. Special attention must be given to the promoting and training in the party and mass organizations of leading cadres of women comrades who could during war replace mobilized comrades. The work among women must receive the systematic attention of all the units, factions and leading committees, and in addition to this, comrades must be assigned to lead the work among women in all units, sections, districts and trade union factions."

You will agree these decisions are correct. There was no opposition to any of them at the congress, but they were not carried into life. Can we say, however, that the work of our women comrades slackens. No. We must all agree that splendid work was done by the women from coast to coast [...]

The Task among Us

If we are to draw the industrial women into our party we will have to tackle the organization of the unorganized women. We will have to head the struggles for their immediate economic needs. We must do systematic recruiting of women workers into the unions. Every district will have to work out a concrete plan of work, concentrating on the basic war industries. On the unemployed field we can form broad organizations which will fight against relief cuts and for higher relief, clothing, better housing, hot lunches for children at school. On these issues we can draw in a broad strata of women.

The housewives can be drawn into the work in connection with the high cost of living on such staple foods as meat, milk, etc. While we must orientate on the organization of the unorganized factory women, we must also give more attention to the work among unemployed women, to the housewives, and to the middle class and intellectual women who are dissatisfied with the burden they are forced to carry. We will have to draw in the foreign-born women into general mass work, in order to break the barrier which exists between the native and foreign-born women. To insure the carrying out of our decisions and once and for all give the work among women the attention it deserves, we will have to do the following;

1 Establish a women's department in each district with a capable comrade in charge, who will be responsible to the district committee and who will be a member of the district committee.

2   Each District to start a recruiting campaign in the trade unions and mass organizations.
3   Each district to promote women comrades to leading positions.
4   Twenty-five percent of the students in the district and national schools to be young girls and women.
5   Educational materials to be issued by the National Women's Department.
6   The issuance of a popular women's magazine to be started by the first of May.
7   The united front city conferences on the question of war and fascism be held to which middle class women, intellectuals and church women be invited.
8   That special attention be given to women's work among the foreign-born people, dealing with specific national questions.
9   That a special course for French-Canadian women be organized in Montreal.
10 That our women on the agrarian field join the reformist farm organizations and become the leading force in the struggle of the poor farmers fighting for seed, relief, etc.

The above recommendations by no means cover our field of activity. In each concrete situation we will have to adopt forms of work that will be applicable to the given situation. In other words, we will have to make a serious effort to carry our decisions into life to see that the turn in our women's work is made if we are to take the decisions of the plenum to heart, if we are to work for the line of the C.I. We will have to liquidate some of the old ideas we had in regard to women's work [...]

[Source: Provincial Archives of Ontario, MU 5830, MS 57, Annie Buller, "The Need for Mass Work among Women," in *Toward a People's Front: Reports and Speeches at the Ninth Plenum of the Central Committee, Communist Party of Canada, November 1935*, 139–47.]

Canadian Federation of University Women

Report of Committee on the Legal and Economic Status of University Women, 1935–1936

This committee of your Federation not only is recent in origin, but is one whose functions are not readily understood, and even if understood not readily carried out. This handicap has been in some measure responsible for the difficulty experienced in obtaining the accurate data which is required. Your convener told you last year and once more is compelled to admit that her contacts with active University women are not as widespread as she would desire. Names of members who were likely to be willing to conduct research into this subject have been kindly suggested by the executive committee. These persons have been written to but all have experienced difficulty in securing reliable data. It is of necessity difficult to gather accurate information on the Economic Status of University Women when they are in the employ of private firms or individuals. The fear is that their position be still further prejudiced by the publication of such information. In the professions likewise many admit difficulties, but hesitate to give accurate details of them lest their status become still more untenable through the revelation of the inferior place which they are forced to occupy.

It is only recently that representations have been made to the League of Nations to have the whole matter of the Status of Women discussed.

Investigations made with a view to presenting the case of women before the League of Nations would seem to indicate that the position of woman in most countries of the world is anything but a happy one. She is suffering set-backs of the rights she has gained. The general tendency in European countries has been that the women are the first to suffer. They are thrown out of their posts, married women are not allowed to work, they are told to go back to the kitchen and the nursery, and their opinion is not considered. The conviction appears to be growing that woman must demand her human rights just as man has demanded his. A new age must be brought into being where all human beings men and women alike shall be treated as equals.

One of the objects set out in the preamble of the International Labour Organization founded by the Treaty of Versailles was "the protection of young people, children and women." Its first annual conference drew up conventions concerning women's employment before and after childbirth, during the night and in unsuitable environments. Many countries apparently followed their rulings, others with highly civilized labour conditions have rejected it. Very often special regulations designed as a protection have become a disability.

This attitude is evidenced by literature which has been sent us by the Open Door International a society which is formed for the Economic Emancipation of the Woman Worker. This organization numbers among its branches and affiliated societies most white countries of the world (barring Canada). Its objects are stated as follows:

> To secure that a woman shall be free to work and be protected as a worker on the same terms as a man and that legislation and regulations dealing with conditions

and hours, payment, entry, and training shall be based upon the nature of the work and not upon the sex of the worker.

– and to secure for women irrespective of marriage or childbirth the right to decide whether or not she shall engage in paid work and to ensure that no regulation shall deprive her of that right.

This organization has for many years considered the position of the child-bearing worker and how she may best be helped at the time of the birth of her child in such a way as not to take from her rights as a worker. The result of careful consideration over a period of many years is that woman being an adult human being should be left in full possession of her rights. Neither marriage or pregnancy or childbirth are reasons for depriving her of the human right to decide for herself whether she shall engage in paid work. To refuse this right to a woman or to impose restrictions in her exercise of it does not help her. It is not really protection but a serious attack on the economic interests of the woman earner. As one writer has remarked – "the equalitarians have observed that it was only in well-paid processes where women came into competition with men, that restrictions have been thought desirable. Charwomen have no statutory hours for meal times. There is no prohibition of night work for domestic servants. Nurses may lift heavy weights, and working mothers continue coal-carrying and floor scrubbing through pregnancy till the first pangs of labour, and resume them as soon as they can put a foot to the ground."

The general result of protective measures say the Open Door International is that women's pay is kept low and that some women lose or fail to get paid work. They claim that every burden which by legislation is thought to be imposed on the employer because his employee is about to have a child is in fact borne by the woman herself. He may dismiss her or recoup himself by paying all women employees a low wage and so not only damage their economic interest, but also depress the wage rates of all women in the labour market. The conclusion to which this organization has come then is that a woman who is incapacitated for her usual work by pregnancy or confinement, should be similarly treated to any worker who is incapacitated for his usual work on account of accident or illness.

General Situation in Canada

When we come to a survey of the Canadian situation we are faced with the difficulty of separating the problems and interests of University Women from that of non-graduates. One exception to this is the profession of High School teaching where most of the women are graduates. Last year we submitted schedules showing salary discrimination against women in that profession as compared with men. The desire on the part of Municipal school boards to appoint men in preference to women is undeniable. In many instances men are given their choice of subjects taught and are often given special consideration. One teacher cites a somewhat indicative instance of a school where a male teacher each year is allowed certain days off for his curling activities without loss of salary the principal or other teachers supply for him. A woman in the same school asked for a half day off to attend the funeral of a relative and she was compelled to pay for a substitute:

In the Government and Municipal posts in Canada the feeling and practice is strongly against allowing married women to continue in their work. In reference to the profession of teaching Prof. F. Clarke of London University who visited Canada last summer referred to the short sightedness of discharging women from schools "once they had become really capable by having a child of their own."

No information is available as to how many, if any, University Graduates have entered banks. We are informed that in view of the pressing problems of unemployment among young men it has become the policy of several Canadian banks when woman employees leave through marriage or other natural causes to replace them with men. This does not apply to the machine operators. We are informed that as a result of this policy the number of women employed in the head office and branches of one of the largest banks in Winnipeg is now 28 whereas in 1929 it numbered 98. During this period the number of male employees was relatively small.

It is reported to us that there is no discrimination on the ground of sex in the Civil Service of Canada. In spite of this fact it is observed that women are not appointed to positions having a high salary attached. It must be remembered that there are certain types of work which women are allowed to retain without argument such as stenography and operation of other machines. The number of salaried posts for women in newspaper work is limited as there are comparatively few publications in any one city in Canada. Those who get in seem to stay indicating that women like the work and have considerable aptitude for it. Marriage may interrupt a women's career in newspaper work, but does not prevent her resuming it if she so desires. The society page seems to be the largest field open to women writers. Some but not many, do general newspaper reporting.

Winnipeg has afforded women newspaper writers rather rare opportunities. Dr E. Cora Hind, Agricultural Editor of the Manitoba Free Press, initiated and developed her own department of this paper to the point where she has become an international figure. The Free Press has likewise one full time editorial woman writer and a woman telegraph editor as well. The Western Municipal news has as its editor Miss Nan Moulton. Another Winnipeg woman the late

Mrs Genevieve Lipsett Skinner, was the first and only woman to sit in the Press Gallery at Ottawa. In the important matter of salary women in newspaper work get less pay than men for jobs of equal or greater responsibility. Promotion into high salaried posts is most uncertain for women.

Employment of women in Canada is menaced not by legislation but by misinformed public opinion and prejudice which believes that employment of women outside the home is one of the major factors prolonging the depression. Speaking on this argument Miss Catherine I. Mackenzie, Principal of the Montreal High School for Girls addressing a meeting of the Professional and Business Women of Montreal recently said: "Blame for having caused the depression was one of the reasons for the attack on the status of women. We used to think it was war debts and post-war speculation – but no it is women who have taken men's jobs holding these high-salaried executive positions and all industry and all business stops! – If back to the kitchen will end the depression then by all means let us go back to the kitchen. She then pictured the result of the back to the kitchen movement! The baker does not come, the shops close because we are at home spinning our own cloth, the hairdresser ceases to exist because we have no time to go and be made beautiful. One by one the big industries, the small shopkeeper, all the things that make up the life of our community will close.

"– Then there will be nothing but depression, we will be back to 1830. That is the logical result of the back-to-the kitchen movement. It would soon bring men to a realization of what a silly scheme it is."

When we come to discuss the political field we may be ill pleased that so few women entered the political arena in the last Federal election, and that so little of success attended the efforts of those who did. We have just cause for disappointment yet we must also admit that since our last report our representation in the Senate and in the House of Commons has doubled. We now have two in the place of one representative in each House. To the rank of Senators has been added Mrs Fallis, and to that of members of the House of Commons Mrs Black, whose husband retired from his office as speaker of the House due to ill health.

In the field of public service we express gratification at the election of an outstanding leader of women in the person of Mrs Plumptre, an Alderman of the City of Toronto. All University women in the City of Winnipeg are justly proud of the outstanding leadership in public service given our city by Alderman Margaret McWilliams.

[Source: LAC, MG 28 II96, vol. 19, file 1, Canadian Federation of University Women, "Report of the Committee on the Legal and Economic Status of University Women," 1935–6.]

PART SEVEN
Pacifism

In July 1937 women from countries bordering the Pacific rim gathered in Vancouver for a conference hosted by the Pan-Pacific Women's Association. This organization encouraged greater cultural understanding between the nations represented and addressed a wide range of women's issues of mutual concern. Against a backdrop of ever-growing international conflict, the promotion of peace proved one of the most pressing topics of discussion at this conference, as illustrated in a cartoon that appeared in the *Vancouver Sun*. Drawing upon the phrase "the hand that rocks the cradle rules the world," the cartoon visually represented the PPWA as a mother attempting to protect the globe, in the form of a child, from imminent threat. While many feminists continued to be dismissive of this phrase, as it falsely, from their point of view, accorded power to women that in many respects they had yet to achieve, the illustration captured the long-standing affinity between women's reform organizations and pacifism. Women were active in peace movements in North America and Europe from early in the nineteenth century onward, with the first all-female pacifist organizations originating later in the century. The illustration further captured one of the key justifications for feminist involvement with this issue throughout much of the first wave, that as mothers women "had a natural desire to preserve peace and had a special mission to fulfill in peace education."[1]

The first national women's organization in Canada to take up the cause of peace activism was the WCTU. Following the lead of the WCTU in the United States, the Dominion Union formed a Peace and Arbitration Committee in 1894 and encouraged local unions to support this issue. The concept of arbitration linked to peace held special appeal for women activists, as it denoted a method of conflict resolution within and between nations by way of negotiation. The report by the Nova Scotia Superintendent on Peace and Arbitration, Margaret McKay, for 1896 connected the recently inaugurated peace work in the province to an already well-established international pacifist movement that had been making tangible advances. With regard to Nova Scotia, McKay admitted that as of yet little had been accomplished, but proposed a future program of activities with particular emphasis placed on the education of children at home, church, and school. As part of its focus on education, the WCTU advocated a policy against military training in schools in the 1890s that would be adopted and pursued by many other women's organizations up to the Second World War.

Demonstrating its ongoing leadership in the realm of peace activities, the WCTU expressed concern over the decision of the Canadian government to send troops to South Africa at the onset of the Boer War in 1899. This war marked the first time Canadian soldiers were sent abroad and, in this initial instance, to support the British military's armed conflict against the Dutch Boers. As demonstrated by the resolution passed by the provincial union in Ontario, the WCTU stated their regret over the government's decision and called upon the women of Canada "to proclaim the principles of peace." In distinct contrast, the National Council of Women of Canada articulated no such regret; instead, as directed by its executive under the leadership of Lady Aberdeen, the council passed a resolution to arrange for the comfort of the troops and made a broad commitment to assist the Canadian government in whatever way was deemed necessary. In the discussion leading up to the passage to the resolution, the council also pledged their cooperation with a group of women who were referred to as "ladies of the Militia" that soon afterward formed the Imperial Order Daughters of the Empire. Not for the first or last time expressions of loyalty to nation and empire took precedence over the goals of pacifism within the Canadian women's movement.

After the end of the Boer War the NCWC did form its own Peace and Arbitration Committee in 1904 under the direction of Ada Courtice, a Quaker and long-time member of the WCTU. Reporting on peace activities within the Local Council of Women of Toronto several years later, Gomer White provided an account of a recent conference which she had attended with Courtice in the United States. She praised the "'world' outlook" of the diverse group of leaders gathered together for this event who were seeking peaceful solutions to international differences. Indicating that a formal commitment to peace work was only in the beginning stages within the NCWC and her own local council, White lauded the leadership of the International Council of Women on this issue. As Heloise Brown has insightfully noted, though, the particular strand of pacifism supported by the ICW at the turn of the century held internationalism as an ideal, "but it also tied individuals closely to their own national identity and origin."[2] And thus within the ICW, nationalism and imperialism, which were effectively coterminous for many feminists during this period, took precedence over a commitment to international cooperation. In large measure the ICW approach was replicated within the NCWC.

With the onset of armed hostilities in Europe in 1914 there was little hesitation on the part of the leading women's reform organizations in Canada to endorse the war. In a pattern replicated in other belligerent countries, many Canadian feminists suspended their involvement in the developing national and international peace networks and concentrated their energies on supporting the war effort. A number of high-profile female reformers, however, initially adopted an anti-war position, including Nellie McClung and Flora MacDonald Denison. In a political tract entitled *Women and War* (1914) Denison made an impassioned plea for pacifism, arguing that despite assurances from the leading powers involved in the conflict, "there is no such thing as 'civilized warfare.'" Condemning the long-standing connection between masculinity and militarism, which she attributed to both heredity and environment, she argued that women were deleteriously affected by war and needed to be granted equal partnership with men in seeking solutions. According to Deborah Gorham and Janice Williamson, Denison in time changed her stance, as she concluded that "the Germans were inherently more militaristic than the British, and therefore more responsible for the war."[3]

Feminist opposition to the First World War gained considerable impetus beyond the borders of Canada with the announcement of an International Congress of Women, later renamed the Women's Peace Conference, that was held at the Hague in April 1915. Under the leadership of Jane Addams, American women's groups played a major role in the organization of the conference, one that was far less complicated than for female reformers elsewhere, given that the United States was still then a neutral country. Invitations were made to various Canadian organizations and individuals to attend, but as the letter and accompanying pamphlet sent to Jane Addams from the National Committee of Women for Patriotic Service attest, there was considerable hostility to the idea of a women's peace conference. Arguing that peace overtures were greatly premature, this group defended at length Canadian involvement in the war, which they characterized as a struggle "to preserve our soul as an Empire," and more generally endorsed the notion of armed conflict "in defence of the rights of the weak and the principles of truth, honour and liberty." Not surprisingly given such sentiments, none of the leading national women's organizations sent a representative to the Hague.

Yet as Barbara Roberts has contended, such a patriotic militarist response to the war was far from universal among women reformers in this country.[4] A small number of Canadian women actually attended the Women's Peace

Conference, including Julia Grace Wales. A professor of English at the University of Wisconsin and a staunch pacifist, Wales wrote an account of her trip to Europe and her experiences while at the conference. Travelling with a large contingent of American delegates, she described the enormous sense of purpose and responsibility the women felt and the "collective mind" that developed en route as ideas were debated. A key resolution widely endorsed at the peace conference was one authored by Wales herself. It advocated the concept of continuous mediation without armistice that involved gathering intellectuals from neutral nations to meet for the duration of the war and prepare proposals to bring about its end. Following extended interactions with other women pacifists, Wales expressed a degree of optimism that an era of world consciousness could soon be ushered in that would create a "family of nations." She carried this message back to Canada, where she gave speeches about the conference.[5]

A feminist-pacifist network of upwards of several hundred Canadian women developed during the midst of the war, with Gertrude Richardson being one of the most committed and eloquent. From her farm in Swan River, Manitoba, Richardson wrote numerous articles opposing the war in women's social-reform journals such as *Woman's Century* and the socialist newspaper *Canadian Forward*. In one 1917 piece she specifically condemned the intended plan of the federal government to impose conscription. Richardson joined the national debate on conscription in which long-standing divisions of class, race, ethnicity, and language were being further revealed by framing it explicitly as a feminist issue. Depicting the introduction of a mandatory draft as submitting men "to the slaughter," she called upon all Canadian women to object to this measure. Of additional significance, she characterized military service as a form of slavery in which militarism was directly linked with imperialist goals.

In the wake of the massive human devastation of the First World War and with the intention of preventing future armed conflicts, women's reform groups reactivated peace work after the armistice. They were joined by a new organization whose central purpose was peace activism, the Canadian section of the Women's International League for Peace and Freedom. Representative more generally of the expanded commitment to transnational collaborations among feminists during the interwar period, Canadian women in WILPF dedicated themselves to a diverse range of educational measures aimed at combating militarism and promoting peace. Most women who joined this organization identified as a socialist or social democrat and, as evidenced by the pamphlet produced by the family court judge and early WILPF Canada member Rose Henderson, employed a class and gender analysis in discussions of war and peace. In this pamphlet that appeared in a number of different versions in the early 1920s, Henderson declared that women needed to be fully informed of both the causes and consequences of war in order to more effectively pursue the goal of peace. She characterized the Great War not as a quest for freedom but as a quest for economic wealth by capitalists, and documented at length the enormous costs most especially for working-class men and women. Henderson pointedly addressed, for example, the physical and moral degradation of women "of the masses" during wartime as the result of sexual violence and the spread of venereal diseases.

Other women's organizations adopted a more moderate stance than WILPF Canada in their peace work. The NCWC heralded the newly formed League of Nations as the surest means of preventing war by forming a committee under this name at the national level and in most of its locals; it also worked in close allegiance with the League of Nations Society of Canada.[6] In a report on peace activism within the NCWC for 1932 Hilda Laird touted the recent appointments of Adelaide Plumptre to the Assembly of the League of Nations and Winnifred Kydd (at the time NCWC president) as a delegate to the disarmament conference, two among a growing number of prominent female social reformers selected for international posts by the federal government in the interwar period. Such appointments were not only a measure of the legitimacy at least some feminists had achieved with the governing political parties, but also recognition that elements within the women's movement in Canada had secured a place in discussions over collective security and international cooperation. Laird also noted that in the past year the NCWC had devoted itself almost exclusively to the "problems of disarmament," which included playing a major role in garnering over 400,000 signatures on the Petition for World Disarmament by International Agreement, a further indication of the organization's ongoing faith in resolving conflicts by way of diplomatic solutions. At the same time, it is evident that the NCWC had been shifting away from emphasizing close ties to Britain on military matters and foreign affairs. Although some affiliated groups resisted this change, statements of allegiance to the British Empire became ever more muted and much less frequent over the course of the 1920s and 1930s.

As international tensions increased during the 1930s, many women's groups expended even greater time and effort on peace matters. On the subject of developing public opinion on peace in 1937, Laura Jamieson was not only quite critical about the contributions of women's reform groups in this realm, she also argued that far more intense academic study was required to ensure "education toward Peace." As an active member of WILPF Canada since the early 1920s, and serving for a time as its national president, Jamieson viewed the efforts of women's groups for whom pacifism was only a partial aim as superficial and intermittent. Along with a growing number of other feminists inside and outside Canada during the 1930s, she challenged the long-held assumption that women had a natural affinity for pacifism and instead argued that a commitment to non-violent solutions was premised on reasoned conviction aided by close examination of academic subjects such as economics, history, and international relations. Echoing the strategy adopted by WILPF during this period, Jamieson also attempted to reformulate patriotism as adhering to universal principles of humanitarianism, not pledging loyalty to nation and empire.

NOTES

1 Janice Williamson and Deborah Gorham, "Peace History," in *Up and Doing: Canadian Women and Peace*, ed. Janice Williamson and Deborah Gorham (Toronto: Women's P, 1989), 28.
2 Heloise Brown, *The Truest Form of Patriotism: Pacifist Feminism in Britain, 1870–1902* (Manchester: Manchester UP, 2003), 156.
3 Williamson and Gorham, "Peace History," 30.
4 Barbara Roberts, *A Reconstructed World: A Feminist Biography of Gertrude Richardson* (Montreal: McGill-Queen's UP, 1996), 8.
5 See, for example, LAC, MG 30, 3238, vol. 1-23, Julia Grace Wales, "Address given by Miss Wales at Point Fortune, August 1915, [after] International Congress of Women at the Hague, April 1915."
6 Veronica Strong-Boag, "Peace-Making Women: Canada, 1919–1939," in *Women and Peace: Theoretical, Historical and Practical Perspectives*, ed. Ruth Roach Pierson et al. (London: Croom Helm, 1987), 178.

Margaret McKay

Report of Provincial Superintendent on Peace and Arbitration (1896)

Woman's Christian Temperance Union

The many international and national congresses held during this year, testify to the advance the peace movement is making all over this round world. From far-away India comes the tidings of woman's practical work along the lines. Belated Spain is drawing up her forces and taking a very unspanish view of the situation, in proof thereof we give the following from a Madrid journal: – "The Queen Regent has been chosen by the South American Republics of Ecuador, Columbia and Peru to act as arbitrator in determining a disputed portion of their respective boundaries." "The world do move." From the Sovereign Pontiff of Rome, there are words of cheer for peace workers. His Holiness expresses the wish "That God may happily crown your praiseworthy efforts with success." In England, France and Germany women are in the forefront of the battle for sweet peace. Recently an inter-Parliamentary assembly representing fourteen European States met to urge the settling of international disputes by arbitration.

The English House of Commons, for the first time in its history, has unanimously declared itself for arbitration. The two great statesmen, Lord Salisbury and President Cleveland, are in close consultation, looking in the same direction. This is in strong contrast to ten years ago, when the Japanese embassy sent to London to investigate the Christian religion with the view to its adoption as the national religion of Japan. Their report was terse and to the point: "Too much fight in the Christian religion, Japan would better stick to her time-honored Shintoism."

Just here the impeachment of the Apostle Paul occurs irresistibly to me, "The name of Christ is blasphemed among the Gentiles by you, as it is written."

The movement in favor of establishing a permanent High Court of Nations, to settle all international difficulties between English speaking nations, is meeting with less opposition that its promoters anticipated. The jingoites are much exercised as to how these decisions shall be enforced. The reply is, in the same way as the Alabama claims were settled, not with threats of glittering swords and deadly guns, but by the moral force of civilized mankind, which has won seventy-six victories for peace during the century.

In WCTU circles, Peace and Arbitration work is, comparatively speaking, new. The Congress held in Chicago 1893, gave the work an impulse, and from this front it was generally adopted by American Unions. The Dominion Union too, joined the forces the following year, and is forging ahead to an encouraging degree. Two years ago the Maritime Union fell into line. The report for that year was a meagre one, and now, at the close of the first year of the existence of the Provincial Union, your Superintendent's report seems as lean as the illusioned king of Pharaoh's dream.

Seven Unions report peace sermons preached, eight report "nothing done along the lines of Peace and Arbitration." One Union reports a Peace Band organized in connection with the existing Juvenile Society, 300 pages of literature numbered, peace sermon preached, the residue of Unions preserve a masterly silence in matter. Your Superintendent forwarded early in November a "Program and Lesson and other Literature for Peace Day," the third Sabbath in December, also copy of notice for local papers to every Union in the Province. Twelve copies of Diamond's Essay on War, was mailed with other literature to ministers and influential persons. One dollar was received from a prominent Christian worker to be expended in anti-Brigade literature. A large package was sent to the Secretary of Boy's Brigades for the Dominion, this was selected by Mrs Baillie, World's Superintendent Peace and Arbitration. Five hundred pages literature was presented and fifty pamphlets.

Experienced peace workers suggest the home and school as the most suitable camping ground on which to urge our peaceful war. The children are our greatest hope, but we do not leave it to the children. We must show up the fallacies and deceits of the Ghoul Militarism by making it a live topic in our homes and schools.

Mrs Frances Lester, National Superintendent Physical Culture, in her last annual report says, "The increasing popular demand among boys for the introduction of military training in schools is to be deplored. Its tendency is to displace physical discipline of a more comprehensive character, it is a detriment to the progress of the work, and an unfortunate influence in favor of war. Children should be trained to believe that the interests of the nation can be better served by settling difficulties as far as possible by arbitration. The WCTU should bring its influence to bear against this innovation in our schools." These words will apply with exact propriety to the brigades of our churches which the *London Christian Advocate* says is an attempt to aid the Kingdom of Christ by its apposite suggestion for substitutes. Calisthenics offer a wide choice as a substitute for these organizations.

Revd Myron Forbush, Yarmouth, offers, through the Boston Peace Advocate, to supply all information necessary in organizing Knights of the Round Table.

Fire Drill for boys and girls is meeting with a large measure of success. Your Superintendent was greatly interested in reading in The Women's Signal of an exhibition given by a girls' Fire Brigade, in a suburb of London. In every particular the drill was as well conducted as that of the boys – a girl of 18 being Captain. The Industrial School in Cambridge, Massachusetts, is making a grand success of this helpful and practical drill. A London daily says it is just the thing to develop the British youth in the way they should go.

[Source: Margaret McKay, "Report of Provincial Superintendent on Peace and Arbitration," in *Report of First Annual Convention of the Nova Scotia WCTU, 1896*, 55–7.]

Ontario Women's Christian Temperance Union
Resolution Regarding the South African War (1899)

Resolved, that we place on record our deep regrets that our country has recently deemed it necessary to engage in war, that we earnestly recommend the women in our country to proclaim the principles of peace, and that we do all in our power to discourage the fostering of the military spirit in our families, in our schools and in our churches and also resolved, that we favor the settlement of international disputes by arbitration instead of war.

[Source: *The Globe*, 4 November 1899.]

National Council of Women of Canada
Resolution and Discussion Regarding Canadian Contingent to the Transvaal (1899)

Lady Aberdeen: –
    May I ask as a matter of urgency that resolution be considered which was adopted for recommendation to you at the Executive yesterday? *Agreed.*
    Resolved: – That a Standing Committee of the National Council of Women of Canada be appointed, which shall be empowered to offer assistance on behalf of the Women of Canada to the Dominion Government in making arrangements for the comfort of the Canadian Contingent, which is about to proceed to the Transvaal War; or to offer co-operation on behalf of the Council, now, or in the future, in any way that the Government may deem desirable."

I know that it will meet with immediate response from all here. Since this resolution was adopted by the Executive yesterday for presentation yesterday to you, I have had a telegram from Mrs Minden Cole, which I think might require that this resolution be somewhat altered – "The ladies in connection with the Militia throughout Canada, with Mrs Hutton at their head, are forming a Society to do all that is possible for the men who got to the Transvaal and for the families that are left. They hope that this will meet with the goodwill of the National Council." I would suggest therefore that we telegraph as a response that we desire to be co-operative with them.

Mrs Willoughby Cummings: – I would suggest that both these be acted upon; that we offer ourselves to the Dominion Government as a National Council, and also that we co-operate with the ladies who are forming other plans. It seems to me that we shall be placing ourselves in the right position to offer our services directly to the Government, and that we ought also to co-operate with any who are already making plans. (Applause.)

Mrs Boomer (London): – I think that was the spirit of the Resolution drafter yesterday. Are we to stand by the original Resolution?

Lady Aberdeen: – To pass that first, I think, and then to pass another resolution accepting the invitation to do anything we can. We shall be able to help the society most effectively through our Local Councils. They will probably be glad to rely on our Councils where they exist.

Mrs Reid (Montreal): – Does not our Resolution cover the ground completely? If we offer our co-operation to the Government is not that quite sufficient? The Government will indicate in what way we had better act.

Lady Aberdeen: – This society is practically a society formed by the ladies of the Militia with Mrs Hutton at their head. Their telegram is an answer to our resolution and indicates the way in which it will be carried out officially. Certainly, we can pass the Resolution.

The Resolution was moved by Lady Thompson, seconded by Mrs Edward Griffin and carried by a standing vote.

Lady Aberdeen – You will then decide that I send a telegram to this Association that the Council will be glad to co-operate with them in any way they can?

Mrs McEwen (Brandon) moved, seconded by Mrs Willoughby Cummings, that a telegram be sent in response to the telegram from the ladies of the Militia, undertaking to co-operate in any way in our power. (Carried unanimously.)

[Source: National Council of Women of Canada, *Yearbook of the National Council of the Women of Canada, 1899*, 47–8.]

M. Gomar White
Peace and Arbitration (1907)

In reviewing the work of the past year there seems to have been very little tangible result, and yet your Committee feels that progress has been made towards bringing this large and vital subject before the minds of the members of the council.

The Convener accompanied by the convener of the National Council on this subject, Mrs A.T. Courtice, attended a Peace and Arbitration council, held at Mohonk Mountain House, Catskill Mountains, N.Y., in June last.

The Convention called annually to meet at this beautiful summer resort, by Mr Charles Smiley, a Friend, has grown from a little party of twenty-five friends at the first meeting, 1894, to a large Convention of two hundred and fifty delegates in 1906. The most magnificent feature of this growth being the character of the individuals whose interest leads them to assemble to discuss, on the broadest lines, the best methods of promoting educationally and politically the cause of peace. At the Council board on the opening morning the generous host, Mrs Smiley, Friend, sat shoulder to shoulder with Cardinal Gibbons, the Supreme Head of the Roman Catholic church in America; Dr Lyman Abbott, the most eminent Congregational divine; Bishop McVickers of Rhode Island, one of the most prominent Episcopal clergyman; the President of Brown's University, Justice Brewer of the Supreme Court of the United States; while eminent jurists, clergy and university Presidents and professors, and prominent business men from all over the Union were in attendance, which as a whole represented the finest ethical and social ideals of a nation. [The] interested listen[ed] for four days to the discussion of this question by such minds, and from every possible point of view always with the large "world" outlook premiered and hearing in conclusion such opinions as that expressed by Cardinal Gibbons, when he said: – My friends, we are here to consider the most vitally important subject that can engage the minds and hearts of men to-day" – and Justice Brewer when he said, "the time *has* come – not will come – when the peace of the world could be secured by an agreement of among the first-class powers of the world to submit all questions of international difference to a Congress or Parliament of the nations." "When the love of peace and prosperity becomes stronger in the hearts of the masses, than the love of power and expansion is in the minds of politicians and statesmen, there will be no further delay in the peace adjustment of all international matters." Do you wonder, Madam President, that the Convener of this committee and her companion returned to Toronto with hearts burning with the desire to have this council take its stand with the positive ways as the advocate of peace and arbitration. With a view to securing such an expression of the National Council, as well as our Local Council, a resolution was submitted to the Executive Committee previous to the meeting in Hamilton, in which the National council was asked to suggest and aid in every possible way methods for active educational work in the Local Councils. Through some technicality the resolution was ruled out, but your Committee is satisfied, from the temper of the Council when the subject was indirectly touched upon at several different times, that if such a resolution had been submitted to the body at large, it would certainly have been adopted.

Already as you know, the International Council of Women has a strong and active standing Committee on Peace and Arbitration. In every country having a National Council of Women, this subject is one of the foremost in the minds and hearts of those it represents; and in every such country, I think without exception, there are active Peace Societies and organizations similar in purpose to the Mohonk Conference to which I have referred; also there should be borne in mind the large international movements such as the Interparliamentary union, the Hague court, and the Peace Congress, that meet in some one of the larger centers of life every year. The past year the meeting was in Milan – I believe this year it is to be in New York City; to this Congress every Peace Society in the world is invited to send a representative. Canada many now share in the great and eminent gathering year after year by sending a delegate from the Canadian Peace Society, of which Sir William Mulock is the President. It is a matter for congratulation that this society is now fully organized and is entering upon its noble campaign of education. All who long for the day when matters of serious international difference the appeal will be made to brain and not to brawn for adjustment should become members of the Society, and held with a fee of a $1.00 a year, and their personal influence to educate the sentiment of a small segment of the great Circle of the nations; feeling assured that when the entire Circle is completed there will dawn the permanent day of peace and prosperity. But to return to the efforts of your Committee. It is along this line that we are now working. A start has been made. Two Societies, the Woman's Alliance of the Unitarian Church, and the Household Economic Association, have appointed each a member on the Committee.

When called upon one year from now to make our annual report we hope to speak for a large and representative Committee and to report much progress made in some one or more of the following directions: – Getting the ministers of the city to observe a Peace Sunday each year, thus following the example of England where the Sunday next before Christmas is so observed; by encouraging editors to advocate peace measures rather than appeal to the belligerent feeling in times of disturbance; by persuading legislators to support arbitration and all laws that strengthen Peace; by discussing the subject as a part of a programme of each winter's work in the various affiliated societies; by petitioning the Board of Education to establish a Peace Day in all schools, a step already accomplished in some of the States, notably in Massachusetts, where the 18th of May is so observed under the title, "Hague Day." These are directions, Madame President, in which Committee, when fully formed, hopes to work, and the Convener begs that various societies affiliated will give an early opportunity for a presentation of the matter at a regular meeting, with the hope that their members may be appointed, or that they will take action on their own initiative and at once appoint a representative on the Committee, notifying the Convener promptly, giving name and address of the appointee.

Respectfully submitted,
M. Gomar White, Convener.

[Source: M. Gomar White, "Peace and Arbitration," in *Report of the Local Council of Women of Toronto*, issue 15 (1909), 27–9.]

A detailed biography of Flora MacDonald Merrill Denison (1867–1921) may be found on page 128.

Flora MacDonald Denison

War and Women (1914)

In recent years it has dawned on the consciousness of all well-meaning people that war is not only Hell, kept alive and burning by hatred and malice, but that as malice and hatred can be evolved out of human beings by love and common sense, so war can be evolved out of nations by the same method.

In a few short years so rapidly did this peace idea grow that in 1913 a palace of peace was actually dedicated to mankind in the city of The Hague in the quaint little country of Holland.

Representative delegates congregated in that charming city and not only "Peace on Earth, Goodwill to Men" was shouted through the length and breadth of the land but also the cry for general disarmament.

To-day the United States and Canada are celebrating a hundred years of peace.

Three thousand miles of frontier stretches between two young nations without a fort or gun or ship to guard or menace.

A gigantic river flows peacefully to the ocean, great lakes wash peaceful shores, tremendous boundary lines are peace blessed, and the wonderland of Giant Mountains war only with the thunder clouds that burst and kiss their snow-capped summits.

The peace idea has been tried out and not found wanting, and with this splendid New World revelation and celebration which was going to culminate with a great world exhibition to celebrate all commerce joined in peace by the completion of the Panama Canal – just as the world seemed ready for a step up the ladder of progress – behold a war cloud bursts, and eight nations – five of which are major powers, are involved in war.

The poor little white Dove of Peace fluttered and fell at the first cruel scratch from the talons of the Eagle of War, and the world is wondering and suffering and gasping with horror and terror.

The peace conference even laid down rules and regulations for "civilized warfare," and the cannon and the bomb, the rifle and the bayonet have hissed back their cruel laugh and shown us all that there is no such a thing as "civilized warfare."

And what does it all mean?

Have the Altruists all lived and worked and thought for nothing?

Have women come into the game of life in the past generations with their wondrous power of organization as shown at their world's represented congresses and passed resolutions of peace and arbitration to be absolutely ignored by the sons to whom they have given birth?

Has Democracy appeared on the stage only to have the curtain rung down at the beginning of the first act and slapped in the face by autocracy?

Is there any meaning to the great platitudes about the "Brotherhood of Man" and "Love your Neighbor as Yourself," and "We're all one human family."

Is Nietzsche right and will war eternally return to tell its gruesome story?

Faith has been wrested from the faithful.

Hope has been buried by the hopeful.

Ambition no longer builds and aspiration receives no inspiring help.

But – It is only yesterday that a social conscience was born.

It is only yesterday since a gleam of light entered the human brain relative to the meaning of psychology and suggestion – of heredity and environment, and the evolutionary theory is still in its infancy.

A barbarian race of human beings evolved through stress and strain of the necessities of existence, has carried the attributes of combat continuously because it meant primarily self protection and self preservation.

The human, and especially the male, has thought in terms of combat and of dominance through force.

But through it all the better and greater thinkers have been planning a wiser war.

When the brain of man was able to conceive and materialize a great Ocean Liner, it was not expressly to carry guns with which to destroy life and property.

When the brain of man invented a heavier-than-air ship to sail above the clouds it was not simply to carry bombs to drop and destroy life and property.

Steel was not tempered to unheard of hardness to pierce through an army of human flesh.

But the male through centuries upon centuries has been combative and war has resulted and how quickly this dominant note took advantage of the inventions of the keenest brains and utilized them to the killing industry.

To-day we do know something of psychology and the subtle telepathy which reaches mind after mind tuned to the same key, and we can explain scientifically the mob spirit and the war spirit.

Tribes grew into greater tribes through dominance and conquest, nations grew into greater nations by the same methods, and ever and ever the worshipped hero was the warrior.

Travel over Europe and who are the heroes flaunted in the face of the people.

Look at Wellington and Nelson in Great Britain. In Germany Frederick the Great is heralded in statue and story the length and breadth of the land, and Napoleon's tomb in Paris is awe inspiring beyond description.

When we studied history, what was the key-note of it all? Battles, battles, battles.

A reign was of importance or not according to the degree and length of the wars.

If we cultivate a piece of land and sow it with thistles and nettles we cannot expect to reap a crop of roses and lilies.

If we cultivate race hatred and militarism we will get war.

No one nation is to blame, it is the outcome of the custom of generations, the outcome of false and cruel standards.

That this war is so much more deadly than all previous wars is that the world has reached the maximum degree of efficiency in warfare.

In its deadliness lies our hope, and when it is all over a new standard of values will have to be written.

In writing this another pen than that held by Mars will have to be used.

Venus must be the star in the ascendant and the mothers of the race must assist in tracing out a new code of ethics.

Woman's thought and action have always been constructive.

They have made the homes in which all sons are born, and they know the cost of life.

Every man who went to battle meant that some woman had gone down into the shadow of the valley of suffering to give him birth.

Women paid the first great price and at last women are demanding that she have some say as to how her property and her sons shall be treated.

Woman demands a say in the social scheme which has cost her so much.

She demands not only protection for her young but the conservation of human life by a more humane civilization.

The women of England have no quarrel with the women of Germany.

Both were standing together like sisters asking, pleading, and petitioning that International Arbitration keep peace between nations and that women be given the power of the ballot to assist in protecting their homes and making their laws.

The world howled and shrieked in derision at a little property being destroyed in order to awaken it to the existence of unjust conditions, but now, with whole cities being destroyed and lives swept away by the thousands, women can only bear the burden of slaughtered sons and husbands and ruined homes.

Their voices were not yet strong enough to make a dent in the murderous giant of militarism.

What now of woman's place being in the home, and what will home be with the darling boy rotting in the trench, the devoted husband crippled for life and the brother diseased and ruined.

For every man killed there is also killed a wife – a mother and a family of children.

Dead men will make no homes, and widows and childless women will take little heart in just houses.

Many women are not filled with the spirit of patriotism, and the primal instinct to conserve and help is meritoriously showing itself in the work being done, but let not the glamour of victory nor the sorrow of defeat blind women to the real important issue.

The important issue before, during, and after the war is Democratic Freedom, and there is no freedom and no democracy while women are a disfranchised class.

Had women stood shoulder to shoulder with men in thinking out world problems this war would never have been.

This war is the most conclusive argument that has ever blazed its electric message across the sky of human consciousness in favor of political equality.

"Prevention is better than cure." We are learning to apply this great truism, and besides, war never cured.

The conquered Napoleon left behind a legacy of hate which is bearing fruit to-day.

The battle of Waterloo was not decisive and the only decisive battle will be a bloodless one, fought out by representatives from nations who will be elected by the whole people.

In that court of arbitration great men and great women will discuss side by side what is best for their children – best for the human race.

[Source: Flora MacDonald Denison, *War and Women* (1914).]

Adelaide Wynne Plumptre (1871-1948) was born in Surrey, England and with her Anglican minister husband immigrated to Canada in 1901. Involved in various women's reform issues in Toronto, including suffrage, she was also one of the founders of the Canadian Girl Guides. Plumptre was appointed Superintendent of Supplies and Corresponding Secretary of the Canadian Red Cross at the outset of the First World War. In 1919, she became President of the CRC. She served several terms on the Toronto School Board from 1926 to 1934 and was the third female alderman for the City of Toronto elected in 1936.

Adelaide Plumptre

Letter Regarding Canadian Involvement in the Women's Peace Conference (1915)

April 15, 1915

Miss Jane Addams
President, International Congress of Women
C/O Executive Committee,
Damrak 28-30
Amsterdam, Holland

Dear Madam:

I am instructed as Secretary of the National Committee of Women for Patriotic Service in Canada to write to you as President of the International Congress of Women. The Committee of which I have the honour to be Secretary is composed as you will see by the enclosed circular of the presidents or their representatives of the nationally organized societies of women in Canada.

Many of the women represented on this Committee have received invitations to be present, or to elect delegates to represent them at the Congress. None of these Canadian societies of women have felt able to accept the courteous invitation of your Committee because they believe that the time for peace has not yet arrived, and therefore, no woman from Canada can speak as representing the opinion of Canadian women.

The enclosed Open Letter concerning Peace has been issued by thousands amongst the women of Canada, and we have received many resolutions endorsing the views therein expressed. It has also been commented upon by most of the women editors of our newspapers, and I have not seen any comment which did not express approval of the position taken in the matter.

Madam President, when we look at Belgium we cannot speak of peace. We speak often of the horrors of war, but there are also the horrors of peace.

In war there is material and physical loss, but what of the spiritual loss involved in a peaceful acquiescence in the devastation of an unoffending country whose sole crime was her geographical position.

The women of the Empire whose husbands, sons and brothers are bleeding on the battle field have no need to learn from other nations of the horrors of war, but they would appeal to the women of other nations, before they condemn all belligerent nations alike, to consider once more the causes of the war as set forth in the official documents issued by various Chancelleries of the nations at war.

We would ask you once more the old question. "What shall a man or a nation give in exchange for his soul?" The soul of any nation is the value that it places upon the defence of the weak, the freedom of the many, and the keeping of its plighted word. It is to preserve our soul as an Empire that we are at war.

This letter is sent to your care as we understand that you are the elected President of the Congress, but if we are mistaken we would be glad if you would kindly hand this to the President.

Yours truly,
Adelaide M. Plumptre, Secretary.

AN OPEN LETTER CONCERNING PEACE

The National Committee for Patriotic Service desires to call attention to a Peace propaganda, emanating from certain neutral countries, and being now circulated in Canada.

Letters and circulars in praise of peace have been issued, calling on women all over the world to stop the war. In some cases signatures to a petition are requested; in others, membership in a Peace Society. In these circumstances, the Committee calls your attention to the following considerations:

Few indeed are the men or women who would hesitate to declare themselves "in favour of peace." No neutral nation can hate war with half of the intensity of hate felt by nations who are bearing war's burdens. But declarations in favour of peace may be represented as condemning all who fight, and such use has been made of them during the war. Though we may hate war, and though we may admit that there is always wrong at the root of war, yet we cannot unconditionally condemn all war, nor regard all belligerents as equally guilty. History teaches us that nations and individuals have been compelled to draw the sword in defence of the rights of the weak and the principles of truth, honour and liberty, holding these dearer than peace, and even life itself.

The war in which we are now engaged is no more scramble for gain, nor quarrel over rights in which all parties are alike to blame, it is rather a struggle between the principles of law and of force – between the policeman and the armed criminal whose liberty is a menace to the neighbourhood. In such a conflict, neutrality has no particular merit; while to entreat the policeman to stop fighting does not tend to promote peace, but only tends to prolong a period of terror and insecurity.

We have drawn the sword to defend the rights of the weak, the liberty of the many, and pledged the honour of the Empire. To sheathe the sword before these ends are achieved is to render useless the sacrifice of countless lives already laid down in defence of these great principles; for could we at this juncture secure peace, we should but leave to our children a dreadful legacy of hate and uncertainty. It would be, in truth, not a peace but a truce, lasting only until the nations have recovered sufficiently to test the issue once more by an appeal to arms; and, worse than all, we should leave Belgium to its fate as a German province.

Shall not the women of this country bear their part in this war with the same high courage and steadfastness of purpose as animate our troops?

And what is our share?

To possess our souls in patience during war's hardships and uncertainties; to refrain from embarrassing our rulers by demands for a premature and illusory peace; to prepare ourselves for the new conditions and duties which peace will inevitably bring, while applying ourselves to the peculiar tasks imposed by war; and, above all to bear ourselves as to be an inspiration in courage ad self-sacrifice to the men who are fighting for our Empire – and for us.

This is our share.

When Germany has learned that right is stronger than might; when the mailed fist no longer threatens Europe, then may we hope for peace which our children's children may inherit. And with such a peace, we may hand on, unbroken, the great traditions of our Empire – honour unstained, liberty safeguarded, justice vindicated.

Such are the conditions to be considered before we unreservedly condemn war, or make petitions for immediate peace.

> Signed on behalf of National Committee,
> Mary R. Gooderham, President
> Adelaide M. Plumptre, Secretary

[Source: SAB, Violet McNaughton Papers, AI, E-18, Letter to Jane Addams, 15 May 1915.]

Julia Grace Wales (1881–1957) was born in the Eastern Townships of Quebec. She received a BA from McGill University and an MA at Radcliff College before being appointed to a teaching position in the Department of English at the University of Wisconsin in 1909. While Wales was a long-time member of the WCTU, it was not until after the outbreak of the First World War that she became actively involved in the women's movement. Distressed by the war, she became a committed pacifist and developed a plan for mediation by an international commission of neutrals. Initially referred to as the "Canadian plan," Wales's proposal was adopted as part of the "Program for Constructive Peace" by American feminists in January 1915, and even more, consequently, by the International Congress of Women at the Hague in April 1915. Wales went on to a long academic career at the University of Wisconsin, where she received her PhD in 1926.

Julia Grace Wales

A Participant's View on the Women's Peace Conference at the Hague (1915)

One sunny afternoon in April a band of forty American women sailed away from New York on the Holland-American steamship Noordam, bound for the woman's International Conference at the Hague.

I should not be right in trying to tell you how all those women felt as we steamed out of the harbor: I may only speak for the few whose thoughts I had opportunity to know intimately. For one thing we felt that we were in a sense taking a leap in the dark: going against the advice of many people who thought our enterprise foolish, following a conviction which had established itself in our minds only after a hard struggle with perplexity, but which, nevertheless, we felt bound to follow. There was a sense of freedom, of course, in that very abandonment to a dimly discerned purpose, in breaking with our traditional way of doing things as we were breaking the link with shore, and in committing ourselves to the uncertainties of the adventure. We could not help thinking of the tragic background of war, of the momentous historical crisis. Most of all we were conscious of a sound in our ears as of all the voices of humanity, as of the ascending prayers of the suffering peoples. It was the sound that we heard in our hearts for many long months, that had made us forget our own powerlessness and insignificance, and had driven us out to seek a way by which those prayers might be answered.

The forty women, who were delegates from many American organizations, were going to the conference not as individuals, but as representatives of the enthusiasm of thousands of people. It was the sense of a strong sentiment behind us that gave us confidence. We had come from all parts of the continent. By degrees as we chatted in our steamer chairs, or tramped on the decks in twos and threes, we grew better acquainted, and the delegation developed a kind of group consciousness that had not been there at first. Every morning we did three hours hard work, assembled in the dining-room of the steamer.

At first the meetings took the form of lectures on the history of the International movement. Later we worked carefully through the resolutions which the International Committee at Amsterdam (the organizers of the Conference) had sent out. Day after day we discussed and debated, rejecting a clause here and there, or adding ideas of our own. Doubtless delegations from the other countries prepared themselves in the same way, and that is perhaps one reason why the work went so smoothly at the conference itself. The other passengers, some of them men of affairs from different parts of the world, who had at first regarded our effort with no small skepticism, gradually grew interested and dropped in to listen to the discussions and sometimes take part in them. It was interesting even under these imperfect conditions to watch the workings of the collective mind. One felt a growing conviction that if the experience and knowledge, the scientific judgment and inventiveness of the world could be concentrated in an International thinking organ, a way might be found even now to establish a just and permanent peace.

And what were our feelings when after a calm voyage and many days of stimulating intercourse, we found ourselves approaching the shores of the Old World, that old world so much loved, and idealized by all dwellers in our hemisphere? I think it was with feelings of awe and heartbreak that we entered the dark shadow of the tragedy, realized around us the clash of incalculable forces, heard the roll of artillery in the distance.

After the conference began our brains were kept so busy that we had no time to realize our feelings. The "collective mind" was at work under more complex conditions. Despite difficulties of language and point of view, the work went forward almost without misunderstandings. During the first day or two we were all timorous, more fearful of wounding each other, however, than of being wounded, but as we proceeded, we gained confidence, for we found that every woman, because she knew her own national sensitiveness, was prepared to take infinite pains in her consideration for the sensitiveness of others. Much might be written about the work of individual leaders. Whenever we shall live over again in imagination those four memorable days, we shall always feel that no words can express what the conference owed at every stage of the proceedings, to the presence and inspiration of the President Miss Jane Addams.

I have not space here to discuss the resolutions which we adopted. But that the reader may understand their spirit and import I will quote three from the pamphlet issued by the International Committee after the Conference.

> That no territory should be transferred without the consent of the men and women in it, and that the right of conquest should not be recognized.
>
> That the government of all nations should come to an agreement to refer future international disputes to arbitration or conciliation, and to bring social, moral, and economic pressure to bear on any country which resorts to arms.
>
> That foreign politics should be subject to democratic control.

One resolution should perhaps be specially mentioned, since it concerns immediate action – that on Continuous Mediation. The Conference advocated the establishment of an international commission of experts to sit throughout the war. The commission should make a thorough study of the issue involved in the war and on the basis of its findings should prepare and put before the belligerent governments simultaneously, proposals for settlement based on principles making for the welfare of the family of nations as a whole, and favourable to the establishment of a permanent peace. If some proposals should fail, others would be framed and put forward until some basis could be found for the opening of actual peace negotiation.

The social life of the conference was even more valuable than the formal meetings. At the hotels, in the homes of the Dutch ladies, at receptions and dinner parties, we met women of many nationalities, and in sympathetic intercourse convinced ourselves of a vital truth that we are sometimes in danger of forgetting, that human nature is essentially the same the world over.

It was impressive to feel around us the historic associations of the Hague. One day a few of us visited the Peace Palace. We looked at the conference rooms, the massive tables and chairs, even the ink wells, all the equipment for mental work on an international scale. We thought of the long table in the dining-room of the Noordam, thought of the forty women busy with pencils and papers, the "collective mind" working in a very small and inadequate way, though with surprising effectiveness. But these vast and beautiful rooms of the Peace Palace were silent and empty. Here was the mechanism, "like an inanimate human brain" as a friend said to me, but where was the consciousness to make it alive? This Peace Palace should be the seat of a world intelligence. When civilization as a whole would seem to be threatening to destroy itself, surely a world brain is urgently needed. We comforted ourselves with the thought that sometime that world consciousness, even now nearly ready to break through, stirring even now like a sleeper, in a dream, will come into permanent being.

When the conference closed, we realized that the work had just begun. The women went away to their homes, carrying the seed of the thought of the Conference onto many lands. A little group remained in Amsterdam for a time, to attend to the work of editing the detailed report. Special committees visited the capitals of Europe to lay the resolutions of the conference before the governments.

And now I think we have all come home feeling that this effort, though undertaken with hesitation, carried out under difficulty, and somewhat widely misunderstood, was well worth while, and that future efforts will be better worth while: that the time has come when the women of the world and the men of the world must set themselves very consciously to begin their task – "that great task of the race, to make the world a home," to bring in the time when there shall be a family of nations, when Christianity shall be the rule between nations as between individuals, "when a new love shall be born, a love never yet known on the earth, the love of a people for a people, of strong nations for strong nations, the chivalry of the strong nations to the weak, the trust of the weak in the strong."

[Source: LAC, MG30, C238, vol.1-22, Julia Grace Wales, Untitled paper, 1915.]

A detailed biography of Gertrude Twilley Richardson (1875–1946) may be found on page 48.

Gertrude Richardson

The Cruelty of Conscription: A Letter to Women (1917)

Who Made the Law that men should die in the mead?
Who spoke the Word that blood should splash in lanes?
Who gave it forth that gardens should be boneyards?
Who spread the hills with flesh and blood and brains?
Who made the Law?

Who made the Law that death should stalk the valleys?
Who spake the Word to kill among the sheaves?
Who gave it forth that Death should lurk in hedgerows?
Who flung the dead amid the fallen leaves?
Who made the Law?

The above lines were found on the body of the author, a young soldier, who died on the field of battle. He was killed in the Somme fighting last October.

Well may we ask "Who made the Law?" – the law that drives such boys as these to death, with sorrow and wonder in their hearts.

Women of Canada – in Ottawa to-day they are planning to thrust upon us this cursed law. Perhaps the hellish deed will be accomplished before your eyes fall upon this page!

What shall we do? Are we calmly to submit when our boys are driven out to the slaughter?

In the "Forward" of June 12th there was an account of the sufferings of my dear young brother, under the Conscription Law in England. He is a life-long pacifist, a conscientious objector. Dragged from his business (he is a yarn merchant) and his widowed mother, whose other boy is with the troops. He has already spent more than thirteen months in the brutal hands of the military authorities. The story would break a heart of stone, and he is but one of the many thousands.

Do you realize what Conscription means? Oh women, women with mother-hearts, this war was arranged and is dominated by the blood-stained capitalists of the world, not by any means those of our nation only.

Their hands, red with the murder of the flower of earth's young, are held up by the apostate "ministers" of the sweetest Teacher of Love and Brotherhood this world has ever known, Christ the Toiler, Christ the Carpenter, who gave back the sick and the dead, healed and restored to their loved ones.

The world is submerged in a sea of madness. And so, I send forth from my breaking heart a call to Canada's women. Do you realize that they will make of your own sons, not only soldiers, but slaves. Militarism is already enslaving men all over our Empire. The poor people of India are dragged to the colors, or to indentured labor. In England, after serving terms of imprisonment, those who from Christian or Socialist motives refuse to submit are offered "alternative service" – a dignified name for a most degrading condition. Here, men are treated worse than convicts – men of the higher refinement – placed under the control of unthinkable brutes, mocked, forced to labor under conditions that would shame negro slavery. Of course, many refuse this "alternative" and are returned to prisons: though the law of England expressly states that the "genu-ine" conscientious objector is entitled to absolute exemption. But militarism knows no law. The best and noblest men of England and Germany to-day are behind prison bars.

Are we going to endure this here? Three times the women of Germany massed in the thousands, have stormed the palace of the Hohenzollerns, demanding that the slaughter of the men shall cease. Bayoneted, sabred, shot – they are for all time the example to all true motherhood. Women of Canada, shall we arise and save our men?

From my little farm home where I weep and pray and suffer, I call to the women with mother-hearts. If you will help, write to me, enclosing a stamped, addressed envelope; and let us form our plans to resist this accursed slavery.

(Mrs.) Gertrude Richardson,
Swan River, Manitoba

[Source: Gertrude Richardson, "The Cruelty of Conscription: A Letter to Women," *Canadian Forward*, 10 July 1917.]

Rose Wills Henderson, 1871–1937, was born in Dublin, Ireland, and immi-grated to Montreal in 1885. After her husband, an accountant, died prematurely in 1904, Henderson taught at a mission school, and in 1912 became a proba-tion officer of the Montreal Juvenile Court. Increasingly involved in left-wing political activities, she was pressured to give up her job in 1919, and thereaf-ter she travelled widely and devoted herself to various women's and socialist issues. Henderson ran unsuccessfully as a federal labour candidate in Montreal in 1921 and in New Westminster, British Columbia, in 1925. After travelling to the Soviet Union in the early 1920s, she wrote and spoke widely on conditions in that country. A member of the Women's International Federation of Peace and Freedom as well as the Women's Peace Union, she wrote a number of ver-sions of the pamphlet *Woman and War*, in the 1920s. Altogether, 10,000 copies of *Woman and War* were sold.

Rose Henderson

From *Woman and War* (192?)

If the women of the world are ever to organize themselves or their children for peace, they must become conscious of the forces making for war.

Too long have women been fed on the romance and glory of war. Too long have its realities been hidden from them by hypocrisy and lies. The death agonies of the dying have been drowned by the din of martial music. The scars of body and soul have been covered up by gaudy uniforms, gold lace, plumes and medals.

The war mongers have fooled and flattered women into the belief that their men folk were fighting for *their honor – their home – their God*, when in reality they were fighting for oil wells, coal fields, new markets to plunder and new "spheres of influence" to exploit.

So far, peace societies have dealt with the problem of making an end of war from the sentimental point of view. They have attempted to tame the beast of militarism with honeyed words – approaching it in a "diplomatic way" – courting the approval of "leading citizens" and being scrupulously careful not to "antagonize" and always loudly proclaiming their loyalty to the "Empire," the "Republic," or whatever form of government prevails in the country they live.

I do not question the sincerity of these people. I have met and talked with many such men and women and one and all conveyed the impression of sincerity and devotion to the cause of peace. But sincerity and devotion is not enough. A mother may be a devoted slave to her child, yet see it die by inches because she lacks the knowledge of child welfare and fails to understand its needs and constitution. Likewise, a mother, through her ignorance, may feed her children a mental poison which may be the cause of sorrow down to the "third and fourth generation."

If women would be the spirit of life, light and truth, which they were destined to be, they must no longer be fooled by illusions, misled by catch phrases, deceived by speculators, cajoled by politicians and lulled into a "God's-will-be-done" attitude by ministers of the Gospel.

Economic conditions have forced women to face the question of poverty, unemployment, infant mortality and prostitution, but in comparison to War these pale into insignificance.

Resolutely and fearlessly the women of the world must understand the causes of war or see the race exterminated.

Woman bears the burden of the race in time of peace as well as war. She does not arm nor does she destroy armies, but she bears and nurtures armies, both industrial and military, before, during and after the war.

The following is a table of the cost of the last war in blood and treasure. These figures are not taken from any pacifist journal nor from the tabulations of a peace organization, but from *The Militiaman*, official organ of the Vancouver Military Institute.

Add to these figures the toll of the world-wide influenza epidemic which

The Cost of the Great War

Countries Involved	Human Cost[a]		Prisoners and Missing[b]	Financial Cost[c]
	Killed	Wounded		
British Empire	800,000	2,000,000	65,000	$ 39,703,000,000
France	1,500,000	3,000,000	450,000	24,265,000,000
Russia	2,750,000	5,000,000	2,500,000	22,600,000,000
Italy	50,000	950,000	1,400,000	12,413,000,000
Serbia	700,000	350,000	100,000	400,000,000
Belgium	250,000	150,000	10,000	3,000,000,000
Japan	300	900	3	40,000,000
United States	80,000	225,000	4,500	22,482,000,000
Rumania	350,000	200,000	100,000	1,600,000,000
Greece	15,000	40,000	45,000	270,000,000
Belgium	250,000	150,000	10,000	3,000,000,000
Japan	300	900	3	40,000,000
United States	80,000	225,000	4,500	22,482,000,000
Rumania	350,000	200,000	100,000	1,600,000,000
Greece	15,000	40,000	45,000	270,000,000
Portugal	4,000	17,000	200	
Germany	1,600,000	3,800,000	800,000	40,000,000,000
Austria-Hungary	900,000	3,000,000	450,000	20,622,000,000
Turkey	450,000	400,000	100,000	1,500,000,000
Bulgaria	100,000	150,000	10,000	815,000,000
Allied Powers' Total	3,050,000	7,350,000	1,360,000	62,935,000,000
Central Powers' Total	3,050,000	7,350,000	1,360,000	62,935,000,000
Grand Totals	9,999,300	19,282,900	6,034,703	$189,860,000,000

[a] Founded on "Direct and Indirect Costs of the Great World War," by E.L. Bogart.
[b] It is estimated that fifty per cent of those listed as "prisoners and missing" are dead.
[c] The cost has been estimated on the increase during the period of the war over normal peace expenditures. Reparations paid by the Central Powers increase their costs and decrease the costs of the Allied Powers.

cost 6,000,000 lives – not counting the 8,000,000 in India and without reckoning those who have died since peace was declared from cholera, typhus, famine blockades, civil wars and malnutrition.

The life-blood – yea, life itself, of some woman was given to bring forth and nurture these millions, the victim of man's ruthless folly; given not in the cause of freedom, but in the cause of mammon. What a waste of woman's life;

what a waste of love; what a waste of labor and sacrifice; what a toll; what a condemnation of man's religion, morality and government.

Reflect, oh, mothers of the world, reflect! These are your children, your men and your boys, the babes you have put to bed and pulled the covers over, a thousand times petted, and nursed, and fed, and brought up to be men. The human blossoms of love for whom you have scrimped and saved and worked to give a trade, profession or a better education so that they might have a better opportunity in life than their forebearers had.

The March of the Dead

If the dead of the Great War could be assembled in one great army this is the spectacle they would present:

"At daybreak they start, twenty abreast. Until sundown they march ... and the next day, and the next, and the next. For ten days the British dead pass in review. For eleven days more the French dead file down 'the Avenue of the Allies.' For the Russians it would require the daylight of five more weeks. Two months and a half would be required for the Allied dead to pass a given point. The enemy dead would require more than six weeks. For four months men actually killed in the war, passing steadily twenty abreast –"

The war claimed, says one journal, 10,000 miles of dead.

If these dead, as they passed by in the melancholy procession, could look into your eyes or could speak to you, what do you imagine their message would be? Would they tell you of the victories and heroics of war, or would they tell you that in war there are no victories for the common people, who supply the cannon fodder and pay the cost – 95 percent of all the cost – in life, suffering and taxation for generations after the war is over.

They would tell you that for every Victoria Cross on the breast of the living there are 100,000 wooden crosses on the graves of the dead!

Rather would they demand that the women of the world search out the causes of war, where the germs of war are hatched and nurtured, and having found the source of disease, join with the mothers of every land to wipe from the face of the earth the bestial game of wholesale-legalized and sanctified slaughter.

If the war's dead could but return for one hour, that hour would be spent in shocking the women of the world into a sense of their responsibility!

Flower of Manhood Sacrificed

Women must scorn to accept the sacrifice of millions of the flower of the manhood of the world in the name of their "honor," "homes" and "God." The cost to the world for generations to come is too great a price; this is but one of the illusions and catch phrases of the war mongers. Instead of war protecting women, it poisons and befouls the very air they breathe. It desecrates all that is noblest, robs them of home and security of the love and companionship of father, husband, lover and son. It spreads disease, famine and desolation in its tracks. Its law is the law of the jungle. It rapes, robs, burns, plunders, poisons and lays waste all that comes within reach of its fiery breath and cloven hoof.

Men assert that during the war women were fiercer in their passions, stooped to meaner and crueler methods of attack, and were more relentless in their desire for revenge against the "enemy" than were the men.

Scarcely anyone able to retain their sanity during the war and watch the effect of its psychology on women will dispute this accusation. In times of peace, at best, women are, with notable exceptions, but the echo, the product of man's laws, man's morality, man's education, political, industrial and religious institutions.

In time of war when the world goes mad, when all restrictions are let down, when men mock and laugh at their own moral and ethical codes, when the only appeal is to woman's primitive emotions, ... she is swept into every excess. She becomes the blind, senseless tool of blind, senseless men, who rule the world. Men who march in their millions to fight unknown enemies, and to fill unknown graves, because someone told them so to do. Woman's "because," in face of this kind of male logic, is reason indeed.

Men are ignorant because women are ignorant. Men are slaves because the creatures who gave them birth and trained them are slaves, and the human race must remain in ignorance and slavery so long as women are looked upon as inferiors and do not take their full responsibility with man for the welfare of the race.

Who can portray the realities of war? Its cost in life, its moral degradation, its foul miasma of lies, hate and fear! The scars of the body are minute as compared to the scars that corrupt the mind, blacken the soul, and poison both soul and body of generations yet unborn.

If these dead heroes could speak, they would tell of romance – yea, of heroic deeds of bravery and sacrifice, yes – but they would concern themselves far more with the side of war that is shrouded in silence, and of which women are kept in ignorance, for good reasons. They would unfold a story that would shock women with a greater sense of responsibility towards their children, and arouse in them a hatred and loathing for the whole horrible game of war that would make war well nigh impossible. Let mothers once understand the horrors of war and there will be few so inhuman as to turn their sons over to it by the millions, unquestioningly, as they do today.

They would tell of their mangled comrades writhing in trenches tormented by lice, rats and mice, wallowing like swine in the blood, mud and filth of the battle fields. They would speak of barbed wire entanglements, shell-holes, guns, tanks, bombs, grenades, liquid flame, disease germs, poison gas, the babblings of the insane, and the ungodly spectacle of millions of men, armed with every device known to science, doing one another to death over the length and breadth of a continent.

And yet this picture but lifts the curtain on the first act of the drama of war. It would convey only a glimmer of the suffering that men endure.

Back of the millions of men are millions of women – mother, wife, sister or sweetheart. Back of these women are millions of children, the mute, outraged, exploited victims of an accursed system making for war.

The Social Cost of War

Bankers figure the cost of war in money; manufacturers in lost labor-power and raw materials; merchants in ruined commodities and lost markets; humanitarians in loss of life; money changers barter and wrangle over their profits and losses. Ministers of the gospel speculate on their heavenly gain in departing souls or acquired virtues in war, but, so far, no one has dared to estimate the cost of war to those helpless victims who bear the greatest burden. The mother heart sinks as she catches a glimpse of the babe she has borne on his way to "embark." The wife stifles the anguish and terror that clutches at her heart when she hears the words, "I'm called up." The maiden's heart sinks when she questions, "Will he ever return?" and sees her dreams of home and children shattered perhaps forever.

In her heart of hearts every intelligent woman questions if her men folk will be strong enough to withstand the moral degradation of the battlefield, and fears that when they are returned to their homes their moral and physical fitness to be fathers and husbands will be undermined.

For the women of the middle and ruling classes, generally speaking, war exists for them in conversations, military balls, reviews, anniversary banquets, organizing and raising patriotic funds, and kindred activities. Their husbands and sons go to war, but keep well away from the danger zones. They are officers, or subordinates. They fight the war by telephone, from arm chairs, and luxurious clubs, the best that can be provided is theirs by "divine right," and their wives and families are especially favored in many ways. They belong to a different class, many having large investments in munition works, railroads, shipping, etc.

For the women of the masses, however, who supply 93 per cent of the army, the story is a different one. The women of the masses, during the war were used to do the meanest work. They were flattered, cajoled, threatened. While the blood of their men folk was being coined into profits on the battle fields, their labor, sex, and necessities were the object of profit extortion, and barter at home. In munitions, garment and packing factories, they toiled incessantly; doing the work of men, but receiving "woman's pay." Ministers of the gospel grew wrathy and demanded that they "do their duty to replenish the loss of war," illegitimacy was winked at and excused as "one of the inevitable results of war." Politicians tricked and deceived them with promises they never intended to carry out. They were told to knit socks, scarfs, sweaters and other garments "to keep the boys warm," but when they went to buy the yarn they found the price had soared. They were advised by sleek well-fed men, and diamond, fur bedecked ladies, not to forget the "dear boys fighting for our home and honor," to send them chocolates, cigarettes, and fruit-cake, but alas when after scrimping a few cents from the pay envelope or "patriotic allowance" they went forth to purchase these things, they found the prices 20 to 100 per cent higher than before the war – some one had been "doing their bit" profiteering in a perfectly patriotic way.

They were told to eat less sugar and bacon, whereupon, after denying themselves and their children they found a corner on both these necessities and huge fortunes being made at their expense, and while men were being shot and jailed for military treason, no one was being hanged, jailed or shot for treason to those men and their dependants who were shedding their life-blood and wading through hell to "make the world safe for democracy" – or Plutocracy?

We can approximate the number killed and wounded; we can count the cost of making new garments, procuring food, furnishing implements of destruction; we may calculate the value of cities laid waste, crops ruined, the cost of constructing new homes, ships and railways, but who can measure, who describe, the suffering of the women and children whose homes are laid in ashes, who flee in terror before the advancing army, to hills and valleys, who crouch and shiver in ruins and dugouts, who forage on garbage heaps and feed off putrid flesh and roots, who are raped and famished, but who may not die by the bullet, or the swift thrust of the sword. Speak not to such as these, oh ye hypocrites, ye befoulers of all that is holy and sacred of the "glories of war," what a desecration of virtue; what a mockery of the home! To the women of the masses, war is a grim reality. It sinks its poisonous fangs deep into their quivering flesh, and pulsating hearts; it desecrates the marriage vow, breaks up their home, and poisons through venereal diseases the very well springs of life.

A well-known physician who for the past ten years has given his life to war work and its after effects, said to me when discussing this matter, "If I could by some means touch a button and put out of life quickly three-fourths of the babies born since 1914, I would consider I was conferring a benefit on mankind."

Think of the untold agony woman silently endures when she realizes that she and her children are the innocent victims of a foul disease, cursed from the cradle to the grave. And to add to her suffering the terrible thought is focusing itself upon her imagination, that it is her own men folk, husband, son or brother, the dupes and tools of mammon, who are bringing upon her and her babies this unspeakable burden of poverty, disease and woe.

The basis upon which war rests are foul – the principles of the thug, the robber, the morals of the jungle.

The duty of the soldier is to kill, the more he kills the greater his reward. A "glorious battle" is heralded, "enemy vanquished," "spectacular heroism," "territory captured" and all eagerly watch to see who will be the honored, the recipients of medals, crosses and higher commissions.

War is organized human butchery and its handmaidens are hypocracy [*sic*], robbery, rape[,] lies, obscenity, profanity, dope. It desecrates virtue and religion, laughs at honesty and mocks the commandment, "Thou shalt not kill." [...]

[Source: Rose Henderson, *Woman and War* (Vancouver: Federated Labor Party, 192?), 3–8.]

Hilda Laird received a BA from Queen's University in 1918 and a BLS from the Pratt Institute in New York City soon afterward. She worked as a cataloguer in the League of Nations Library in Geneva, Switzerland, in the early 1920s before returning to serve as the first dean of women at Queen's University from 1925 to 1933. She resigned from this position to become a full-time faculty member in the Department of German. She received a PhD from Cornell in 1939.

Hilda C. Laird

League of Nations (1932)

It is a great pleasure to be able to report that during the past year the Canadian Government has twice named women as members of important delegations to Geneva.

Mrs H.P. Plumptre of Toronto was a member of the Canadian delegation to the Twelfth Assembly of the League of Nations in September 1931. She was, moreover, made "rapporteur" of the Fifth Committee of the Assembly and in that capacity presented the report on the traffic in women and children. Mrs Plumptre was one of three women to speak at a plenary session of the Assembly. Since her return she has been good enough to give a number of stimulating addresses, which have done much to arouse interest in the League of Nations and to inform public opinion concerning its work.

Miss Winnifred Kydd, President of our National Council, was named a member of the Canadian Delegation to the Disarmament Conference and has just returned from Geneva. In her appointment the Council feels that it too has been highly honoured. The knowledge that Miss Kydd was at the Conference made every account of it in daily paper or monthly magazine of real personal interest, as we look forward eagerly to the time when she will herself be able to give us first-hand information concerning the work done. Her personal charm and the vivid picture of the Geneva setting which she will be able to give will win for the cause of disarmament the interest and the support of many people, who find newspaper reports and discussions but dull reading. We have already had the pleasure of hearing an address by Miss Kydd, which was broadcasted from Geneva.

The Disarmament Conference has before it problems of a magnitude and complexity which the layman can scarcely grasp. The general debate was concluded before Easter. At present, five technical commissions, which have been set up to consider definite ways and means of accomplishing a limitation or reduction of armaments, are at work. These commissions are dealing with,

a) Political questions
b) Land forces and armaments
c) Naval forces and armaments
d) Air forces and armaments
e) Moral disarmament

Miss Kydd was appointed a member of the last named committee.

The most important achievement of the Conference up to the present time has been the decision to outlaw chemical and bacteriological warfare. This decision is one of vital importance and deserves to be welcomed with prayers of thanksgiving and public expressions of joy in every civilized country. May it be followed by decisions radically to reduce armaments, for mutual reductions will not affect the security of any country and will bring financial relief and lessen the danger of war.

The League of Nations Committee has this year devoted itself almost exclusively to the study of the problems involved in disarmament and to an attempt to create a strong body of public opinion in its favour.

In July more than 3500 forms for the Petition for World Disarmament by International Agreement issued by the League of Nations Society in Canada were sent out to all presidents of Local Councils for distribution among their affiliated societies. This was done in accordance with the decision reached by the National Council at its last annual meeting. The Local Councils took up the task of filling the forms with a will and a large number of signatures were secured. Mrs J.A. Wilson, Girl Guides representative on the League of Nations Committee, sent the form and a covering letter to 102 Girl Guides Commissioners with excellent results. In January the Canadian petitions with 430,000 names was presented to the Rt. Hon. R.B. Bennett by a delegation from the League of Nations Society led by Dr H.M. Tory, the president. On February 6th the Canadian petition, together with petitions from many other countries of every continent, was presented to the Disarmament Conference in Geneva. There were millions of signatures. Representatives of women's organizations alone carried in volumes with 8,000,000 names. The Canadian volumes were deposited before the president of the assembly by four Canadian women resident in Geneva, Mrs W.A. Riddell, wife of the Canadian Advisory Officer at Geneva, Mrs Eastman, wife of Dr Eastman of the International Labour Office; Mrs Rasminsku, wife of O. Rasminsku of the League secretariat and Mrs Fellows.

In October a circular letter was sent to all Local League of Nations conveners and to the Presidents of Local Councils making suggestions for the work of the local committees during the winter. With the letter were enclosed (1) a pamphlet entitled "Disarmament" compiled by G.A. Innes, giving information concerning the Disarmament Conference, (2) a list of dramatic sketches issues by the Women's League of Nations, (3) a short list of books, periodicals, magazine articles and pamphlets, which might be used by study groups. The copies of the pamphlet "Disarmament" were supplied by the League of Nations Society.

In November a resolution was passed by the Provincial Council of Alberta asking that the Canadian delegates to the Disarmament Conference be chosen without delay and that they be persons who would adequately represent the peace sentiment of the Canadian people. This resolution was approved by the National sub-executive and was forwarded to the Federal Government. Similar resolutions were passed by the Ottawa Local Council and the Toronto and York Township Local Councils.

In November, too, a report of the work done by the Canadian League of

Nations Committee was sent to Lady Aberdeen for the International Council Bulletin [...]

May I, in conclusion, thank my committee for the efforts which they have made this year in the good cause of world peace and ask them to continue those efforts another year, if possible to redouble them. For the present the main subject of study should still be disarmament. Miss Kydd has suggested that each local council should send to the League Secretariat for a copy of the Draft Convention and should use this as a basis of discussion just as the Disarmament Conference itself is about to do.

[Source: Hilda C. Laird, "League of Nations," in *National Council of Women Yearbook 1932*, 55–7, 58.]

Laura Marshall Jamieson, 1882–1964, was born in Brant County, Ontario. She graduated from the University of Toronto in 1908 with a degree in philosophy. She eventually married and moved to Vancouver, where she became active in the University Women's Club and the suffrage movement. In 1921 she helped to found a local chapter of the Women's International League for Peace and Freedom and went on to serve as this organization's national president. After her husband's death in 1926 she succeeded him as a juvenile court judge, the first woman in British Columbia to hold such a position. In 1939 she entered provincial politics and was elected as a Canadian Commonwealth Federation MLA in Vancouver Centre.

Laura Jamieson
Developing Public Opinion on Peace (1937)

Vancouver, BC, May 14, 1937

Reply to Questionnaire re Technique of Developing Public Opinion on Peace

First of all, I believe the best work in educating public opinion on Peace is done by organizations or groups whose specific aim is such education. Many organizations have Peace as a partial aim, or have a committee on Peace. Unless that committee is an extremely active one, the efforts toward peace are apt to be very superficial and usually spasmodic.

Again, such organizations must be made up of members all of whom are devoted to the cause of peace. The great weakness of many of the League of Nations Societies is that they invariably have some members whose chief aim is to keep the organization from doing too much for Peace – that is, to keep it from doing anything which might be considered "unpatriotic" or "anti-British"; hence the society remains negative, its energies are dissipated; and earnest workers for peace drop out.

I shall confine my remarks chiefly to the WIL as it has worked for Peace in Vancouver, as I know that best, having been an active member since its inception in 1921. In the early years of the WIL we conceived its great work as trying to arouse the public to the *need* for Peace. So we had:

(a) Demonstrations in the park on the anniversary (or the nearest Sunday to it) of the opening of the Great War. Holding these immediately after the Band Concert we got a large audience of the rank and file of the public. Several speakers representing various sections of the public addressed the people. Such demonstrations undoubtedly reached many and aroused their thoughts regarding Peace!

(b) Pageants. For several years we had large indoor gatherings where children of the various national groups put on a loosely connected pageant or play, stressing goodwill and Peace.

(c) Goodwill Day in schools. Our members in the Parent Teacher Federation urged the celebration of May 18 as Goodwill Day and the WIL gave a prize for the best essay on Peace, thereby getting the pupils to think on Peace lines.

(d) Conferences. The WIL got other Peace groups to co-operate in holding an All Day Conference on Peace on or near Armistice Day.

(e) Radio programs; good music combined with short speeches on Peace.

As the WIL worked out some particular techniques or function in developing public opinion on Peace, we turned over this particular function to some other group, and tried to develop new ones, and to work along some line which seemed more fitting for us, or more in tune with new conditions.

So the Pageants finally became the Folk Art and Dance Festival, developed to a much larger scale than the WIL could have done, and broadening the influence of good-will.

Goodwill Day was taken up by the Department of Education and has become an Annual affair.

The All Day Peace Conference was turned over to the League of Nations Society, as it had many affiliated groups, and is still carrying on.

The WIL, making a constant study not only of Peace, but of the conditions in the world, came to realize in later years that the *will to peace* needed now very little stressing in Canada at least, where it was well established in the public mind. But now it seemed to us, the public mind needed to be educated regarding *those policies which were necessary for Governments to follow if Peace were to be attained.* So in the past several years our studies are directed to this latter purpose. It is not easy to come quickly to a definite conclusion as to such policies; but following up our study in former years, and assisted by the WIL headquarters in Great Britain, the U.S. and Geneva, as well as by outstanding economists and experts, we can feel fairly sure of our ground. Books and literature are collected and distributed to individuals and groups.

The same methods can be used as formerly to educate public opinion, only we must get the public to think more deeply than before. That *reason* must be appealed to, rather than the emotion. So along with demonstrations and public meetings etc, we now stress the *study group.* Only by study and discussion can individuals and groups learn the causes of war, the economic conditions in the world today leading to peace and war, the policies which must be followed to bring peace. Adult Education, therefore, in almost any form, will help Peace education; because a heightening of man's intelligence and increasing his information will enable him to judge the conditions and movements more clearly and he is more likely to realize those policies necessary to peace and to advocate them.

Particularly study groups in economics, current history, current events, and of course in Peace itself, will, I believe, do more than any other one thing to educate public opinion toward Peace.

In conclusion I want to state that vague admonitions to "Good-will," impassioned speeches on the desirability of Peace today "cut little ice." Even Governments that want Peace are devoting themselves to policies that must inevitably lead to war. People must learn *why* these things are. Only study and an exercise of the *reason* can show them what must be done for Peace. And only pressure from enlightened citizens will force governments to change their policies into those assigned to bring peace. No doubt the emotion has a place in the cause of Peace, but my experience is that the appeal to the emotion alone does nothing to bring Peace. Only study and the conviction that comes from knowledge will lead men to take the steps necessary to bring Peace.

It is for this reason that I conclude as I began, in stating that groups whose specific aim is Peace do the best work in educating public opinion. Their members have *conviction* first, based upon study. This leads them to study more and spread abroad the knowledge thus attained. "Knowledge is power" is particularly true in regard to education toward Peace. Such a group becomes a centre for information and inspiration to weaker groups.

If such groups, besides studying within their own national boundaries, educating public opinion there, and influencing their governments, are also affiliated with similar groups in other countries, the work for Peace is thus strengthened. The WIL is such a group. By its friendship and co-operation it strengthens the hands of its groups in countries where the war spirit is perhaps stronger. It tends to make *friends* of possible enemy nations, which is the strongest defense against war yet devised. Such affiliations of groups in many countries make a united movement for Peace, and a united acceptance of certain policies as those necessary to bring Peace. All of this helps education toward Peace much more than isolated groups working for Peace within national boundaries. Especially by international conferences, where such policies are worked out and accepted by groups from many countries, education for Peace is furthered. Also where groups in the various parts of Canada unite in conferences, individuals return to their centres stimulated; and the unity of outlook and of policy strengthens the work for Peace.

These groups doing intensive study and closely affiliated with similar groups in other lands act as leaders and "inspirers" to other groups less keen on Peace. The WIL and similar groups are the advance groups of the whole peace movement.

[Source: SAB, Violet McNaughton Papers, A1, E-50-2, Laura Jamieson, "Reply to Questionnaire re Technique of Developing Public Opinions on Peace," 14 May 1937.]

"The Hand That Rocks the Cradle" (1937)

[Source: *Vancouver Sun*, 14 July 1937.]

Index

communism and, 11, 70, 97–102, 241,
274–6; organizing and, 71, 102–11;
pacifism and, 102–3, 287–9, 292,
301–3, 315–19; socialism and, 11, 70.
See also nationalism.
International Labour Organization (ILO),
71, 72, 106–8, 110, 277.
International Woman Suffrage Alliance.
See International Alliance of Women.
International Women's Day, 70, 96–7,
100, 101

Jamieson, Laura, 285, 315–18
Jewish refugees, 63–4, 72–3, 111–12
Jewish women, 47, 112, 158, 178–9
Johnson, E. Pauline – Tekahionwake, 22,
37–40, 49–50
Jousssaye, Marie, 237
Judaism, 47, 63–4, 72–3, 111–12, 158,
178–9

Kerr, Dora Forster, 201, 220–2
Knights of Labour, 10, 237–8, 243–6
Kydd, Winnifred, 203, 285, 313

labour. *See work*
labour unions, 11, 100, 150, 237–9,
241–2, 243–6, 275–6
Ladies Empire Club (London GB), 23,
40–4
Ladies of the African United Baptist
Association (Halifax), 158, 179–82.
See also organizations, local
Laird, Hilda, 185, 312–15
League of Nations, 71, 102, 103,
105–10, 128, 192, 277, 285, 312–15.
League of Nations Society of Canada
(LNSC), 285, 312–15, 316. *See also*
organizations, national
Leathes, Sonya, 114, 135–9

Liasion Committee of International
Women's Organizations, 72, 106–9.
See also organizations, international
Local Council of Jewish Women
(Toronto), 158, 178–9. *See also* organ-
izations, local
Local Council of Women of, Medicine
Hat, 227; Montreal, 46–7, 200, 239;
Toronto, 282. *See also,* organizations,
local

Machar, Agnes, 250–2
MacMurchy, Violet, 203, 232–5
Macphail, Agnes, 159, 188–92
MacVicar, Katie, 238, 243–6
marriage, 35–6, 143, 173–4, 201, 209–
10, 218–19, 220–2, 271, 273; divorce
and, 141; maternity and, 143–4, 210,
233–4, 278; nationality and, 14, 60,
159, 188–92; polygamy and, 35–6;
property and, 21, 28–30, 120, 176
Matheson, Sarah Robertson, 159, 183–4
McClung, Nellie, 5 116, 144–7, 155,
186–7, 192, 227, 283
McDonnell, Mary, 114, 119–23
McGeachy, Mary, 71–2, 102–3
McKay, Margaret, 281–2, 287–9
McKinney, Louise, 186–7
McNaughton, Violet, 10, 71, 102–3
Methodist Department of Social Service
and Evangelism, 202, 224–8
Methodist Women's Missionary Society
(MWMS), 157, 168–70, 208, 211. *See
also* organizations, national
minority rights. *See* rights
missionaries, 7, 23, 31–3, 81–2, 124,
157, 162, 168–70, 200, 208–11
Mokray, Anna, 70–1, 99–102
Montreal Women's Club, 46. *See also*
organizations, local

STUDIES IN GENDER AND HISTORY

General editors: Franca Iacovetta and Karen Dubinsky

9 780802 094148